From Digital Disruption to Dominance

TECHNOLOGICAL INNOVATION AND SUSTAINABILITY FOR BUSINESS COMPETITIVE ADVANTAGE

Series Editors: Allam Hamdan and Reem Khamis

Innovation and sustainability are broad terms that describe many interdisciplinary sciences – business success and competitiveness may not be separated from social and cultural aspects that interfere with any future development prospects. Research in across areas would provide a better understanding of international experiences, bridging the gap between developing and developed nations. This series promotes new visions for business research prospects that work in favour of innovation and sustainability in terms of governance, environment and ethics.

Technological Innovation and Sustainability for Business Competitive Advantage highlights business problems faced by institutions in a scientific way, finding possible practical solutions. Contributing to setting and improving business theories and practices and encouraging scientific research in technological innovation and sustainability, volumes activate dialogue between academics, practitioners and individuals and provide recommendations to improve institutions.

Previous Volumes

Technological Innovations for Business, Education and Sustainability
Edited by Allam Hamdan

Technological Horizons: Technological Skills and Knowledge for Practitioners Within Business Environment
Edited by Hashem Alshurafat and Claire Beattie

Technological Horizons: Insights for Accounting, Auditing and Internal Control in Emerging Markets
Edited by Hashem Alshurafat and Claire Beattie

Forthcoming Volumes

The Tech-Driven Future: Navigating Sustainability in the Digital Age
Edited by Jaheer Muthkar K.P., Berenika Byczek, Felix Claudio Julca-Guerrero and Roger Pedro Norabuena-Figueroa

The Role of Artificial Intelligence Applications in Business
Edited by Ra'ed Masa'deh

Ethical Standards for Technological and Business Education Sustainability
Edited by Esra Saleh AlDhaen, Vishanth Weerakkody, David Gallear and Weifeng Chen

Sustainability in Light of Governance and Artificial Intelligence Applications
Edited by Bahaa Subhi Awwad

Comprehensive Insights in Technological Sustainability, Education and Business: Exploring Diverse Perspectives and Impactful Strategies
Edited by Allam Mohammed Hamdan

From Digital Disruption to Dominance: Leveraging FinTech Applications for Sustainable Growth

EDITED BY

MAHA SHEHADEH

Al-Ahliyya Amman University, Jordan; Bangor University, UK

AND

KHALED HUSSAINEY

Bangor University, UK

emerald
PUBLISHING

United Kingdom – North America – Japan – India – Malaysia – China

Emerald Publishing Limited
Emerald Publishing, Floor 5, Northspring, 21-23 Wellington Street, Leeds LS1 4DL

First edition 2025

British Library Cataloguing in Publication Data
A catalogue record for this book is available from the British Library

ISBN: 978-1-83549-609-1 (Print)
ISBN: 978-1-83549-608-4 (Online)
ISBN: 978-1-83549-610-7 (Epub)

Printed and bound by CPI Group (UK) Ltd, Croydon, CR0 4YY

Contents

Part 2: Innovations and Applications of FinTech

Part 3: The Future of FinTech: Sustainability and Challenges

About the Editors

Dr Maha Shehadeh is an Assistant Professor in FinTech at the Al-Ahliyya Amman University in Jordan and a Visiting Scholar at Bangor University Business School, UK. Renowned for her research in FinTech, digital transformation and financial inclusion, she has received the Al Qasimia University Research Award for Islamic Economics (2021) and was recognised as the Most Published Researcher in the Scopus Database at her business college (2023). Dr Shehadeh is the editor of the book 'From Digital Disruption to Dominance: Leveraging FinTech Applications for Sustainable Growth' and a guest editor for the *Journal of Financial Reporting and Accounting*. Her extensive publications in high-impact journals focus on integrating Artificial Intelligence (AI), big data and blockchain into financial services, significantly contributing to the academic and professional FinTech community. She is also an active member of the Innovation Center and Entrepreneurship (ICE) at her university, promoting innovation and entrepreneurship in the financial sector.

Khaled Hussainey is a Professor of Accounting at Bangor Business School, Bangor University. Formerly, he held positions at Portsmouth University, Plymouth University, Stirling University, Manchester University and Ain Shams University. He has over 25 years of teaching experience across undergraduate and postgraduate levels. He has a growing research reputation in the field of Accounting. His research interests focus on corporate narrative reporting. He has been featured in the 'World Ranking of Top 2% Researchers' database created by Stanford University (USA) experts. He has published more than 250 articles in peer-reviewed journals and has written several book chapters and edited several books. His articles have appeared in journals such as *Accounting and Business Research*, *British Accounting Review*, *Business Strategy and the Environment*, *European Financial Management*, *International Journal of Finance and Economics*, *International Review of Financial Analysis*, *Journal of Accounting and Public Policy*, *Journal of Accounting Literature*, *Journal of Corporate Finance*, *Journal of Environmental Management*, *Journal of International Accounting, Auditing and Taxation*, *Review of Quantitative Finance and Accounting* and *Technological Forecasting and Social Change*. He has received external research grants from the Economic and Social Research Council (ESRC), British Academy, Qatar National Research Foundation (QNRF), Financial Reporting Council (FRC) and Abu Dhabi University. He is a co-editor of the *Journal of Financial Reporting and Accounting* and an editor of the *International Journal of Emerging Markets* and the *Journal of Sustainable Finance and Accounting*. He is an associate editor of the *International Journal of Finance and Economics, Journal of Applied Accounting Research, Accounting Research Journal* and *International Journal of Accounting, Auditing and Performance Evaluation* and *Review of Accounting and Finance*.

About the Contributors

Khaled Abd ElAlim is an Assistant Professor of Accounting at Faculty of Political Science, Economics and Business Administration, May University in Cairo (MUC). Prior to joining MUC, Dr Abd ElAlim worked as Assistant Professor of Accounting and Finance, Faculty of Commercial Studies and Business Administration, Egyptian E- Learning University. He also joined School of Business, Canadian International College, Cairo campus of Cape Breton University as an Assistant Professor of Accounting. In Addition to his teaching experience, Khaled is a member of editorial team of *Corporate Ownership and Control Review* and external reviewer of *Corporate Governance and Organizational Behavior Review*.

Tahreer M. Abu Hmeidan is a passionate Digital Marketing Professor and an industry expert dedicated to fostering the next generation of digital marketing strategists, with a PhD from the University of Bedfordshire, UK.

Faeyz Abuamria is an Associate Professor of Economics and currently serves as the Vice President for Academic Affairs. He also coordinates the Master's Programme in International Economics and Development. Dr Abuamria holds a PhD in Economics and a Master's in Applied Economics from the University of Granada, Spain, as well as a Bachelor's Degree in Financial Economics. His research interests span Financial Economics, FinTech, Applied Economics, Finance and Islamic Economics. He has published numerous research papers in his areas of specialisation.

Mousa Ajouz is an Assistant Professor and the Coordinator of the FinTech Programme at Palestine Ahliya University. He also serves as a Research Fellow at INTI International University, Malaysia. Dr Ajouz earned his PhD in Islamic Banking and Finance from the Institute of Islamic Banking and Finance, IIUM. He holds a BSc in Economics and an MSc in Finance. He is an active member of the General Union of Palestinian Economists. Dr Ajouz focuses his research on FinTech, Islamic FinTech, InvestTech, InsurTech and PayTech. Throughout his career, he has participated in various indexed conferences and published numerous papers in his areas of interest.

Abdullah M. Al-Ansi is an Assistant Professor at the College of Commerce and Business Administration (CCBA) at Dhofar University, Oman. He holds a PhD in Management, and his main research interest is in Entrepreneurship, Strategic

Management, Virtual Reality (VR), Augmented Reality (AR) and Artificial Intelligence (AI) Applications in Management practices.

Budiman Al Iman is an Assistant Professor at the Faculty of Psychology, Mercu Buana University in Yogyakarta, Indonesia. He holds a PhD from Universitas Muhammadiyah Yogyakarta. As a dedicated researcher, his expertise lies in the intersection of interpersonal trust, mental health and management. His work focuses on exploring how interpersonal trust and spiritual values influence organisational dynamics and employee well-being, providing valuable insights that bridge the fields of Psychology and Management.

Anas Al Mulla is a PhD student at the University of Gloucestershire with over 12 years of experience in the UAE education sector. He spent six years as a Lecturer at Liwa College in Abu Dhabi, where he significantly contributed to student development and academic excellence. Currently, he served as the School Operations Manager at Brighton College Abu Dhabi. His role involves overseeing daily operations, ensuring efficient administrative processes and maintaining a conducive learning environment. His extensive experience includes operations, administration, finance, facilities management and project management. His work is marked by his dedication to improving educational standards and practices, making significant contributions to the advancement of education in the UAE. Additionally, he is a co-author of a research book on entrepreneurship in emerging economies, highlighting his broad expertise and commitment to educational, research and economic development.

Salsabila Aisyah Alfaiza is a Lecturer and a researcher in a School of Economics and Business, Telkom University, Indonesia, and a PhD student in Management at University Utara Malaysia. Her main focus is on digital business and marketing.

Fadi Alkaraan is a Professor of Accounting and Finance, currently working at the University of Lincoln as an Associate Professor of Accounting, Governance and Sustainability. He has been appointed as a Visiting Professor AT EM Normandie Business School, Dubai. He is an Affiliate Professor at Gulf Finance Centre, Gulf University for Science and Technology, Kuwait, and an Affiliate Professor at the Institute of Management Technology (IMT), Dubai. He is a DBA/PhD supervisor at the University of Gloucestershire. Fadi is Certified Global Business Analyst and a Certified Management Accountant. His research interests focus on governance, sustainability and business model transformation in large UK companies towards eco-systems, environmental, social and governance (ESG), Sustainable Development Goals (SDGs), corporate social responsibility (CSR), innovation strategies and companies' dynamic capabilities, green sustainable strategic investment decision-making and investment appraisal techniques. His research has appeared in 3*ABS leading journals including *The British Accounting Review*, *Technological Forecasting and Social Change* and *Business Strategy and the Environment*. He is an associate editor for the *Journal of Applied Accounting Research*.

Ibrahim Alnafrah is an Associate Professor and a Research Fellow at the Graduate School of Economics and Management, Ural Federal University. His research covers the Knowledge-Based Economy, National Innovation Systems, Intellectual Property Rights Management, Green Innovations, Blockchain Technology, Machine Learning in Economics and Post-Conflict Development Policies. He has co-authored two books on the Knowledge Economy and published a book on blockchain's economic applications.

Neha Arora is currently working as an Assistant Professor at School of Commerce and Finance, Geeta University, Panipat, Haryana (India). She did her PhD in Management from M.D. University Rohtak. She has completed her M.Phil, M.com from M.D. University Rohtak. She got fellowships Like Junior Research Fellowship (JRF) in Management and Commerce. She qualified UGC-NET in Management and Commerce. She has 5 years of teaching experience. She has published various research papers in national and international journals of repute. She has presented various research papers at National and International conferences in the area of Commerce and Management.

Israa Badr is a faculty member in the Department of Accounting at Ain Shams University, Egypt's Faculty of Commerce. He specialises in accounting and is particularly interested in integrating AI technologies into the finance sector. The research involves quantitative studies that investigate the impact of AI on corporate financial decision-making (CCFD). This study advances accounting practices by incorporating cutting-edge AI methodologies.

Tat-Huei Cham is currently a Professor and the Dean at the UCSI Graduate Business School, UCSI University, Malaysia. Professor Cham also holds the position of a Visiting Professor at Tashkent State University of Economics in Uzbekistan, Chongqing University of Arts and Sciences in China, Krirk University of Thailand, Universitas Multimedia Nusantara and Symbiosis International (Deemed University) of India. His research interests include medical tourism, marketing, advertising, consumer behaviour, branding, and technology management. His work has been published in various international journals, including the *Journal of Hospitality Marketing and Management, Journal of Hospitality and Tourism Research, Journal of Business Research, International Journal of Tourism Research, Internet Research, Journal of Retailing and Consumer Services* and *International Journal of Bank Marketing*, among others. Besides serving as a member of the editorial review board for various reputable international journals, Professor Cham is also actively involved in training, consultancy projects and supervision of postgraduate students.

Tamer Darwish is a Professor in Human Resource Management (HRM), and the Head of HRM Research Centre in the Business School, University of Gloucestershire. He is also an Academic Fellow of the Chartered Institute of Personnel and Development (CIPD) and a Fellow of the Higher Education Academy (FHEA). His research interests lie in the areas of strategic HRM, international and comparative HRM and measurement of organisational performance, with a particular focus on emerging markets. His research has appeared in leading management and HRM journals such as *Human Resource Management*, *British Journal of Management*, *Management International Review*, *Asia Pacific Journal of Management*, *European Management Review* and the *International Journal of Human Resource Management*. He is also an Associate Editor of the *International Journal of Manpower* and serve on the Editorial Boards of a number of academic journals, including the *International Journal of Human Resource Management and Management Decision*.

H.M. Dawood is a versatile professional with a solid 24-year record spanning various sectors, including banking and technology. His expertise lies in spearheading impactful initiatives within the Fintech and AI realms. He holds a Doctorate in Fintech from UCSI University, a Bachelor's degree in Computer Science and an MBA. Dr Hatim completed his doctoral research under the guidance of Prof Dr Liew, Dr Marcia and Prof Dr Cham at UCSI University. His career highlights include managing pivotal national projects in digital transformation and leading the implementation of the Dhamani platform for health insurance information exchange. Dr Hatim has demonstrated a knack for navigating intricate challenges, harnessing emerging technologies and fostering positive change. His dedication is centered on advancing the fusion of technology and business for sustainable growth and innovation. Furthermore, Dr Hatim has authored five articles in reputable journals on topics within the Fintech and AI domains. He maintains a strong interest in ongoing research and publication pursuits.

Ahmed Riyadh Dhaif holds a Bachelor's degree in banking and finance from Bangor University/Bahrain Institute of Banking and Finance and a Master's degree in management and finance from Bangor University, UK. He is currently a researcher at Bangor Business School, with ongoing projects in FinTech, sovereign ratings and demography. He is an active member of the credit risk research group at the Institute of European Finance www.bangor.ac.uk/bbs/research/ief

Nermin Nour El-din Farghaly is a Research Assistant. He graduated from the Cairo University in 2019 with a Bachelor's degree in Accounting. She also obtained a Master's degree in Accounting and Finance from Cairo University in 2022. I have completed the courses required for the PhD in Accounting, Specialisation (Financial) in 2024. She has experience in analysing the narrative content of banks' annual reports and collecting financial and governance data from these reports. She is an ad hoc reviewer for the *Journal of Financial Reporting and Accounting*. She also participated with Professor Khaled Hussainey in authoring two research papers, one of which was published in the *Sadat City University Journal* entitled 'Accounting for the Financial Effects of Foreign Exchange Rate Changes', and the other was published in the *Arab Journal of Administrative Sciences* in Kuwait entitled 'The Structure of Research Papers and Types of Research Contributions'.

Askar Garad is a Yemeni scholar based in Indonesia and earned his Doctoral Degree in Management from Universitas Muhammadiyah Yogyakarta, graduating as the best in 2022/2023. He now serves as a Lecturer and a researcher at Universitas Muhammadiyah Yogyakarta and STIKes Muhammadiyah Cirebon.

With expertise in IT and Telecommunication Engineering, his impactful contributions span systems management, investment, economics, business, e-services, e-learning systems and international education. As a versatile educator, a consultant and a mentor, Dr Garad's influence extends beyond academia.

Imene Guermazi is an Assistant Professor of Finance at the Institute of Higher Commercial Studies, Sfax, Tunisia. She teaches courses on Finance and Accounting. His current research focuses on Corporate Finance, FinTech, Financial Economics, Sustainability and Islamic Finance. She has authored and co-authored several papers published in indexed international journals.

Rawnaa Ibrahim is affiliated with the School of Economics and Finance at HSE University, Russia, and the Egyptian Russian University (ERU), Egypt. I have extensive experience in Economics and Finance, with a particular focus on applying AI techniques to Accounting and Finance. I contributed to various research projects. This research project aims to bridge the gap between traditional financial practices and innovative AI solutions, enhancing the efficiency and accuracy of financial analysis and decision-making processes.

Md. Abu Jahid is a Visiting Assistant Professor of Accounting at Universitas Muhammadiyah Yogyakarta, Indonesia. He received his PhD with the best thesis award from the same university in the 2023/24 academic year. Before that, he worked as an academician in Bangladesh, Saudi Arabia and Indonesia. His research interests include Managerial Accounting, CSR and Corporate Governance (CG).

Rita Kusumawati, an Associate Professor in the Management Programme at Universitas Muhammadiyah Yogyakarta, is currently completing her doctoral programme at the Graduate Programme of Muhammadiyah University of Yogyakarta. Her research interests include: financial management, FinTech and entrepreneurship.

Emad Masoud is a skilled Associate Professor of Marketing with 16 years of teaching experience in business programmes throughout Jordan and the Gulf region. Holding a PhD in Marketing, he merges academic expertise with 10 years of industry practice, offering a valuable mix of theory and real-world insight.

Sulaiman Mouselli is an Associate Professor in Finance at Finance, Investment and Banking Department at the Faculty of Business Administration, Arab International University. His research spans the areas of asset pricing, information risk, corporate governance and FinTech.

Peterson K. Ozili is a Senior Policy Economist in the Advisory Services Group at the Central Bank of Nigeria. He has wealth of experience in Banking Supervision and Economic Policy. He does extensive research on topics of global interest in Economics, Finance, Business and Accounting. He has more than 100 publications in Economics and Finance journals, and he is widely known for his contributions to financial inclusion research and digital finance research. He is an international speaker and has been an invited speaker at the International Monetary Fund (IMF). He holds a PhD in Accounting and Finance from the University of Essex in the United Kingdom. He also holds a PhD in Economics from Nile University of Nigeria as well as an MSc in Accounting and Financial Economics from the University of Essex in the United Kingdom. He is a certified associate Professional Risk Management (PRM) holder.

Hosam Alden Riyadh is an Assistant Professor and a faculty member, a researcher, at School of Economics and Business, Telkom University, Indonesia. He holds a Doctoral degree in Accounting, currently a Certified Sustainability Reporting Specialist (CSRS) and a Certified Sustainability Reporting Assurer (CSRA). His main research interest CSR, ESG, and information system.

Moamen A. Shazly is an Assistant Professor of Accounting and a Faculty of Business Studies Arab Open University, Egypt. Prior to joining Arab Open University, he worked as an Assistant Professor of Accounting in Ahram Canadian University (ACU). In addition to his teaching experience, he has great experience in Quality Assurance and Scientific Research.

Nedaa Shhadah is a Master's candidate at the Financial and Banking Department of the Higher Institute of Business Administration. Her research is centred on the potentials of crowdfunding for economic growth and financial inclusion in emerging economies.

Arni Surwanti, MSi, leads the Magister Management Programme at Universitas Muhammadiyah Yogyakarta, with impactful publications emphasising community-based rehabilitation, financial dynamics and empowering persons with disabilities. Noteworthy works include 'Increasing the Role of Community-Based Rehabilitation Groups' (2020) and 'Dynamic Model of Dividend Payout Companies in Indonesia' (2019). Dr Surwanti's dedication to advocacy, especially in entrepreneurship and regional regulations, makes substantial contributions to societal welfare.

Ruchika Vermani is a staunch academician and a research scholar with the perfect blend of interest in curricular, co-curricular activities and research. She has over 14 years of experience in the academic and corporate world. She has been dedicated to the teaching community for over 12 years. She is a UGC NET qualifier, has an MBA from GGSIPU New Delhi, an MCom from MDU Rohtak and has graduated from the University of Delhi. Ms Vermani has numerous research papers to her credit in diverse areas at various national and international conferences. She has authored a book titled *Retail Management and Sales Procedure for the Students of Commerce*. She was conferred the Best Teacher Award for her distinguished services in 2017. She received her award on the eve of Teacher's Day from Haryana Granth Academy, Panchkula. She was also awarded for exemplary work by the Punjab Kesari group and Rashtriye Punjabi Mahasabha in 2023.

Hesham Zakaria is an Assistant Professor of Accounting, College of Administrative and Financial Sciences, Imam Jafar Al- Sadiq University, Baghdad, Iraq and an Assistant Professor of Accounting, Higher Institute of Administrative Sciences Elbeihera, Egypt. Prior to joining his university, he joined School of Business, Canadian International College, Cairo campus of Cape Breton University as an Assistant Professor of Accounting. In addition to his teaching experience, he has great experience in Quality Assurance and Scientific Research.

Foreword

In the post-COVID-19 era, the global shift towards digital transformation and sustainable processes has become increasingly critical across all sectors, including finance. Financial Technology (FinTech) has rapidly emerged as a pivotal force driving this transformation, reshaping the financial landscape and creating new models for sustainable growth. The importance of FinTech is not only in its capacity to improve efficiency and inclusivity but also in its potential to foster long-term economic and social sustainability.

The role of FinTech in achieving sustainable growth is the central theme of this book, 'From Digital Disruption to Dominance: Leveraging FinTech Applications for Sustainable Growth'. This volume offers a detailed exploration of how innovative FinTech solutions are revolutionising financial services. The chapters, written by experts in the field, explore various aspects of FinTech, including mobile banking, AI, financial inclusion and social impact investment. They provide valuable insights into how these technologies are addressing contemporary challenges and creating new opportunities for sustainable development.

The digital transformation of the financial sector, driven by FinTech, aligns closely with the United Nations Sustainable Development Goals (UNSDGs), particularly those related to economic growth, industry innovation and reduced inequalities. By leveraging digital technologies, financial services can become more accessible and equitable, thus promoting financial inclusion and economic resilience.

This book is a crucial resource for academics, practitioners and policymakers seeking to understand the dynamic interplay between FinTech and sustainable growth. The insights presented in these chapters highlight technology's transformative power and capacity to drive positive change in the financial sector.

As you explore the comprehensive analyses and case studies within this volume, you will gain a deeper appreciation of how FinTech innovations are not just disrupting traditional financial models but are also paving the way for a more sustainable and inclusive future. This book serves as a guide to navigating the complexities of the digital economy and leveraging the potential of FinTech to achieve sustainable growth.

Sincerely,

Dr Maha Shehadeh, Al-Ahliyya Amman University, Jordan;
Bangor University, UK
Professor Khaled Hussainey, Bangor University, UK

Preface

In the dynamic landscape of modern finance, the intersection of technology and financial services, commonly known as Financial Technology or FinTech, has emerged as a transformative force. This book, 'From Digital Disruption to Dominance: Leveraging FinTech Applications for Sustainable Growth', aims to provide a comprehensive exploration of the ways in which FinTech is reshaping the financial sector and driving sustainable growth across various economies.

The motivation for this book came from recognising that while FinTech's impact on daily transactions and consumer behaviour is frequently discussed, its potential to sustain long-term economic, social and environmental growth is less frequently the subject of scholarly inquiry. This gap in the literature calls for a thorough examination, which this book aims to offer through diverse perspectives and a multidisciplinary approach.

The chapters within this book are designed to guide readers through the historical evolution of FinTech, present opportunities and challenges and explore specific applications and innovations that demonstrate FinTech's capacity to drive sustainable growth. Our contributing authors, who are esteemed experts from academia, industry and policymaking, offer extensive knowledge and insights covering the theoretical foundations of FinTech innovations to practical case studies and empirical reviews.

In Part One, the book sets the stage with a foundational overview of FinTech, tracing its historical roots and expanding into its current global landscape. This section aims to establish a solid understanding of the core concepts and frameworks that define FinTech operations and strategies.

Part Two addresses specific innovations and applications within FinTech, including cutting-edge developments in AI, the role of digital payment systems in fostering financial inclusion and the psychological and cultural dynamics influencing the adoption of FinTech services. This section emphasises the diverse applications of FinTech and its potential to revolutionise traditional financial and banking practices.

Part Three shifts focus towards sustainability and future challenges, examining how FinTech not only responds to but also anticipates the needs of the modern economy. It looks at sustainable and social finance, the impacts of global disruptions such as the COVID-19 pandemic and the evolving role of technology in meeting these challenges.

This book is intended for a wide audience that includes financial professionals, policymakers, researchers and students. It seeks to provide not just a snapshot of current FinTech applications but also a vision of future possibilities. As we present this comprehensive guide to the ever-evolving world of FinTech, we invite our readers to reflect on the transformative potential of technology in finance and consider how these innovations can be utilised to ensure robust, inclusive and sustainable growth for future generations.

With each chapter, we hope to inspire new discussions, ideas and research that will contribute to the thriving landscape of FinTech. This book is evidence of the power of interdisciplinary knowledge and the importance of embracing technological advances in shaping tomorrow's financial services.

Sincerely,

Dr Maha Shehadeh, Al-Ahliyya Amman University, Jordan;
Bangor University, UK
Professor Khaled Hussainey, Bangor University, UK

Acknowledgement

We are deeply thankful to everyone who contributed to the making of this book.

First and foremost, we extend our deepest appreciation to the editorial team at Emerald Publishing for their exceptional professional support and for providing a distinguished platform to share this work. Special thanks to Prof Allam Hamdan, the editor of the book series 'Technological Innovation and Sustainability for Business Competitive Advantage', for his invaluable guidance and support.

Our sincere thanks also go to Bangor University and the Al-Ahliyya Amman University for their significant support and for providing environments that are highly conducive to academic research and collaboration. Your commitment to advancing scholarly efforts has greatly improved the quality of this work.

We extend our deepest gratitude to all the contributing authors. Your contributions, enriched with varied viewpoints and creative ideas, have substantially enhanced the quality of this book. Your dedication to rigorous research and scholarly excellence is truly commendable, and it has been an honour to collaborate with such esteemed colleagues.

Thank you all for your invaluable contributions and support.

Sincerely,
Dr Maha Shehadeh and Professor Khaled Hussainey

Part 1

Foundations and Adoption of FinTech

Chapter 1

Exploring the Landscape of Financial Technology: Innovations, Regulatory Challenges and the Disruptive Impact of Fintech on Traditional Financial Services

Ahmed Riyadh Dhaif

Bangor University, UK

Abstract

This chapter provides a comprehensive examination of financial technology (fintech) firms, exploring their background, features, products and services. Framed within the themes of financial innovation, disintermediation and disruption, the chapter examines the transformative impact of fintech on the financial industry. Fintech firms leverage advanced technology to offer innovative financial solutions, such as mobile payment systems, robo-advisors and peer-to-peer (P2P) lending platforms, thereby enhancing accessibility and efficiency in financial services. The regulatory environment is highlighted, noting that while traditional banks are heavily regulated, fintech firms often operate with more flexibility, raising potential concerns about regulatory arbitrage and associated risks. The continued evolution of fintech, driven by advances in artificial intelligence (AI), blockchain and data analytics, holds significant potential for further transforming the financial industry. This chapter sets the stage for ongoing exploration of fintech's implications and future developments.

Keywords: Fintech; financial innovation; financial disintermediation; financial disruption; blockchain

1. Introduction

The purpose of this chapter is to present a comprehensive background on financial technology (fintech) firms and review the relevant literature in this

From Digital Disruption to Dominance, 3–44

Published under exclusive licence by Emerald Publishing Limited
doi:10.1108/978-1-83549-608-420251001

dynamic field. The review of fintech is formulated within three distinct themes: financial innovation, disintermediation and disruption. In addition, this chapter acknowledges the 'technology-enabled financial solutions' adopted by fintech firms to fill gaps in the provision of financial services within the traditional banking model. Fintech leverages the rapid advancement of technology to offer a wide range of financial services. These services include online payment solutions, corporate and consumer lending, asset management, financial consultancy through robo-advisors, equity crowdfunding and alternative financial services (Ajouz et al., 2023, 2024; Alkhazaleh et al., 2023; Alkhwaldi et al., 2022; Brandl & Hornuf, 2017; Cantu & Ulloa, 2020; Philippon, 2020; Rehman et al., 2023). By employing innovative technology, fintech firms are increasing competition within the financial industry. For instance, Brazil's banking sector, renowned for being one of the most profitable globally, is experiencing significant shifts due to higher mobile internet penetration. According to Fitch Ratings (2016), depositors are increasingly favouring digital-only fintech firms over traditional banks. This trend is pressuring incumbent banks to adapt to the evolving landscape of technology-enabled financial services (S&P, 2018).

The evolution of fintech is a story of the seamless integration of finance and technology, marked by key events that have shaped the current state of this longstanding relationship. Initially, fintech was focused on back-end systems of established financial institutions. Over time, it has evolved to cover a broader spectrum of services directly accessible to consumers and businesses. In the early days, fintech revolved around automating the processes within traditional banks. However, with the advent of the internet and mobile technologies, fintech has expanded its reach, transforming how financial services are delivered and consumed. This chapter aims to provide an overview of fintech firms through the lenses of financial innovation, disintermediation and disruption, highlighting how these firms have redefined the financial services landscape.

One of the core themes explored in this chapter is financial innovation. Fintech firms are at the forefront of developing new products and services that traditional financial institutions have been slow to adopt. For instance, mobile payment systems and digital wallets have revolutionised how people conduct transactions. Services like Apple Pay, Google Wallet and various mobile banking apps have made it possible for consumers to pay for goods and services without needing physical cash or cards. Moreover, fintech has introduced new methods of lending and borrowing. Peer-to-peer (P2P) lending platforms such as LendingClub and Prosper connect borrowers directly with lenders, bypassing traditional banks. This not only reduces the cost of borrowing but also provides more favourable terms for both parties. Additionally, robo-advisors like Betterment and Wealthfront offer automated, algorithm-driven financial planning services with minimal human intervention, making investment advice more accessible and affordable.

Another significant theme is financial disintermediation, where fintech firms adopt methodologies that differ from the traditional approach of prior incumbents. Disintermediation refers to the removal of intermediaries in the supply chain, a phenomenon fintech firms have effectively leveraged. By using technology to connect consumers directly with financial services, fintech firms bypass traditional banks, thereby reducing costs and increasing efficiency. For example, in the realm of payments, companies like PayPal and Stripe allow businesses and individuals to transfer money and process payments without going through traditional banking channels. Similarly, blockchain technology and cryptocurrencies, exemplified by Bitcoin and Ethereum, offer decentralised financial systems that operate independently of traditional banks. These innovations not only provide faster and cheaper transaction methods but also introduce new paradigms in financial intermediation.

The third theme, financial disruption, examines how fintech firms disrupt the primary functions of incumbents and introduce new risks. Traditional banks have long held a monopoly over financial services, but fintech firms are challenging this dominance by offering superior customer experiences, lower costs and innovative products. Fintech's impact on the financial industry is multifaceted. On the one hand, it forces traditional banks to innovate and improve their services. On the other hand, it amplifies certain risks and introduces new ones. For example, the rise of fintech has led to increased cyber threats, as the digital nature of these services makes them susceptible to hacking and fraud. Additionally, the regulatory landscape struggles to keep pace with rapid technological advancements, creating uncertainties and potential vulnerabilities. Despite these challenges, the disruptive influence of fintech is undeniable. It has democratised access to financial services, empowering individuals and small businesses that were previously underserved by traditional banks. Equity crowdfunding platforms like Kickstarter and Indiegogo enable entrepreneurs to raise capital directly from the public, bypassing conventional funding sources such as banks and venture capitalists. This not only provides new opportunities for funding but also fosters innovation and entrepreneurship.

The chapter underscores the transformative role of fintech in reshaping the financial services industry. By examining fintech through the themes of financial innovation, disintermediation and disruption, we gain a comprehensive understanding of how technology is driving changes in finance. Fintech firms are not merely adapting to existing paradigms; they are creating new ones, challenging traditional banks to evolve or risk obsolescence. The marriage of finance and technology has brought about unprecedented changes, offering more efficient, accessible and innovative financial solutions. As we delve deeper into the intricacies of fintech, it becomes clear that its impact extends beyond mere technological advancements. It represents a fundamental shift in how financial services are conceptualised, delivered and consumed, marking a new era in the financial industry. This chapter aims to provide a thorough understanding of this shift, setting the stage for further exploration of fintech's implications and future developments.

2. Fintech Evolution

The use of technology in the financial industry is not new to the scene. However, the current degree of reliance on fintech through technology-enabled and nonbanks to provide superior and new financial services and products that meet customers' needs and expectations is on an unparalleled level. Although 'fintech' has been widely appearing in multiple sources such as the press, communication media and the scientific literature, a global consensus among regulators, supervisors, practitioners and researchers about what 'fintech' means is yet to be found. Some researchers attempted to tackle the matter and noticed that 'fintech' was used in many business contexts and with a lack of consistency and open to many interpretations (Schueffel, 2016). In addition, Gomber et al. (2017) justify the lack of consensus surrounding what 'fintech' means as simple neologism.

Moreover, the lack of theoretical foundation, academic literature tackling the issue and structure of scientific knowledge in this area contributes to the lack of consensus (Milian et al., 2019). However, the definitions brought forward so far drew a thick line of distinction between financial innovation and financial disruption, one fitting within the current regulations and the other would require a new set of regulations in place. The literature consists of several different definitions and interpretations of 'fintech' many of which developed their own and some have cited or referred to others' work (Allen et al., 2020; Barberis, 2014; Bettinger, 1972; BIS, 2018; Brandl & Hornuf, 2017; Čižinská et al., 2016; FSB, 2017; IMF, 2019; Maier, 2016; Micu & Micu, 2016; Oxford Learning Dictionary, 2021; Shim & Shin, 2016). Table 1.1 reviews the definitions identified across different sources (journal articles, industry reports, websites and oxford dictionary).

Table 1.1. Summary of 'Fintech' Definitions.

Source	Definition
Bettinger (1972, p. 62)	'Is an acronym which stands for financial technology, combining bank expertise with modern management science techniques and the computer.'
Barberis (2014, p. 5)	'Fintech refers to the application of technology within the financial industry. The sector covers a wide of activities from payments (e.g. Contactless) to financial data and analysis (e.g. Credit scoring), financial software (e.g. Risk management), digitised processes (e.g. Authentication) and perhaps most well-known to the wider public, payment platforms (e.g. P2P lending).'
Čižinská et al. (2016, p. 461)	'"Fintech" is an economic industry composed of companies that use technology to make financial services more efficient.'
Micu and Micu (2016, p. 380)	'Financial technology also known as Fintech, is a new sector in the finance industry that incorporates the whole plethora of technology that is used in finance to facilitate trades, corporate business or

Table 1.1. *(Continued)*

Source	Definition
	interaction and services provided to retail consumer.’
Maier (2016, p. 143)	‘Driven by technological advances new service models have developed in the financial industry which offer additional opportunities to customers. Under the common denominator “fintech,” these businesses aim to challenge existing financial institutions by using technology to deliver value to the customer in an alternative way.’
Shim and Shin (2016, p. 170)	‘Fintech is an emerging financial services sector that includes third party payment, MMF, insurance products, risk management, authentication and peer-to-peer (P2P) lending.’
Schueffel (2016, p. 45)	‘Fintech is a new financial industry that applies technology to improve financial activities.’
Brandl and Hornuf (2017, p. 2)	‘An acronym for start-ups that commercialise technological financial innovations.’
FSB (2017, p. 7) and BIS (2018)	‘Technologically enabled financial innovation that could result in new business models, applications, processes, or products with an associated material effect on financial markets and institutions and the provision of financial services.’
IMF (2019, p. 8)	‘Advances in technology that have potential to transform the provision of financial services spurring new business models, applications, processes and products.’
Allen et al. (2020, p. 3)	‘A form of intermediation that is characterised by a shift from reliance on the balance sheet to instead utilise information technology in order to allocate capital, i.e. a shift from a dealer to a broker model of financial intermediation.’
Oxford English Dictionary (2021)[a]	‘Computer programs and other technology used to support or enable banking and financial services.’

[a]See Oxford Learner’s Dictionaries. https://www.oxfordlearnersdictionaries.com/definition/english/fintech#:~:text=fintech-,noun,provide%20banking%20and%20financial%20services

The IMF/World Bank came up with their own definition of fintech due to fintech being a very broad term that covers so many aspects regarding banks, supervisors and other industry participants. To the best of my knowledge, the most used 'fintech' definition was established by the Financial Stability Board (FSB, 2017). The definition was also adopted by the Basel Committee on Banking Supervision (BIS, 2018) and appeared in various institutional and academic papers (Agarwal & Zhang, 2020; FSB, 2019; Wang et al., 2020). Both IMF/World Bank, Financial Stability Board and Basel Committee on Banking Supervision definitions contain a handful of commonalities, most importantly is the focus of technology being the first part of the definition and the core inceptor to financial innovation/financial transformation. In addition, both definitions agree that it is not with complete certainty that the development in technology can lead to stimulating new business models inclusive of new products, services and processes. Hence, the words 'could result' and 'have potential' are used. However, FSB's definition defers marginally in highlighting the fact that there could be a material effect on the financial markets and the participants of these markets, perhaps such addition to the definition is a result of FSB's role in monitoring the global financial system and providing recommendations that are very much concerned with enhancing financial stability.

The most simple and inclusive definition was proposed by Schueffel (2016): 'fintech is a new financial industry that applies technology to improve financial activities'. This scientific definition captures new/improved financial services (device independent technology, e-trading, etc) and new disruptive technologies (blockchain, robo-advisors, cryptocurrency, etc). Yet, this definition differs widely from others mentioned above by overlooking certain words such as new products, services, processes and business models. Nonetheless, BIS (2018) emphasised on the fact that no umbrella definition is needed but perhaps what matters the most is a clear definition of the related products and services. As a result, regulators would be able to establish an approach for regulation. Still, definitions evolve over time and only an agreed upon and a shared definition will bring in significance to the word and that is highly necessary to science, reduction of miscommunication and eliminating misperception among users (regulators, practitioners, researchers, etc) (Waugh, 1997). It is also important to point out that there are substantial differences in defining fintech in the literature and perhaps it is due to the swappable use of the word 'fintech' in practice.

The association of finance and technology is widely regarded as 'fintech' and is very much misunderstood, especially when fintech is assumed as solely an outcome of the global financial crisis (GFC) of 2007–2010 rather than the crisis continue to act as a catalyst to the rapid growth of this very long-established relationship (Agarwal & Zhang, 2020; Choi, 2020). Certain events across history, dating back to 1866, set the foundation for the current state of this relationship: First, the transatlantic cable, the exogenous shock with immediate impacts on financial market operations at that point of time.[1] That said, bills of exchange

[1]See The Struggle for Control of Global Communication, The Formative Century, 2002. https://www.jstor.org/stable/10.5406/j.ctt2ttcks

came to an end and were labelled 'obsolete' and trading communications between merchants across the Atlantic fell from over a week in time to a few seconds. The introduction of the automatic teller machine (ATM) by Barclays back in 1967 is the second event that marks the development of the modern day relationship between finance and technology.[2] Although these events have impacted the industry drastically, after extensive research they are often forgotten and barely recognised in the recent literature on fintech. For this brief historical timeline, the main focus will be on two specific areas only, i.e. payments and consumers.

Within a period of five years from 1968 to 1973, the payment systems went through radical changes. The Inter-Bank Computer Bureau concerned with all transactions between UK banks was established to minimise human error, reducing time of processing payments/transactions and most importantly to streamline the entire process. Three years later, the company's name changed to Bankers Automated Clearing Services (BACS) (Welch, 1999).

On the other side of the Atlantic, the Clearing House Interbank Payment System (CHIPS) incepted in the United States during 1970.[3] The difference between the two nations is that throughout the period before the establishment of both systems to handle payments, the transactions between UK banks were mainly paper based. However, the United States had Fedwire which is a real-time gross settlement funds transfer system overseen by Federal Reserve Banks based on telegraph, 1970 recorded that system taking an electronic approach. An important fact to mention is that CHIPS is a private clearing house for transactions of large values whereas Fedwire is part of a regulatory body. In addition, the CHIPS clearing system is based on netting the transactions and consolidating them while Fedwire clears every transaction separately.

In 1973, the Society of Worldwide Interbank Financial Telecommunications (SWIFT) was established.[4] This system was created to link financial institutions across different geographical locations together for the purpose of sending/receiving financial transactions in a secure, reliable and a streamline method. However, as beneficial as this system is certain drawbacks are elevated in terms of terror financing and money laundering. Banks had to 'de-risk' which can result in a spread of risk to individuals, by forcing them to reach out for alternative sources to carry out transactions, which are less regulated leading to the same problem in the first place. In addition, increasing other sources of risks such as systemic risk.

The way technology is rapidly changing the shape of the financial industry especially regarding the close linkages between financial institutions and fintech institutions continues to be a vibrant discussion for policymakers and surely is affecting systemic risk. FSB (2017) suggests that fintech activities could run an intensified contagion of risk in the financial system and as a result denting

---

[2]See Thomas Lerner, Mobile Payment, 2013. https://link.springer.com/book/10.1007/978-3-658-03251-7

[3]See CHIPS, Federal Reserve Bank of New York. https://www.newyorkfed.org/aboutthefed/fedpoint/fed36.html

[4]See SWIFT History, Society of Worldwide Interbank Financial Communications. https://www.swift.com/about-us/discover-swift?AKredir=true

financial stability. Furthermore, Li et al. (2020) find that fintech's risk spread to financial institutions correlated directly with the increase of financial institutions' systemic risk. However, the existing literature remains premature in such regards. Payments are being transformed rapidly by digital innovation, an area where incumbent banks dominated throughout history.

In the consumer area, the first notable change was introduced back in 1980 and 1983 when online banking was first introduced in the United States and United Kingdom, respectively. Undoubtedly, the two and a half decades starting from 1980 recorded major changes in the financial industry; it is the period where technology was more integrated in financial services. Telegraph was replaced by the fax by the late 1980s; the introduction of the internet reshaped the industry and continues to restructure it to this day. The first online account checking was introduced by Wells Fargo back in 1995, and finally, the first direct bank without any physical branch emerged in 2005.[5]

The major differentiation is that using technology to provide financial services in the past was somehow expected to be by supervised banks. However, at present times and even with the high entry barriers to this industry which seem to be deteriorated, today's highly digitalised world could have acted as a catalyst along with the outcome of the GFC of 2008 to shake up the industry and allow non-bank firms to enter the industry and to some degree complement many financial services that banks provide. Moreover, Schueffel's (2016) acknowledgement of fintech as a new financial industry clearly describes the current scene of events, especially in terms of new and change in regulations. In the consumer area, certainly technology played a major role in reshaping the industry. However, post 2008 GFC, trust gained more momentum than technology and innovation for consumers. Telegraph's (2017) survey regarding the future of fintech reported that reliability and trust remain as the most important to financial services for consumers (Telegraph, 2017).[6]

3. Financial Innovation

The current level of digitalisation in our lives set the foundation for fintech firms to target certain banking services and products and provide them to certain market niches that traditional incumbent banks were unable to reach. Two of the core functions of financial services that Merton (1992) identified are 'moving funds across time and space' and 'pooling of funds', which were traditionally done through a savings account and the stock market; for the latter, financial innovation combined both core functions through crowdfunding.[7] Brandl & Hornuf (2017)

---

[5]See Wells Fargo, Wells Fargo celebrates 20 years of Internet Banking. https://stories.wf.com/wp-content/uploads/20years-of-internetbanking-at-WellsFargo-timeline.pdf

[6]See The Telegraph, Future of Fintech, 'What consumers really think', Consumer Survey 2017. https://www.telegraph.co.uk/content/dam/business/spark/Fintech/Telegraph_Fintech_Report%202017.pdf

[7]Crowdfunding is a method of raising finance by pooling a large number of people each for a small sum of money. See United Kingdom Crowdfunding Association (UKCFA) https://www.ukcfa.org.uk/what-is-crowdfunding/

argued that integrating sophisticated technology into financial services raised the question about the relationship between the lenders and borrowers and ultimately the role of the 'intermediator', which here refers to the traditional incumbent bank.

3.1 Technology-Enabled Financial Services

Several studies attempted to establish a fintech taxonomy in regard to the products and services, area of coverage and areas of activity (Arner et al., 2015; Gomber et al., 2017; He et al., 2017; Milian et al., 2019). To the best of my knowledge, the most suitable framework to describe fintech's products and services was established by BIS (2018). Fig. 1.1 shows fintech's innovation in each sector of financial services in the industry.

Although technological innovations in the financial industry date back to 1866, the years following the GFC of 2008 witnessed a very rapid development of technological innovation in the industry.[8] While Fig. 1.2 presents a framework to describe the underlying products and services of fintech firms, Table 1.2 illustrates the foundations of the technological innovations and how they result in some of the new financial products and services provided by fintech firms.

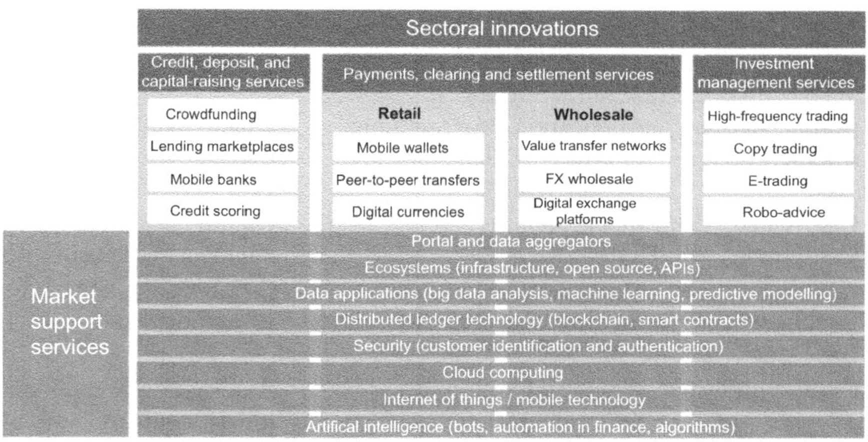

Fig. 1.1. Fintech's Products and Services and the Sector of Innovation Services. *Source:* BSCS. (See Basel Committee on Banking Supervision, Sound Practices, Implications of fintech developments for banks and bank supervisors, Bank for International Settlements, (February 2018)).

[8]The framework developed by BIS in Fig. 1.1 maps the scope of financial technology and embedded it is within the core financial services provided by the incumbents. More recent advanced in technology enabled all the market support services highlighted by BIS.

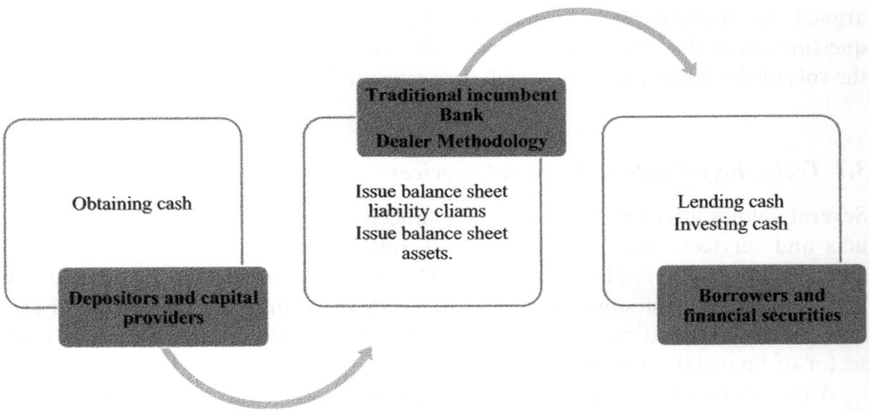

Fig. 1.2. Dealer Methodology Used by Traditional Banks. *Source:* Author's own.

Table 1.2. Foundation of Technology Innovation in Fintech Products and Services.

Technological Foundation	Technological Innovation	Innovative Financial Product/Service
Mobile Access Internet	Application Programming Interface (APIs) Digital Wallets	Digital Wallets Crowdfunding Peer to Peer
Distributed Computing	Blockchain	Digital currencies Payment settlement
Artificial Intelligence Big Data	Machine learning Predictive analytics	E-trading Robo-advisors
Cryptography	Biometrics Smart contracts	Automatic transaction Identity authentication/protection

Source: He et al. (2017).

The technological innovations presented in the table are the pure drivers of the current change in the financial industry, most if not all the innovations are understood to be intersecting. Artificial intelligence (AI), big data and cryptography are essential for distributed computing to successfully function to run effective blockchain services. As a result, digital wallets utilise the latter services to renovate mobiles and cell phones into payment devices or 'points of sale' (He et al., 2017). However, this directly implicates the high barriers of entry to financial intermediaries in the industry. The ability of the underlying technological innovation to bring together parties of transaction and more importantly reduce the cost of transaction resulted in decreasing the cost of intermediation in recent years and evidently amplified the competition in the industry (Philippon, 2020).

Under the theme of financial innovation with technology-enabled financial services in focus, the wider literature investigates the application of the technology rather than the technology itself. Consequently, Chen et al. (2019) provide an overall empirical work on fintech innovation, and others focused on certain elements of fintech innovation such as cryptocurrencies and initial coin offerings (Cahill & Liu, 2021; Foley et al., 2019; Howell et al., 2020), robo-advisors (D'Acunto et al., 2019) and AI (Ashta & Herrmann, 2021; Zhang et al., 2021). In addition, a set of papers focus on financial innovation and how it can affect the performance of banks (Beck et al., 2016; Chen & Du, 2016; Lee et al., 2021; Zouari-Hadiji, 2021).

The emergence of fintech firms into the financial industry have received mixed reaction by market participants and observers, as some fintech startups are selling their technology-enabled financial solutions to the incumbents while others are targeting the customer base of the incumbents. The implication of fintech firms on the incumbents is yet to be quantified as the industry continues to develop, but a key issue is how financial innovation brought forward by fintech firms can cause disruption or recalibrate the financial industry.

Chen et al. (2019) tackle the question of how valuable is fintech innovation precisely in the US market. They contribute to the developing fintech's taxonomy and empirical literature by defining fintech as 'the set of recently developed digital computing technologies that have been applied – or that will likely be applied in the future – to financial services'. The empirical results of this unique study contribute meticulously to the developing fintech literature, finding that fintech innovation are value to market participants and the industry. Yet certain sectors of the industry show negative implications such as blockchain technology can increase efficiency for the banking and insurance sectors while negatively implicating payment systems. In addition, data analytics shows significant disruption to all sectors in the financial industry suggesting a recalibration in the industry by new business models and fostering competition. More importantly, the study suggests that fintech innovation can yield incremental implications to the industry when originated by possible entrants while it also finds that incumbents with larger market shares will suffer less if it invests in innovation and R&D.

3.1.1 Blockchain and Cryptocurrencies

The strand of empirical literature based on the application of such technology in the banking industry is scarce because of its early stages in application; however, the dependency on the technology and applying it in the banking industry may benefit the incumbents and parallelly elevate cyber-related risks as prudential regulators suggest (BIS, 2018; FSB, 2017). However, the literature shows some important understandings of blockchain, suggesting that the two most important advantages of the technology when embedded within financial services is the ability simplify and reduce time costs with any financial transaction. On the other hand, blockchain is simply a distributed digital ledger with sophisticated protocols that are impeccable to alter, making it very beneficial in many functional areas (Schuetz & Venkatesh, 2020). Additionally, it is important to highlight that the first blockchain ledger was deployed to support the electronic system of Bitcoin (Nakamoto, 2008).

Cryptocurrencies remain a vital topic among users, investors, academics and regulators around the world, and in early 2021, the total market capitalisation of cryptocurrencies attained the $2 trillion benchmark with Bitcoin itself accounting for more than 50% of that market as Chavez-Dreyfuss (2021) reports. However, regulatory scrutiny on cryptocurrencies trading and usage by regulators in China resulted in a significant decrease in value of the highly volatile asset class losing nearly 50% of its market capitalisation (Reuters, 2021). Basel Committee on Banking Supervision suggests that banks with exposure to the asset class should endure tougher capital requirements while also acknowledging the limited exposure, yet it remains potentially capable of undermining financial stability and breed risks faced by the banks (BIS, 2021b).

While the volatility and financial stability risks are of great importance, Foley et al. (2019) attempt to measure and quantify the value and size of illegal activities in cryptocurrencies trading, which directly justify the concern by prudential regulators. The quantification of the illegal activity in Bitcoin based on the empirical analysis shows 29.12%, and 23.23% of Bitcoin users are involved in illegal activities. It also approximates 25% of the users, and 50% of the transactions are for illegal purposes, which represents 27 million users and $76 billion per year with most of the transactions taking place on the dark web. More importantly, they argue that the true intrinsic value of Bitcoin is a means of payment that facilitate illegal trade rather than financial innovation.

Bitcoin's trajectory has laid the path for other cryptocurrencies to enter the market, such as Ethereum (the second most popular cryptocurrency by market share), and more recently, Dogecoin is gaining momentum rapidly (Szalay & Venkataramakrishnan, 2021). Yeung (2020) suggests that demand, risk appetite of buyers and technical factors drive the price of cryptocurrencies, yet the value and survivability seem to be extremely heterogeneous among the asset class. Regulations played an important role in shaping project Libra by Facebook (the digital currency launched in June 2019), recently rebranded and relocated from Switzerland to the United States, due to global regulatory scrutiny as a result of concerns of becoming a platform for money laundering and more importantly, implicating monetary stability as Murphy (2021) reports.

Examining the performance and survivability of cryptocurrencies in relation to imitating Bitcoin, Cahill and Liu (2021) are able to show some empirical findings of the asset class volatility and other determinants of its longevity and success. The study classifies cryptocurrencies in two categories, copycat (CC) if it includes either 'Bit' or 'Coin' or non-copycat (NCC) if otherwise. They find 1,161 CCs and 2,248 NCC and that during 2017, the number NCC overtook CC justified by the growing attention by stakeholders to cryptocurrencies during that point of time. The empirical results shows that CCs are associated with highly yielding early periods and lower longevity, and this performance diminishes after passing the six-month period where NCC shows longer longevity. Such results can be interpreted as cryptocurrencies buyers are recognising that CCs may potentially yield similar returns as Bitcoin. In contrast, Cahill and Liu (2021) argue that the empirical findings of NCC's survivability can be interpreted that those coins may have the advantage of unique purposes, which plays an important role in mitigating the risks for the buyers. More importantly, due to the vast amount of initial coin offerings, the empirical results also suggests that coin buyers may prefer CC cryptocurrencies over NCC cryptocurrencies due to the current success of Bitcoin, faster higher yields and the difficulty in differentiating between NCCs and their aims.

According to Gorton and Zhang (2021), financial innovators have created more than 8,000 cryptocurrencies with many aiming towards democratising finance and achieving financial liberty. However, BIS (2021c) advocates that central bank digital currencies (CBDCs) will become prominent in the future and offers an adequate representation of money in the current digital economy. As the use of cash continues to decrease, time shall tell how central banks will transform from cash and notes to their respective CBDCs and how will the transformation affect the market capitalisation of current cryptocurrencies in the likes of Bitcoin, Ethereum, etc.

3.1.2 Artificial Intelligence and Robo-Advisors

Technology-enabled financial services have provided a pathway for different technological innovations, for instance robo-advisors. Robo-advisors collect information on their clients by asking various questions in relation to investment objectives, financial situation and other portfolio-related matters such as rebalancing and refinancing activities (Al-Araj et al., 2022; Al-Gasaymeh et al., 2023; Alkhaldi et al., 2023; Chebbi et al., 2024; Hatamlah et al., 2023). The introduction and adoption of robo-advisors precisely in wealth-management shed the light on issues concerning behavioural bias, following investment trends, risk appetite and diversification.

In such regards, D'Acunto et al. (2019) examine the wealth management robo-advisor tool which focuses on portfolio optimisation of Indian equities at a large brokerage house in India. The study, though limited to India only, provides substantial empirical findings where adopting robo-advisors with previously well-diversified investors shows no significant effect, yet it increases trading activities with no translation to superior performance. In contrast, undiversified investors show significant diversification and greater performance. D'Acunto et al. (2019) also suggest that after investors adopted the robo-advising tool, the exhibition of behaviour biases did not disappear. The interpretation of this study requires caution as the focus was on one asset class in one country only, and financial market dynamics and performance differ substantially across developing vs developed markets.

Basel Committee on Banking Supervision allocates AI as market support service; however, the application of the technology in the banking industry extends far beyond market support. For instance, financial institutions deploy AI to tackle uncertainties and increase both efficiency and productivity while the industry is undergoing constructive changes as they become more collaborative and open towards change. Yet, the empirical literature on technologies embedded in financial services in the likes of blockchain, robo-advisors and AI remains limited at this stage.

Ashta and Herrmann (2021) examine the opportunities and risks of applying AI in banking and investments, by using a case study methodology based on reviews of news articles, annual reports of financial institutions, business literature and a questionnaire responded to by six CEOs of organisations deploying AI in their operations.[9] They find that AI will provide substantial opportunities and dominates three areas (risk management, customer targeting and customer engagement) though AI benefits banks in cutting costs, and it also leads to more mergers among the incumbents to boost their customer bases. More importantly, Ashta and Herrmann (2021) suggest that the prerequisite for AI to be accepted in the financial industry is to 'learn how to learn' as customers will choose more function specialised fintech.

3.2 Financial Innovation and Banks' Performance

The quality of risk management plays a major role in banks' performance and stability, and it is important to be well maintained as the industry shifts further towards digitisation and adoption of technology-enabled financial products and services. In such regards, Zouari-Hadiji (2021) examines the direct and indirect implication of financial innovation on banks' performance through their risk management practices. This study deploys a sample of 10 Tunisian banks with data ranging from 2009 to 2018, obtained from publicly available financial statements and banks' reports from the Tunisian financial market council. Noteworthy, banks' performance is measured by return on assets (ROA) and market to book (MTB) financial indicators while risk management is measured by an annual value-at-risk (VaR). On the other hand, financial innovation characteristics are quantified using standard deviation of ROA for innovation risk, price-to-earnings ratio (PER) for innovation horizon and a ratio of tangible assets to total assets to measure the innovation horizon.

Zouari-Hadiji (2021) shows important empirical results where there is a positive relationship between the three financial innovation indicators and performance of banks with noticeable risk management practices. Furthermore, the results show that financial innovation drives the banks to mitigate the risks predominantly to achieve better performance. It is important to note that the direct and indirect effects of financial innovation on banks' performance under risk management practices is more significant in private banks that accounts for 7 of 10 banks in this study, which can be explained by their annual (VaR) to manage risks more effectively.

In a thorough cross-country study, Beck et al. (2016) review financial innovation and its implication on banks' growth, fragility and economic growth, by employing a sample of 32 countries over the period of 1996–2010. Their study

---

[9]The companies of the CEOs consist of AI service provides, digital solutions, analytics and fintech.

quantifies financial innovation more significantly than others in this strand of empirical literature, where four variables are used to measure financial innovation, including value added of financial R&D, cost of financial R&D, ratio of securitisation over GDP and off-balance sheet items over total assets, measure. Beck et al. (2016) find that all financial innovation variables exhibit positive effects on banks' growth; however, banks in countries with higher levels of financial innovation show faster pace of growth. Furthermore, banks in countries with rigorous entry requirement into the industry show low levels of growth. However, the results suggest negative implications on banks' fragility and performance under severe economic conditions. While the study shows heterogenous empirical results, it concludes a net progressive impact of financial innovation on economic growth in countries with better growth opportunities. Furthermore, the study also proposes that financial innovation is significantly associated with private bank ownership where Zouari-Hadiji (2021) also shows consistent results.

Lee et al. (2021) examine how fintech innovation development in China is affecting cost efficiency and the adoption of the technology with the Chinese banking industry. The study utilises data covering 5 state-owned commercial banks (SOCBs), 12 joint stock commercial banks (JSCBs) and 69 city commercial banks (CCBs) from 2003 to 2017. Very importantly, this empirical study is the first to deploy the Basel Committee on Banking Supervision fintech innovation taxonomy (BIS, 2018) to classify the fintech firms in the data based on their innovation. Efficiency is measured based on three different parameters, group-specific cost efficiency (CE), Metafrontier cost efficiency (MCE) and technology gap ratio (TGR).

The results indicate that adequately capitalised banks demonstrate cost efficiency while banks with less investments in their technology tend to agonise more from non-performing loans. Accounting for the management structures of the banks in the sample, Lee et al. (2021) find varied results as fintech innovation exhibit stronger negative impact on CCBs due to their limited funds to invest in technology while fintech innovation shows weaker implication on JSCBs, in comparing both types of commercial banks to SOCBs. However, it is important to understand the banking industry in China, fintech innovation and investment in technology are capable in yielding an advantage for the adaptor, yet the position of SOCBs supported by national credit guarantee and monopolistic features are providing defensive capabilities against the fintech innovation development in the nation. Consequently, under different circumstances there may have been a different empirical finding.

4. Financial Disintermediation

Financial intermediation by traditional incumbent banks contributed significantly to sustainability and growth throughout the years and in particular reducing inequality and poverty and improving overall economic performance (Beck et al., 2007; Demirgüç-Kunt & Levine, 2009). However, the impact of technological advancements on the cost of financial intermediation resulted in minor gains in efficiency if not none (Bazot, 2018; Philippon, 2015). It is possible that cost efficiency gains are little to no due to systemic stability being the underlying expense, and banks are of great importance to the overall economy along with the fact that they are given 'safety net regulatory subsidies' (Allen et al., 2012). The facts undoubtedly explain why fintech innovation is originating outside the regulated banking industry, in particular the shadow banking sector (Ari et al., 2017).

4.1 Dealer and Broker Financial Intermediation

Financial intermediaries' main function is to draw together lenders and borrowers or providers and users of capital; this is done through information and communication (Boot et al., 2020).[10] Traditionally, incumbent banks utilise their branch network to be the first point of contact to provide financial services to individuals functioning as an intermediator. However, fintech firms employ innovative financial products and services using the underlying technological advancements to take on the role of the intermediator that traditional banks always did by eliminating the presence of physical branches. The methodology of intermediation applied by incumbent traditional banks and fintech firms differs. Successively, fintech firms use 'broker' methodology and traditional banks use 'dealer' methodology (Allen et al., 2020). Figs. 1.2 and 1.3 explain the intermediation function using dealer and broker methodology, respectively.

As evident from Figs. 1.2 and 1.3, traditional incumbent banks obtain cash from lenders (for example: depositors, investors, savers, etc) and then use a leveraged balance sheet to function as an intermediator. In the process, banks endure high costs to maintain their financial resources, and a handful of risks, for example credit risk, liquidity risk, interest rate risk, etc. In contrast, fintech firms capitalise on the underlying technological innovations to provide new financial products and services to individuals with zero balance sheet commitment, less risks and lower cost to maintain financial resources. As a result, this methodology reduces the cost of intermediation and potentially disintermediate the incumbent banks (Allen et al., 2020; Brandl & Hornuf, 2017). Although technology's role in traditional incumbent banks have grown throughout the years (Feng & Wu, 2018), this was offset by the heavy regulations imposed on the banks especially after the GFC of 2008 and perhaps can explain why the foundation of intermediation by traditional banks remained constant.

4.2 Vertical and Horizontal-Integrated Financial Intermediation

The recent steep innovation in information and communication is presenting structural challenges for traditional incumbent banks' business model.[11] Horizontally, fintech firms are able to enter the industry and compete with traditional

---

[10]Traditional incumbent banks acting as financial intermediaries overcome moral hazard and adverse selection in order to match lenders and borrowers.

[11]Traditional banks are vertically and horizontally integrated financial intermediaries. Vertically, banks utilise their balance sheet to network with customers through deposit taking and lending. Horizontally, banks depend on 'informational and communication synergies' to offer services that do not require the balance sheet of the bank. See Boot et al. (2020).

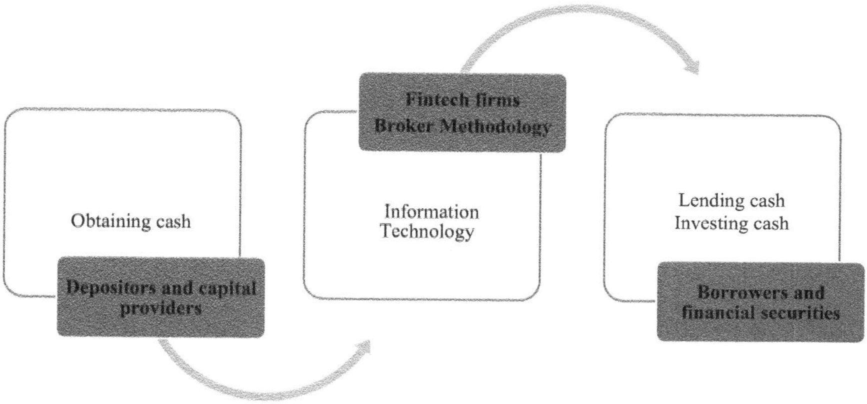

Fig. 1.3. Broker Methodology Used by Fintech Firms. *Source:* Author's own.

incumbent banks by focusing on providing financial services that don't require operating a balance sheet. Vertically, fintech firms are competing through reaching out to customers openly (Berlin & Mester, 1998). In horizontal terms, fintech firms are potentially capable of disintegrating banking services for two main reasons. First, regulation is playing a crucial role in the disintegration process since most jurisdictions allow non-financial firms to provide specific financial services such as electronic payments. However, traditional incumbent banks have been outsourcing back-office operations and in recent years started outsourcing 'pre-sales and information technology' (BIS, 2014). In contrast, the current disintegration we are witnessing is propelled by communication and can potentially produce tangible structural changes in integrated financial intermediaries such as banks. Second, the broker methodology of financial intermediation used by fintech firms in addition to the lack of balance sheet prerequisite to provide these services are facilitating the disintegration of the traditional incumbent bank's business model.[12] Moreover, fintech firms can overcome inefficiencies of large traditional banks by specialising in offering certain financial services. By utilising innovative underlying technology, fintech firms are able to be more robust and efficient and compete with the incumbents in terms of suitability, time and price (Boot et al., 2020; Fuster et al., 2020).

Despite all the rapid advances in the underlying technological innovations and their impact on finance and continuously changing regulations in recent times, traditional incumbent banks continue to engage in many intermediation activities (such as payment services, information processing, maturity transformation and

[12]The broker methodology refers to the practice of connecting borrowers and lenders directly through digital platforms, bypassing the need for traditional balance-sheet-based intermediation. This allows fintech firms to operate with lower regulatory and capital requirements compared to incumbent banks.

risk pooling) that meet their objectives and structure their balance sheet accordingly (Roengpitya et al., 2014). The challenges to traditional incumbent banks are not new; however, only lately fintech firms have started using digital platforms to provide a wide range of products and services which are customer-oriented. Banks have always invested in fintech platforms to achieve higher efficiency and such investments resulted in growth throughout the years. Nevertheless, fintech firms focusing on more customer-oriented products and capitalising on the damaged reputation of traditional incumbent banks after the GFC of 2008 are aiming to disrupt and potentially replace the banks (Petralia et al., 2019).

4.3 Financial Disintermediation

Industry observers argue that fintech firms are capitalising on the technology-enabled financial services and innovative products in areas where banks face higher fixed costs and a damaged reputation in the aftershock of the GFC of 2008. While the methodology of intermediation among the incumbents and fintech firms was reviewed in earlier, the implications of fintech firms entering the credit market globally may yet to be realised. However, some empirical studies show a glimpse of fintech's effect on the credit market and their implications on the incumbents' performance and lending behaviour.

Di Maggio and Yao (2021) examine the personal credit market in the United States by using data from one of the top three credit bureaus with a sample of 3,792,757 loans originating from both fintech and traditional lenders from 2012 to 2017. They find important empirical results suggesting that fintech lenders tend to start off their operations by lending less creditworthy individuals which gradually changes to more creditworthy individuals. The understanding of such behaviour from fintech lenders is to establish a pool of borrowers and book revenues; while such lending activity may aggravate the levels of risk, they also find that fintech lenders seem to price their loans better in comparison to the incumbents. Surprisingly, they show that fintech lenders depend on hard information available in the credit bureau reports rather than advancement in technology, indicating insufficiency in soft information. However, they show that as fintech lenders gain market share they shift away from hard information, and they become integrated in the market.

Furthermore, Di Maggio and Yao (2021) find that loan defaults from fintech lenders are higher in comparison to the incumbents. The interpretation of such result is complex; they justify such result by finding that individuals are likely to borrow from a fintech lender within a short period after unemployment. In addition, based on their underlying mechanism they suggest that fintech borrowers acquire the funds for additional spending rather than servicing other outstanding debt. As a result, prudential regulators are concerned with expansion of credit and lack of safety nets.

4.3.1 P2P Lending and Crowdfunding

In 2016, technology-enabled lending platforms accounted for the largest share of lending in the United States, standing at 30% of unsecured instalment loans as the credit bureau agency as TransUnion (2017) reports.[13] However, the question remains unanswered to whether fintech activities such as P2Plending would replace or complements the incumbents lending activities. As researchers and academics endeavour into the discussion, few studies provide important suggestions empirically.

Tang (2019) examines whether P2P lending platforms can substitute or complements the incumbents in the consumer credit market in the United States, by developing a conceptual framework where P2P and incumbent lenders harmonise.[14] The study uses data from LendingClub and Call Reports under FAS 166/167 from (FDIC) for 59 banks,[15] from 2009 to 2012. By using a negative regulatory shock to bank credit supply, Tang (2019) shows that the technology-based platforms can capitalise and grow their business as a result of less creditworthy borrowers shifting to the P2P platforms from the incumbents. In contrast, the study also finds a complementary relationship among both parties given that P2P platforms are able to finance small loans. It can be seen from such results that possible changes in regulations in the coming years will determine the relationship between the technology-enabled financial platforms and the incumbents.

Fraud, financial misconduct and diminishing trust in the banks is arguably playing a vital role along other variables in restructuring the banking industry (Petralia et al., 2019). In one of the earliest studies to examine the implication of bank misconduct and fintech (characterised by online lending platforms), Bertsch et al. (2020) examine the relationship between bank misconduct and the growth of online lending in the United States. Using data from LendingClub, Prosper and a proxy of bank misconduct exemplified by complaints received by the Consumer Financial Protection Bureau (CFPB). The study finds that bank misconduct is significant in explaining the rise of online lending in the United States under a local and a national setting examination and that fraud and misconduct by the bankers are driving borrowers to alternative sources of credit while accounting for the loan pricing.

Furthermore, trust seems to play an important role in the relationship of bank misconduct and the rise of online lending. Bertsch et al. (2020) provide empirical evidence suggesting that in regions where the general trust is high, traditional lending remains preferable. Additionally, the association between bank misconduct and online lending is significantly referable to CFPB complaints and bank service quality. It is possible to see from these results a different view on explaining borrowers' choice of credit. While Tang (2019) shows that borrowers may find online lending platforms more welcoming for their small size loan

---

[13]For further details, see Newsroom, TransUnion (2017, November 2). https://newsroom.transunion.com/fintechs-taking-larger-share-of-personal-loan-market-while-increasing-portfolio-risk-return-performance/

[14]The conceptual framework considers that banks and P2P lending platforms compete with each other in the market.

[15]FAS 166/167 require banks to consolidate variable interest entities (VIEs) that are not consolidated under the generally accepted accounting practices (GAAP). For further details, see FDIC (2009, June). https://www.fdic.gov/news/financial-institution-letters/2010/fil10003a.pdf

offerings, Bertsch et al. (2020) show that trust remains more important than loan size and prices in some regions in the United States.

4.3.2 Declining Cost of Intermediation and Potential Disintermediation of Traditional Banks

Prior studies investigating the unit cost of intermediation throughout historical time periods include (Bazot, 2018; Philippon, 2015). In addition, Berg et al. (2020) show how alternative credit scoring methods are implicating credit scoring, underlining a main function of financial intermediaries. Moreover, Hodula (2022); Koranteng and You (2024); Pampurini et al. (2024); Strebinger and Treiblmaier (2024) and Yang and Zhou (2024) focus on possible disintermediation.

Philippon (2015) studies the role of intermediation performed by the finance industry by focusing on the theory and measurement of financial intermediation precisely in the United States. Various sources of data are used in the paper which include Securities Industry and Financial Markets Associations (SIFMA), Federal Reserve's Flow of Funds, Humane Society of the United States, US Bureau of Economic Analysis, etc.[16] The result contributes by quantifying and examining the changes in the unit cost of intermediation, income of financial intermediation and the quantity of intermediated assets.[17] With the rapid advancement in technology and innovation in the finance industry, Philippon (2015) shows that the unit cost of intermediation remains constantly high as it was back in early 1900s. Furthermore, the income of financial intermediation is driven by the significant increase in quantity and quality of intermediated assets throughout the years, which also appears to fluctuate across different periods due to different economic cycles.

On the other hand, Bazot (2018) attempts to measure the unit cost of financial intermediation across Germany, France and the United Kingdom based on data from OECD running from 1950 to 2007. The approach in measuring the unit cost of financial intermediation differs slightly from Philippon (2015), the unit cost is calculated using a ratio of financial income to financial output.[18] The results shows a significant positive correlation between the unit cost of intermediation and nominal interest rates across the three different nations, which can be distinguished from the

---

[16]For further data sources used in this paper, please refer to Philippon (2015) Data Appendix, See https://www.aeaweb.org/articles?id=10.1257/aer.20120578

[17]Income of financial intermediation is estimated by dividing value added of finance industry over GDP. Quantity of intermediated assets is estimated by accounting for outstanding consumer credit, holding of liquid assets, and value of intermediated corporate assets. The measurement of this indicator is based on principal of including instrument on balance sheets of three parties, nonfinancial firms, households, and end users. Unit cost of intermediation is estimated by dividing income of financial intermediation over the adjusted intermediated assets. See Philippon (2015) for further details.

[18]Financial income is measured as a percentage of the GDP, while financial output measures the quantity of financial services obtained from the financial industry, main through credit provision, securities issuance, and wealth management. See Bazot (2018) for further details.

increase in the unit cost of intermediation from 1970s and 1980s parallelled by an increase in nominal interest rates. In contrast, nominal interest rates declined across the 1990s and early 2000s while the unit cost of intermediation remained high due to further development of credit intermediation and wealth management in the financial industry.

In comparison to Philippon (2015), Bazot (2018) show that the unit cost of the three major European economies increased since the 1960s. However, the increase is significantly in smaller quantities than in the United States. It remains as an open question of how fintech firms will affect the unit cost of financial intermediation and potential disintermediation of banks. Prudential regulators are concerned with potential disintermediation of the incumbents (BIS, 2018; FSB, 2017, 2019).

Through examining the impact of fintech on financial stability across multiple nations, Koranteng and You (2024) find that the emergence of fintech has the potential to disrupt the existing structure of the financial industry by fostering strategic disintermediation, which can expose the financial system to increased interconnections and financial network complexities. While Yang and Zhou (2024) show that fintech emergence can enhance financial disintermediation by reducing the role of financial intermediaries, helping to relieve financing constraints for private enterprises, which is a mechanism by which fintech development can improve industrial ownership structure and narrow internal economic disparities in China. In contrast, Strebinger and Treiblmaier (2024) provide empirical evidence on the likelihood of full disintermediation of B2C industries through blockchain technology. The result suggests that a full disintermediation in the financial industry is highly unlikely; however, there is strong indication of disruption to traditional financial services by introducing and embedding decentralised P2P transactions.

Hodula (2022) address the possibility of fintech credit replacing traditional credit through examining 78 countries. The work finds that fintech credit can act as both substitute and complement for traditional incumbents' credit. However, this result is well driven by the banking industry's characteristics where in less concentrated and more stable markets, fintech credit acts as a compliment to traditional banking credit and severs different niche in the market. Oppositely, in a concentrated banking industry, fintech credit acts as a direct substitute either by competing for similar borrowers or through extending credit to a gap in the market. Pampurini et al. (2024) show that in Italy, the emergence of fintech firms has led to increased disintermediation in the financial sector. This was evident through the creation of new business opportunities that have changed the way users access financial services, leading to increased demand for cheap, accessible and technology-enabled financial solutions.

5. Financial Disruption

5.1 Disruption to Primary Functions of Traditional Incumbent Banks

Highly competitive challenges, macroeconomic slump and lower interest rates combined with the Covid-19 pandemic pressurised traditional banks and the industry as a whole. As innovative digital technologies continue to lower the barriers to entry, the incumbents are facing major disruption to their most primary functions of payment services and maturity transformation (Petralia et al., 2019; Thakor, 2020a, 2020b). The loss of the payment services business is significantly disrupting traditional incumbent banks; World Economic Forum (2015) implied that it could also lead to the loss of client relationships and cross-selling opportunities. Fintech innovations are potentially capable of adversely affecting the financial system and developing micro- and macro-financial risks.[19] However, the impact is yet to be supported by any evidence (FSB, 2017), but Sahay et al. (2020) distinguished the limited disruption caused by fintech firms through filling the gaps in traditional incumbent banks' services using digital solutions. Moreover, the current trend in disruption of fintech innovation has been bounded at a regional level rather than a global level as result of the complexity in regulations across various jurisdictions (Galvin et al., 2018).[20]

5.1.1 Maturity Transformation

The competition in lending in recent years increased radically, and it is undeniably a result of the rapid innovation within this function of traditional banks. In this area, fintech firms have expanded the access to credit through the application of innovative credit review techniques with the backing of data, machine learning models and automation of the decisions on loan approval, which all resulted in streamlining the process and decreasing the time taken to approve a loan drastically (De Roure et al., 2016; Jagtiani & Lemieux, 2018).[21]

However, fintech's P2P lending through digital platforms is causing decentralisation in the financial services aligned with the fact of disruption and absence of traditional risk and maturity transformation (Navaretti et al., 2017). As a result, more attention is directed towards fraud events, cyber risk, higher rate of defaults and breakdown of the platforms (Claessens et al., 2018).[22]

As beneficial fintech lending to the overall competition and expansion of credit, it sets the scene for major disruption and spillovers of risks to the incumbent banks. Lending standards can be undermined substantially, the undiversified nature and procyclicality of the lending model of fintech lenders, lack of fintech firms' access to safety nets and an increase in lending activity outside the regulatory net can all lead to disruption in traditional banks' profitability and overall financial stability (Claessens et al., 2018).

---

[19]Micro-financial risks are categorised as financial risks (such as: maturity mismatch), and operational risks (such as: cyber risk, regulatory risk). Macro-financial risks such as: contagion, procyclicality, and excess volatility.

[20]In terms of payments, European fintech firms find it difficult to expand their business to the US due to the fact that individual states require separate money transfer licenses.

[21]These innovative credit review techniques leverage non-traditional data sources, such as social media activity and transaction histories, to assess creditworthiness. The use of machine learning algorithms further enhances the accuracy of credit risk evaluation, enabling faster and more efficient decision-making.

[22]Higher default rates slumped investors' returns in China, United Kingdom, Australia, Korea, and the United States, similar periods where non-performing loans are at low levels.

5.1.2 Payment Services

For some time now, fintech firms have been offering payment services to users mainly through mobile applications, and these services are offered in both domestic and cross jurisdictions. The increase in involvement of fintech firms in this area could potentially erupt risks and cause disruption in the system (BIS, 2014). Nevertheless, fintech firms' investment in infrastructure technology to create systems and platforms to offer payment services decreases the cost of servicing the clients (Philippon, 2020). Consequently, fintech firms are capable of improving efficiency of the payment systems, offering more payment options, using data (such as: payment patterns) to offer bespoke services and with all these benefits at a lower cost in comparison to the incumbents (Petralia et al., 2019).

In any payment service, offered by traditional banks or fintech firms, certain risks rise, such as fraud, operational, legal, settlement, credit, systemic and liquidity (CPSS, 2000). The major difference in the potential impact of disruption in case of any of these risks are triggered is the risk mitigation measures in place. Emphasising on the importance of risk mitigation measures among regulators (BIS, 2014, 2018) is a result of the growing involvement of fintech firms in the payment service business and their presence at some stage in the payment chain.

Therefore, fintech firms could potentially focus on providing a specific service and achieving a large network and economies of scale leading to concentration which may affect operational risk. In addition, traditional banks collaborating with fintech firms through outsourcing payment services may result in an increase in operational risk (BIS, 2014). The focus on operational risk in both scenarios Fintech firms' involvement in the payment services business is merely a beginning to other risks that are yet to be identified or understood (FSB, 2017).[23]

5.2 Key Risks

The magnitude of the risks surfacing from embedding advanced innovative technology in the delivery of financial services is yet to be clear, along with the entry of non-banks or fintech firms into the financial industry (Allen et al., 2020). However, some research was able to pinpoint certain risks that may potentially lead to disintermediation of the incumbents and disruption to the global financial system (Adelmann et al., 2020; Aldasoro et al., 2020, 2021; BIS, 2018; FSB, 2017, 2019).

5.2.1 Strategic Risk

The main concern of regulators in terms of strategic risk lies within the capability and potential of fintech firms to disassemble financial services using innovative underlying technologies to offer services that banks usually bundle and offer and directly implicate the profitability of the traditional incumbent banks (BIS, 2018). Therefore, the risk of lower profitability for the incumbents raises regulators'

[23]First, fintech firms specialise in a specific payment service and become concentrated. Second, incumbent banks rely on outsourcing payment services to fintech firms.

concern in regard to their ability to endure severe economic conditions. In addition, such conditions may potentially motivate traditional incumbent banks to engage in riskier activities to offset the decline in their profitability (Khan & Malaika, 2021).

5.2.2 Compliance Risk

The complexity of compliance with regulatory requirements puts the burden on the incumbents to adapt appropriate monitoring processes in place. The incumbents processing transactions on behalf of fintech firms are held accountable to authentication and may risk finding themselves involved in illegal transactions. The degree of automation, responsibility and delivery of financial products and services by fintech firms and the incumbents can potentially undermine transparency and therefore compliance risk soars drastically, especially when one party is operating outside the regulatory net (Khiaonarong & Goh, 2020; BIS, 2021a).

5.2.3 Cyber and Operational Risk

Traditional incumbent banks have had pressures from numerous sources encountering high levels of operational risks but post the GFC of 2008 losses from operational risk declined (Aldasoro et al., 2023). However, the developments are different due to new players with advanced technological innovations which are capable of offering financial services outside the regulatory net (FSB, 2019). Consequently, the rise of outsourcing to third party service providers by the incumbents is gaining momentum and becoming highly critical, and in most cases, these third-party service providers consist of fintech firms that fall outside the regulatory net. As a result, FSB (2017) suggested that higher levels of operational risk may potentially cause disruption and directly affect financial stability. BIS (2018) advocated that such risk could lead to a systemic crisis within the industry and may create a new dimension of operational risk with great potential of causing financial disruption. Cyber risk and operational risk are integrated, and perhaps cyber risk falls under a wide range of operational risks for financial institutions. In such regards, research in this domain is scarce, and researchers are yet to empirically examine the implications of cyber risks on targeted organisations such as banks because of limited data on cyber incidents and their trust costs.

As we move further in the era of the digitised economy, cyber risk is becoming more of a major threat and cause for disruption in the global financial system; however, it remains under the perception of being a subclass of operational risks (Kopp et al., 2017). Cyber risk as a term covers a wide range of information technology related failures or breaches and is normally defined as 'the risk of financial loss, disruption or reputational damage to an organisation resulting from the failure of its IT systems' (Aldasoro et al., 2022). Higher levels of digitalisation coming into our lives is developing and extending cyber risks beyond the global financial system (Aldasoro et al., 2021, 2023).

Some studies were able to allocate the sectors in the economy where cyber-attacks are more likely to take place, and it is without surprise the financial sector, consisting of the traditional incumbent banks, financial services firms, fintech firms and insurance companies and subsequently of their critical role of financial intermediation and high degree of IT dependency (Kamiya et al., 2021; Kopp et al., 2017). In addition, Bouveret (2018) was able to quantify the underlying VaR linked to cyber risks. Cyber risks continue to pose an imminent threat and a driver of financial disruption in the system. FSB (2017) emphasised on embedding cybersecurity mechanisms in the early stages of fintech firms' operations and the incumbents due to the higher dependency on advanced technology in their operations.

Nonetheless, supervision will play a greater role in the coming years as Aldasoro et al. (2022) suggested that adequate quality of supervision of financial services is positively correlated with lower loses from operational risks; however, there seems to be no relationship between the quality of supervision and the frequency and number of losses associated with cyberattacks. Fintech literacy will play an important role in terms of cyber risks as fintech firms continue their endeavour into the industry, and FSB (2019) noted that the higher literacy and risk awareness among users, regulators and supervisors will decrease the probability of financial disruption. It is also important to mention that cyber risk is very often stressed upon in financial stability reports and research published by prudential authorities and central banks around the world (Adelmann et al., 2020).

Historical operational risk losses have been correlated with human error or fraud in several forms; few notable examples include the case of internal fraud which set back Barings Bank a billion US dollars in 1995 and by JP Morgan Chase with $6 billion in 2012 (RBNZ, 2019). Operational losses are extremely relevant to banking supervision and regulation. In the United States, the Federal Reserve require the largest Banking Holding Companies (BHCs) with assets above $10 billion benchmark to participate in an annal Comprehensive Capital Analysis and Review (CCAR) programme complemented by Dodd-Frank Act Stress Testing (DFAST) and to determine the adequacy of BHCs' capital to withstand economic and financial stress and resume operations (Federal Reserve, 2021).

Consequently, Curti and Migueis (2021) concentrate on the possibility of information of past operational losses in predicting future operational losses by focusing on US banks. They depend on a sample of 38 publicly traded BHCs that participate in both (CCAR and DFAST) programs and reports of their operational losses in the FR Y-14Q form to the Federal Reserve. The form includes significant amount of information that is useful to conduct empirical research.

Furthermore, internal fraud may have caused mayhem in notable cases, but Basel II defined and classified operational losses into seven types, and Curti and Migueis (2021) study follows these forms. The study shows that asset size is significant with operational losses, and two types of operational losses (CPBP and EDPM) are more prominent in the losses, while BDSF shows no significance to operational losses. The study's empirical evidence support the usefulness of historical data to predict future exposure, yet certain factors related operational exposure such as the risk culture and appetite remain difficult to quantify (Curti & Migueis, 2021).

In line with the view that cyber risk falls under operational risk, Aldasoro et al. (2023) approach operational risk losses and cyber risk losses by using VaR methods and consequently compare the results to Basel II accords' Basic Indicator Approach (BIA). The first empirical result suggests operational risks can be valued between 6% and 12% of total gross income of the banks, and regularly, it takes on minimum a year to be uncovered and registered in the books of the banks. The results also show that the periods followed by expanding monetary policies show a significant increase in number of operational losses and their value, defended by the risk-taking behaviour of the banks under such economic conditions.

On the other hand, Aldasoro et al. (2023) estimate cyber risk losses as a proportion of total operational losses, and the empirical result indicates a significant spike in cyber risk events around 2016, suggesting a similar period in regard to fintech rapid growth. The second empirical result shows that cyber risk losses are valued at 0.25–0.65% of total gross income of the banks. While this study finds empirical evidence to correlate operational losses with the macroeconomic conditions, this does not hold for cyber losses. However, it suggests stringent supervision can mitigate cyber risks so does the broader operational risk.

Due to the growing attention to cyber risk by prudential regulators and researchers, the Bank for International Settlements published another paper in the same year focusing mainly on cyber risk across 21 sectors including (the financial and insurance sector) using a dataset consisting of 115,416 cyber incidents. Aldasoro et al. (2022) show that the majority of the incidents took place in the American regions with Africa have the least figure.

Cyber events can take a wide range of forms; hence, the study classifies events into security incidents, data breach, IT implementation errors, phishing/skimming, privacy violation, and others which include any other cyber event not recognised in any of the categories. In order to find an inference of the drivers of cyber incidents and provide suggestions for mitigating such events, the study uses cloud dependency, technological skills and IT spending by each sector to conduct the investigation. In terms of technological skills, they find that organisations in sectors with developed technological skills are superior at overseeing the costs incurred from cyber incidents. While for cloud services, they show that higher levels of investment and dependency on the services can lower the cost of cyber incidents, they justify such result by suggesting that the cloud's cybersecurity services provide protection for the user. Aldasoro et al. (2022) present important empirical results that should be interpreted with caution as cyber-related incidents remain very difficult to quantify and measure. Yet, the increase in cloud services dependency can expose the users to new forms of risks through malware, viruses, etc.

Uddin et al. (2020) investigate whether spending on technology can alter the stability of banks. Like Wang et al. (2020), they use Z-score to represent a stability proxy of the banks. They argue that the first variable measures the total spending on cyber technology outlined by the strategy of a bank, and the second variable is able capture a bank's budget allocation policy in comparison to other expenses. The study shows that Chinese banks spent the most dollar amount on cyber technology throughout the period of the study, with Bangladeshi Banks spending the least amount.

Uddin et al.'s (2020) study differs from others reviewed earlier as it finds spending on cyber technology proposes no gains but rather increases risk of banks from all sizes and affects their stability. Uddin et al.'s (2020) finding is related to the fintech era as it suggests significant effects on banks from all sizes operating in technologically advanced countries. The empirical literature on cyber risk and financial institutions is very scarce due to limitation and accuracy of data and shortage of reporting cyber-related incidents by targeted firms. Yet, Aldasoro et al. (2022) and (2023) present imperative results and methodologies to build upon. However, other studies also focusing on cyber risk, such as Eling and Wirfs (2019); Makridis and Dean (2018), argue that there seems to be no long-run economic effect on targeted firms. More importantly, breaches in cybersecurity of the firms are only recognised when the targeted firm reports them and that does not necessarily imply that there have been zero cybersecurity breaches in any form, within periods that show no reports on cyber-related incidents.

In brief, this strand of empirical literature is gaining the attention of academics and researchers, and the availability and accuracy of the data will shape its pace. Moreover, empirical findings should be interpreted with caution as historical data used in the reviewed paper doesn't not quantify the potential number and magnitude of future cyber-related incidents as firms from different sectors continue to digitalise their operations more rapidly than the past.

Under the theme of financial disruption, a substantial number of empirical research is present that is concerned with fintech's impact on banks' risk taking and fostering competition in the banking industry through studying different aspects of fintech. However, the current empirical literature indicates a geographical division due to the varying levels of fintech development across the world.

China is leading the world in terms of fintech development as a result of certain key factors that helped the fintech sector to develop at a rapid pace. The Chinese authorities exhibited through their policies and actions through the years facilitated this rapid pace. Hua and Huang (2021) suggest that the accommodative regulations and the government support to utilise the technology-enabled financial services as a tool to promote financial inclusion to supply the shortage in the Chinese financial markets, contributed thoroughly to such prominent fintech development. In such regards, this can be observed by the fact that Alipay commenced its business in 2004, yet only in 2011, it required to attain an official license. Furthermore, FinVolution Group, the first peer to peer lending platform in China, established in 2007 and experienced 9 years without any scrutiny from the regulators.

Fitch Ratings (2021) also suggest that due to the sizable market in China, the authorities in the years leading up to failure of P2P lending platform Ezubao in 2016 side-stepped disrupting financial innovation through the rapidly developing fintech sector as it is important to support the overall economic growth in China.

An early and fast development of the fintech sector may be providing adequate data for researchers to conduct their research. In addition, most of the empirical literature focusing on China's fintech and its implications on commercial banks secured grants by the National Natural Science Foundation of China (NSFC) and Beijing Municipal Social Science Foundation (BMSSF). In NSFC's latest guidance to its programs under economic sciences, it emphasises that the priority and more attention will be paid to those research proposals focusing on an array of disciplines with specific elaboration on fintech and China's economic structural adjustments.[24] All these key factors are playing an important role in the quantity and quality of fintech research focusing on China in recent years being published in a variety of high-quality journals, such as the *European Journal of Finance*, *International Journal of Finance and Economics*, *Technological Forecasting & Social Change*, etc.

Consequently, the majority of the recent empirical research is focusing on China (Chen et al., 2021; Cheng & Qu, 2020; Cho & Chen, 2021; Hua & Huang, 2021; Meifang et al., 2018; Sheng, 2021; Wang et al., 2020, 2021; Wang & Huang, 2018; Yao et al., 2021; Yao & Song, 2021) in comparison to the US (Bunea et al., 2018; Jagtiani & Lemieux, 2018; Li et al., 2020), Indonesia (Phan et al., 2020), Latin America and the Caribbean (Tambunlertchai et al., 2022), North America and the European Union (Carlini et al., 2022). Fung et al. (2020)'s study is unique in having a wide sample comprising 84 countries.

5.2.4 Payments, Lending, and Spillover of Risk

Bunea et al. (2018) explore the attitude of US banks towards the fintech sector, using the annual 10-K forms filed in the 12 months ending in 2017 with the SEC by the publicly listed banks and several explanatory variables (bank size, ROE, ROA and CEO characteristics) to determine which variable is more relative to a bank mentioning fintech in their forms. Bunea et al. (2018) show that only in 2016, the banks in their study raised up concern of the fintech sector potentially implicating their business. In 2016, 14 banks filed concerns and the number increased to 66 banks representing 14% of the sample in their study. Moreover, they show that bank size is significantly related to the banks concerned with the fintech sector.

The incumbent filers show concern about fintech's implication on two main areas, namely payments and lending. Such concern can be interpreted in different perspectives. While fintech's eminence soared in the past decade might be able to explain the incumbent's reaction, it seems that the decision to grant fintech firms a bank charter in December 2016 by the Office of the Comptroller of the Currency (OCC) in the US is certainly a justifiable interpretation to the growing concern of the incumbents. However, Bunea et al. (2018) may have concluded differently if it was extended beyond 2017, the announced fintech charter would grant fintech

[24]See National Natural Science Fund Guide to Programs 2020 for further details, http://www.nsfc.gov.cn/english/site_1/pdf/NationalNaturalScienceFundGuidetoPrograms2020.pdf

firms operation without the burden of state-by-state regulations and licencing causing a legal action by the New York Department of Financial Services (DFS).[25]

In regard to payment, Meifang et al. (2018) study the implications of financial innovation in payments using a sample of 73 commercial banks listed at the Shanghai and Shenzhen stock exchanges, from 2007 to 2014. Innovation in payments is represented as third party payment (TPP) and the implication on the economic value added (EVA) per share of the commercial banks in the sample. Meifang et al. (2018) find a positive relationship between value creation abilities (EVA) of financial institutions and internet TPPs. Their study also supports the understanding that technology innovations in methods of payment promote the development of the financial industry in emerging economies such as China in this instance, a finding that is consistent with the institutional literature and prior technological advancements in payments. However, the characteristics of the Chinese market differ significantly to other emerging economies, e-commerce platforms are more developed and the level of spending and transactions is unparalleled due to the large population of the country.

In lending terms, using loan-level data from LendingClub and Y-14M loan-level data reported by US banks, Jagtiani and Lemieux (2018) show that LendingClub, a major fintech lender in the US, has infiltrated areas that are underserved by traditional banks. An important justification to their conclusion is supported by the uncovering that fintech lending rises steeply in areas where bank branch per capita declines for the incumbents and the incumbents' market concentration. The study's findings are consistent with the fact that fintech start-ups are focusing on the unbanked and specific communities that are underserved by traditional banks.

Nonetheless, the most pertinent cause for LendingClub's soaring market share is due to growing demand for extra credit. Many fintech lending consumers demanding unsecured loans state that the funds are used to refinance other outstanding debt such as credit cards, suggesting that the areas where bank branch per capita declines are characterised by difficult economic variables such as local unemployment rate.

While the US financial markets are developed and fintech firms are rapidly growing, it is important to examine a different market and how can fintech firms implicate the incumbent's operations, in terms of lending activities. Tambunlertchai et al. (2022) examine fintech and their implication on lending and competition using the net interest margin (NIM) as an indicator in Latin American and the Caribbean (LAC) and data on 692 banks from 1988 to 2018.[26]

---

[25]The New York DFS filed a lawsuit disputing the OCC's decision to grant a fintech charter, stopping the OCC from accepting applications. However, only recently in June 2021 the decision has been reversed and the OCC started accepting application for its proposed fintech charter. For further details see. https://www.jdsupra.com/legalnews/occ-s-fintech-charter-survives-after-8818861/

[26]The sample includes Argentina, Bolivia, Brazil, Chile, Colombia, Costa Rica, Mexico, Peru, and Uruguay.

Deploying a difference-in-difference model and using fintech lending introduction as an exogenous shock to examine the difference, they find that NIM of the incumbents decreases significantly after fintech lending has been introduced.

The institutional literature shows growing concern from prudential regulators regarding fintech disrupting the incumbents' intermediation process and declining revenues. Accordingly, Tambunlertchai et al. (2022) provide empirical evidence supporting the regulators' view. In addition, fintech firms are rapidly developing in markets where alternative financial solutions are scarce compared to developed financial. Nonetheless, any interpretation of the empirical results on fintech especially for the LAC region, where fintech is yet to be developed in comparison to other regions, should be approached with prudence as more data becomes available and possible market changes in the future.

The Covid-19 global pandemic has played an important role in escalating demand for credit across households and businesses, especially for small and medium-sized enterprises (SMEs), which are disrupted mainly because of lock-downs, decline in revenues and deteriorating economic conditions. Sheng (2021) investigates the impact of fintech on the competence of traditional banks to supply credit to SMEs using an annual data of 31 regions in China from 2011 to 2018.

Maturity transformation and overcoming information asymmetry are two of the primary functions of traditional banks that fintech firms are targeting. Sheng (2021) suggests that fintech have helped the incumbents of all sizes to convert soft information to hard information, yet the empirical result shows that large size banks seem to benefit more from fintech in extending credit to SMEs, mainly due to fintech development as it overcomes the 'technical original advantages' of small size banks.[27]

While the reviewed studies can illustrate a close relationship between fintech activities and traditional banks based on empirical assessment, the weakness of this strand of empirical literature is due to the focus on only a specific business segment (payment and lending) of the incumbents. Consequently, Li et al. (2020) use a sample of US market-based fintech firms extracted from KBW Nasdaq Financial Technology Index and financial institutions in the S&P 500 index and the daily stock returns from 2011 to 2018, with the final sample consists of 129 institution including fintech firms, banks, insurance firms, real estate lenders and diversified financials.

Li et al. (2020) estimate fintech risk spillover using Granger causality of stock returns and measures financial institutions' systemic risk by employing SRISK indicator. As a result, they find a positive correlation between both indicators when financial institutions' systemic risk increases. Although their study examines a broader spectrum of financial institutions inclusive of banks, insurance firms and real estate lenders, which go beyond the scope of this thesis, the results

---

[27]Soft information refers to information about a borrower that is of nonstandard, hard information on borrowers include credit scores based on their historical payments and other data.

emphasise the importance of risk spillover from fintech firms and potential undermining of financial stability.

5.3 Further Implications of Fintech for Commercial Banks

A cluster of the empirical literature focuses on fintech's implications on commercial banks in China. In a study which focuses on fintech adoption by different types of commercial banks based on their size and its implication on the economic capital of commercial banks' risk estimated by using VaR, Yao and Song (2021) employ a sample of 16 listed commercial banks of which five are large state-owned commercial banks, eight joint-stock commercial banks and three city commercial banks. They show significant heterogeneity in the impact on the different types of commercial banks. The empirical result favours large state-owned commercial banks and show significant decrease in the economic capital of those commercial banks' risk and increasing their profits. While this empirical study advocates collaborations among fintech firms and traditional banks, the empirical analysis does not include any type of risk rising from the technology-enabled financial solutions.

Cheng and Qu (2020) focus on commercial banks' credit risk and potential implication by banks' inhouse fintech. Their sample entails data on 6 state-owned commercial banks, 12 joint-stock commercial banks, 33 city commercial bank and 9 rural commercial banks in China from 2008 to 2017. They show important empirical results which suggest that large state-owned commercial banks are rapidly developing their own fintech, resulting in a decline in banks' credit risk measured by default risk of banks' loans (NPL). The study shows stronger negative effects on smaller, private and non-listed banks. In addition, the study also suggests that bank's developed fintech promote negative effects by elevating regulatory risks but does not provide any empirical work on the matter.

However, large banks generally employ more efficient governance structures and are able to tackle regulatory risks in comparison to smaller banks precisely after Basel II and III Capital Accord implementation. Though the economic capital of commercial banks' risk and banks' credit risk are two different domains, the implication of external fintech firms or inhouse developed fintech shows negative effects on smaller banks in both studies.

Like Cheng and Qu (2020), Wang et al. (2021) examine banks' internally adopted fintech and its implication on commercial banks' efficiency, showing a positive increase across a range of indicators; profitability, innovation, risk controls and service efficiency. However, this study differs by categorising the sample of 113 commercial banks in China into national, urban and rural commercial banks, finding stronger negative effects on rural commercial banks due to deficiency in understanding and applying fintech. Though this study diverges in the sampling process and scope, the empirical result is consistent with Cheng and Qu's (2020) finding; the effect of internally developed banks' fintech is affecting smaller banks predominantly in comparison to large banks.

In a study involving fintech and banks' risk taking in China, Wang et al. (2020) use bank-level data from 2011 to 2018 to empirically examine whether fintech development increases or decreases commercial banks' risk-taking behaviour. Covering a panel of 320 commercial banks the study shows a greater negative impact on banks with lower operational efficiencies and banks with higher exposure and involvement in shadow banking. More importantly, they find an increase in bank risk-taking behaviour, which settles down when fintech develops furthermore. The study quantifies fintech using news headlines searches inclusive of the word 'fintech' and deploys a factor analysis to construct a fintech index. This original approach merely represents the rapid development of the fintech industry in China. Nonetheless, they find negative impacts of fintech developments on banks of all sizes and more prominently, on large size banks in China due to the high costs and complex organisational structure.

Focusing on commercial banks' fintech products and their impact on efficiency, Chen et al. (2021) employ non-financial performance indicators to examine the implications of fintech's products. This study differs from several others discussed earlier for deploying a questionnaire for both customers and employees of commercial banks and using non-financial performance measures. They show a positive relationship among deploying fintech products and commercial banks meeting customer needs and commercial banks' recalibrating their operations while also underscoring employees' acceptance. The study also tackles the difficulties Covid-19 have had on traditional banking operations, focusing on the fact that the global pandemic has accelerated the digitisation process of many banking services and reshaped operations, with employees accepting the recalibrated operations.

The studies reviewed in this section all shed light on fintech firms' implications on several aspects of commercial banks in China under different perspectives. In such regards, Cho and Chen (2021) adopt the metafrontier cost Malmquist productivity index to measure the implication of the fintech sector on commercial banks performance in China from the viewpoint of cost metafrontier.[28] The data from 2011 to 2017 consist of 6 state-owned commercial banks, 7 joint-stock commercial banks and 21 more commercial banks. Given the metafrontier, this study like others reviewed in this section shows heterogenous results among the groups in the sample; however, it empirically suggests positive effects on the three groups of commercial banks. The group-specific cost efficiency results indicate better performance by the joint-stock commercial banks in comparison to others. Furthermore, considering the cost Malmquist productivity index, the study suggests that joint-stock commercial banks are relatively closer to their prospective output. The result is due to increase in variables such as scale cost efficiency change, pure technological change and the scale cost for technological cost for the joint-stock commercial banks in the sample.

[28]Cho and Chen (2021) deploy data envelopment analysis (DEA) to construct the index under violence risk scale (VRS), such approach is used to examine and quantify the change in cost productivity side of China's banking industry and their implications.

In contrast, Phan et al. (2020) show opposing results on fintech firms' implications on bank performance using financial measures. The study uses data of 41 banks in Indonesia from 1997 to 2017 and four financial performance indicators; ROA, return on equity (ROE), ratio of net interest income to total assets (NIM) and yield on earning assets (YEA). They find significant negative effects on all four financial performance indicators of all the banks. However, large and state-owned banks are more effected by fintech firms in comparison to small and private banks, conflicting most of the empirical literature focusing on China's commercial banks discussed earlier. Wang et al. (2020) show similar empirical results on larger Chinese banks, but Phan et al. (2020) justify the result differently arguing that small size banks are faster to adopt technological innovation and bear less cost than larger banks under such circumstances.

While both China and Indonesia are strong grounds for fintech firms, their implication on the incumbents at this point seem to differ across the two nations. However, in a cross-continent study consisting of 80 banks across North America and Europe, Carlini et al. (2022) examine the effects of bank equity investment in fintech firms on banks' stock returns. They consider the size of investment in each transaction and categorise fintech firms into two categories: finance oriented and technology-oriented fintech firms. The empirical results show that European banks suffer a stronger negative abnormal market returns in contrast to the North American banks. Furthermore, tech oriented fintech firms show additional significant negative effect on bank stock returns. Carlini et al. (2022) explain that the negative reaction is associated with the risk and time needed for such bank equity investment to produce tangible lucrative returns. It can be prudent to accept this empirical conclusion, when aligned Wang et al. (2020) similar result by showing that fintech requires time for development and implementation to demonstrate positive effects on the Chinese banks.

Prudential regulators are concerned with the potential negative impact of fintech on the incumbent's profitability and financial stability. In such regards, Fung et al. (2020) use a panel data of 1,375 banks from 84 countries around the world and focus on fintech's implications on the fragility of the incumbents through their profitability. The empirical results show that after a regulator introduces a regulatory sandbox for start-up fintech firms, banks in emerging financial markets benefit from financial stability exhibited through their profitability. However, the empirical results show contrasting effects on banks in developed markets where fintech firms implicate financial stability and subsequently the profitability of the banks. The explanation for such divergent result between both types of markets is exhibited well in the literature as prior studies (Beck et al., 2016; Brei et al., 2020) show that a declining GDP tend to increase banks' risk and banks' distress. Fung et al. (2020) also suggest that market specifications can determine the implication of fintech development on the stability of the financial institutions.

This strand of empirical literature is developing rapidly as empirical data about fintech is emerging, more research fundings are available and the priority is given to fintech related research. Empirical findings from the different studies reviewed in this section at this stage of fintech development should be interpreted with caution. However, the empirical literature provides constructive methodologies that can be built on to conduct further research and identify the gaps within this strand. Based on the reviewed articles, the implication of fintech firms on the incumbents at this stage seem to be propelled by market specific characteristics and instituting a negative impact on the profitability of the incumbents.

6. Conclusion

This chapter provides a comprehensive overview of fintech firms, delving into their background, features and the array of products and services they offer. The investigation of fintech is framed within three distinct themes: financial innovation, financial disintermediation and financial disruption. The main fintech taxonomy and definitions, as presented by the Basel Committee on Banking Supervision and the Financial Stability Board (BIS, 2018; FSB, 2017), are crucial for understanding the regulatory and operational landscape within which these firms operate.

Financial innovation, the first theme explored, highlights the pioneering efforts of fintech firms in introducing novel financial products and services. These innovations have transformed the way consumers and businesses engage with financial services. From mobile payment solutions and digital wallets to robo-advisors and P2P lending platforms, fintech firms have harnessed the power of advanced technology to create more accessible, efficient and user-friendly financial solutions. These innovations have not only improved the customer experience but also increased competition within the financial industry, compelling traditional banks to enhance their own offerings.

The second theme, financial disintermediation, addresses the shifting dynamics of financial intermediation. Traditional banks have long served as the primary intermediaries in financial transactions, relying heavily on their balance sheets and established processes. In contrast, fintech firms utilise information technology to connect consumers directly with financial services, effectively bypassing traditional intermediaries. This disintermediation has reduced costs and increased efficiency in various financial transactions, from payments to lending. However, it is important to note that while fintech firms leverage advanced technology, the overall cost of intermediation has not significantly decreased, and efficiency gains remain modest. This underscores the complex nature of financial services and the challenges inherent in transforming established processes.

The third theme, financial disruption, examines the profound impact of fintech firms on traditional banking functions. Traditional banks are being disrupted by fintech firms, particularly in areas such as payment services and maturity transformation. Fintech firms, with their technology-enabled financial products and services, are rapidly taking over these primary functions. For example, digital payment platforms and cryptocurrencies have revolutionised the way payments are made, challenging the dominance of traditional banks in this area. Similarly, P2P lending and crowdfunding platforms are providing alternative avenues for raising capital, disrupting traditional banking models of lending and borrowing.

A significant factor in the evolution of fintech is the regulatory environment. Traditional banks are heavily regulated due to their crucial role in the economy, which has resulted in a relatively stable intermediation process over the years. The stringent regulatory framework ensures the stability and reliability of traditional financial institutions but also limits their ability to innovate rapidly. In contrast, fintech firms often operate outside the umbrella of traditional financial regulation, allowing them greater flexibility to innovate and adapt to changing market demands. However, this also raises concerns about regulatory arbitrage and the potential risks associated with less regulated entities providing critical financial services.

Despite the disruptions caused by fintech, traditional banks continue to play a vital role in the financial ecosystem. Their extensive networks, deep customer relationships, and trust built over decades provide them with significant advantages. Moreover, traditional banks are increasingly adopting fintech innovations to enhance their own services. Many banks are partnering with fintech firms or developing their own technology-driven solutions to remain competitive. This convergence of traditional and fintech models is creating a more integrated and dynamic financial landscape.

Looking ahead, the interplay between fintech firms and traditional banks will likely continue to evolve. Regulatory frameworks will need to adapt to ensure a level playing field and address the emerging risks associated with new financial technologies. Collaboration between regulators, traditional banks and fintech firms will be crucial in shaping a sustainable and inclusive financial ecosystem. The future of fintech holds immense potential. Advances in AI, blockchain and data analytics are poised to drive further innovation in financial services. These technologies can enhance the accuracy and efficiency of financial transactions, improve risk management and provide more personalised financial solutions. As fintech firms continue to push the boundaries of what is possible, they will play an increasingly important role in shaping the future of finance.

In conclusion, this chapter has provided a detailed examination of the transformative impact of fintech on the financial industry. By exploring the themes of financial innovation, disintermediation and disruption, we have gained insights into how fintech firms are redefining financial services. Ultimately, the evolution of fintech represents a fundamental shift in how financial services are conceptualised, delivered and consumed. As we move forward, the continued collaboration and adaptation between traditional financial institutions and fintech firms will be essential in creating a resilient and inclusive financial ecosystem.

References

Adelmann, F., Elliott, J., Ergen, I., Gaidosch, T., Jenkinson, N., Khiaonarong, T., Morozova, A., Schwarz, N., & Wilson, C. (2020). *Cyber risk and financial stability: It's a small world after all.* International Monetary Fund, Staff Discussion Note, (7).

Agarwal, S., & Zhang, J. (2020). FinTech, lending and payment innovation: A review. *Asia-Pacific Journal of Financial Studies*, *49*(3), 353–367.

Ajouz, M., Abuamria, F., Al Zeer, F., Salahat, M., Shahadeh, M., Binsaddig, R., Al-Sartawi, A., & Al-Ramahi, N. M. (2023). Navigating the uncharted: The shaping of FinTech ecosystems in emerging markets. *Cuadernos de Economía, 46*(132), 189–201.

Ajouz, M., Shehadeh, M., Jabarin, R., Sharar, S. A., Jawabra, S., & Salman, W. (2024, February). Is FinTech catalyst or constraint for banking performance? In *2024 2nd International conference on cyber resilience (ICCR)* (pp. 1–5). IEEE.

Al-Araj, R. E. E. M., Haddad, H. O. S. S. A. M., Shehadeh, M. A. H. A., Hasan, E., & Nawaiseh, M. Y. (2022). The effect of artificial intelligence on service quality and customer satisfaction in Jordanian banking sector. *WSEAS Transactions on Business and Economics, 19*(12), 1929–1947.

Al-Gasaymeh, A. S., Almahadin, H. A., Shehadeh, M., Migdady, H., & Atta, A. A. B. (2023, March). Investigating the role of artificial intelligence in embedded finance on improving a nonfinancial customer experience. In *2023 International conference on business analytics for technology and security (ICBATS)* (pp. 1–6). IEEE.

Aldasoro, I., Frost, J., Gambacorta, L., & Whyte, D. (2021). *Covid-19 and cyber risk in the financial sector*. Bank for International Settlement. Bulletin, (37).

Aldasoro, I., Gambacorta, L., Giudici, P., & Leach, T. (2020). *The drivers of cybers risk* (p. 865). Bank for International Settlements, Monetary and Economic Department.

Aldasoro, I., Gambacorta, L., Giudici, P., & Leach, T. (2022). The drivers of cyber risk. *Journal of Financial Stability, 60*, 100989.

Aldasoro, I., Gambacorta, L., Giudici, P., & Leach, T. (2023). Operational and cyber risks in the financial sector. *International Journal of Central Banking, 19*(5), 340–402.

Alkhaldi, F., Shehadeh, M., Abu-AlSondos, I. A., & Almazaydeh, L. (2023, December). Artificial intelligence applications and roles in supply chain sustainability. In *2023 Asia conference on cognitive engineering and intelligent interaction (CEII)* (pp. 120–124). IEEE.

Alkhazaleh, A., Assaf, A., Shehada, M., Almustafa, E., & Allahham, M. (2023). Analysis of the impact of fintech firms' lending on the expansion of service base companies in Jordan. *Information Sciences Letters, 12*(8), 2891–2902.

Alkhwaldi, A. F., Alharasis, E. E., Shehadeh, M., Abu-AlSondos, I. A., Oudat, M. S., & Bani Atta, A. A. (2022). Towards an understanding of FinTech users' adoption: Intention and e-loyalty post-COVID-19 from a developing country perspective. *Sustainability, 14*(19), 12616.

Allen, L., Bali, T. G., & Tang, Y. (2012). Does systemic risk in the financial sector predict future economic downturns? *Review of Financial Studies, 25*, 3000–3036.

Allen, F., Gu, X., & Jagtiani, J. (2020). *A survey of fintech research and policy discussion*. Federal Reserve Bank of Philadelphia. Working Papers, 21.

Ari, A., Darracq-Paries, M., Kok, C., & Zochowski, D. (2017). *Shadow banking and market discipline on traditional banks*. International Monetary Fund. Working Paper, 285.

Arner, D. W., Barberis, J. N., & Buckley, R. P. (2015). *The evolution of fintech: A new post-crisis paradigm?* University of Hong Kong Faculty of Law Research Paper No. 2015/047, UNSW Law Research Paper No. 2016-62.

Ashta, A., & Herrmann, H. (2021). Artificial intelligence and fintech: An overview of opportunities and risks for banking, investments, and microfinance. *Strategic Change, 30*, 211–222.

Barberis, J. (2014). *The rise of fintech: Getting Hong Kong to lead the digital financial transition in APAC*. https://thefintechbook.com/media/uploads/resources/reports/fintech.hk/2015/07/14/05_30_48/The%20Rise%20of%20FinTech%20-%20Nov%20-14.pdf

Bazot, G. (2018). Financial consumption and the cost of finance: Measuring financial efficiency in Europe. *Journal of the European Economic Association*, *16*(1), 123–160.

Beck, T., Chen, T., Lin, C., & Song, F. M. (2016). Financial innovation: The bright and the dark side. *Journal of Banking & Finance*, *72*, 28–51.

Beck, T., Demirgüç-Kunt, A., & Levine, R. (2007). Finance, inequality and the poor. *Journal of Economic Growth*, *12*(1), 27–49.

Berg, T., Burg, V., Gombovic, A., & Puri, M. (2020). On the rise of FinTechs: Credit scoring using digital footprints. *Review of Financial Studies*, *33*(7), 2845–2897.

Berlin, M., & Mester, L. J. (1998). Intermediation and vertical integration. *Journal of Money, Credit, and Banking*, *30*(3), 500–519.

Bertsch, C., Hull, I., Qi, Y., & Zhang, X. (2020). Bank misconduct and online lending. *Journal of Banking & Finance*, *116*, 105822.

Bettinger, A. (1972). FINTECH: A series of 40-time shared models used at manufacturers Hanover Trust Company. *Interfaces*, *2*(4), 62–63.

BIS. (2014). *Non-banks in retail payments*. Bank For International Settlements, Committee on Payments and Market Infrastructures.

BIS. (2018). *Sound practices implications of fintech developments for banks and banks supervisors*. Bank for International Settlements, Basel Committee on Banking Supervision.

BIS. (2021a). *Changing patterns of capital flow*. Bank for International Settlements. Committee on the Global Financial System Papers, (66).

BIS. (2021b). *Prudential treatment of cyrptoasset exposures*. Bank for International Settlements, Basel Committee on Banking Supervision.

BIS. (2021c). *CBDCs: An opportunity for the monetary system*. Bank for International Settlement. Annual Economic Report.

Boot, A., Hoffmann, P., Leaven, L., & Ratnovski, L. (2020). Financial intermediation and technology: What's old, what's new? *Journal of Financial Stability*, *53*.

Bouveret, A. (2018). *Cyber risk for the financial sector: A framework for quantitative assessment*. International Monetary Fund. Working Paper, (143).

Brandl, B., & Hornuf, L. (2017). *Where did fintechs come from, and where do they go? The transformation of the financial industry in Germany after digitalization*. University of Jena, University of Bremen.

Brei, M., Gadanecz, B., & Mehrota, A. (2020). SME lending and banking system stability: Some mechanisms at work. *Emerging Markets Review*, *43*, 100676.

Bunea, S., Kogan, B., Kund, A. G., & Stolin, D. (2018). Fintech and the banking bandwagon. *The Capco Institute Journal of Financial Transformation*, *47*, 25–34.

Cahill, D., & Liu, Z. (Frank) (2021). Limitations of imitation: Lessons from another Bitcoin copycat. *Journal of Corporate Finance*, *69*, 101992.

Cantu, C., & Ullou, B. (2020). *The dawn of fintech in Latin America: Landscape, prospects and challenges* (p. 112). Bank for International Settlements, Monetary and Economic Department.

Carlini, F., Del Gaudio, B. L., Porzio, C., & Previtali, D. (2022). Banks, fintech, and stock returns. *Finance Research Letters*, *45*, 102252.

Chavez-Dreyfuss, G. (2021). Crypto market cap surges to record $2 trillion, bitcoin at $1.1 trillion. *Reuters*.

Chebbi, T., Migdady, H., Hmedat, W., & Shehadeh, M. (2024). Another look at the price clustering behavior: Evidence from the Muscat stock exchange. *Review of Behavioral Finance*, *16*(5), 773–791.

Chen, Q-A, & Du, F. (2016). Financial innovation, systematic risk and commercial banks' stability in China: theory and evidence. *Applied Economics*, *48*(41), 3887–3898.

Chen, M. A., Wu, Q., & Yang, B. (2019). How valuable is FinTech innovation? *Review of Financial Studies*, *32*(5), 2062–2106.

Chen, X., You, X., & Chang, V. (2021). FinTech and commercial banks' performance in China: A leap forward or survival of the fittest? *Technological Forecasting and Social Change*, *166*, 120645.

Cheng, M., & Qu, Y. (2020). Does bank FinTech reduce credit risk? Evidence from China. *Pacific-Basin Finance Journal*, *63*(July).

Cho, T.-Y., & Chen, Y.-S. (2021). The impact of financial technology on China's banking industry: An application of the metafrontier cost Malmquist productivity index. *The North American Journal of Economics and Finance*, *57*, 101414.

Choi, Y. (2020). *Digital banks: Lessons from Korea*. World Bank Group, Innovation and Technology Note Series.

Čižinská, R., Krabec, T., & Venegas, P. (2016). FieldsRank: The network value of the firm. *International Advances in Economic Research*, 1–3.

Claessens, S., Frost, J., Turner, G., & Zhu, F. (2018). *Fintech credit markets around the world: Size, drivers, and policy issues*. Bank for International Settlement.

CPSS. (2000). *Clearing and settlement arrangements for retail payments in selected countries*. Bank for International Settlements, Committee on Payment and Settlement Systems.

Curti, F., & Migueis, M. (2021). *The information value of past losses in operational risk*. Federal Reserve Bank of Richmond, and Federal Reserve Board.

D'Acunto, F., Prabhala, N., & Rossi, A. G. (2019). The promises and pitfalls of robo-advising. *Review of Financial Studies*, *32*(5), 1983–2020.

De Roure, C., Pelizzon, L., & Tasca, P. (2016). *How does P2P lending fit into the consumer credit market?* Deutsche Bundesbank. Discussion Papers, (30).

Demirgüç-Kunt, A., & Levine, R. (2009). *Finance and inequality: Theory and evidence*. World Bank. Policy Research Working Paper, 4967.

Di Maggio, M., & Yao, V. (2021). Fintech borrowers: Lax screening or cream-skimming? *Review of Financial Studies*, *34*, 4565–4618.

Eling, M., & Wirfs, J. (2019). What are the actual costs of cyber risk events? *European Journal of Operational Research*, *272*, 1109–1119.

Federal Reserve. (2021). *Stress tests and capital planning*. Supervision and Regulations. https://www.federalreserve.gov/supervisionreg/stress-tests-capital-planning.htm

Feng, Z., & Wu, Z. (2018). *Bank technology: Productivity and employment*. Florida International University.

Fitch Ratings. (2016). *Brazil banks to rethink digital strategy as fintechs grow*. https://www.fitchratings.com/research/banks/brazil-banks-to-rethink-digital-strategy-as-fintechs-grow-15-08-2016

Fitch Ratings. (2021). *China's fintech evolves on fast track, diversified applications.* https://www.fitchratings.com/research/banks/china-fintech-evolves-on-fast-track-diversified-applications-18-04-2021

Foley, S., Karlsen, J. R., & Putnins, T. J. (2019). Sex, drugs, and bitcoin: How much illegal activity is financed through cryptocurrencies? *Review of Financial Studies, 32*(5), 1798–1853.

FSB. (2017, June). *Financial stability implications from fintech, supervisory and regulatory issues that merit authorities' attention* (pp. 1–61). Financial Stability Board.

FSB. (2019, February). *Fintech and market structure in financial services: Market developments and potential financial stability implications* (pp. 1–37). Financial Stability Board.

Fung, D. W. H., Lee, W. L., Yeh, J. J.-H., & Yuen, F. L. (2020). Friend or foe: The divergent effects of fintech on financial stability. *Emerging Markets Review, 45*, 100727.

Fuster, A., Goldsmith-Pinkham, P., Ramadorai, T., & Walter, A. (2020). *Predictably unequal? The effects of machine learning on credit markets.* Swiss National Bank, Federal Reserve Bank of New York, Imperial College London.

Galvin, J., Han, F., Hynes, S., Qu, J., Rajgopal, K., & Shek, A. (2018). *Synergy and disruption: Ten trends shaping fintech.* McKinsey & Company, Global Banking. https://www.mckinsey.com/industries/financial-services/our-insights/synergy-and-disruption-ten-trends-shaping-fintech

Gomber, P., Koch, J. A., & Siering, M. (2017). Digital finance and fintech: Current research and future research directions. *Journal of Business Economics, 87*, 537–580.

Gorton, G. B., & Zhang, J. Y. (2021). *Taming wildcat stablecoins.* Yale School of Management; National Bureau of Economic Research (NBER), Board of Governors of the Federal Reserve System.

Hatamlah, H., Allan, M., Abu-AlSondos, I., Shehadeh, M., & Allahham, M. (2023). The role of artificial intelligence in supply chain analytics during the pandemic. *Uncertain Supply Chain Management, 11*(3), 1175–1186.

He, D., Leckow, R., Haksar, V., Griffoli, T. M., Jenkinson, N., Kashima, M., Khiaonarong, T., Rochon, C., & Tourpe, H. (2017). *Fintech and financial services: Initial considerations.* International Monetary Fund. Staff Discussion Note, (5).

Hodula, M. (2022). Does fintech credit substitute for traditional credit? Evidence from 78 countries. *Finance Research Letters, 46*, 102469.

Howell, S. T., Niessner, M., & Yermack, D. (2020). Initial coin offerings: Financing growth with cryptocurrency token sales. *Review of Financial Studies, 33*(9), 3925–3974.

Hua, X., & Huang, Y. (2021). Understanding China's fintech sector: Development, impacts and risks. *The European Journal of Finance, 27*(4–5), 321–333.

IMF. (2019). *Fintech: The experience so far.* International Monetary Fund. Policy Paper.

Jagtiani, J., & Lemieux, C. (2018). Do fintech lenders penetrate areas that are underserved by traditional banks? *Journal of Economics and Business, 100*, 43–54.

Kamiya, S., Kang, J.-K., Kim, J., Milidonis, A., & Stulz, R. M. (2021). Risk management, firm reputation, and the impact of successful cyberattacks on target firms. *Journal of Financial Economics, 139*(3), 719–749.

Khan, A., & Malaika, M. (2021). *Central bank risk management, fintech, and cybersecurity*. International Monetary Fund. Working Paper, 105.

Khiaonarong, T., & Goh, T. (2020). *Fintech and payment regulation: analytical framework*. International Monetary Fund. Working Paper, (75).

Kopp, E., Kaffenberger, L., & Wilson, C. (2017). *Cyber risk, market failures, and financial stability*. International Monetary Fund. Working Paper, 185.

Koranteng, B., & You, K. (2024). Fintech and financial stability: Evidence from spatial analysis for 25 countries. *Journal of International Financial Markets, Institutions and Money*, *93*, 102002.

Lee, C.-C., Li, X., Yu, C.-H., & Zhao, J. (2021). Does fintech innovation improve bank efficiency? Evidence from China's banking industry. *International Review of Economics & Finance*, *74*, 468–483.

Li, J., Li, J., Zhu, X., Yao, Y., & Casu, B. (2020). Risk spillovers between FinTech and traditional financial institutions: Evidence from the U.S. *International Review of Financial Analysis*, *71*, 101544.

Maier, E. (2016). Supply and demand on crowdlending platforms: Connecting small and medium-sized enterprise borrowers and consumer investors. *Journal of Retailing and Consumer Services*, *33*, 143–153.

Makridis, C. A., & Dean, B. (2018). Measuring the economic effects of data breaches on firm outcomes: Challenges and opportunities. *Journal of Economic and Social Measurement*, *43*, 59–83.

Meifang, Y., He, D., Xianrong, Z., & Xiaobo, X. (2018). Impact of payment technology innovations on the traditional financial industry: A focus on China. *Technological Forecasting and Social Change*, *135*, 199–207.

Merton, R. C. (1992). Financial innovation and economic development. *The Journal of Applied Corporate Finance*, *4*(4), 12–22.

Micu, I., & Micu, A. (2016). Financial technology (fintech) and its implementation on the Romanian non-banking capital market. *SEA-Practical Application of Science*, (11), 379–384.

Milian, E. Z., Spinola, M. D. M., & Carvalho, M. M. D. (2019). Fintechs: A literature review and research agenda. *Electronic Commerce Research and Applications*, *34*.

Murphy, H. (2021). Facebook-backed digital currency project narrows focus to US. *Financial Times*. https://www.ft.com/content/4c5a72fe-48e9-467c-8a9e-cd2d3a3deafd

Nakamoto, S. (2008). *Bitcoin: A peer-to-peer electronic cash system*. https://bitcoin.org/bitcoin.pdf

Navaretti, G. B., Calzolari, G., Mansilla-Fernandez, G., & Pozzolo, A. F. (2017). Fintech and banking. Friends or foes? *European Economy*, *2017*(2).

Oxford Learning Dictionary. (2021). *Fintech noun – Definition, pictures, pronunciation and usage notes*. Oxford Advanced Learner's Dictionary. https://www.oxfordlearnersdictionaries.com/definition/english/fintech#:~:text=fintech-,noun,provide%20banking%20and%20financial%20services

Pampurini, F., Pezzola, A., & Quaranta, A. G. (2024). Lending business models and fintech efficiency. *Finance Research Letters*, *65*, 105519.

Petralia, K., Philippon, T., Rice, T., & Véron, N. (2019). *Banking disrupted? Financial intermediation in an era of transformational technology*. International Center for Monetary and Banking Studies. Geneva Reports on the World Economy, (22).

Phan, D. H. B., Narayan, P. K., Rahman, R. E., & Hutabarat, A. R. (2020). Do financial technology firms influence bank performance? *Pacific-Basin Finance Journal*, *62*, 101210.

Philippon, T. (2015). Has the us finance industry become less efficient? On the theory and measurement of financial intermediation. *The American Economic Review*, *105*, 1408–1438.

Philippon, T. (2020). *On fintech and financial inclusion*. Bank for International Settlements. Working Paper, (841).

Rehman, S. U., Al-Shaikh, M., Washington, P. B., Lee, E., Song, Z., Abu-AlSondos, I. A., Shahadeh, M., & Allahham, M. (2023). FinTech adoption in SMEs and bank credit supplies: A study on manufacturing SMEs. *Economies*, *11*(8), 213.

RBNZ. (2019, May). *Financial stability report*. Royal Bank of New Zealand.

Reuters. (2021). *Bitcoin, Ethereum plunge; crypto market cap losses nearly $1 trillion*. https://www.reuters.com/technology/bitcoin-ethereum-plunge-crypto-market-cap-losses-nearly-1-trillion-2021-05-19/#:~:text=Bitcoin%2C%20ethereum%20plunge%3B%20crypto%20market%20cap%20losses%20nearly%20%241%20trillion,-By%20Reuters&text=NEW%20YORK%2C%20May%2019%20(Reuters,cryptocurrency%20sector%20approaching%20%241%20trillion

Roengpitya, R., Tarashev, N., & Tsatsaronis, K. (2014, December). Bank business models. *BIS Quarterly Review*.

S&P. (2018). *Fintech proliferation, evolving clients compel bank branch closures in Brazil*. https://www.spglobal.com/marketintelligence/en/news-insights/trending/DMW6HCaqpnfumBfaj5TJWg2

Sahay, R., Allmen, U. E. V., Lahreche, A., Khera, P., Ogawa, S., Bazarbash, M., & Beaton, K. (2020). *The promise of fintech, financial inclusion in the post Covid-19 era*. International Monetary Fund, Monetary and Capital Markets Department.

Schueffel, P. (2016). Taming the beast: A scientific definition of fintech. *Journal of Innovation Management*, *4*(4), 32–54.

Schuetz, S., & Venkatesh, V. (2020). Blockchain, adoption, and financial inclusion in India: Research opportunities. *International Journal of Information Management*, *52*, 101936.

Sheng, T. (2021). The effect of fintech on banks' credit provision to SMEs: Evidence from China. *Finance Research Letters*, *39*, 101558.

Shim, Y., & Shin, D.-H. (2016). Analysing China's fintech industry from the perspective of actor–network theory. *Telecommunications Policy*, *40*(2–3), 168–181.

Strebinger, A., & Treiblmaier, H. (2024). Disintermediation of consumer services through blockchain? The role of intermediary brands, value-added services, and privacy concerns. *International Journal of Information Management*, *78*, 102806.

Szalay, E., & Venkataramakrishnan, S. (2021). What are cryptocurrencies and stablecoins and how do they work? *Financial Times*. https://www.ft.com/content/424b29c4-07bf-4612-b7d6-76aecf8e1528

Tambunlertchai, S., Bejar, P., Ishi, K., Komatsuzaki, T., Shibata, I., & Sin, J. (2022). Can fintech foster competition in the banking system in Latin America and the Caribbean? *Latin American Journal of Central Banking*, *3*(2), 100061.

Tang, H. (2019). Peer-to-peer lenders versus banks: Substitutes or complements? *Review of Financial Studies*, *32*(5), 1900–1938.

Telegraph. (2017). Future of fintech. The telegraph, consumer survey 2017. https://www.telegraph.co.uk/content/dam/business/spark/Fintech/Telegraph_Fintech_Report%202017.pdf

Thakor, A. V. (2020a). Fintech and banking: What do we know? *Journal of Financial Intermediation, 41*.

Thakor, A. V. (2020b). Corrigendum to: Fintech and banking: What do we know? *Journal of Financial Intermediation, 43*, 100858.

TransUnion. (2017). *FinTechs taking larger share of personal loan market while increasing portfolio risk-return performance*. https://newsroom.transunion.com/fintechs-taking-larger-share-of-personal-loan-market-while-increasing-portfolio-risk-return-performance/

Uddin, M. H., Mollah, S., & Ali, M. H. (2020). Does cyber spending matter for bank stability? *International Review of Financial Analysis, 72*, 101587.

Wang, J., & Huang, Y. (2018). Measurement of fintech media sentiment and its implications for online lending. *China Economic Quarterly, 17*(4), 339–366.

Wang, R., Liu, J., & Luo, H. (2020). Fintech development and bank risk taking in China. *The European Journal of Finance, 27*(4–5), 397–418.

Wang, Y., Xiuping, S., & Zhang, Q. (2021). Can fintech improve the efficiency of commercial banks? —an analysis based on big data. *Research in International Business and Finance, 55*.

Waugh, L. R. (1997). Roman Jakobson's work as a dialogue: The dialogue as the basis of language, the dialogue as the basis of scientific work. *Acta Linguistica Hafniensia, 29*(1), 101–120.

Welch, B. (1999). *Electronic banking and treasury security* (2nd ed.). https://shop.elsevier.com/books/electronic-banking-and-treasury-security/welch/978-1-85573-336-7

World Economic Forum. (2015, June). *The future of financial services* (pp. 1–176). https://www3.weforum.org/docs/WEF_The_future__of_financial_services.pdf

Yang, T., & Zhou, B. (2024). Local FinTech development, industrial structure, and north-south economic disparity in China. *International Review of Financial Analysis, 93*, 103119.

Yao, Y., Li, J., & Sun, X. (2021). Measuring the risk of Chinese Fintech industry: Evidence from the stock index. *Finance Research Letters, 39*, 101564.

Yao, T., & Song, L. (2021). Fintech and the economic capital of Chinese commercial bank's risk: Based on theory and evidence. *International Journal of Finance & Economics, 28*, 2109–2123.

Yeung, T. (2020). 3 important factors driving the price of Bitcoin. *NASDAQ*. https://www.nasdaq.com/articles/3-important-factors-driving-the-price-of-bitcoin-2020-10-09?amp

Zhang, B. Z., Ashta, A., & Barton, M. E. (2021). Do fintech and financial incumbents have different experiences and perspectives on the adoption of artificial intelligence? *Strategic Change, 30*, 223–234.

Zouari-Hadiji, R. (2021). Financial innovation characteristics and banking performance: The mediating effect of risk management. *International Journal of Finance & Economics*, 1–14.

Chapter 2

An Overview of Fintech: Opportunities, Challenges and Potential Development

Askar Garad[a], *Hosam Alden Riyadh*[b], *Abdullah M. Al-Ansi*[c], *Rita Kusumawati*[a] *and Md Abu Jahid*[a]

[a]Universitas Muhammadiyah Yogyakarta, Indonesia
[b]Telkom University, Indonesia
[c]Dhofar University, Oman

Abstract

This systematic review aims to identify procedures, risks, growth opportunities, gaps, challenges, trends and potential of financial technology (fintech) in modern businesses. This study reviews existing literature and synthesises the related findings about fintech in modern businesses. To extract more valuable financial data and give clients better services, this review considers combining AI and IoT technologies used in modern business. To accomplish the review objectives, we analysed 61 Scopus-indexed articles from 2016 to 2023 using the meta-analysis methodology. We conducted content analysis in addition to thematic analysis to validate the literature standard. However, we have identified and discussed opportunities, challenges, trends and future developments in fintech. The findings of this study provide a theoretical foundation for information systems-based fintech research, including fintech concept formulation and growth. The findings of this review offer insights into the ways that emerging technologies are changing financial markets and shaping consumer behaviours. This includes studying things like blockchain technology, digital wallets and peer-to-peer lending platforms. This study contributes to the improvement of fintech services by identifying procedures for absorbing contemporary financial technologies, mitigating their risks and identifying the latest ones.

Keywords: Financial technology; information systems; financial services; artificial intelligence; fintech industry; financial innovation

From Digital Disruption to Dominance, 45–73

Published under exclusive licence by Emerald Publishing Limited
doi:10.1108/978-1-83549-608-420251002

1. Introduction

Financial technology (fintech) is a set of modern technologies used to provide financial services and products (Hu et al., 2019). Fintech includes innovative and developed practices aimed at providing new financial products and services, or those currently available, by reducing expenses, enhancing security aspects and improving the process of financial inclusion, which leads to stimulating financial development and economic growth (Abdul-Rahim et al., 2022). Fintech is a new financial industry that applies technology to improve financial activities, driven by advances in e-finance and mobile technology (Alhajjaj & Ahmad, 2022). It challenges traditional financial institutions and provides an opportunity for start-ups to enter the industry. Fintech is an important innovation in the financial services industry, driven by economic sharing, regulation, policy and information technology. It has caused controversy in communities due to moral hazards, loan defaults and information asymmetry. Regulators should encourage innovation and apply consumer protection and risk management to ensure safe and appropriate financial services (Banerjee et al., 2022; Bayram et al., 2022).

Therefore, adopting these adjustments has become vital as a result of the exceptional financial sector revolution brought on by rapid technological advancements (Cao & Zhai, 2022). Banks and financial service providers have consequently prioritised the advancement of fintech and the encouragement of innovation in the financial industry. Banks and financial service providers accomplish this through the utilisation of the Fintech Regulatory Sandbox project, other initiatives and the establishment of suitable regulatory frameworks and techniques (Chen et al., 2022). Systemic risk is rising among digital banks in their native economies (Chen et al., 2021). These banks, also referred to as neo-banks, are more vulnerable than their conventional counterparts to the risks associated with consumer lending, which frequently comes with less loss insurance because it is unsecured. In addition to their higher liquidity concerns, their exposure also includes their tolerance for a higher level of risk in the stock portfolio (especially since liquid assets as a proportion of digital bank deposits are often lower than their ratio with conventional banks) (Chen & Chen, 2022; Chen et al., 2023).

However, the risk management systems and general resilience of the majority of digital banks have not been tested in economic downturns, which presents a problem for regulators as a result of these considerations (Wang & Wu, 2021). Fintechs are not only taking on more risk, but they are also exerting pressure on established rivals in the market. Take the United States as an example, where fintech originators adopt a growth strategy that becomes active during times when mortgage lending is expanding, like during the epidemic (Edbert et al., 2023; Niya et al., 2022). Fintech companies are posing competitive challenges to traditional banks, leading to a decline in their profitability, and this trend is expected to continue (Mwemezi et al., 2022).

The inherent risk increases as more financial services operations shift from heavily regulated banks to businesses and platforms that are either barely or not at all regulated (Kumar et al., 2022). Although fintech has entered this sector and is competing with traditional banks there, it also brings with it other factors. Furthermore, there remains a strong interconnection between the two, particularly in terms of providing liquidity and financing bank loans for fintech firms. Due to their interconnection, which may necessitate regulatory action, including better consumer and investor protection, and regulatory arbitrage (where businesses relocate operations to less regulated industries and areas), these entities provide difficulties for financial authorities (Abdul-Rahim et al., 2022; Bayram et al., 2022; Imerman & Fabozzi, 2020). Policies have been required to target both traditional banks and fintech firms fairly. These actions improve the opportunities provided by fintech while reducing the risks associated with them. This calls for stronger capital, liquidity and risk management standards for digital banks that are proportionate to fintech threats. It might be necessary for established banks and other established institutions to concentrate greater prudential control on the soundness of less technologically sophisticated banks as their current business models might be less long-term viable (Katyayani & Varalakshmi, 2019; Ozili, 2023).

Decentralised finance presents a barrier to effective regulation and control due to the absence of regulating bodies. In this case, regulatory action should concentrate on the organisations that are accelerating the decentralised finance sector's explosive expansion, such as stablecoin issuers and central exchanges for trading crypto-assets. Supervisory agencies should also promote strong governance, including adherence to the laws governing this activity and the self-regulatory bodies. These organisations would make good starting points for regulatory scrutiny (Gao & Jin, 2022; Putra et al., 2022; Su & Xu, 2023). Based on the above, we note that a management framework that can regulate fintech innovations without restricting their economic potential is urgently needed to increase the competitiveness of the fintech sector globally. Therefore, this study aims to (1) identify current research trends in the field of fintech; (2) identify procedures for absorbing modern financial technologies and mitigating their risks; (3) determine the latest growth opportunities in financial technologies; (4) identify gaps in fintech research and (5) identify challenges and trends for future research potential.

2. Research Methodology

The study employed content analysis, a qualitative and interpretive form of text analysis. Discourse analysis involves making interpretations based on the specifics of the source material and the context (Booth et al., 2016). The steps taken for the discourse analysis are shown in below.

Step 1:	Define the research aims and select the content of the analysis:	The study designed the research questions based on the aims identified in the fintech context to provide relevant skills to fintech service providers that help them attain regulatory fintech innovations without restricting them to increase the competitiveness of the fintech sector globally.
Step 2:	Gather Information:	The documents for analysis were extracted from Scopus research papers.
Step 3:	Analyse the Content:	This step involved a close examination of a variety of elements from the collected material, such as words, sentences, paragraphs and the overall structure of the content extracted for analysis, and then retaining the ones that were relevant to the research aims of the study. The study undertook a narrative approach to analysing the content. The study adopts a thematic analysis of fintech in preparing Identify current research trends in the field of fintech; identify procedures for absorbing modern financial technologies and mitigating their risks; determine the latest growth opportunities in financial technologies; identify gaps in fintech research and identify challenges and trends for future research potential.
Step 4:	Review the Strategy:	Limited to only English articles Fintech only Review of an abstract, methodology, data collection and analysis based on the aims of the research.

The authors applied the meta-analysis method in this article. Next, we analyse the findings from the selected literature in a meta-analysis literature review. According to Polit and Beck (2006), methods of meta-analysis aid in reaching conclusions and identifying features and connections among data. It is a non-statistical method that assesses and analyzes study results with the goal of advancing prior theories and interpretations. This study is based on publications from peer-reviewed scientific journals that are included in the Scopus database.

The review process, according to Cronin et al. (2008), entails five different steps used to select articles. Table 2.1 shows 61 scientific articles chosen for evaluation between 2016 and 2023. After selecting the articles to be included in the review, the Wordstate8 programme is used to analyse the articles and extract the most frequent

Table 2.1. Search Strategy and Inclusion/Exclusion Criteria.

Steps of Process Collection Articles	**Inquiries**	**Result/ Articles**
First stage: Inter Keywords in Scopus and Downloaded	(TITLE-ABS-KEY ((Fintech AND procedure) OR (Fintech AND risk) OR (Fintech AND growth AND opportunities) OR (Fintech AND gap) OR (Fintech AND challenge) OR (Fintech AND trend) OR (Fintech AND potential) OR (Financial AND technology AND procedure) OR (Financial AND technology AND risk) OR (Financial AND technology AND growth AND opportunities) OR (Financial AND technology AND gap) OR (Financial AND technology AND challenge) OR (Financial AND technology AND trend) OR (Financial AND technology AND potential)) AND LIMIT-TO (PUBYEAR, 2023, 2022, 2021, 2020, 2019, 2018, 2017, 2016)) AND LIMIT-TO (PUBSTAGE, "final")) AND LIMIT-TO (DOCTYPE, "article")) AND LIMIT-TO (LANGUAGE, "English")) AND LIMIT-TO (SRCTYPE, "j"))	1,365

(Continued)

Table 2.1. *(Continued)*

Steps of Process Collection Articles	Inquiries	Result/ Articles
Second stage: Start to download	Records excluded (*n* = 464), with reasons: Don't focus on fintech	901
Third stage: Records screened	(Title and abstract check) Records excluded (*n* = 462), with reasons: Don't focus on research aims	439
Fourth stage: Full-text articles assessed for eligibility	(Full-text articles check) Records excluded (*n* = 173), with reasons: Don't focus on research aims	266
Fifth stage: Check finding of articles based on keywords	(Finding/Results-text articles Check) Records excluded (*n* = 205), with reasons: Don't focus on research aims	61

words in the articles, the frequency of keywords and the topics that the selected articles focus on. The following are the outputs of articles analysed by Wordstate8.

The frequency of keywords in relation to the primary texts used for this study stands out in Fig. 2.1. The most frequently used words are fintech, risk, financial, banks, services and technology, which indicates that these are the primary study axes in recent years.

Fig. 2.2 shows the distribution of articles over the years of publication. As can be noticed in the figure, there has been increasing research into fintech in the last two years. This means that there is a focus on research on fintech after the Covid-19 pandemic.

Table 2.2 shows the frequency of keyword processing. Researchers can examine the link between two signals or datasets using a statistic called coherence. It is widely used to figure out how significant the difference between articles selected as input and the output of a literature review is. If the signals are ergodic and the system function is linear, the causality between the input (articles) and output (results) can be inferred.

3. Results and Discussion

The authors analysed the full text of the articles in this section, based on the objectives of this research. In Table 2.3, the results of the analysis are presented.

Fig. 2.1. Cloud of Frequency Keywords.

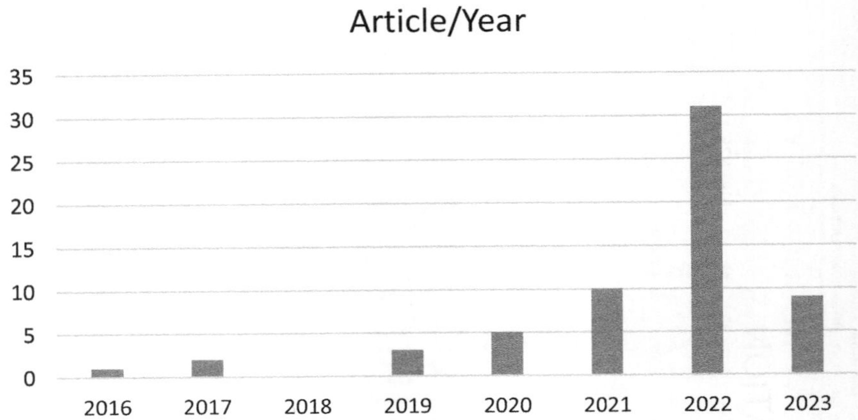

Fig. 2.2. Frequency of Articles by Year.

Table 2.2. Statistics Analysis of Topics.

No	Topic	Keywords	Coherence	Freq.	Cases	% Cases
1	*Fintech Services Products*	Services; Products; Financial; Companies; Fintech; Traditional; Consumers; Provide; Fintech services; Financial services; Fintech companies; Products and services;	0.393	3,240	61	100.00%
2	*Adoption of Fintech Services*	Adoption; TAM; Trust; Attitudes; Adopt; Fintech; Usage; Fintech services; Adoption of fintech services; Fintech adoption; Fintech companies; Technology adoption; Fintech service;	0.366	1,190	55	90.16%
3	*Financial Institutions Threats*	Threats; Losses; Fund; Institutions; Financial; Financial	0.339	868	55	90.16%

Table 2.2. *(Continued)*

No	Topic	Keywords	Coherence	Freq.	Cases	% Cases
		institutions; Financial services; Financial technology; Financial system; Traditional financial; Financial service; Financial market; Traditional financial institutions; Financial products;				
4	*Commercial Banks*	Commercial; Banks; Reduce; Risk; Efficiency; Commercial banks;	0.384	2,449	51	83.61%
5	*Credit Risk Information Asymmetry*	Credit; Flow; Information; Borrowers; Personal; Processing; Credit risk; Information asymmetry; Credit flow; Credit risk management; Credit information; Personal credit; Personal information;	0.355	714	50	81.97%
6	*Market Share Traditional Banks*	Share; Ideal; Market; Traditional; Market share; Traditional banks; Traditional commercial banks; Digital transformation; Traditional banking;	0.340	643	47	77.05%
7	*Data Quality*	Performance; AI; Company; Quality; Management; Risk management; Data quality;	0.326	386	46	75.41%

(Continued)

Table 2.2. *(Continued)*

No	Topic	Keywords	Coherence	Freq.	Cases	% Cases
8	*Mobile Money*	Mobile; Money; Payment; Payments; Transactions; Mobile money; Mobile payment; Mobile payments; Payment services; Payment systems; Electronic money; Mobile payment services;	0.358	701	43	70.49%
9	*Risk Platforms Peer Lending*	Platforms; Lending; Peer; Transition; Crowdfunding; Industry; Risk platforms; Peer lending; Lending industry; Transition platforms; Types of platforms; Lending platforms; Peer to peer lending;	0.342	518	42	68.85%
10	*Interest Rate Liberalisation CPI Growth*	Liberalisation; Interest; Signif; Growth; Interest rate liberalisation; CPI growth;	0.338	275	38	62.30%
11	*Blockchain Technology Distributed*	Distributed; Blockchain; Securities; Settlement; Central; Blockchain technology; Distributed ledger technology;	0.355	359	37	60.66%
12	*Cloud Computing Big Data*	Cloud; Computing; Big; Cloud computing; Big data; Mobile technology;	0.346	270	36	59.02%

Table 2.2. *(Continued)*

No	Topic	Keywords	Coherence	Freq.	Cases	% Cases
13	*Actual and Predicted Values*	Predicted; Actual; Values; Prediction; Degree; Actual and predicted values; Degree of deviation; Prediction accuracy;	0.339	179	33	54.10%
14	*Planning and Execution Optimal Resolution Strategy*	Execution; Planning; Actions; Optimal; Def; Dif; Automated; Algorithms; Planning and execution; Optimal resolution strategy; Insolvency estate;	0.384	167	32	52.46%
15	*Venture Capital Fintech Start*	Ups; Start; Venture; Capital; Venture capital; Fintech start; Capital funds;	0.339	322	31	50.82%

Table 2.3. Literature Review Results.

Fintech Procedures	Fintech procedures are the measures taken in order to ensure the accuracy and security of financial transactions. These steps are essential for the successful implementation of technology within the financial sector as they help reduce fraud and minimise operational risks associated with handling money. The factors that need to be taken into account when considering fintech procedures include data quality control, compliance standards related	(Alhajjaj & Ahmad, 2022; Banerjee et al., 2022; Bayram et al., 2022; Cao & Zhai, 2022; Gao & Jin, 2022; Guermond, 2022; Hu et al., 2019; Jonker & Kosse, 2022; Khuong et al., 2022; Kim & Hong, 2016; Kong & Loubere, 2021; Pintér et al., 2021; Putra et al., 2022; Saksonova & Kuzmina-Merlino, 2017; Su & Xu, 2023; Syed et al., 2021; Tiwari et al., 2023; Upreti et al., 2023; Wan et al., 2023)

(Continued)

Table 2.3. *(Continued)*

	to regulations, application testing processes, authentication protocols, system resilience architecture, data encryption and storage protocols, risk mitigation approaches and cybersecurity strategies. It is crucial for companies to invest in these measures to protect their operations from mismanagement or malicious activities. Furthermore, frequent audits can help organisations stay on top of these necessary procedures in order to function optimally and remain compliant with modern financial regulations. The procedures for absorbing modern financial technologies and mitigating their risks: (1) Providing training programs and building self-capabilities in this field, especially with regard to confronting cyber risks, which are the most important measures that can be taken in this field. (2) Developing a specific legislative and regulatory framework for this purpose, as it is the most important measure that can be taken to absorb financial technologies and mitigate their risks. (3) Encourage innovation and create sandbox incubators to this end. (4) Establishing special observatories to monitor the new technology	

Table 2.3. *(Continued)*

	of financial markets. Opportunities for growth in financial technologies: (1) Dealers are interested in more complex financial products, including integrated financial services. (2) Digital banking, wealth management, remittances and digital payments constitute an important segment of the financial technology sector.	
Fintech Risks	Financial Technology (Fintech) risks are inherent to the industry due to the global, integrated nature of these digital finance solutions and services. These risks arise from deficiencies in the design, implementation, testing, operation, control and governance of existing IT systems. There are four primary types of fintech-related risks: strategic risk associated with changes in the competitive landscape or market demand; operational risk related to potential breakdowns in internal processes for developing or operating fintech systems; compliance risk linked to regulations regarding data privacy and disclosure; and financial crime risk posed by sophisticated fraudsters exploiting weaknesses in security controls. Ultimately, it is crucial for organisations to be	(Abdul-Rahim et al., 2022; Chen & Chen, 2022; Chen et al., 2022; Edbert et al., 2023; Geranio, 2017; Guermond, 2022; Hu et al., 2019; Katyayani & Varalakshmi, 2019; Mascarenhas et al., 2021; Mwemezi et al., 2022; Ozili, 2023; Pintér et al., 2021; Putra et al., 2022; Razak et al., 2021; Vučinić & Luburić, 2022; Wan et al., 2023; Wang & Wu, 2021; Zheng et al., 2022)

(Continued)

Table 2.3. *(Continued)*

	aware of these risks and have a comprehensive plan for managing them effectively. Also, there are five risks in managing fintech, which are: Cyberattacks, product inappropriateness, regulatory non-compliance, unexpected market events and increased global competition. There are five risks in managing fintech, which are cyberattacks, product inappropriateness, regulatory non-compliance, unexpected market events and increased global competition.	
Fintech Growth Opportunities	Fintech is a rapidly evolving sector that holds great potential for growth opportunities. With advancements in technology and the increased adoption of digital channels, fintech start-ups are able to offer innovative solutions that cater to the changing demands of consumers. These solutions range from mobile payment apps, robot-advisory platforms, online lending platforms, and blockchain-based systems. Fintech firms have gained momentum by transforming traditional financial services through a customer-centric approach that emphasises speed, security, affordability and convenience. The emergence of open banking	(Bayram et al., 2022; Cao & Zhai, 2022; Chen et al., 2023; Guermond, 2022; Hogan, 2022; Imerman & Fabozzi, 2020; Katyayani & Varalakshmi, 2019; Khuong et al., 2022; Kim & Hong, 2016; Kong & Loubere, 2021; Liu et al., 2021; Muganyi et al., 2022; L. Nguyen et al., 2022; Niya et al., 2022; Putra et al., 2022; Ringe & Ruof, 2020; Saksonova & Kuzmina-Merlino, 2017; Sidaoui et al., 2022; Tiwari et al., 2023; Upreti et al., 2023; Wan et al., 2023; Wang & Wu, 2021)

Table 2.3. *(Continued)*

	APIs has enabled fintech firms to collaborate with established financial institutions thereby providing new revenue streams for banks while allowing fintech firms access to large customer bases. In summary, the fintech industry presents a world of possibilities for entrepreneurs seeking to disrupt traditional ways of banking and investing whilst driving innovation across financial services.	
Fintech Gaps	As the fintech sector increases in complexity and sophistication, it is essential that the research agenda accompanying this industry keeps up with the pace of development. Although there have been extensive reviews of existing studies into fintech conducted, many gaps remain in our understanding of these rapidly evolving markets. One particularly important area which needs further exploration is the implications of fintech for consumer protection and financial inclusion. Additionally, due to its global scope, another key area requiring greater study is the cross-border impacts associated with fintech services. Moreover, one such gap could be focussing on the benefits and risks of blockchain in the context of finance. Although blockchain has already been	(Alhajjaj & Ahmad, 2022; Banerjee et al., 2022; Chen et al., 2021; Guermond, 2022; Katyayani & Varalakshmi, 2019; Kumar et al., 2022; Li, 2022; Li et al., 2022; L. Nguyen et al. 2022; Y. T. H. Nguyen et al., 2022; Su & Xu, 2023; Syed et al., 2021)

(Continued)

Table 2.3. *(Continued)*

	added to financial institutions' systems, research needs to focus on its optimal uses, security breaches, and operational limitations that may arise during transactions. Another area that can be explored is how AI has impacted customer experience in banking services. While AI enables innovative applications like chatbots, it also presents ethical concerns around big data and privacy protection for customers. Identifying these gaps means closing them with more extensive analysis that could help researchers predict future trends or even aid in the development of regulations to keep up with emerging technologies. Finally, a detailed examination into the relationship between Big Data Analytics strategies and consumer behaviour should also be undertaken to ensure that opportunities are maximised without compromising consumer privacy or data security.	
Fintech Challenges	Fintech is the new buzzword in the finance industry, driven by innovations in technology and disruption. However, with the increasing number of fintech start-ups entering the market every day, challenges have emerged that require urgent attention. One of these	(Alhajjaj & Ahmad, 2022; Chen et al., 2021, 2022; Geranio, 2017; Gerrans et al., 2022; Guermond, 2022; Mascarenhas et al., 2021; Mwemezi et al., 2022; Ozili, 2023; Rupeika-Apoga & Wendt, 2022; Saksonova & Kuzmina-Merlino, 2017; Su

Table 2.3. *(Continued)*

	challenges is cybersecurity threats as financial systems are often targeted by hackers seeking unauthorised access to sensitive data. Another significant challenge is regulation and compliance as traditional financial institutions tend to be more rigorously regulated than their fintech counterparts. Lastly, customer acquisition and retention pose a challenge as consumers are increasingly selective about where they invest their money, expecting secure platforms with personalised services that cater to their specific needs. Ultimately, fintech companies must devise innovative strategies to overcome these obstacles for long-term success in an increasingly crowded marketplace.	& Xu, 2023; Syed et al., 2021; Tut, 2023; Vasenska et al., 2021; Vučinić, 2020; Wan et al., 2023; Yu, 2022; Zheng et al., 2022)
Fintech Trends	Fintech has been revolutionising the financial industry in recent times, and it is likely to continue doing so for many years to come. One of the most significant trends in fintech is the rise of digital payments, making transactions fast, easy, and more secure than ever before. Moreover, mobile banking usage has soared due to the convenience and ease of use offered. Another emerging trend is that of cryptocurrencies like Bitcoins	(Chen et al., 2022; Fahy, 2022; Gao & Jin, 2022; Gerrans et al., 2022; Guermond, 2022; Imerman & Fabozzi, 2020; Khuong et al., 2022; Kim & Hong, 2016; Loiacono & Rulli, 2022; Niya et al., 2022; Razak et al., 2021; Suzianti et al., 2022; Tut, 2023; Upreti et al., 2023; Vučinić & Luburić, 2022; Wang & Wu, 2021; Zhao et al., 2022; Zhou & Li, 2022)

(Continued)

Table 2.3. *(Continued)*

	which are changing the future landscape of transactions by providing quick transfers around the world with lower fees. Another trend is the use of AIAI to improve fraud prevention and enhance customer experience. Robo-advisors, which rely on algorithms to provide investment advice or portfolio management services, are also gaining popularity among investors who seek low-cost and automated financial solutions. AI-based automated customer services have increased customer satisfaction levels as they do not have to wait in long queues for simple inquiries regarding their accounts. All such trends are transforming finance into a more technology-driven sector that caters better to consumer preferences and lifestyle choices resulting in the effective use of resources and safer economic practices alike.	
Fintech Potential	Fintech has the potential to revolutionise the financial industry. Fintech companies can deliver personalised services that traditional banks may struggle to match due to the ever-increasing demand for digital and mobile solutions. The rise of blockchain technology, AI and machine learning is	(Cao & Zhai, 2022; Chen et al., 2023; Gao & Jin, 2022; Guermond, 2022; Hogan, 2022; Imerman & Fabozzi, 2020; Khuong et al., 2022; Kim & Hong, 2016; Kong & Loubere, 2021; Liu et al., 2021; Mishchenko et al., 2021; Muganyi et al., 2022; Niya et al., 2022; Ozili, 2023; Putra et al., 2022; Sidaoui

Table 2.3. *(Continued)*

	allowing these companies to offer innovative products like robo-advisors, mobile payment solutions and cryptocurrency platforms. These tools provide greater access, convenience and transparency for consumers while also increasing efficiency and reducing costs for service providers. This shift towards digitisation has opened up a world of possibilities for fintech start-ups that can leverage data analysis to create tailored solutions for specific market niches. By staying ahead of the curve in terms of technological advancements, fintech companies have the potential to transform traditional banking models into more flexible and accessible systems that can better serve customers' needs.	et al., 2022; Su & Xu, 2023; Tiwari et al., 2023; Upreti et al., 2023; Zhou & Li, 2022; Zveryakov et al., 2019)

4. Fintech Procedures

Fintech procedures are revolutionising the world of finance by helping to create new efficiencies, reduce paperwork and expedite transactions (Alhajjaj & Ahmad, 2022; Bayram et al., 2022; Cao & Zhai, 2022; Khuong et al., 2022; Wan et al., 2023). These procedures enable smooth, automated financial operations that can be conducted 24/7 with minimal human intervention. They enable faster access to funds and more safety due to enhanced security features such as biometrics, cryptography and two-factor authentication. Furthermore, fintech procedures allow for better data management, leading to improved lending decisions based on a deeper understanding of customers' financial histories. This provides an opportunity for financial institutions to offer beneficial services tailored to individual customer needs in order to drive customer retention and satisfaction (Edbert et al., 2023; Hu et al., 2019; Syed et al., 2021; Wan et al., 2023).

5. Fintech Risks

With the increasing popularity of fintech and its expansion into personal banking, there is a growing risk of data breaches and privacy issues. Financial institutions must have safeguards in place to protect customer information from hackers and malicious actors who intend to use such data for nefarious means (Abdul-Rahim et al., 2022; Kumar et al., 2022; Mwemezi et al., 2022). As cybercriminals are becoming more sophisticated with their methods of attack, companies must secure their digital platforms against fraudulent activity. Finally, fintech should establish procedures for addressing customer disputes and conduct ongoing due diligence on the products and services they provide to safeguard customers' assets (Bayram et al., 2022; Imerman & Fabozzi, 2020; Katyayani & Varalakshmi, 2019; Ozili, 2023).

Fintech risk management is an important tool for companies in the financial services industry to protect themselves from potential losses. It involves assessing, monitoring and managing the various aspects of fintech operations that may introduce risk, including technological risks due to cyberattacks, operational risks due to a lack of resources or procedural errors and market risks due to changing customer behaviours or environmental factors (Gao & Jin, 2022; Kong & Loubere, 2021; Putra et al., 2022; Su & Xu, 2023). Companies must employ a comprehensive approach to identify their current risk profile and use robust tools such as machine learning algorithms for real-time risk analysis. Additionally, companies should create complete plans detailing response protocols in the case of unanticipated incidents or events. This could include adhering to security standards across all platforms and using encryption technologies to reduce the chance of data breaches (Alhajjaj & Ahmad, 2022; Chen et al., 2023; Mohsin et al., 2022; Zheng et al., 2022).

Fintech has led to a variety of changes in the financial services industry. However, with these advances come a range of risks that must be considered by those operating in this space (Upreti et al., 2023; Zhou & Li, 2022). Elements of these fintech risks include cybersecurity, regulatory compliance and data integrity (Chen et al., 2021). Cybersecurity entails protecting systems from attacks or tampering by unauthorised actors while regulatory compliance involves meeting applicable regulations set out by regulatory bodies (Vučinić & Luburić, 2022). Moreover, maintaining accurate and complete data is essential to ensuring accuracy and trustworthiness in fintech services. Because of this, businesses that use fintech need to lower the risks that come with it by taking precautions like tightening access controls and encrypting data, and they also need to have good plans for how to quickly handle any problems that may arise (Li et al., 2022; Vučinić & Luburić, 2022; Yu, 2022).

6. Fintech Growth Opportunities

Fintech offers immense growth opportunities for companies due to its ability to significantly reduce costs and increase efficiency throughout the financial services industry (Gao & Jin, 2022; Kim & Hong, 2016; Vasenska et al., 2021). The growing penetration of mobile devices, increasing availability of APIs and open banking standards, broadening access to capital markets for SMEs and adoption of new technologies such as AI, blockchain and cloud computing are drastically changing the way consumers interact with financial products (Chen et al., 2021; Imerman & Fabozzi, 2020; Khuong et al., 2022; Upreti et al., 2023). Fintech can be leveraged to launch customised solutions tailored to specific target audiences or business requirements that can create unique value propositions that traditional banks cannot offer (Abdul-Rahim et al., 2022; Gao & Jin, 2022; Vasenska et al., 2021; Zhou & Li, 2022). With the drive towards digital transformation in all industries, fintech continues to present a formidable opportunity for growth (Abdul-Rahim et al., 2022; Fatmawati & Garad, 2023; Kim & Hong, 2016; Mishchenko et al., 2021).

The areas of fintech growth opportunities have been particularly visible in a variety of areas, ranging from payments and capital markets to insurance and banking (Alhajjaj & Ahmad, 2022; Imerman & Fabozzi, 2020; Kong & Loubere, 2021). As technology continues to enable smarter ways to transact business and interact with customers, the space is evolving rapidly (Edbert et al., 2023; Vasenska et al., 2021). Everything from automated investment advice, improved credit scoring systems, peer-to-peer loans and online exchanges for stocks and bonds is becoming commonplace (Abdul-Rahim et al., 2022; Vasenska et al., 2021; Zhou & Li, 2022). Additionally, improvements in authentication methods are offering greater financial inclusion to underserved demographics as well as improving security measures (Chen et al., 2022; Mwemezi et al., 2022; Putra et al., 2022). These trends highlight the immense potential for both start-ups and established corporations within the fintech landscape who can leverage these technologies to provide better services that improve customer experience (Abdul-Rahim et al., 2022; Guermond, 2022).

7. Fintech Gaps

The use of fintech remains a key factor in modernising existing banking, payments and security systems (Ringe & Ruof, 2020; Vasenska et al., 2021). Despite the pace of fintech advancements, there remains a gap between what is available on the market and what banks or merchants need in terms of improved access to both digital products and services (Abdul-Rahim et al., 2022). Financial institutions are challenged with enhancing customer service, minimising cost overhead and managing increasing security risks (Bayram et al., 2022; Khuong et al., 2022; Ringe & Ruof, 2020). These fintech gaps can range from legacy system capabilities to consumer demand for mobile-friendly solutions to implement innovation at scale. As such, stakeholders must act rapidly to recognise existing technological advantages, underline potential risks associated with fintech integration and ultimately prioritise the right mix of strategic investments that yield long-term benefits (Imerman & Fabozzi, 2020; Putra et al., 2022; Vasenska et al., 2021).

Fintech research gaps remain a pressing issue within the industry, as existing studies often focus on generic topics with limited attention paid to micro- and macro-specific questions. To truly understand how the industry is evolving, researchers must identify new and innovative methods of collecting data and develop deep insights into specific areas such as banking, fintech start-ups, capital markets and regulations (Khuong et al., 2022; Putra et al., 2022; Yu, 2022; Zhou & Li, 2022). Doing so will enable them to uncover unique opportunities in different geographical markets while also creating opportunities for prospective students to build comprehensive expertise in their chosen area. Research must therefore become increasingly focused on achieving an appropriate balance between what is quantifiable and qualitative so as to accurately portray the current landscape of finance technology worldwide (L. Nguyen et al., 2022; Garad et al., 2021).

8. Fintech Challenges

As a rapidly growing industry, fintech brings with it many unique challenges. From the perspectives of both incumbents and new entrants to the financial services space, these range from regulatory considerations and technological infrastructure to customer acquisition and marketing (Abdul-Rahim et al., 2022). Furthermore, data privacy concerns over customer information held by existing or emerging players must be taken into account, meaning a great deal of consideration must be given to forming proper partnerships between institutions in order to protect customers from all kinds of malicious behaviours (Gao & Jin, 2022; Vasenska et al., 2021). Security, both physical and virtual, is another ongoing challenge in this sector that should not be overlooked. Finally, interoperability between fintech firms, legacy banks and even different countries' banking systems can create significant obstacles when launching innovative products into different markets (Putra et al., 2022; Rahmawati et al., 2023).

Fintech challenges largely revolve around the need to identify and implement new technology solutions, balance shifting regulations and ensure security for consumers (Abdul-Rahim et al., 2022; Bayram et al., 2022). While technology can offer unique advantages, such as increased speed of transactions or customisation on a consumer level, it also comes with risk; for example, cyberattack resilience is a significant challenge that can lead to data being stolen from both the provider and the consumer (Putra et al., 2022; Upreti et al., 2023). Furthermore, different jurisdictions repeatedly adjust their regulations relating to fintech based on public opinion or corporate pressure from other institutions. This dynamic results in a fluidity of required compliance standards that providers must keep abreast of in order to remain competitive and secure (Vučinić, 2020; Vučinić & Luburić, 2022). Finally, consumer trust is paramount when dealing with financial technologies; a provider must ensure their platform is secure against potential breaches while also providing assurance that their user data won't be exploited without consent (Kim & Hong, 2016; Rupeika-Apoga & Wendt, 2022).

9. Fintech Trends

Fintech trends continue to shape the financial services industry and create an ever-changing competitive landscape (Abdul-Rahim et al., 2022; Kim & Hong, 2016).

As the demand for customer-centric solutions, accessible mobile banking technologies, open APIs, cloud computing capabilities and comprehensive risk management systems grows exponentially, organisations are increasingly turning to emerging fintech innovations to stay ahead of the competition (Kong & Loubere, 2021; Vasenska et al., 2021). The growth of automated processes such as algorithmic trading allows investors to access new products faster than ever before while machine learning helps banks quickly identify emerging customer behaviour patterns in real time. Furthermore, blockchain has become a cornerstone of digital ledger solutions and is revolutionising identity management obligations. Organisations must remain agile and ensure they are leveraging these technologies to maximise effectiveness in order to stay on top of the rapidly advancing digital finance ecosystem (Abdul-Rahim et al., 2022; Kong & Loubere, 2021; Putra et al., 2022).

Fintech trends have continued to revolutionise the financial sector. In recent years, we've seen a rise in fintech applications ranging from direct banking services, such as payment processing and investment management, to revolutionary financial products leveraging blockchain technology for cryptocurrency investments (Al-Ansi et al., 2023; Imerman & Fabozzi, 2020; Ringe & Ruof, 2020). Emerging technologies such as AI, automated data analysis tools and distributed ledger systems are reshaping how firms process transactions and interact with customers. With real-time data analytics comes greater transparency into customer behaviour, which can enable companies to create tailored experiences for their users. Moreover, the advancement of data security measures ensures that individual information remains secure even when companies choose to open up their data capabilities to other parties. These advancements will lead us into an era of faster payments, better financial inclusion and a myriad of cost-effective fintech options available globally (Abdul-Rahim et al., 2022; Guermond, 2022; Khuong et al., 2022).

10. Fintech Potential

Fintech has the potential to revolutionise the entire financial industry. With advancements in AI and machine learning, it is now possible to automate processes that were previously done manually and with error-prone manual input (Edbert et al., 2023; Vasenska et al., 2021). Financial technologies also have great potential to create more efficient services for customers, increasing speed and accuracy while decreasing wait times and errors. It is likely that fintech will offer improved insights into customer behaviours and risk profiles, enabling businesses to better manage their finances. Additionally, fintech could make it easier for customers to access banking services, making them more user-friendly and less intimidating (Abdul-Rahim et al., 2022; Chen et al., 2021; Gao & Jin, 2022).

Fintech has revolutionised how businesses operate and allocate capital in the current climate. Its potential to disrupt existing financial services models is immense, from creating digital portfolios for consumers to providing peer-to-peer lending and other forms of credit to SMEs. Fintech also has a wide reach in terms of customer base, with technological advances enabling access by anyone with an internet connection (Mohsin et al., 2022; Saksonova & Kuzmina-Merlino, 2017; Vasenska et al., 2021). With an estimated 20% of global banking revenues facing disruption pressure from developing technologies like blockchain, fintech will continue to gain traction over traditional banking systems. As the industry matures, it creates more opportunities for customers to leverage smart technology solutions and industry tools, improving economic decision-making and mitigating risk while also offering significant cost savings and greater customer choice. Taken together, these factors make it clear that there is considerable potential in leveraging fintech in order to remain competitive in today's markets (Garad et al., 2022; Li, 2022; Vučinić, 2020).

11. Conclusion and Implications

Through an organised study of the literature, we pulled a total of 1,365 articles from the Scopus databases. We selected the titles and abstracts of the articles. After conducting a thematic analysis and an annotated bibliography, we evaluated 124 final papers. The findings of the literature review led to the division of fintech research into a number of subprocesses, including the following: Identifying current research trends in the field of fintech, identifying procedures for absorbing contemporary financial technologies and mitigating their risks, determining the most recent growth opportunities in financial technologies, determining gaps in fintech research and determining challenges and trends for future research potential. This research contributes to the improvement of fintech services by identifying procedures for absorbing contemporary financial technologies, mitigating their risks and identifying the latest ones. The experiences gained from technology practices are an important point for expanding the scope of fintech services. In practice, selecting articles from the Scopus database and procedures can provide a technology search reference for high-quality literature. Other researchers can follow how technology-related research changes over time. The classification of articles can help future researchers review previous studies according to their research needs. If articles are categorised, future researchers can review references according to their specific study needs. In future research, it is still necessary to research the original issues brought up by the emergence of fintech, such as moral hazard, loan defaults and information asymmetry.

References

Abdul-Rahim, R., Bohari, S. A., Aman, A., & Awang, Z. (2022). Benefit–risk perceptions of FinTech adoption for sustainability from bank consumers' perspective: The moderating role of fear of COVID-19. *Sustainability*, *14*(14). https://doi.org/10.3390/su14148357

Al-Ansi, A. M., Hazaimeh, M., Hendi, A., AL-hrinat, J., Adwan, G., & Garad, A. (2023). Innovative responses to exogenous shocks in Indonesian transportation firms: Mediating role of sustainable performance and outcomes. *Planning*, *18*(9), 2663–2672. https://doi.org/10.18280/ijsdp.180905

Alhajjaj, H., & Ahmad, A. (2022). Drivers of the consumers adoption of Fintech services. *Interdisciplinary Journal of Information, Knowledge, and Management*, *17*, 259–285. https://doi.org/10.28945/4971

Banerjee, R., Majumdar, S., & Albastaki, M. (2022). Ideal self-congruence: Neo-banking by traditional banks and the impact on market share – A case of UAE banks. *International Journal of Professional Business Review*, *7*(4), 1–21. https://doi.org/10.26668/businessreview/2022.v7i4.e779

Bayram, O., Talay, I., & Feridun, M. (2022). Can fintech promote sustainable finance? Policy lessons from the case of Turkey. *Sustainability*, *14*(19). https://doi.org/10.3390/su141912414

Booth, A., Sutton, A., & Papaioannou, D. (2016). Taking a systematic approach to your literature review. *Systematic Approaches to Successful Literature Review*, 9–35.

Cao, Y., & Zhai, J. (2022). A survey of AI in finance. *Journal of Chinese Economic and Business Studies*, *20*(2), 125–137. https://doi.org/10.1080/14765284.2022.2077632

Chen, Y. J., & Chen, Y. M. (2022). Forecasting corporate credit ratings using big data from social media. *Expert Systems with Applications*, *207*(i). https://doi.org/10.1016/j.eswa.2022.118042

Chen, X., Wen, C., & Lu, K. (2023). Does an imbalance in the population gender ratio affect FinTech innovation? *Technological Forecasting and Social Change*, *188*, 2018. https://doi.org/10.1016/j.techfore.2022.122164

Chen, B., Yang, X., & Ma, Z. (2022). Fintech and financial risks of systemically important commercial banks in China: An inverted U-shaped relationship. *Sustainability*, *14*(10). https://doi.org/10.3390/su14105912

Chen, K. C., Yu, C. M., & Dargahi, T. (2021). Evaluating the risk of disclosure and utility in a synthetic dataset. *Computers, Materials & Continua*, *68*(1), 761–787. https://doi.org/10.32604/cmc.2021.014984

Cronin, P., Ryan, F., & Coughlan, M. (2008). Undertaking a literature review: A step-by-step approach. *British Journal of Nursing*, *17*(1), 38–43. https://doi.org/10.12968/bjon.2008.17.1.28059

Edbert, I. S., Ramdhan, D., Putri, N. L. P. Y. A., Salsabila, B. A., Susanto, I. R., & Rumagit, R. Y. (2023). Analysis of user trust in the security of sensitive data provided to financial technology companies. *ICIC Express Letters*, *17*(1), 41–47. https://doi.org/10.24507/icicel.17.01.41

Fahy, L. (2022). Regulator reputation and stakeholder participation: A case study of the UK's regulatory sandbox for fintech. *European Journal of Risk Regulation*, *13*(1), 138–157. https://doi.org/10.1017/err.2021.44

Fatmawati, I., & Garad, A. (2023). An analytical study of the relationship between network capability and e-marketing to achieve the competitive advantage of MSEs. In *The implementation of smart technologies for business success and sustainability* (pp. 3–12). https://link.springer.com/chapter/10.1007/978-3-031-10212-7_1

Gao, Y., & Jin, S. (2022). Corporate nature, financial technology, and corporate innovation in China. *Sustainability*, *14*(12), 1–22. https://doi.org/10.3390/su14127162

Garad, A., Rahmawati, A., & Pratolo, A. (2021). The impact of board directors, audit committee and ownership on financial performance and firms value. *Universal Journal of Accounting and Finance*, *9*(5), 982–994. https://doi.org/10.13189/ujaf.2021.090509

Garad, A., Yaya, R., Pratolo, P., & Rahmawati, A. (2022). The relationship between transformational leadership, improving employee's performance and the raising efficiency of organizations. *Management and Production Engineering Review*, *13*(2), 15–30. https://doi.org/10.24425/mper.2022.142052

Geranio, M. (2017). Fintech in the exchange industry: Potential for disruption? *Masaryk University Journal of Law and Technology*, *11*(2), 245–266. https://doi.org/10.5817/MUJLT2017-2-3

Gerrans, P., Baur, D. G., & Lavagna-Slater, S. (2022). Fintech and responsibility: Buy-now-pay-later arrangements. *Australian Journal of Management*, *47*(3), 474–502.

Guermond, V. (2022). Whose money? Digital remittances, mobile money and fintech in Ghana. *Journal of Cultural Economy*, *15*(4), 436–451. https://doi.org/10.1080/17530350.2021.2018347

Hogan, A. (2022). Financialisation of schooling in Australia through private debt: A case study of Edstart. *Australian Educational Researcher*, *49*(5), 897–913. https://doi.org/10.1007/s13384-021-00470-8

Hu, Z., Ding, S., Li, S., Chen, L., & Yang, S. (2019). Adoption intention of Fintech services for bank users: An empirical examination with an extended technology acceptance model. *Symmetry*, *11*(3). https://doi.org/10.3390/sym11030340

Imerman, M. B., & Fabozzi, F. J. (2020). Cashing in on innovation: A taxonomy of FinTech. *Journal of Asset Management*, *21*(3), 167–177. https://doi.org/10.1057/s41260-020-00163-4

Jonker, N., & Kosse, A. (2022). The interplay of financial education, financial inclusion and financial stability and the role of big tech. *Contemporary Economic Policy*, *40*(4), 612–635. https://doi.org/10.1111/coep.12578

Katyayani, J., & Varalakshmi, C. (2019). Cognitive computational model for evaluation of fintech products and services with respect to Vijayawada city, AP. *International Journal of Innovative Technology and Exploring Engineering*, *8*(10), 1733–1736. https://doi.org/10.35940/ijitee.J9074.0881019

Khuong, N. V., Phuong, N. T. T., Liem, N. T., Thuy, C. T. M., & Son, T. H. (2022). Factors affecting the intention to use financial technology among Vietnamese youth: Research in the time of COVID-19 and beyond. *Economies*, *10*(3). https://doi.org/10.3390/economies10030057

Kim, K., & Hong, S. (2016). The data processing approach for preserving personal data in Fintech-driven paradigm. *International Journal of Security and Its Applications*, *10*(10), 341–350. https://doi.org/10.14257/ijsia.2016.10.10.30

Kong, S. T., & Loubere, N. (2021). Digitally down to the countryside: Fintech and rural development in China. *Journal of Development Studies*, *57*(10), 1739–1754. https://doi.org/10.1080/00220388.2021.1919631

Kumar, A., Srivastava, A., & Gupta, P. K. (2022). Banking 4.0: The era of artificial intelligence-based fintech. *Strategic Change*, *31*(6), 591–601.

Li, C. (2022). Quantitative measurement and analysis of FinTech risk in China. *Economic Research-Ekonomska Istrazivanja*, *35*(1), 2596–2614. https://doi.org/10.1080/1331677X.2021.1970606

Li, G., Elahi, E., & Zhao, L. (2022). Fintech, bank risk-taking, and risk-warning for commercial banks in the era of digital technology. *Frontiers in Psychology*, *13*(July), 1–13. https://doi.org/10.3389/fpsyg.2022.934053

Liu, C., Fan, Y., & Zhu, X. (2021). Fintech Index prediction based on RF-GA-DNN algorithm. *Wireless Communications and Mobile Computing, 2021*. https://doi.org/10.1155/2021/3950981

Loiacono, G., & Rulli, E. (2022). ResTech: Innovative technologies for crisis resolution. *Journal of Banking Regulation, 23*(3), 227–243. https://doi.org/10.1057/s41261-021-00154-4

Mascarenhas, A. B., Koda Perpétuo, C., Barrote, E. B., & Perides, M. P. (2021). The influence of perceptions of risks and benefits on the continuity of use of fintech services. *Brazilian Business Review, 18*(1), 1–21. https://doi.org/10.15728/BBR.2021.18.1.1

Mishchenko, S., Naumenkova, S., Mishchenko, V., & Dorofeiev, D. (2021). Innovation risk management in financial institutions. *Investment Management and Financial Innovations, 18*(1), 191–203. https://doi.org/10.21511/imfi.18(1).2021.16

Mohsin, A., Sheikh, M. D. R. I., Tushar, H., Iqbal, M. M., Hossain, S. F. A., & Kamruzzaman, M. (2022). Does FinTech credit scale stimulate financial institutions to increase the proportion of agricultural loans? *Cogent Economics and Finance, 10*(1). https://doi.org/10.1080/23322039.2022.2114176

Muganyi, T., Yan, L., Yin, Y., Sun, H., Gong, X., & Taghizadeh-Hesary, F. (2022). Fintech, Regtech, and financial development: Evidence from China. *Financial Innovation, 8*(1). https://doi.org/10.1186/s40854-021-00313-6

Mwemezi, J., Senadjki, A., & Sea, L. L. (2022). Augmenting Bank credit flow to agro-processing SMEs through financial technology (FinTech): Evidence from Tanzania. *WSEAS Transactions on Business and Economics, 19*, 1914–1928. https://doi.org/10.37394/23207.2022.19.172

Nguyen, Y. T. H., Tapanainen, T., & Nguyen, H. T. T. (2022). Reputation and its consequences in Fintech services: The case of mobile banking. *International Journal of Bank Marketing, 40*(7), 1364–1397. https://doi.org/10.1108/IJBM-08-2021-0371

Nguyen, L., Tran, S., & Ho, T. (2022). Fintech credit, bank regulations and bank performance: A cross-country analysis. *Asia-Pacific Journal of Business Administration, 14*(4), 445–466. https://doi.org/10.1108/APJBA-05-2021-0196

Niya, H., El Bousaadani, A., & Mohamed, R. (2022). Adoption of technological solution on fintechs using training engineering: Case of health sector. *Journal of Theoretical and Applied Information Technology, 100*(18), 5274–5285.

Ozili, P. K. (2023). CBDC, Fintech and cryptocurrency for financial inclusion and financial stability. *Digital Policy, Regulation and Governance, 25*(1), 40–57. https://doi.org/10.1108/DPRG-04-2022-0033

Pintér, É., Bagó, P., Berényi, L., Molnár, L., Deutsch, N., Szigeti, G., & Pintér, T. (2021). How do digitalization and the Fintech phenomenon affect financial decision-making in the younger generation? *Acta Polytechnica Hungarica, 18*(11), 191–208. https://doi.org/10.12700/APH.18.11.2021.11.11

Polit, D. F., & Beck, C. T. (2006). The content validity index: Are you sure you know what's being reported? Critique and recommendations. *Research in Nursing & Health, 29*(5), 489–497. https://doi.org/10.1002/nur.20147

Putra, R. D., Mulyani, S., Poulus, S., & Sukmadilaga, C. (2022). Data quality analytics, business ethics, and cyber risk management on operational performance and fintech sustainability. *International Journal of Data and Network Science, 6*(4), 1659–1668. https://doi.org/10.5267/j.ijdns.2022.4.008

Rahmawati, A., Wahyuningsih, S. H., & Garad, A. (2023). The effect of financial literacy, training and locus of control on creative economic business performance. *Social Sciences & Humanities Open*, *8*(1), 100721. https://doi.org/10.1016/j.ssaho.2023.100721

Razak, M. I. Ab, Dali, N. A. M., Dhillon, G., & Manaf, A. W. A. (2021). Fintech in Malaysia: An appraisal to the need of Shariah-compliant regulation. *Pertanika Journal of Social Sciences and Humanities*, *28*(4), 3223–3233. https://doi.org/10.47836/PJSSH.28.4.40

Ringe, W. G., & Ruof, C. (2020). Regulating fintech in the EU: The case for a guided sandbox. *European Journal of Risk Regulation*, *11*(3), 604–629. https://doi.org/10.1017/err.2020.8

Rupeika-Apoga, R., & Wendt, S. (2022). FinTech development and regulatory scrutiny: A contradiction? The case of Latvia. *Risks*, *10*(9). https://doi.org/10.3390/risks10090167

Saksonova, S., & Kuzmina-Merlino, I. (2017). Fintech as financial innovation – The possibilities and problems of implementation. *European Research Studies Journal*, *20*(3), 961–973. https://doi.org/10.35808/ersj/757

Sidaoui, M., Bouheni, F. B., Arslankhuyag, Z., & Mian, S. (2022). Fintech and Islamic banking growth: New evidence. *The Journal of Risk Finance*, *23*(5), 535–557. https://doi.org/10.1108/JRF-03-2022-0049

Su, F., & Xu, C. (2023). Curbing credit corruption in China: The role of FinTech. *Journal of Innovation and Knowledge*, *8*(1). https://doi.org/10.1016/j.jik.2022.100292

Suzianti, A., Haqqi, F. R., & Fathia, S. N. (2022). Strategic recommendations for financial technology service development: A comprehensive risk-benefit IPA-Kano analysis. *Journal of Modelling in Management*, *17*(4), 1481–1503. https://doi.org/10.1108/JM2-11-2020-0297

Syed, A. A., Ahmed, F., Kamal, M. A., & Segovia, J. E. T. (2021). Assessing the role of digital finance on shadow economy and financial instability: An empirical analysis of selected South Asian countries. *Mathematics*, *9*(23). https://doi.org/10.3390/math9233018

Tiwari, A. K., Abakah, E. J. A., Shao, X., Le, T. N. L., & Gyamfi, M. N. (2023). Financial technology stocks, green financial assets, and energy markets: A quantile causality and dependence analysis. *Energy Economics*, *118*. https://doi.org/10.1016/j.eneco.2022.106498

Tut, D. (2023). FinTech and the COVID-19 pandemic: Evidence from electronic payment systems. *Emerging Markets Review*, *54*(3), 2022. https://doi.org/10.1016/j.ememar.2023.100999

Upreti, K., Syed, M. H., Khan, M. A., Fatima, H., Alam, M. S., & Sharma, A. K. (2023). Enhanced algorithmic modelling and architecture in deep reinforcement learning based on wireless communication Fintech technology. *Optik*, *272*. https://doi.org/10.1016/j.ijleo.2022.170309

Vasenska, I., Dimitrov, P., Koyundzhiyska-Davidkova, B., Krastev, V., Durana, P., & Poulaki, I. (2021). Financial transactions using Fintech during the Covid-19 crisis in Bulgaria. *Risks*, *9*(3), 1–28. https://doi.org/10.3390/risks9030048

Vučinić, M. (2020). Fintech and financial stability potential influence of FinTech on financial stability, risks and benefits. *Journal of Central Banking Theory and Practice*, *9*(2), 43–66. https://doi.org/10.2478/jcbtp-2020-0013

Vučinić, M., & Luburić, R. (2022). Fintech, risk-based thinking and cyber risk. *Journal of Central Banking Theory and Practice*, *11*(2), 27–53. https://doi.org/10.2478/jcbtp-2022-0012

Wan, Q., Miao, X., Wang, C., Dinçer, H., & Yüksel, S. (2023). A hybrid decision support system with golden cut and bipolar Q-ROFSs for evaluating the risk-based strategic priorities of fintech lending for clean energy projects. *Financial Innovation*, *9*(1). https://doi.org/10.1186/s40854-022-00406-w

Wang, R., & Wu, Y. (2021). Application of blockchain technology in supply chain finance of Beibu Gulf region. *Mathematical Problems in Engineering*, *2021*. https://doi.org/10.1155/2021/5556424

Yu, K. (2022). Risk evaluation of the new fintech institutions in China based on fuzzy analytical hierarchy process. *Mathematical Problems in Engineering*, *2022*. https://doi.org/10.1155/2022/9338032

Zhao, J., Li, X., Yu, C. H., Chen, S., & Lee, C. C. (2022). Riding the FinTech innovation wave: FinTech, patents and bank performance. *Journal of International Money and Finance*, *122*, 102552.

Zheng, Z., He, J., Yang, Y., Zhang, M., Wu, D., Bian, Y., & Cao, J. (2022). Does financial leverage volatility induce systemic financial risk? Empirical insight based on the Chinese fintech sector. *Managerial and Decision Economics*. https://doi.org/10.1002/mde.3738

Zhou, H., & Li, S. (2022). Effect of COVID-19 on risk spillover between fintech and traditional financial industries. *Frontiers in Public Health*, *10*. https://doi.org/10.3389/fpubh.2022.979808

Zveryakov, M., Kovalenko, V., Sheludko, S., & Sharah, E. (2019). FinTech sector and banking business: Competition or symbiosis? *Economic Annals-XXI*, *175*(1–2), 53–57. https://doi.org/10.21003/ea.V175-09

Chapter 3

Unravelling the Dynamics: A Theoretical Exploration of the Role of Unified Payment Interface (UPI) in Digital Inclusion

Ruchika Vermani and Neha Arora

Geeta University, India

Abstract

The Unified Payments Interface (UPI) has emerged as a transformative force within the digital payment landscape, revolutionising how individuals and businesses conduct financial transactions in India. This research paper embarks on a theoretical journey to elucidate the growth trajectory of UPI by delving into secondary data sources. Through meticulous analysis and synthesis of existing literature, regulatory reports and industry insights, this paper constructs a comprehensive narrative that traces the evolution of UPI from its inception to its current status as a cornerstone of the Indian digital payments ecosystem. The theoretical framework employed in this study draws upon concepts from innovation diffusion theory, network effects and technological adoption models to elucidate the factors driving the adoption and proliferation of UPI. By examining key milestones, regulatory interventions, technological advancements and market dynamics, this paper unveils the intricate interplay of various stakeholders, including banks, fintech firms, government bodies and consumers, in shaping the trajectory of UPI growth. Furthermore, this research delves into the utility of UPI as a payment infrastructure by exploring its implications for financial inclusion, efficiency, security and economic development. By facilitating seamless, real-time and interoperable transactions, UPI has democratised access to financial services, empowered small businesses and catalysed the transition towards a less-cash economy. This paper fills a critical gap in the literature by providing a holistic and theoretically grounded analysis of UPI's evolution and its broader implications. It contributes valuable insights into the mechanisms driving digital payment innovations and their socio-economic impacts, thereby informing policy decisions to foster inclusive and sustainable financial ecosystems.

From Digital Disruption to Dominance, 75–102

doi:10.1108/978-1-83549-608-420251003

Keywords: Digital payment; Unified Payment Interface; perceived value; intention to use; intention to recommend

1. Introduction

The digital payment system appeared as a new normal. Technological advancements do wonders for the upliftment of society along with the nation (Najib & Fahma, 2020). Since Unified Payments Interface (UPI) is reliant on technology, prospective users must be pleased with all facets of this technology (Fahad & Shahid, 2022). UPI is a home-grown payment mechanism launched by the National Payments Corporation of India (NPCI) in 2016 (Balakrishnan, 2023). It is continuing to garner popularity and is now universally accepted (Saha & Kiran, 2022).

According to the announcement made by our Honourable Prime Minister Sh. Narender Modi during his visit to France in September 2023, India's UPI will be adopted by France which means a ticket to the Eiffel Tower can be bought by direct payment in rupees using UPI, which will certainly boost the economy of India. UPI is named as the biggest innovation in creating a digital ecosystem (Ranpariya et al., 2021), which in turn raises financial inclusion and financial literacy and is facilitated by financial stability (Rastogi et al., 2021). A revolution in the digital payment ecosystem has paved the system for the growth and advancement of the Indian economy (Mukhopadhyay & Upadhyay, 2022).

There is a transformation happening in the way people shop and people make payments in our country. People are immersed in technology, paving the mode for advancement in the banking industry (Wong et al., 2022). There has been tremendous growth in the volume and value of UPI transactions in the recent past. UPI has shattered records with an astonishing 11 billion-plus transactions with a total transaction amount of ₹17.16 lakh crores in October 2023 with the potential to hit 20 billion transactions per month. This is an incredible milestone and the power of digital payments. There have been studies on digital payment systems and m-wallets, but there has been a dearth of studies evaluating the effect of a UPI. UPI took over the m-wallets as well as the traditional banking payments mechanism in India (Bagla & Sancheti, 2018).

The worldwide race to cashless transactions is underway. Sweden is acing the charts in becoming a cashless economy. It is now 100% cashless. Merchants can lawfully deny the acceptance of payments in cash. India is doing wonders too, and Indian UPI is now accepted by various countries like Singapore, UAE, Nepal, Sri Lanka, France and Bhutan. In this study, we have explored the components that influence the usage of UPI and its recommendation factors, the effect of usage of UPI system on the marginalised sector of the country and the measures to push the cashless mechanism in the country.

There is no proven relationship between economic development, financial inclusion, financial literacy and the rising digital payment mechanism UPI (Kumari & Biswas, 2023).

In the year 2004, The Apex Bank of our country, the Reserve Bank of India (RBI), introduced the Real-Time Gross Settlement (RTGS) (Narsapur & Parasar, 2020) system to facilitate immediate payments exceeding ₹2 lakhs. They used NEFT for smaller payments; but, in this case, payments could only be made in batches of 30-minute increments. Customers lacked patience and wanted to find quick ways to make expenditures to save time. With all of these objectives in mind, in the year 2008, the NPCI National Payment Corporation of India was established to handle the nation's payment system and subsequently broaden its scope with an eye on UPI-based international payments. Numerous countries have already embraced Indian UPI (Kumar & Yadav, 2022).

Furthermore, a new method had to be developed so that tiny direct merchant payments could be made without the need to add beneficiaries. The NPCI developed UPI, an improved version of Immediate Payment Service (IMPS), in 2016. It is the baby product of Raghuram Rajan and Dilip Asbe. Here, a UPI ID, often called a Virtual ID, is necessary. This technology makes it easy to make rapid payments around the clock, without incurring additional fees, without accessing the internet and even without using a smartphone (Venkatesh et al., 2003).

UPI got a strong push by the country's pandemic-related constraints, demonetisation (NIC, 2024) and the popular Digital India Campaign. UPI's goal is to make monetary transactions simple, economical and safe for clients while also fostering digitisation and financial inclusion in India (Thomas & Chatterjee, 2017). Online direct transfers took on a life of their own and UPI gained enormous traction.

The first nation to implement UPI 2021 was Bhutan, enabling Indian visitors to make UPI-based payments (TOI, 2021). Having more than 100 billion transactions in 2023, India led the global list of countries having online payment systems (ET, 2023; NPCI, 2023). Its exceptional feature of interoperability – that is, the ability to send money instantly and without incurring fees – made it more widely used. Unavoidably, UPI payments were promoted because they were supported by all financial institutions. All the banks operating in the country are promoting UPI payments.

India's second-largest population of internet users has spurred a growing need for digital financial services. This has propelled India into the global fintech arena, where it now holds the third position in the world for the number of fintech companies as of 2023. UPI proves to be a masterstroke in the digital payment system. UPI is serving the low-income group well and adding to the financial inclusion of the unserved community.

Table 3.1 exhibits the most commonly used digital payment platforms in India.

Launched in 2010, the IMPS platform made mobile banking the foundation. It was used for instant fund transfers of less than ₹2 lakhs using your phone. The drawback with IMPS was that smaller amounts could not be paid directly to merchants; additionally, adding beneficiaries took approximately 30 minutes, and there was no option to scan and pay, which has become people's favourite nowadays espousal UPI.

Table 3.1. Digital Payment Platforms.

Platform	Digital Payment Option	Description
CBDC 1 December 2022	Central Bank Digital Currency	The RBI began a pilot run of the e-rupee, India's central bank digital currency (CBDC), for both the wholesale and retail sectors. RBI's approach to the fintech ecosystem is customer-centric, with a focus on strong governance, effective oversight, ethical behaviour and risk management, as well as supporting self-regulation by fintech through a self-regulatory organisation.
BHIM 30 December 2016	Bharat Interface for Money	BHIM is a standalone mobile wallet programme. BHIM provides a more simplified approach that is largely focused on person-to-person payments whereas UPI includes a larger range of transaction possibilities, such as bill payments and merchant transactions. It does not require any bank information, such as an account number.
UPI 11 April 2016	Unified Payments Interface	It is a payment system that allows customers to join several bank accounts in a single smartphone app and transfer funds without providing an IFSC code or account number. Through a single-window interface, you may send or receive payments, pay invoices, and authorise recurring payments. UPI is free to use, instantaneous and available 24*7 in a fraction of a second using the IMPS foundation.

USSD November 2012	Unstructured Supplementary Service Data	It allows users without smartphones or the internet to use mobile banking through *99#; this can be used for fund transfers, checking account balances and generating statements.
IMPS 22 November 2010	Immediate Payment Service	Instant, real-time, 24*7 electronic fund transfer system using mobile, internet and ATM
AEPS November 2010	Adhaar-enabled Payment System	To enable a bank customer to use Aadhaar as an identity to access respective Aadhaar-enabled bank account and perform basic banking transactions such as cash deposit, cash withdrawal, intrabank or interbank fund transfer, balance inquiries and obtain a mini statement via a Business Correspondent.
NEFT November 2005	National Electronic Funds Transfer	It operates during banking hours, used in one-to-one funds transfers like salary transfers, bill payments, etc.
RTGS March 2004	Real-Time Gross Settlement	Real-time money transfer, without any delay. It is considered the best payment method for the amount of Rs. 2 lakhs or more. It works 24*7.
M-Wallets July 2004	Mobile Wallets like HDFC Payzapp, MobiKwik and Paytm	A mobile wallet is a digital storage space for credit, debit, ID and gift cards, allowing purchases to be performed with a mobile device rather than a physical card. In the event of theft, no one will be able to use the mobile device to make a payment without supplying the

(Continued)

Table 3.1. *(Continued)*

Platform	Digital Payment Option	Description
		necessary security credentials which makes it more secure.
M-Banking 22 November 2002	Mobile Banking through SMS	Access and operate bank accounts through a bank app or browser
PPI 1987	Prepaid Payment Instruments Debit Card	PPIs include online wallets, smart coupons, smart cards and many others. They hold a specific prepaid amount that users can use to purchase products and recharge mobile phones.
Plastic Money 1980	Credit Card	Plastic money is a payment mechanism that uses plastic cards to replace cash transactions. These pocket-sized cards are constructed of plastic/metal. The cards permit electronic transactions by securely storing financial information on the card and allowing you to access your accounts on the go.

Source: Author's Derivation.

The UPI got a strong push from the country's pandemic-related constraints, demonetisation and the popular Digital India Campaign. UPI's goal is to make monetary transactions simple, economical and safe for clients while also fostering digitisation and financial inclusion in India (Thomas & Chatterjee, 2017). Online direct transfers took on a life of their own, and the UPI gained an enormous grip (Neema & Neema, 2016). The first nation to implement Indian UPI in the year 2021 was Bhutan, enabling Indian visitors to make UPI-based payments.

Having more than 100 billion transactions in 2023, India led the global list of countries having online payment systems (NPCI, 2023). Its exceptional feature of interoperability – that is, the ability to send money instantly, compatible with all platforms and without incurring fees – made it more widely acceptable. Unavoidably, UPI payments were promoted because they were supported by all financial institutions (Nabila et al., 2018). All the banks operating in the country are supporting the platform. India's second-largest population of internet users has spurred a growing need for digital financial services (Mahesh & Bhat, 2022). This has propelled India into the global fintech arena where it now holds the third position in the world for the number of fintech companies as of 2023.

UPI proves to be a masterstroke in the digital payment system. UPI is serving the low-income group well and adding to the financial inclusion of the unserved community. The massive growth of smartphones has impacted numerous mobile-based services (Kumar & Yadav, 2022). The most significant of them is the expansion of the Internet in India, which is supported by an increase in mobile transactions. UPI is based on the idea of one-click two-factor authentication (2FA). The first factor is the user's cell phone, and the second is MPIN or biometrics. It is based on IMPS. To make the Indian economy cashless, it enables consumers to transfer funds in real time. It has played a significant part in India's cashless transaction revolution. Table 3.2 exhibits UPI Monthly Product Statistics from 2016 to 2024.

India has the world's second-largest internet user base, which has had a direct impact on demand for digitised financial services. India has appeared as a worldwide fintech force, ranking third in the standings of total fintech companies. This enormous growth of smartphones has had a ripple effect on a host of mobile-based services (Sivathanu, 2019). However, India is named as the world's most fascinating internet market. Mobile devices are the main factor driving this growth. India surged to mobile browsing, skipping the entire desktop and laptop browsing period. While over a third of internet users in the United States and the United Kingdom accessed the internet via mobile devices, Indians accessed the internet around 80% of the time, indicating a strong preference for mobile use.

Around 1.35 billion UPI transactions were recorded in the first 20 days of October 2023, a 13% increase from the previous month, while 1.8 million transactions worth 3.29 trillion were recorded in September alone, owing primarily to faster adoption of contactless payments during the COVID-19 crisis, which was accompanied by the festive season shopping spree (ET, 2023a, 2023b; Indbiz).

Table 3.2. NPCI – UPI Product Statistics.

Month	No. of Banks Live on UPI	Volume (in Mn)	Value (in Cr.)
Mar-24	572	13,440.00	19,78,353.23
Feb-24	560	12,102.67	18,27,869.35
Jan-24	550	12,203.02	18,41,083.97
Dec-23	522	12,020.23	18,22,949.42
Nov-23	516	11,235.29	17,39,740.61
Oct-23	505	11,408.79	17,15,768.34
Sep-23	492	10,555.69	15,79,133.18
Aug-23	484	10,586.02	15,76,536.56
Jul-23	473	9,964.61	15,33,645.20
Jun-23	458	9,335.06	14,75,464.27
May-23	445	9,415.19	14,89,145.44
Apr-23	414	8,898.14	14,07,007.55
Mar-23	399	8,685.30	14,10,443.01
Feb-23	390	7,534.76	12,35,846.62
Jan-23	385	8,036.89	12,98,726.62
Dec-22	382	7,829.49	12,82,055.01
Nov-22	376	7,309.45	11,90,593.39
Oct-22	365	7,305.42	12,11,582.51
Sep-22	358	6,780.80	11,16,438.10
Aug-22	346	6,579.63	10,72,792.68
Jul-22	338	6,288.40	10,62,991
Jun-22	330	5,862.75	10,14,384
May-22	323	5,955.20	10,41,520
Apr-22	316	5,583.05	9,83,302.27
Mar-22	314	5,405.65	9,60,581.66
Feb-22	304	4,527.49	8,26,843.00
Jan-22	297	4,617.15	8,31,993.11
Dec-21	282	4,566.30	8,26,848.22
Nov-21	274	4,186.48	7,68,436.11
Oct-21	261	4,218.65	7,71,444.98
Sep-21	259	3,654.30	6,54,351.81
Aug-21	249	3,555.55	6,39,116.95
Jul-21	235	3,247.82	6,06,281.14
Jun-21	229	2,807.51	5,47,373.17

Table 3.2. *(Continued)*

Month	No. of Banks Live on UPI	Volume (in Mn)	Value (in Cr.)
May-21	224	2,539.57	4,90,638.65
Apr-21	220	2,641.06	4,93,663.68
Mar-21	216	2,731.68	5,04,886.44
Feb-21	213	2,292.90	4,25,062.76
Jan-21	207	2,302.73	4,31,181.89
Dec-20	207	2,234.16	4,16,176.21
Nov-20	200	2,210.23	3,90,999.15
Oct-20	189	2,071.62	3,86,106.74
Sept-20	174	1,800.14	3,29,027.66
Aug-20	168	1,618.83	2,98,307.61
July-20	164	1,497.36	2,90,537.86
June-20	155	1,336.93	2,61,835.00
May-20	155	1,234.50	218,391.60
Apr-20	153	999.57	151,140.66
Mar-20	148	1,246.84	206,462.31
Feb-20	146	1,325.69	222,516.95
Jan-20	144	1,305.02	216,242.97
Dec-19	143	1,308.40	202,520.76
Nov-19	143	1,218.77	189,229.09
Oct-19	141	1,148.36	191,359.94
Sept-19	141	955.02	161,456.56
Aug-19	141	918.35	154,504.89
July-19	143	822.29	146,386.64
June-19	142	754.54	146,566.35
May-19	143	733.54	152,449.29
Apr-19	144	781.79	142,034.39
Mar-19	142	799.54	133,460.72
Feb-19	139	674.19	106,737.12
Jan-19	134	672.75	109,932.43
Dec-18	129	620.17	102,594.82
Nov-18	128	524.94	82,232.21
Oct-18	128	482.36	74,978.27
Sep-18	122	405.87	59,835.36

(Continued)

Table 3.2. *(Continued)*

Month	No. of Banks Live on UPI	Volume (in Mn)	Value (in Cr.)
Aug-18	114	312.02	54,212.26
July-18	114	273.75	51,843.14
June-18	110	246.37	40,834.03
May-18	101	189.48	33,288.51
Apr-18	97	190.08	27,021.85
Mar-18	91	178.05	24,172.6
Feb-18	86	171.40	19,126.2
Jan-18	71	151.83	15,571.2
Dec-17	67	145.64	13,174.24
Nov-17	61	105.02	9,669.33
Oct-17	60	76.96	7,057.78
Sep-17	57	30.98	5,325.81
Aug-17	55	16.80	4,156.62
July-17	53	11.63	3,411.35
June-17	52	10.35	3,098.36
May-17	49	9.36	2,797.07
Apr-17	48	7.20	2,271.24
Mar-17	44	6.37	2,425.14
Feb-17	44	4.38	1,937.71
Jan-17	36	4.46	1,696.22
Dec-16	35	1.99	707.93
Nov-16	30	0.29	100.46
Oct-16	26	0.10	48.57
Sep-16	25	0.09	32.64
Aug-16	21	0.09	3.09
Jul-16	21	0.09	0.38
Jun-16	21	0.00	0.00
May-16	21	0.00	0.00
Apr-16	21	0.00	0.00

Image Source: npci.org.in

UPI was set up with a vision of migrating towards a 'less cash' and more digital society. It is a system that enables peer-to-peer online payments for users holding different bank accounts, to send/receive money or to pay directly to merchants from their Smartphone without the need to enter bank account information or net banking User ID/Password, so we call it convenient and efficient.

UPI is quickly becoming a global favourite since it is the quickest, safest and most convenient way to pay. UPI is gaining acceptance worldwide because it is not only inexpensive and interoperable but also scalable and customisable, making it simple for other countries to adopt. It surpasses even conventional cash payment methods, providing an unrivaled level of convenience (Sankaran & Chakraborty, 2021).

Table 3.3 represents some prominent literature reviews on UPI.

UPI has played a pivotal part in India's fintech boom. Its success story has become an international model. Its ability to instantaneously transfer money between bank accounts via mobile applications has revolutionised how consumers conduct digital transactions. The interoperability of UPI across banks and payment platforms has resulted in the formation of a unified payment ecosystem.

It has enabled digital payments for small enterprises and street sellers, resulting in increased financial inclusion (Tombini, 2023). UPI has also accelerated the creation of new payment goods and services. Furthermore, efforts are being made to connect the UPI with quick payment systems in other nations.

2. Prospects of Unified Payment Interface in India

India has the world's second-largest internet user base, which has had a direct impact on demand for digitised financial services. India has appeared as a worldwide fintech force, ranking third in the standings of total fintech companies (Sivathanu, 2019). This enormous growth of smartphones has had a ripple effect on a host of mobile-based services. The surge in UPI transactions has revealed that the prospects of UPI in India are enormous.

- *Financial Inclusion* – The UPI has played an important role in achieving financial inclusion in India by bringing unbanked persons into the formal financial system (Ofosu-Mensah Ababio et al., 2021). Our country's robust digital public infrastructure, including Aadhaar, affordable internet access, pervasive mobile phone services and PMJDY, has enabled more people to access financial services, independent of location or socioeconomic position.
- *Push to Cashless Economy* – According to the Governor of the RBI Sh. Shantikanta Das, UPI is the backbone of India's digital payments. The rapid expansion of digital technologies in India over recent years cited their transformative impact on the country's financial system. The rise of digital payments signals a shift to a cashless, technologically driven-future (Ofosu-Mensah Ababio et al., 2021). The convenience and security they offer provide benefits both for consumers and for the broader financial system.
- *Acceptance by Foreign Country* – With its robust startup ecosystem, vibrant talent pool and unwavering commitment to digital transformation, India is now focusing on leveraging technology to bridge gaps, empower individuals and promote financial inclusion. Various countries now accept Indian UPI payments.

Table 3.3. Table Representing Literature Reviews on Unified Payments Interface.

Author(s) and Year	The Context of Study	Theoretical Framework	Constructs	Key Findings
Thakur and Srivastava (2013)	Perceived Risk, Adoption Readiness, Usage Intention, and Individual Innovativeness among Consumers for M-Payment Solutions in India.	TAM UTAUT	AR, EU, PR, PIN	The study discovered that PU, PEoU, social impact and conducive factors are all characteristics of perceived preparedness. These factors have a positive impact on the intention to use mobile payments. Personal Ingenuity has a beneficial impact on the intention to utilise mobile payments. Innovative users are more inclined to use mobile payment systems. Three dimensions of PR were established in the study: perceived security risk, perceived privacy risk and perceived monetary risk. Addressing security and privacy concerns is critical for increasing mobile payment use. Overall, the study emphasises the significance of perceived preparedness, personal innovation and addressing perceived risk in influencing consumer behaviour and desire to utilise mobile payment services.
Kakade and Veshne (2017)	Steps Towards Cashless Economy UPI.	Theoretical Study		UPI's objectives include facilitating instant payments using mobile and web applications, providing a secure and convenient payment service, supporting the expansion of e-commerce, and encouraging financial inclusion. The ability to use personal mobile devices for all payments, the use of unified identifiers such as Aadhaar numbers and virtual payment addresses, the ability to make payments without sharing account details and the use of 1-click 2-factor authentication. UPI has made digital transactions as simple as sending text messages and is available 24*7, unlike other payment systems such as RTGS and NEFT.

				UPI improves system efficiency and contributes to India becoming a cashless economy. It covers the issues that India has in the e-banking business, such as low literacy rates and difficulties in obtaining banking services.
Sivathanu (2019)	Digital Payment System Adoption during demonetisation.	UTAUT2 IRT	BI, IR, ST, AU, CX	The use of digital payment systems is influenced by Behavioural Intention and Intention to Recommend. Stickiness to cash payment moderates the link between BI and the Actual Usage of digital payment systems. Factors such as PU, Perceived Simplicity of Use, social impact, facilitating conditions and Trust influenced the adoption and use of digital payment systems. Challenges to digital payment system acceptance and usage include a lack of understanding, security concerns and Complexity. The study emphasises the importance of policymakers and digital payment system service providers developing strategies to increase digital payment system acceptance and adoption.
Sun et al. (2017)	Trust Model of Mobile Banking Users in China.	DOI Trust Theory Trust Evaluation Model	UB, PU, EU, INQ, T	Structure assurance, ubiquity, information quality, Trust, Ease of Use and experience were identified as major elements influencing trust in mobile banking in the study on the initial trust model of mobile banking customers. Structure certainty was discovered to be the most critical component influencing trust tendencies. Other characteristics that influence early trust and experience include ubiquity, information quality, reported contentment and perceived simplicity of use. Concluded that mobile banking customers' initial trust affects their perception of experience and their predisposition to trust, which affects their actual use of mobile banking services.

(Continued)

Table 3.3. *(Continued)*

Author(s) and Year	The Context of Study	Theoretical Framework	Constructs	Key Findings
				To improve customer acceptance and trust in mobile banking, suppliers should focus on developing early trust and offering a great user experience.
Bagla and Sancheti (2018)	Sustainability of Digital Wallets.	Inferential Analysis	Descriptive Research Methods.	There are many gaps between user expectations and their satisfaction with digital wallets in India. Customers are more satisfied than their mean expectation level in only two areas: The ability to withdraw funds and the minimum information required to begin using a digital wallet. Customers' mean satisfaction level is lower than their mean expectation level in six areas: Easy user interface, security features, appealing reward programme, wide acceptability, no transaction cost and collecting interest on money stored in the wallet. These discrepancies in client satisfaction constitute a risk to the survival of digital wallets unless wallet service providers take meaningful initiatives to bridge these gaps.
Kaur et al. (2020)	Investigation of factors influencing adult's intentions to use and suggest mobile wallets.	DOI TAM TAM2 UTAUT TPB TRA	RA, CM, CX, TR, OBV	The convenience and efficiency of mobile wallets affected their intention to recommend them to others. Users' intentions to use and suggest mobile wallets were linked to their compatibility with their lives. Users' intent to use mobile wallets was found to be influenced by intuitive user interface (IU). In promotional campaigns and commercials, the particular advantages of mobile wallets, such as security, dependability and anytime-anywhere transactions, should be stressed. The study's findings are

				essential for mobile payment service providers since the behaviour of young adults is critical in technology adoption and usage-related decisions. Service providers should concentrate on increasing potential customers' willingness to use mobile wallets by taking into account compatibility with users' lifestyles, convenience of learning and use, and promoting the benefits of mobile payments.
Najib and Fahma (2020)	Adoption of Digital Payments System by SME Restaurants in Indonesia.	Extended TAM	PEU, PU, PUT, ATT, IU, T	Factors such as PEU, Perceived Utility, ATT and T influence SMEs' intention to use digital payment systems. They find it simple to use and beneficial to their operations, more the trust more the usage. SMEs are concerned about perceived dangers such as delays in receiving money and transaction failures owing to insecure digital connections so digital infrastructure is important. They are also motivated by competitive and consumer demands and government support.
Malaquias and Silva (2020)	Adoption of Mobile Banking by Brazil's Rural Community.	TAM TPB	T, EU, SI, PU	The researchers collected data from 115 farmers in the state of Minas Gerais and analysed the results using confirmatory factor analysis and structural equation modelling. According to the survey, perceived ease of use, perceived utility and trust were the most important factors influencing farmers' adoption of mobile banking. However, the association between social impact and mobile banking use was negative, contradicting earlier studies. This study leads to a better knowledge of the benefits of information technology in the financial routines of Brazilian farmers.

(Continued)

Table 3.3. *(Continued)*

Author(s) and Year	The Context of Study	Theoretical Framework	Constructs	Key Findings
Patil et al. (2020)	Consumer Adoption of Mobile Payments in India.	UTAUT SEM	PEE, EE, SI, FC, PIN, AN, T, ATT, GR, BI	Because of India's cultural and linguistic variety, existing dominant technology adoption models such as TAM and UTAUT may not be easily applicable to the Indian setting. Consumer mobile payment adoption or usage behaviour in India is heavily influenced by factors such as Perceived usefulness, Perceived Ease of Use, Perceived Severity of security Threats, Perceived Cost, Knowledge, and innovation resistance. The study focuses on customer desire to embrace or utilise digital/mobile payment systems, rather than actual adoption or usage. The study focuses on mobile payment technology adopters in India, and future research should include non-adopters to examine the outcomes using the proposed model. The study took a quantitative approach, and future studies could benefit from a mixed-method approach to acquire a more comprehensive knowledge of consumer payment acceptance.
Shankar and Rishi (2020)	Convenience influences mobile banking adoption intentions.	CMR TAM TPB UTAUT I UTAUT II	AC TC SC OOC	Access Convenience, Transaction Convenience, Possession Convenience, EOU, transactional ease and possession/post-possession ease all have a substantial impact on the intention to use mobile banking. Search and evaluation convenience have no major impact on the intention to use mobile banking. The most influential factor in mobile

				banking adoption intention is possession/post-possession convenience, showing that customers are inclined to use mobile banking to save time and effort when conducting banking activities. The intention to use mobile banking has a substantial impact on the actual use of mobile banking. These findings imply that some aspects of online convenience are important in motivating people to use mobile banking services. To encourage the use of mobile banking, banks should focus on improving access convenience, transaction convenience and possession/post-possession convenience.
Saha and Kiran (2022)	Factors affecting the adoption of UPI by Baby Boomers.	UTAUT	PU, EU, SI, UB	According to the study's findings, the commencement of the COVID-19 epidemic was the key drive for baby boomers to choose UPI as a payment channel. The study also revealed numerous elements that influenced baby boomers' behavioural intention to embrace UPI. Performance expectancy, effort expectancy, social impact, and ubiquity are among these criteria. Overall, the analysis reveals that the pandemic was a significant factor in the adoption of UPI among baby boomers.
Mahesh and Bhat (2021)	Investigate the growth and possibilities of UPI in India's digital payment ecosystem.	Descriptive Research	SWOT	UPI has experienced rapid expansion in the retail digital payment market in recent years. Customers have migrated to contactless payments, resulting in greater digital payment use. UPI has considerably aided the growth of digital payments in India. In the digital economy, UPI is regarded as a potentially revolutionary method of transmitting payments. The study emphasises UPI's strengths and future possibilities in the digital payment environment. The study underlines the importance of

(Continued)

Table 3.3. *(Continued)*

Author(s) and Year	The Context of Study	Theoretical Framework	Constructs	Key Findings
				future research into India's whole e-payment infrastructure. According to the research case study on the UPI in India, UPI has demonstrated extraordinary growth in the previous few years, particularly in the retail payment sector. According to the survey, the growth of digital payments on the UPI network has expanded dramatically. The study also sought to comprehend UPI's position in the digital payment ecosystem, as well as to identify its primary strengths and growth potential. Overall, the study underlined UPI's potential contribution to India's digital economy.
Jha and Kumar (2021)	Consumer perception of the use of UPI.	Descriptive Study	PE, EE, SI, BI	The research highlights that the adoption of UPI payments has significantly increased after the demonetisation and government reforms promoting cashless transactions. Factors such as Perceived Enjoyment. Effort Expectancy, Social Influence, facilitating conditions (mobile specifications and network strength) and cashback and rewards have a significant impact on users' Behavioural Intention to adopt UPI payments. Users who value a smooth payment experience, minimal effort requirement, and are facilitated by the latest technology are more likely to embrace UPI payments. The study suggests that UPI optimises financial operations, allows quicker payments, and provides time-saving benefits to users. Learning to use

				UPI payment is perceived as easy, and users have confidence in using the UPI payment service skillfully. Social influence, including the endorsement of UPI payments by friends and family, and the perception of mobile payment as trendy, plays a role in users' adoption of UPI. The study admits its limitations, such as small sample size and data collected during the pre-COVID-19 and COVID-19 eras. Future studies should look at a broader demographic and post-COVID-19 factors driving the migration to digital payments.
Fahad and Shahid (2022)	Determinants of UPI adoption in India.	Diffusion of Innovation (DOI)	RA, CX, OBV, IU, S, IR	The Intention to Use UPI was found to have a substantial positive relationship with Relative Benefit, Complexity, and Observability. Compatibility and Trialability were found to have no significant relationship with UPI Intention to Use. Customer satisfaction was connected with a higher inclination to utilise UPI. Satisfaction was found to be related to the intention to suggest UPI. Customers who are happy with UPI are more inclined to tell others about it.
Wong et al. (2022)	Analysing the Gamification's effectiveness in boosting M Payment Acceptance among China's Silver Generation.	TAM Prospect Theory	ATT, AI, PE, PU, PEG, PEU	Gamification can encourage M payment. Performance Expectancy influences the Perceived Effectiveness of gamification. Furthermore, the gamified experience was found to increase the Perceived Ease of Use and Perceived Usefulness significantly. However, among the silver generation, the perceived danger was identified as a substantial obstacle to translating Attitude and Intention to Use. The importance of an enjoyable gamified experience is increasing the effectiveness of gamification.

(Continued)

Table 3.3. *(Continued)*

Author(s) and Year	The Context of Study	Theoretical Framework	Constructs	Key Findings
Kumari and Biswas (2023)	Satisfaction with M-payments.	SEM TAM ECM	PVC, CP, PU, PST, IU, S, SQL	Participation in Perceived Value co-creation, Service Quality, Cognitive Processing and user pleasure partially mitigates the association and boosts user happiness resulting in stronger IU for M-Payment. Perceived Utility enhances the link between user happiness and Intention to Use. The Perceived Severity of security Threats has no direct impact on customer happiness or Intention to Use.

Source: Author's Derivation.

Note: AC – Access Convenience, AI – Intention to Adopt, AN – Anxiety, AR – Adoption Readiness, ATT – Attitude, AU- Actual Usage, BI – Behavioural Intention, CM – Compatibility, CP – Cognitive Processing, CX – Complexity, EE – Effort Expectancy, EU – Ease of use, FC – Facilitating Conditions, GR – Grievance Redressal, INQ – Information Quality, IR – Innovation Resistance, IU – Intention to Use, IR – Intention to Recommend, OBV – Observability, OOC – Overall Online Convenience, KN – Knowledge, PB – Perceived Benefits, PC – Perceived Cost, PE – Performance Expectancy, PST – Perceived Security Threats, PEU – Perceived Ease of Use, PE – Perceived Enjoyment, PEG – Perceived effectiveness of Gamification, PIN – Personal Innovativeness, PU – Perceived Usefulness, PUT – Perceived Utility, POC – Possession Convenience, PST – Perceived Severity of Security Threats, PSU – Perceived Simplicity of Use, PVC – Perceived Value Co-creation, PEE – Performance Expectancy Effort, RA – Relative Advantage, RB – Relative Benefit, S – Satisfaction, SC – Search Convenience, SI – Social Influence, ST – Stickiness to Cash Payment, SQL – Service Quality, T – Trust, TC – Transaction Convenience, TR – Trialability, UB – Ubiquity, UE – User Experience.

- *Two-Factor Authentication* – UPI is safe to use; to ensure transaction security, UPI has a strong 2FA mechanism. To validate the transaction, users must input their unique Mobile Personal Identification Number (MPIN). Advanced encryption technologies such as TLS, AES and PKI safeguard UPI transactions, ensuring that sensitive information such as user identities and transaction data remain confidential during transmission. You also don't have to divulge your bank account information to anyone because UPI employs VPA, or Virtual Payment Address, as the transaction identifier.
  This lowers the possibility of information leakage and unauthorised access to your bank account. Another advantage of UPI security is that it is device-specific (Gochhwal, 2017). This means you can only access your UPI account from the device with which you registered it. This stops anyone from accessing your UPI account from a separate device, providing an additional layer of protection. Furthermore, the RBI requires UPI transactions to use rigorous authentication techniques.
- *Boost to Digital Economy* – With the launch of the Digital India Campaign, every citizen of the country is becoming more tech-savvy, thereby accelerating the transition to a cashless ecosystem. India leads in digital payments, having recorded 89.5 million digital transactions in 2022, accounting for 46% of global real-time payments (IBEF, 2024), and having more digital payments transactions than the other four leading countries combined.
- *Reduced Cash Dependency* – According to RBI analysts, India has been experiencing new milestones in digital payments, in both value and volume terms, indicating the robustness of India's payment ecosystem and acceptance. India continues to dominate the digital payment landscape! We're paving the path to a cashless economy with innovative solutions and widespread acceptance. Brazil ranked second on the list, with 29.2 million transactions.
  China comes in second with 17.6 million transactions, according to MyGovIndia data. Thailand ranks fourth with 16.5 million digital transactions, followed by South Korea with 8 million. Prime Minister Narendra Modi stated that India is ranked as the leader in digital payments and that the country's rural areas are flourishing (The Hindu, 2023).
- *Withdrawal of denomination 2,000 currency notes* – The RBI has stated that Rs. 2,000 denomination banknotes would be moved out of circulation (pib.gov.in; RBI, 2016) on 19 May 2023 following the November 2016 demonetisation of the former Rs. 500 and Rs. 1,000 notes. The RBI declared that the goal of issuing Rs. 2,000 notes had been met when sufficient amounts of currency notes of various denominations became available. UPI has become a convenient and secure choice for customers and merchants, boosting the digital ecosystem.
- *Enhanced Transparency in the System* – Our honourable Prime Minister has stated that digital payment systems will strengthen the hands of the average man in the battle against corruption, black money and fake currencies.
- *Security of Payments* – UPI is based on the platform of the IMPS. Users must create a Virtual ID or VPA of their choice before linking it to any bank account to use the UPI. This method does not necessitate the exchange of bank information between the payee and the payer. Because the VPA serves as their

financial address, customers do not need to remember the beneficiary account number, IFSC codes or net banking user ID/password when sending or receiving funds (Thomas & Chatterjee, 2017).

- *Convenience and Efficiency* – UPI streamlines payments by eliminating the need for account numbers, IFSC codes and other standard banking information. A single VPA acts as a transaction identifier.
- *Maximum Bank Support* – India's thriving startup ecosystem, its vibrant talent pool and the unwavering commitment to digital transformation. UPI is our landmark example of commitment to innovation. It is a game changer for India's digital payment ecosystem (Sobti, 2019). More than 70 mobile apps and over 50 million merchants across India now accept UPI payments, thereby the UPI platform witnessed and exceeded an impressive 10 billion transactions, solidifying its position as the spinal cord of digital payments.
- *Government Backup* – The RBI is committed to encouraging responsive innovation and has taken strategic steps such as starting a fintech department within the RBI to manage the evolving fintech sector and the reserve bank innovation hub, a wholly owned subsidiary engaged in technology-based projects aimed at benefiting the masses and paying special consideration to the rapidly evolving fintech sector.
- *Rewards and Incentives* – UPI rewards like cashback, discounts coupons, etc. offered by different apps or even banks are a primary reason for its popularity.
- *Vendor Support* – UPI is compatible with several banks and financial organisations. Users may streamline their transactions by linking several bank accounts to a common UPI app, eliminating the need for separate applications for every bank.
- *No/Low Bank Visits* – India's journey towards a digital payment mechanism embodies innovation with a human touch, spanning financial inclusion, digital payments and the use of artificial intelligence for credit assessments. UPI is accessible round-the-clock, even on vacation days and weekends, allowing users to transfer and receive money whenever it's convenient without being constrained by banking hours.

3. Challenges Faced by UPI Ecosystem

Challenges to digital payment ecosystem acceptance and usage include a deficit of understanding, security concerns and system complexity (Sivathanu, 2019). Fraudsters are getting more ingenious day by day. Although UPI is a quick and easy way to transfer funds from different bank accounts, it can also be misused for scams.

- *Lack of Infrastructure* – A significant spike in UPI-based transactions, as well as an increase in the number of rejected payments, necessitates increased investment and focus on banks' capacity to handle increasing volumes. However, the number of failed payments attempts due to network difficulties on the servers of banks and the NPCI has been steadily increasing.

- *Delayed Payments* – Due to the lack of infrastructure, the payments are delayed or deducted money can take up to 48 hours to be credited again. These issues make the user uncomfortable and tend to avoid digital transactions.
- *Limited transaction flexibility* – The maximum UPI daily transfer limit can change from bank to bank between INR 25,000 and INR 1,00,000. A few banks have also set UPI transfer limits per week or month instead of a day. However, these types of regulations and limits limit the transactions of the users.
- *Increased transaction failures* – NPCI must recognise that this is a major concern. September 2023 was particularly problematic for all platforms due to the massive surge in transactions and the bank's inability to support it (BS, 2023; livemint). Infrastructure development must take the pace to carry on the record to higher limits.
- *No Incentives to the Banks* – UPI payments are free for users and merchants since the merchant discount rate, or MDR, is set at zero by the finance ministry, but this also implies that banks have no incentive to invest in improving UPI or gaining new customers. Hence, many banks passively discourage it.
- *Cyber Fraud* – Hackers may opt for fraudulent malpractices. Enemies from across the border run their operations to fake transactions. If digital transactions could curb corruption and black money, Kenya would have been the most transparent country in the world. About 75% of the adult population in Kenya uses mobile phones for payments and money transfers. The value of mobile money transactions and transfers per day is equal to 4.5% of the annualised GDP of Kenya, as per a report published in an *International Monetary Fund (IMF)* journal.

4. Way Ahead

India is perfectly positioned to digitalise its economy and 1.4 billion people while also playing an important role across countries and regions throughout the world, expanding its impact and global status. This enables India to use technology to address societal gaps in financial inclusion and to push grass-roots level entrepreneurship and innovation, all while promoting digital literacy, social issues relating to women's empowerment and governance delivery.

The massive growth of smartphones has impacted numerous mobile-based services. The most significant of them is the expansion of the Internet in India, which is supported by an increase in mobile transactions. UPI is based on the idea of one-click2FA. The first factor is the user's cell phone, and the second is MPIN or biometrics. It is based on IMPS. To make the Indian economy cashless, it enables consumers to transfer funds in real time. It has played a significant part in India's cashless transaction revolution.

Under India's G20 presidency, the RBI and the BIS Innovation Hub have jointly launched the G20 Tech Sprint, a global technology competition focused on improving cross-border payments. This year seeks innovative solutions for three problem statements: addressing illicit finance risks through AML/CFT/Sanctions technology, enabling settlement in emerging market and developing economy (EMDE) currencies and developing technology solutions for multilateral cross-border CBDC platforms. The G20 TechSprint aims to demonstrate how technology can address challenges in this domain, foster innovation and promote seamless payments across borders while maintaining financial integrity.

- *Agile Infrastructure Development* – India is currently witnessing a digital payments revolution (Agrawal et al., 2020; Mehta & Shah, 2020), with $3 trillion worth of digital payments in 2022, which is expected to reach $10 trillion by 2026 (BCG, 2022). This is driven by the combined benefits of its multiple digital efforts, including the most visible ones such as Aadhaar digital ID and UPI. In India, the use of fintech apps such as GooglePay, PhonePe and Paytm has increased dramatically. As a result, India now accounts for 40% of worldwide real-time digital payments.
- *Blockchain Integration* – Blockchain is a distributed ledger technology that enables numerous parties to keep a shared record of transactions without the need for a central authority. Transactions in a blockchain network are grouped into blocks and added to a chain of prior transactions. Blockchain's decentralised nature assures transparency, security and immutability. The decision between blockchain and UPI is highly influenced company's unique requirements. Blockchain is the technology to explore if transactions are complex and require features such as transparency, security and decentralisation.
  On the other hand, if one values simplicity, speed and widespread acceptance in everyday payments, UPI is the better option. One has to investigate the use of blockchain technology in the UPI infrastructure to improve transparency, security and scalability. Smart contracts have the potential to automate transaction processes, minimise the need for intermediaries and enable seamless cross-border transactions.
- *AI-Powered Fraud Prevention* – Using artificial intelligence and machine learning, one can detect and prevent fraudulent UPI transactions in real time. Using powerful anomaly detection algorithms to discover suspicious activity by analysing user behaviour patterns and transaction data.
- *Personalised Financial Insights* – Payment technologies have become an essential element of our daily lives in today's quickly changing digital landscape. One can utilise data analytics and artificial intelligence to empower UPI users with individualised financial insights and provide users with real-time expenditure analysis, budgeting tools and targeted advice to help them make smart financial decisions.

5. Conclusion

However, India is named as the world's most fascinating internet market. Mobile devices are the main factor driving this growth. India surged to mobile browsing, skipping the entire desktop and laptop browsing period. While over a third of internet users in the United States and the United Kingdom accessed the internet via mobile devices, Indians accessed the internet around 80% of the time, indicating a strong preference for mobile use (Najib & Fahma, 2020).

Around 1.35 billion UPI transactions were recorded in the first 20 days of October, a 13% increase from the previous month while 1.8 million transactions worth 3.29 trillion were recorded in September alone, owing primarily to faster adoption of contactless payments during the COVID-19 crisis, which was accompanied by the festive season shopping spree. UPI was set up with a vision of migrating towards a 'less cash' and more digital society (Kirmani et al., 2023).

It is a system that enables peer-to-peer online payments for users holding different bank accounts, to send and receive money or to pay directly to merchants from their Smartphone without the need to enter bank account information or net banking UserID/Password, so we call it convenient and efficient. Because of their compatibility, UPI transactions are superior to mobile wallets (Kumar & Yadav, 2022).

UPI transactions can occur between any two banks or among the accounts of the same bank, but wallet transactions can only occur between two digital wallet accounts. In the case of UPI, a VPA ID serves as the identifier whereas a mobile number serves as the identifier in the event of a wallet transaction. UPI is quickly becoming a global favourite since it is the quickest, safest and most convenient way to pay.

Table 3.4. NPCI – TOP 5 UPI APP Statistics.

		Customer Initiated Transactions	
Sr. No.	**Application Name**	**Volume (Mn)**	**Value (Cr)**
1	PhonePe	6,502.15	10,02,387.84
2	Google Pay	5,061.18	6,95,196.05
3	Paytm	1,210.64	1,33,707.06
4	Cred	132.31	44,991.57
5	Axis Bank Apps	13.59	3,044.92

Image Source: npci.org.in

UPI is gaining acceptance worldwide because it is not only inexpensive and interoperable but also scalable and customisable, making it simple for other countries to adopt. It surpasses even conventional cash payment methods, providing an unrivaled level of convenience.

Table 3.4 exhibits Top 5 UPI APP Statistics.

References

Agrawal, S., Gupta, G., & Zagade, A. (2020). Fintech: A new revolution in India. *JournalNX*, 47–57.

Bagla, R. K., & Sancheti, V. (2018). Gaps in customer satisfaction with digital wallets: Challenge for sustainability. *The Journal of Management Development*, *37*(6), 442–451. https://doi.org/10.1108/JMD-04-2017-0144

Balakrishnan, M. (2023). The Unified Payment Interface and the growth of digital payments in India: An analysis. *Journal of Payments Strategy & Systems*, *17*(3).

Fahad, & Shahid, M. (2022). Exploring the determinants of adoption of Unified Payment Interface (UPI) in India: A study based on diffusion of innovation theory. *Digital Business*, *2*(2). https://doi.org/10.1016/j.digbus.2022.100040

Gochhwal, R. (2017). Unified Payment Interface—An advancement in payment systems. *American Journal of Industrial and Business Management*, *07*(10), 1174–1191. https://doi.org/10.4236/ajibm.2017.710084

Jha, R. R., & Kumar, R. (2021). UPI-an innovative step for making digital payment effective and factors affecting consumer perception on the use of UPI. *Journal of Emerging Technologies and Innovative Research*, *8*(7), 698–705.

Kakade, R. B., & Veshne, N. A. (2017). Unified Payment Interface (UPI) – A way towards cashless economy. *International Research Journal of Engineering and Technology*, *4*(11), 762–766.

Kaur, P., Dhir, A., Bodhi, R., Singh, T., & Almotairi, M. (2020). Why do people use and recommend m-wallets? *Journal of Retailing and Consumer Services*, *56*. https://doi.org/10.1016/j.jretconser.2020.102091

Kirmani, M. D., Haque, M. A., Sadiq, M. A., & Hasan, F. (2023). Cashless preferences during the COVID-19 pandemic: Investigating user intentions to continue UPI-based payment systems in India. *Journal of Science and Technology Policy Management*, *14*(4), 758–779. https://doi.org/10.1108/JSTPM-08-2021-0127

Kumar, N. K., & Yadav, A. S. (2022). A systematic literature review and bibliometric analysis on mobile payments. *Vision*. Sage Publications India Pvt. Ltd. https://doi.org/10.1177/09722629221104190

Kumari, N., & Biswas, A. (2023). Does M-payment service quality and perceived value co-creation participation magnify M-payment continuance usage intention? Moderation of usefulness and severity. *International Journal of Bank Marketing*, *41*(6), 1330–1359. https://doi.org/10.1108/IJBM-11-2022-0500

Mahesh, A., & Bhat, G. (2022). A systematic review and research agenda of digital payment system with reference to Unified Payment Interface. *International Journal of Management, Technology and Social Sciences*, *7*(2), 679–709.

Mahesh, A., & Bhat, G. (2021). Digital payment service in India – A case study of Unified Payment Interface. *International Journal of Case Studies in Business*, *5*(1), 2581–6942. A Refereed International Journal of Srinivas University, India. https://doi.org/10.5281/zenodo.5091207

Malaquias, R. F., & Silva, A. F. (2020). Understanding the use of mobile banking in rural areas of Brazil. *Technology in Society*, *62*, 101260.

Mehta, N., & Shah, S. (2020). Payment banks: Digital revolution in Indian banking system. *International Journal of Management and Humanities*, *4*(6), 110–115. ISSN, 2394-0913.

Mukhopadhyay, S., & Upadhyay, P. (2022). Institutional intervention in technology innovation: The struggle to increase mobile payment adoption. *Digital Policy, Regulation and Governance*, *24*(1), 74–92. https://doi.org/10.1108/DPRG-01-2021-0002

Narsapur, R. R., & Parasar, A. (2020). An analysis of the rise in digital transactions in India. https://ssrn.com/abstract=3660907

Nabila, M., Purwandari, B., Nazief, B. A., Chalid, D. A., Wibowo, S. S., & Solichah, I. (2018, October). Financial technology acceptance factors of electronic wallet and digital cash in Indonesia. In *2018 international conference on information technology systems and innovation (ICITSI)* (pp. 284–289). IEEE.

Najib, M., & Fahma, F. (2020). Investigating the adoption of digital payment system through an extended technology acceptance model: An insight from the Indonesian small and medium enterprises. *International Journal of Advanced Science, Engineering and Information Technology*, *10*(4), 1702–1708. https://doi.org/10.18517/ijaseit.10.4.11616

Neema, K., & Neema, A. (2016). UPI (Unified Payment Interface) – A new technique of digital payment: An exploratory study. *International Journal of Current Research in Multidisciplinary*, *3*(10), 1–10. https://www.india-briefing.com/news/growth-of-digital-payments-systems-in-india-

Ofosu-Mensah Ababio, J., Attah-Botchwey, E., Osei-Assibey, E., & Barnor, C. (2021). Financial inclusion and human development in frontier countries. *International Journal of Finance & Economics*, *26*(1), 42–59. https://doi.org/10.1002/ijfe.1775

Patil, P., Tamilmani, K., Rana, N. P., & Raghavan, V. (2020). Understanding consumer adoption of mobile payment in India: Extending Meta-UTAUT model with personal innovativeness, anxiety, trust, and grievance redressal. *International Journal of Information Management*, *54*, 102144.

Ranpariya, T., Joshi, A., & Rajdev, A. A. (2021). Factors driving the adoption of UPI services based on the UTAUT model. https://www.researchgate.net/publication/359577251

Rastogi, S., Panse, C., Sharma, A., & Bhimavarapu, V. M. (2021). Unified Payment Interface (UPI): A digital innovation and its impact on financial inclusion and economic development. *Universal Journal of Accounting and Finance*, *9*(3), 518–530. https://doi.org/10.13189/ujaf.2021.090326

Saha, P., & Kiran, K. B. (2022). What insisted baby boomers adopt unified payment interface as a payment mechanism?: An exploration of drivers of behavioral intention. *Journal of Advances in Management Research*. https://doi.org/10.1108/JAMR-01-2022-0022

Sankaran, R., & Chakraborty, S. (2021). Factors impacting mobile banking in India: Empirical approach extending UTAUT2 with perceived value and trust. *IIM Kozhikode Society and Management Review*, *11*(1), 7–24. https://doi.org/10.1177/2277975220975219

Shankar, A., & Rishi, B. (2020). Convenience matter in mobile banking adoption intention? *Australasian Marketing Journal*, *28*(4), 273–285.

Sivathanu, B. (2019). Adoption of digital payment systems in the era of demonetization in India: An empirical study. *Journal of Science and Technology Policy Management*, *10*(1), 143–171. https://doi.org/10.1108/JSTPM-07-2017-0033

Sobti, N. (2019). Impact of demonetization on the diffusion of mobile payment service in India: Antecedents of behavioral intention and adoption using extended UTAUT model. *Journal of Advances in Management Research*, *16*(4), 472–497. https://doi.org/10.1108/JAMR-09-2018-0086

Sun, B., Sun, C., Liu, C., & Gui, C. (2017). Research on initial trust model of mobile banking users. *Journal of Risk Analysis and Crisis Response*, *7*(1).

Thakur, R., & Srivastava, M. (2013). Adoption readiness, personal innovativeness, perceived risk, and usage intention across customer groups for mobile payment services in India. *Internet Research*, *24*(3), 369–392. https://doi.org/10.1108/IntR-12-2012-0244

Thomas, R., & Chatterjee, A. (2017). Unified Payment Interface (UPI): A catalyst tool supporting digitalization-utility, prospects and issues. www.ijiras.com

Venkatesh, V., Morris, M. G., Davis, G. B., & Davis, F. D. (2003). User acceptance of information technology: Toward a unified view. *Quarterly*, *27*(3).

Wong, D., Liu, H., Meng-Lewis, Y., Sun, Y., & Zhang, Y. (2022). Gamified money: Exploring the effectiveness of gamification in mobile payment adoption among the silver generation in China. *Information Technology and People*, *35*(1), 281–315. https://doi.org/10.1108/ITP-09-2019-0456

https://www.bcg.com/publications/2022/future-of-digital-payments-in-india

https://www.bis.org/speeches/sp231029.htm#:~:text=Over%202014%E2%80%9321%2C%20the%20share,and%20improving%20access%20to%20credit

https://www.business-standard.com/economy/news/india-s-upi-transactions-fall-marginally-in-sept-hold-on-to-10-bn-mark-123100100516_1.html

https://economictimes.indiatimes.com/tech/technology/total-upi-transactions-cross-100-billion-mark-in-2023/articleshow/106492917.cms

https://www.ibef.org/industry/banking-india

https://indbiz.gov.in/upi-transactions-reach-10-56-billion-in-september/

https://www.livemint.com/industry/banking/rise-in-payment-failures-puts-focus-on-banking-infra-overhaul-11603334098652.html

https://www.nic.in/blogs/digital-payments-driving-the-growth-of-digital-economy/

https://www.npci.org.in/what-we-do/upi/product-statistics

https://pib.gov.in/PressReleaseIframePage.aspx?PRID=1942514

https://rbi.org.in/commonman/English/scripts/PressReleases.aspx

https://sphweb.bumc.bu.edu/otlt/mphmodules/sb/behavioralchangetheories/behavioralchangetheories4.html

https://www.thehindu.com/business/Economy/india-leads-global-digital-payments-with-895-million-transactions-in-2022-mygovindia-data/article66953386.ece

https://timesofindia.indiatimes.com/india/bhutan-adopts-indias-bhim-upi-payment-system/articleshow/84377246.cms

Chapter 4

Users' Intentions of Adopting Fintech Services: Analysis of Trust and Attitude Elements

Askar Garad[a], *Arni Surwanti*[a], *Abdullah M. Al-Ansi*[b], *Hosam Alden Riyadh*[c], *Salsabila Aisyah Alfaiza*[c] *and Budiman Al Iman*[d]

[a]Universitas Muhammadiyah Yogyakarta, Indonesia
[b]Dhofar University, Oman
[c]Telkom University, Indonesia
[d]Universitas MercuBuana Yogyakarta, Indonesia

Abstract

The objective of the article is to extend the applicability of conventional technology acceptance models by thoroughly and specifically analysing the influencing elements and their relationship with the adoption of fintech services. The numerical approach was employed. A total of 573 responses were included in the study. In this study, the sample data were statistically analysed using Smart-PLS 4.0. The study findings indicate that user trust in fintech services is positively influenced directly by perceived ease of use, brand reputation and government support while perceived risk and utility are not significantly correlated with user confidence in fintech services. In addition, user attitudes about fintech services are positively impacted by brand reputation, government support and perceived usefulness. Users' perceptions of risk and usability do not significantly affect how they feel about fintech services. User attitudes regarding fintech services are positively indirectly influenced by perceived utility, brand reputation, and government support, as well as by a considerable amount of trust. Users' attitudes regarding fintech services are not significantly impacted by the indirect impacts of perceived usefulness and risk. The results of this study give financial service providers an empirical foundation and a user assessment for

From Digital Disruption to Dominance, 103–119

Published under exclusive licence by Emerald Publishing Limited
doi:10.1108/978-1-83549-608-420251004

implementing cutting-edge, user-centred services. Additionally, it offers helpful information for financial service providers, fintech company marketing tactics and the accomplishment of strategic objectives.

Keywords: Fintech adoption; user trust; attitudes towards fintech; perceived ease of use; brand reputation; government support

1. Introduction

Fintech, or financial technology, is the application of cutting-edge technological advancements to products and services in the financial industry. It includes activities such as mobile banking, cryptocurrency and blockchain technology, among others, that are fast-developing (Dawood et al., 2021; Railslove GmbH, 2023). Sam Daley and Columbia Engineering asserted that fintech had sped up and simplified financial transactions for both individuals and businesses in 2022 (Daley, 2022). Additionally, the emergence of crowdfunding websites strengthens relationships with clients. Additionally, it has changed a variety of markets, most notably the ones in the banking, trading, insurance and risk management industries. According to Graužinienė and Kuizinienė (2020), the adoption of fintech is influenced by a number of elements, including social impact, risk and trust, user innovation, perceived value and perceived risk, a lack of faith in traditional banking and attention to neglected banking areas.

Since the rise of modern society, fintech has been around. In his 1919 book The Economic Consequences of the Peace, economist John Maynard Keynes allegedly made the first reference to fintech and the future of financial services. Mikhelidze (2020), Payments Ventures (2020) and Zigurat Global Institute of Technology (2022) claim that Fintech 1.0 (1886–1967), the initial stage of the fintech industry, involves building the infrastructure necessary to provide worldwide financial services. This included the first transatlantic wire in 1866 and the creation of the first credit card by Diner's Club in 1950. Between 1967 and 2008, a time known as Fintech 2.0, banks grew more digital and automatic thanks to the launch of ATMs in 1967 and the availability of online banking in 1994. During the Fintech 3.0 era (2008–2014), the number of startups offering cutting-edge financial solutions – like mobile payments and cryptocurrencies – rose. Global improvements in digital banking technology during the Fintech 3.5 period (2014–2017) heralded a departure from Western-dominated financial systems and a move towards globalisation. Fintech 4.0 (2018–present) (C2FO Team, 2023) is concerned with disruptive technologies, like artificial intelligence and machine learning, that are altering how people interact with their finances.

Banks use fintech to enhance customer satisfaction and operational effectiveness. The current study focuses on banking fintech strategy and supply-side risk. A study on the 'peer-to-peer' collaboration paradigm between Indonesian banks and fintech firms was done by Zavolokina et al. (2016). Chang et al. (2016) looked at the competition between Indonesian banks and fintech firms as well as changes to business procedures related to fintech. The generation that makes up the majority of consumers of fintech enterprises is not the same generation that makes up the majority of bank customers, claim Lien et al. (2020). Instead, it is millennials' grandparents and parents. Customers should therefore take into account the consequences of demand-side adoption of fintech services. From a static standpoint, investigating the variables affecting bank users' adoption of fintech can help improve the services offered to them and the relationship between banks and customers. Studying the variables affecting bank users' adoption of fintech can provide fresh perspectives and a thorough understanding of how fintech services are used (Shahzad et al., 2022). Millennials do not yet use fintech to a significant extent since they have a lesser level of financial awareness than their parents and grandparents. However, when millennials' financial capabilities develop, they will overtake baby boomers as the primary users. In order to better serve millennials in the future, banks can do so by knowing the factors that influence their acceptance of fintech services (Putranto & Sobari, 2021; Rahmawati et al., 2023).

The purpose of this work is to thoroughly investigate and discuss the relationship between the adoption behaviour of fintech users and the influence of the technological models used in the aforementioned study. As a result, this paper's original contributions include an in-depth and practical analysis of the elements that influence the adoption of fintech services, expanding the applicability of conventional technological acceptance models. This paper's original contributions include delivering useful data for financial service providers, marketing tactics for fintech companies and aiding in the accomplishment of strategic goals.

2. Conceptual Framework of Hypotheses

Fintech has rapidly revolutionised the financial services sector, allowing providers to offer greater convenience, security and efficiency. However, to allow users to adopt and use these technologies, they must perceive them as easy to use and trustworthy. Research has found that there is a positive relationship between perceived ease of use (PEU) and trust (TRU) in fintech (Alshathry & Almeshal, 2022). Perceived ease of use is the degree to which users feel comfortable and easy to use fintech services (Hutapea & Andista, 2021). Trust is an important factor in the adoption of fintech services as it affects users' attitudes towards financial technologies (Nangin et al., 2020; Yan et al., 2021).

Users are more likely to trust a product if its interface is understandable, intuitively navigable, visibly organised, provides timely feedback after interactions with it and contains adequate instructions on how to use it. Additionally, the perceived trustworthiness of fintech applications increases when users trust both the provider organisation they interact with and its platform itself (Firmansyah et al., 2023). Such trust typically stems from positive experiences previously encountered by customers or from word-of-mouth endorsements from peers in their social network. As such, integrators of fintech technology must focus on building an exemplary user experience by enhancing the perceived ease of use and trustworthiness of their applications (Garad et al., 2022; Lien et al., 2020).

Perceived ease of use plays an important role in the attitude and overall acceptance of a fintech product or service.

By providing simple and intuitive experiences to users, it increases their confidence in the technology and encourages a more positive sentiment towards it. This decreased complexity can also drive greater user engagement since there is less barrier to entry when utilising the product or service. Companies can conduct surveys, usability tests and Net Promoter Score (NPS) to gain insights into user perceptions about the interface design and corresponding attitudes towards using fintech solutions (Juntumaa et al., 2020; Temple et al., 2020). Such data can provide valuable insights as to how best to scale up adoption for new fintech products by developing easier interfaces, features and support services. Overall, research suggests that there is a strong relationship between perceived ease of use and trust in fintech. This relationship is important for understanding user adoption intentions for fintech services as well as for developing strategies to increase user acceptance and usage of fintech services (Shahzad et al., 2022). Based on the above, we can formulate two hypotheses as follows.

H1. There is a positive relationship between perceived ease of use (PEU) and attitude (ATT) in fintech.

H2. There is a positive relationship between perceived ease of use (PEU) and trust (TRU) in fintech.

In the world of fintech, both brand image and trust are crucial components to success. A strong brand image conveys the value of a product or service to potential customers and instils confidence in them to commit to the purchase. Trust is further established when positive attitudes surround a brand, allowing them to communicate its key messaging through word-of-mouth marketing and sustainable business practises. An effective communication strategy ties these elements together by creating an environment of openness and empowerment which builds a solid reputation over time among fintech users. In combination, they provide an unwavering commitment from customers as well as support in navigating the ever-changing regulations of the financial sector (Al-Ansi et al., 2023; Hu et al., 2019).

Research has found that there is a positive relationship between brand image (BI) and trust (TRU) in fintech, and it positively influences users' trust in adopting fintech services (Hu et al., 2019). This is because the brand image can increase the credibility and reliability of products or services, and it can improve the investment in infrastructure for organisational trust in the context of fintech applications (Roh et al., 2022). Additionally, brand image (BI) has a significant impact on users' trust (TRU) in fintech services (Garad et al., 2021; Hu et al., 2019). Companies should invest in establishing an appropriate organisational culture and visual identity complete with website design, logo and general messaging that reflect their unique value proposition. Additionally, offering sustainability-focused products and services will further strengthen brand loyalty among environmentally conscious customers; this can be implemented through content marketing initiatives such as providing resources for financial literacy or launching eco-friendly campaigns. Upholding core values and staying consistent throughout all communication channels is vital for developing a successful brand image within the fintech industry (Chuang et al., 2016).

H3. There is a positive relationship between brand image (BI) and trust (TRU) in fintech.

H4. There is a positive relationship between brand image (BI) and attitude (ATT) in fintech.

Governments around the world are increasingly recognising and embracing fintech, taking steps to provide legal and regulatory frameworks that facilitate innovation and security. Fintech-driven initiatives are providing secure access to financial services to traditionally unbanked populations and helping support economic development. Government support provides legitimacy and trust, which is essential for technology players when moving into new markets (Das & Das, 2020). As trust increases through government backing, the public's attitude towards fintech increases as well. With advances in digital policies and customer protection measures, people become more comfortable using these new technologies and banking products designed to improve their financial lives. This increased comfort sets the stage for further innovation within the fintech space by allowing providers a platform to grow their businesses with an increased customer base ready for new solutions (Das & Das, 2022; Fatmawati & Garad, 2023).

Research suggests that there is a positive relationship between government support (GS) and trust (TRU) in fintech services. Government support can include favourable legislation and regulations, as well as the setting up of infrastructure such as telecom networks. This can help to promote trust in fintech services, which is essential for their adoption (Hu et al., 2019). In addition to government support, other factors, such as innovation in information technology and fintech, can also help to build trust in these services (Chuang et al., 2016). Therefore, it is clear that there is a positive relationship between government support and trust in fintech services. This is due to the fact that government support increases users' attitudes towards fintech adoption, as well as their trust in these services.

H5. There are positive relationships between government support (GS) and trust (TRU) in fintech.

H6. There are positive relationships between government support (GS) and attitude (ATT) in fintech.

Perceived usefulness is an important concept in the realm of FinTech, as it reflects how users evaluate the value and practicality of a given solution. This perception is highly dependent on user experience, which must take into account all aspects of the process, such as ease of access, functionality, aesthetics, security and speed. Quality user experience can help users to trust fintech solutions and build brand loyalty. Additionally, effective marketing strategies can have a significant impact on user perception of usefulness by increasing awareness and conveying use case examples. In order for a fintech solution to truly succeed long term, it is not only important that the product has strong features but also that its purpose and benefits are effectively communicated to customers (Fernando & Touriano, 2018).

Modern fintech applications have generally been well-received in the digital financial world, due in large part to their perceived usefulness and trustworthiness. Such factors are particularly important when users are entrusting their personal information and funds to platforms, as the veracity of risk and security protecting these assets is paramount. Furthermore, since studies show that strong user attitudes alongside high trust can lead to greater financial experiences – such as simpler budgeting, easier payment management and better access to savings methods – it stands to reason that such tools can facilitate greater economic welfare within our society (Lim et al., 2019).

According to Suprapto and Farida (2022), there is a positive relationship between perceived usefulness (PU) and trust (TRU) in fintech. This means that as users perceive the usefulness of fintech services, their trust in them increases. Furthermore, research by Fernando and Touriano (2018) has shown that trust is an essential factor in the adoption of fintech services as it helps build confidence and reduce uncertainty. Perceived trust has been found to positively affect behavioural intention in various digital contexts such as e-commerce, internet banking, mobile banking and mobile payments (Lim et al., 2019). Studies have also found that trust can influence perceived usefulness in the adoption of fintech services (Hu et al., 2019), which in turn can affect users' continuance intention for fintech services (Roh et al., 2022). Overall, research suggests that perceived trust plays a significant role in influencing users' intention and adoption of fintech services.

H7. There are positive relationships between perceived usefulness (PU) and trust (TRU) in fintech.

H8. There are positive relationships between perceived usefulness (PU) and attitude (ATT) in Fintech.

Perceived risk in fintech is a major consideration for both consumers and the financial services industry. Fintech products and services can be impacted by everything from consumer data security to economic volatility, with different levels of perceived risk depending on the type of service or product being provided (Tang et al., 2020). Consumers must assess the level of personal data and financial information they are comfortable providing to a fintech company while industry partners must evaluate their own risk exposures as they collaborate with or adopt new technology into their operations. Fintech startups may face greater scrutiny than traditional institutions due to their unknown track record, so it is important to monitor changing public opinion on product trustworthiness, information security policies and other aspects impacting perceived risk in order to discern any potential risks when entering new markets (Ali et al., 2021; Garad et al., 2021).

According to research results by Saleem (2021) and Tang et al. (2020), risk has a considerable negative impact on the adoption of fintech services. Additionally, research has shown that trust plays an important role in fintech adoption and can help to mitigate the effects of perceived risk. Overall, it appears that while perceived risk can be a barrier to fintech adoption, it can be mitigated by increasing trust in the service. Therefore, strategies such as providing clear information about security measures and emphasising customer service could help to reduce the impact of perceived risk on fintech adoption.

H9. There are negative relationships between perceived risk (PR) and trust (TRU) in fintech.
H10. There are negative relationships between perceived risk (PR) and attitude (ATT) in fintech.
H11. There are positive relationships between trust (TRU) and attitude (ATT) in fintech.

Based of the above, the framework of hypotheses can be drawing as Fig. 4.1.

3. Methodology

This study's goals included using empirical research to examine users' behavioural intentions and the key factors influencing the uptake of fintech services. The researchers adopted a quantitative approach. An extensive assessment of the pertinent literature on technology adoption and online banking led to the creation of a pool of questions that considered the hidden structures. The researchers developed the questionnaire for this study based on the research conducted by Hu et al. (2019), Singh et al. (2020) and Shaikh et al. (2020).

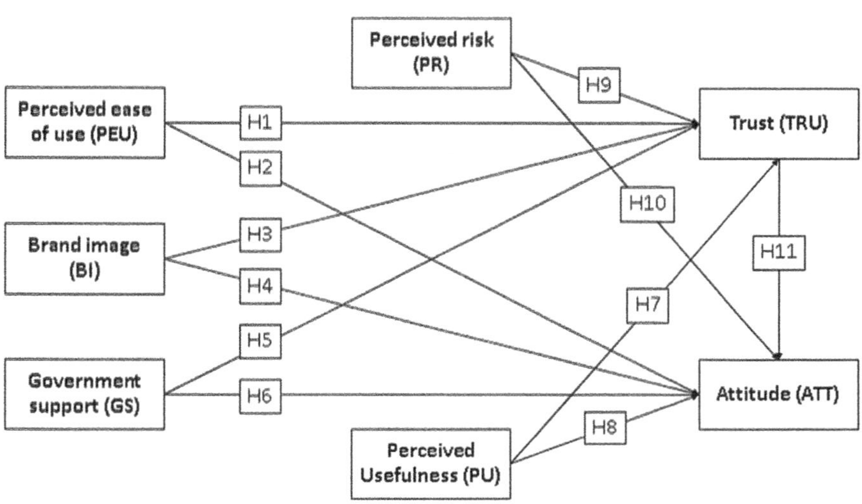

Fig. 4.1. Research Framework Hypotheses.

3.1 Sampling Technique

Using electronic distribution, survey questions were sent to possible respondents who had previously used or had experience with the fintech service. The target respondents were bank clients from the public and private sectors, including small and medium business owners, freelancers, postgraduate students at private universities and employees of public and private institutions and companies.

The characteristics of the respondents were determined to have used one of the following services during the last month from the time of filling out the questionnaire. The following services have been identified: using online money transfers, using online shopping, using mobile banking applications or using online payments. As it is challenging to collect a sampling frame comprising the specifics of all fintech users, a combination of suitable and purpose-based sampling approaches was applied. To prevent bias, all participants were given a general explanation of fintech services and the significance of this study. All items in the final survey instrument were evaluated on a five-point Likert scale (5 = strongly agree and 1 = strongly disagree), with the exception of demographic data and frequency of fintech service usage.

3.2 Distribution of the Questionnaire

The study was conducted in Yogyakarta, Indonesia. The questionnaire was filled out online, but the questionnaire was distributed to the respondents through two methods: sending it to potential respondents through social networks or meeting potential respondents directly in small and medium-sized enterprises (SMEs), universities and public places. Potential respondents are asked to fill out the questionnaire, and after approval, a link to the questionnaire is sent to them via WhatsApp or Instagram.

In Table 4.1, 768 responses in total were collected. After the screening, 573 responses were accepted, giving the survey an effective response rate of 74.6%. Invalid questionnaires with not completed or randomly filled fields were excluded.

Table 4.1. Survey Results.

Question		**Respondents Answer**		
Do you use online financial transaction services like transfers, payments and shopping?		Number	Decision	Total
Options	Never	195	Excluded	195
	Sometimes	35	Included	573
	Usually	391	Included	
	Often in everyday	147	Included	

Table 4.1. *(Continued)*

Question	**Respondents Answer**		
	Yes	No	Total
Have you used online financial transfers in the last month?	571	2	573
Have you used online shopping in the last month?	438	135	573
Have you used online payments in the last month?	289	284	573
Have you used the mobile banking application in the last month?	547	26	573

Source: Primary data.

In this study, the sample data were statistically analysed using Smart-PLS 4.0. Table 4.2 displays the demographic data from 573 surveys in a descriptive statistical style, including sex, age, education level, monthly disposable income and use of fintech services or products.

Table 4.2. Sample Demography.

Demographics	**Variable and Category**	**Frequency**	**Percentage**
Gender	Male	232	40%
	Female	341	60%
Age	18–25	82	14%
	26–35	235	41%
	36–45	91	16%
	46–55	92	16%
	>=56	73	13%
Employer status	Civil employees/Public services	97	17%
	Employees in private institutions and companies	196	20%
	Owners and staff of MSEs	104	18%
	Student	82	14%
	Higher education institutions' staff	77	13%
	Self-employed	97	17%

(Continued)

Table 4.2. *(Continued)*

Demographics	Variable and Category	Frequency	Percentage
Education	Less than diploma	54	9%
	Diploma	162	28%
	Bachelor's degree	296	52%
	Master or more	61	11%
Income (Rp)	Less than 2,000,000	92	16%
	2,000,000–6,000,000	275	48%
	6,000,000–10,000,000	135	24%
	More than 10,000,000	71	12%
Fintech service usage	Occasionally	161	28%
	Usually,	319	56%
	Frequently in everyday	93	16%
Total		*573*	*100%*

Source: Primary data.

4. Results and Discussions

4.1 Validity, Reliability and Discriminant Validity

The model was examined using internal consistency reliability, convergent validity and discriminant validity tests in addition to confirmatory factor analysis. The consistency or stability of measurement results is referred to as reliability, which is equivalent to the dependability of the survey items. In this study, the internal consistency of the data was evaluated using Cronbach's alpha and composite reliability (CR) metrics. Fornell and Larcker (1981) specify that the sample's Cronbach's alpha and correlation coefficient should both be better than 0.7. The sample's AVE values must be higher than 0.5, and the loadings of the measurable variables must be higher than 0.7, according to Chin (1998). The survey items were developed based on research (Hu et al., 2019). The Cronbach's alpha for all indicators in this research was up 0.7 as illustrated in Table 4.3.

From Table 4.3, it appears that the discrimination between the variables is valid. Guntu et al. (2022) assert that item-total correlation statistics can also be used to demonstrate discrimination in the survey items. Between zero and 0.19, the question may not be discriminating very well; between 0.2 and 0.39, it may be discriminating well and between 0.4 and higher, it may be discriminating quite significantly. Cristobal et al. (2007) have verified that the validity is higher than 0.30.

Table 4.3. Discriminant Validity of Variables and Cronbach's Alpha.

Items	ATT	BI	GS	PEU	PR	PU	TRU	Cronbach's Alpha
ATT	0.840							0.790
BI	0.654	0.808						0.740
GS	0.638	0.641	0.843					0.798
PEU	0.532	0.592	0.580	0.889				0.735
PR	0.510	0.715	0.548	0.476	0.834			0.781
PU	0.605	0.568	0.613	0.498	0.534	0.780		0.787
TRU	0.574	0.637	0.577	0.707	0.501	0.480	0.907	0.785

Source: Primary data.

5. Structural Equation Model: Hypothesis Testing

This portion tested the hypothesis using the sample data and a structural equation model after conducting empirical research on the adoption model of fintech services based on the analysis of the sample data. The validity and reliability analysis came before this section.

The test results for the hypotheses have been shown based on Fig. 4.2. The assumptions posed in this research were then evaluated using the Smart-PLS 4.0

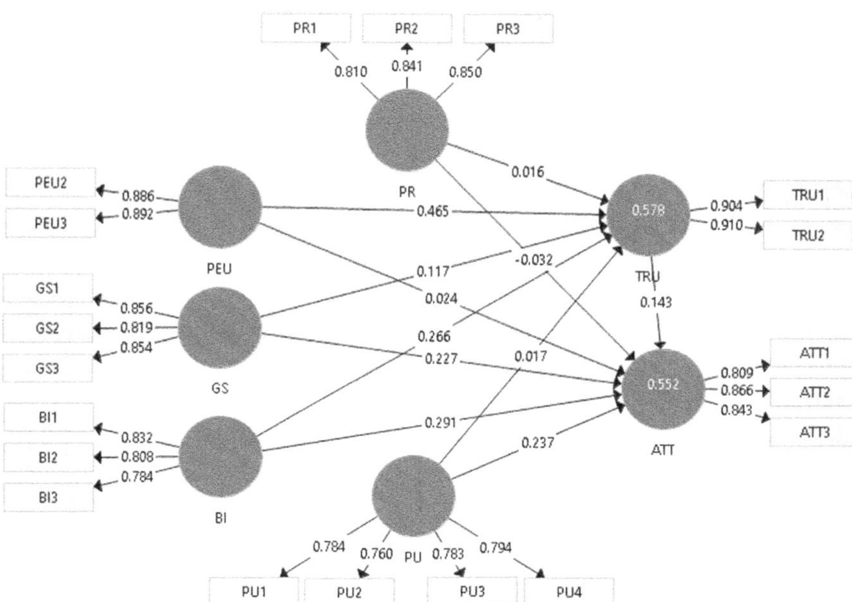

Fig. 4.2. Framework Hypotheses Results.

retrieved standardised path coefficient and t-value from the SEM model. The coefficient test is typically significant at the 0.05 level of significance if $t > 1.96$. The coefficient test is significant if $t > 2.58$ at the level of confidence of p 0.01 is used. The coefficient test is significant if $t > 3.1$ and has a p-value >= 0.001.

Table 4.4 shows that hypotheses of direct effect *H1*, *H3*, *H4*, *H5*, *H6*, *H8* and *H11* are accepted, while *H2*, *H7*, *H9* and *H10* are rejected. In addition, hypotheses of the indirect effect *H12*, *H13* and *H14* are accepted while *H15* and *H16* are rejected.

Table 4.4. Results of Hypotheses.

Hypothesis	**Standard Deviation (STDEV)**	***t* Statistics (|O/STDEV|)**	***p*-Values**	**Outcome/ Support Status**
Direct Effects				
H1: PEU -> TRU	**0.040**	**11.677**	**0.000**	**Supported**
H2: PEU -> ATT	0.043	0.561	0.575	Not supported
H3: BI -> TRU	**0.060**	**4.393**	**0.000**	**Supported**
H4:BI -> ATT	**0.056**	**5.239**	**0.000**	**Supported**
H5: GS -> TRU	**0.045**	**2.638**	**0.009**	**Supported**
H6: GS -> ATT	**0.050**	**4.532**	**0.000**	**Supported**
H7: PU -> TRU	0.037	0.469	0.640	Not supported
H8: PU -> ATT	**0.042**	**5.694**	**0.000**	**Supported**
H9: PR -> TRU	0.050	0.315	0.753	Not supported
H10: PR -> ATT	0.046	0.695	0.488	Not supported
H11: TRU -> ATT	**0.044**	**3.218**	**0.001**	**Supported**
Indirect Effects				
H12: PEU -> TRU -> ATT	**0.022**	**3.032**	**0.003**	**Supported**
H13: BI -> TRU-> ATT	**0.015**	**2.463**	**0.014**	**Supported**
H14: GS -> TRU -> ATT	**0.008**	**2.208**	**0,028**	**Supported**

Table 4.4. *(Continued)*

Hypothesis	**Standard Deviation (STDEV)**	***t* Statistics (|O/STDEV|)**	***p*-Values**	**Outcome/ Support Status**
H15: PU -> TRU -> ATT	0.006	0.444	0.657	Not supported
H16: PR -> TRU -> ATT	0.007	0.309	0.758	Not supported

Source: Primary data.

6. Discussion and Conclusion

According to the results of the model's hypotheses tests, trust in fintech services is positively impacted by brand reputation, perceived usability and government assistance. A customer's attitude may be influenced by how much they trust fintech services, depending on how they perceive risk. The mechanism is that customers are actively motivated to use fintech services by the trust. However, perceived risk has a strong negative impact on trust. To increase customers' desire to use the services, financial institutions that offer Fintech services must take steps to lower the perceived risk to clients. As a result, customers will have more confidence in the products and services they receive. A user's adoption of fintech services is mostly unaffected by the perceived ease of use.

In conclusion, a brand's reputation, governmental support for emerging technologies and other factors all have an impact on consumer behaviour. After assessing the benefits and drawbacks, individuals eventually base their choice on their feelings regarding adoption. The findings of our study provide financial service providers with an empirical basis and a user assessment for putting forward cutting-edge, user-centred services.

The acceptance and use of fintech services by users, as well as how these services alter how clients interact with financial service providers, are all topics covered in this article. This study discovers that PEU, BI and GS have favourable effects on TRU for the adoption of fintech services, which is consistent with Lal et al.'s (2020) findings, while the adoption of fintech services is not strongly predicted by PU and PR, in contrast to the research findings of this article (Hu et al., 2019; Hutapea & Andista, 2021).

This investigation also offers additional proof that BI, GS, PU and TRU have favourable effects on ATT for the adoption of fintech services, in line with the research findings of Nangin et al. (2020). Although there is no significant correlation between the direct effects of PEU and PR and ATT, these results are consistent with those of Hu et al.'s (2019) study. In contrast, there is a strong correlation between ATT and the outcomes of the PEU's indirect action through TRU.

7. Limitations and Future Research

This study forecasts and explains why users will adopt fintech services using the aspects of service trust and attitude. Our research's impacting factors do, however, have certain limitations. It has not been investigated how society and other psychological elements affect people. Therefore, we urge the following researchers to utilise a comprehensive and effective analysis to analyse the acceptance model of fintech services, including financial, privacy and cyber security dangers.

References

Al-Ansi, A. M., Hazaimeh, M., Hendi, A., AL-hrinat, J., Adwan, G., & Garad, A. (2023). Innovative responses to exogenous shocks in Indonesian transportation firms: Mediating role of sustainable performance and outcomes. *Planning*, *18*(9), 2663–2672. https://doi.org/10.18280/ijsdp.180905

Ali, M., Raza, S. A., Khamis, B., Puah, C. H., & Amin, H. (2021). How perceived risk, benefit and trust determine user Fintech adoption: A new dimension for Islamic finance. *Foresight*, *23*(4), 403–420. https://doi.org/10.1108/FS-09-2020-0095

Alshathry, N. A., & Almeshal, S. A. (2022). Fintech perceived usefulness, ease of use among consumers, and its effect on satisfaction and continuous usage: An impractical study on STC Pay and Apple Pay in the Saudi Arabian retail sector. *International Journal of Management and Information Technology*, *17*, 1–14. https://doi.org/10.24297/ijmit.v17i.9197

C2FO Team. (2023, January 31). *The history of fintech: How has the industry evolved?* https://www.c2fo.com/amer/us/en-us/resource-center/article/07212021/the-history-and-evolution-of-the-fintech-industry

Chang, Y., Wong, S. F., Lee, H., & Jeong, S. P. (2016, August). What motivates Chinese consumers to adopt FinTech services: A regulatory focus theory. In *Proceedings of the 18th annual international conference on electronic commerce: E-commerce in smart connected world* (pp. 1–3). https://doi.org/10.1145/2971603.2971643

Chin, W. W. (1998). Commentary: Issues and opinion on structural equation modeling. *MIS Quarterly*, vii–xvi. https://www.jstor.org/stable/249674

Chuang, L. M., Liu, C. C., & Kao, H. K. (2016). The adoption of fintech service: TAM perspective. *International Journal of Management and Administrative Sciences*, *3*(7), 1–15. https://www.ijmas.org/3-7/IJMAS-3601-2016.pdf

Cristobal, E., Flavián, C., & Guinalíu, M. (2007). Perceived e-service quality (PeSQ): Measurement validation and effects on consumer satisfaction and web site loyalty. *Managing Service Quality: International Journal*, *17*(3), 317–340. https://doi.org/10.1108/09604520710744326

Daley, S. (2022, August 18). *What is fintech? A quick definition.* https://builtin.com/fintech

Das, A., & Das, D. (2020). Perception, adoption, and pattern of usage of FinTech services by bank customers: Evidences from Hojai District of Assam. *Emerging Economy Studies*, *6*(1), 7–22. https://journals.sagepub.com/doi/pdf/10.1177/2394901520907728

Das, A., & Das, D. (2022). Adoption of FinTech services amidst COVID-19 pandemic: Empirical evidence from Assam. *Managerial Finance*. ahead-of-print. https://doi.org/10.1108/MF-08-2022-0379

Dawood, H. M., Liew, C. Y., & Lau, T. C. (2021). Mobile perceived trust mediation on the intention and adoption of FinTech innovations using mobile technology: A systematic literature review. *F1000Research*, *10*. https://doi.org/10.12688/f1000research.74656.2

Fatmawati, I., & Garad, A. (2023). An analytical study of the relationship between network capability and e-marketing to achieve the competitive advantage of MSEs. In *The implementation of smart technologies for business success and sustainability* (pp. 3–12). https://link.springer.com/chapter/10.1007/978-3-031-10212-7_1

Fernando, E., & Touriano, D. (2018, November). Development and validation of instruments adoption FinTech services in Indonesia (Perspective of trust and risk). In *2018 International conference on sustainable information engineering and technology (SIET)* (pp. 283–287). IEEE. https://doi.org/10.1109/SIET.2018.8693192

Firmansyah, E. A., Masri, M., Anshari, M., & Besar, M. H. A. (2023). Factors affecting fintech adoption: A systematic literature review. *FinTech*, *2*(1), 21–33. https://doi.org/10.3390/fintech2010002

Fornell, C., & Larcker, D. F. (1981). Evaluating structural equation models with unobservable variables and measurement error. *Journal of Marketing Research*, *18*(1), 39–50. https://doi.org/10.1177/002224378101800104

Garad, A., Rahmawati, A., & Pratolo, A. (2021). The impact of board directors, audit committee and ownership on financial performance and firms value. *Universal Journal of Accounting and Finance*, *9*(5), 982–994. https://doi.org/10.13189/ujaf.2021.090509

Garad, A., Yaya, R., Pratolo, P., & Rahmawati, A. (2022). The relationship between transformational leadership, improving employee's performance and the raising efficiency of organizations. *Management and Production Engineering Review*, *13*(2), 15–30. https://doi.org/10.24425/mper.2022.142052

Graužinienė, S., & Kuizinienė, D. (2020). Research on factors identification in FinTech acceptance: Lithuania context. *Applied Economics: Systematic Research*, *14*(1), 41–57. https://doi.org/10.7220/AESR.2335.8742.2018.12.1.7

Guntu, M., Lin, E. J. D., Sezgin, E., Gregory, M. E., Huang, Y., & Linwood, S. L. (2022). Identifying the factors influencing patients' telehealth visit satisfaction: Survey validation through a structural equation modeling approach. *Telemedicine and e-Health*, *28*(9), 1261–1269. https://doi.org/10.1089/tmj.2021.0372

Hu, Z., Ding, S., Li, S., Chen, L., & Yang, S. (2019). Adoption intention of fintech services for bank users: An empirical examination with an extended technology acceptance model. *Symmetry*, *11*(3), 340. https://doi.org/10.3390/sym11030340

Hutapea, R. S., & Andista, D. R. (2021, November). The effect of perceived ease of use, perceived usefulness, and risk on user interest in using financial technology peer to peer lending. In *2nd International seminar of science and applied technology (ISSAT 2021)* (pp. 619–623). Atlantis Press. https://www.atlantis-press.com/proceedings/issat-21/125963777

Juntumaa, J., Laitinen, M., & Kirichenko, S. (2020). The Net Promoter Score (NPS) as a tool for evaluation of the user experience at culture and library services. *Qualitative and Quantitative Methods in Libraries*, *9*(2), 127–142. http://www.qqml.net/index.php/qqml/article/view/654

Lal, K., Rani, M. S., & Rajini, P. (2020). Factors that influence the customer adoption of Fintech in Hyderabad, India. *International Journal of Recent Technology and Engineering*, *8*. https://www.ijrte.org/wp-content/uploads/papers/v8i5/D9114118419.pdf

Lien, N. T. K., Doan, T. T. T., & Bui, T. N. (2020). Fintech and banking: Evidence from Vietnam. *The Journal of Asian Finance, Economics and Business*, *7*(9), 419–426. https://doi.org/10.13106/jafeb.2020.vol7.no9.419

Lim, S. H., Kim, D. J., Hur, Y., & Park, K. (2019). An empirical study of the impacts of perceived security and knowledge on continuous intention to use mobile fintech payment services. *International Journal of Human-Computer Interaction*, *35*(10), 886–898. https://doi.org/10.1080/10447318.2018.1507132

Mikhelidze, G. (2020, June 7). *A short history of fintech*. https://hackernoon.com/a-short-history-of-fintech 72hs3w7u#:~:text=Fintech%20was%20Born%20(1886%20%2D%201967)&text=In%20the%201950s%2C%20the%20first,new%20era%20of%20financial%20services

Nangin, M. A., Barus, I. R. G., & Wahyoedi, S. (2020). The effects of perceived ease of use, security, and promotion on trust and its implications on fintech adoption. *Journal of Consumer Sciences*, *5*(2), 124–138. https://doi.org/10.29244/jcs.5.2.124-138

Payments Ventures. (2020, October 12). Fintech: The history and future of financial technology. https://thepaymentsassociation.org/article/fintech-the-history-and-future-of-financial-technology/

Putranto, B. D., & Sobari, N. (2021, June). Predicting intention of using fintech lending to bank users in Indonesia. In *18th International symposium on management (INSYMA 2021)* (pp. 206–211). Atlantis Press.

Rahmawati, A., Wahyuningsih, S. H., & Garad, A. (2023). The effect of financial literacy, training and locus of control on creative economic business performance. *Social Sciences & Humanities Open*, *8*(1), 100721. https://doi.org/10.1016/j.ssaho.2023.100721

Railslove GmbH. (2023). *FinTech definition*. https://www.fintechweekly.com/fintech-definition

Roh, T., Yang, Y. S., Xiao, S., & Park, B. I. (2022). What makes consumers trust and adopt fintech? An empirical investigation in China. *Electronic Commerce Research*, 1–33. https://doi.org/10.1007/s10660-021-09527-3

Saleem, A. (2021). Fintech revolution, perceived risks and Fintech adoption: Evidence from financial industry of Pakistan. *International Journal of Multidisciplinary and Current Educational Research*, *3*, 191–205. https://www.ijmcer.com/wp-content/uploads/2021/05/IJMCER_W0330191205.pdf

Shahzad, A., Zahrullail, N., Akbar, A., Mohelska, H., & Hussain, A. (2022). COVID-19's impact on Fintech adoption: Behavioral intention to use the financial portal. *Journal of Risk and Financial Management*, *15*(10), 428. https://doi.org/10.3390/jrfm15100428

Shaikh, I. M., Qureshi, M. A., Noordin, K., Shaikh, J. M., Khan, A., & Shahbaz, M. S. (2020). Acceptance of Islamic financial technology (FinTech) banking services by Malaysian users: An extension of technology acceptance model. *Foresight*, *22*(3), 367–383. https://doi.org/10.1108/FS-12-2019-0105

Singh, S., Sahni, M. M., & Kovid, R. K. (2020). What drives FinTech adoption? A multi-method evaluation using an adapted technology acceptance model. *Management Decision*, *58*(8), 1675–1697. https://doi.org/10.1108/MD-09-2019-1318

Suprapto, Y., & Farida, F. (2022). Analisis pengaruh brand image, trust, security, perceived usefulness, perceived ease of use terhadap adoption intention fintech di Kota Batam. Jesya (Jurnal Ekonomi danEkonomi Syariah), *5*(1), 319–332.

Tang, K. L., Ooi, C. K., & Chong, J. B. (2020). Perceived risk factors affect intention to use FinTech. *Journal of Accounting and Finance in Emerging Economies*, *6*(2), 453–463. https://doi.org/10.26710/jafee.v6i2.1101

Temple, J. G., Burkhart, B. J., & Tassone, A. R. (2020). Does the survey method affect the Net Promoter Score? In *Advances in usability and user experience: Proceedings of the AHFE 2019 international conferences on usability and user experience, and human factors and assistive technology, July 24–28, 2019, Washington DC, USA 10* (pp. 437–444). Springer International Publishing. https://link.springer.com/chapter/10.1007/978-3-030-19135-1_42

Yan, C., Siddik, A. B., Akter, N., & Dong, Q. (2021). Factors influencing the adoption intention of using mobile financial service during the COVID-19 pandemic: The role of FinTech. *Environmental Science and Pollution Research*, 1–19. https://doi.org/10.1007/s11356-021-17437-y

Zavolokina, L., Dolata, M., & Schwabe, G. (2016). The FinTech phenomenon: Antecedents of financial innovation perceived by the popular press. *Financial Innovation*, *2*(1), 1–16. https://doi.org/10.1186/s40854-016-0036-7

Zigurat Global Institute of Technology. (2022). *Evolution of fintech: The 5 key eras.* https://www.e-zigurat.com/innovation-school/blog/evolution-of-fintech/

Part 2

Innovations and Applications of FinTech

Chapter 5

The Application of Artificial Intelligence in Financial Services to Improve Customer Experiences

Nermin Nour El-din Farghaly

Cairo University, Egypt

Abstract

The purpose of this chapter is to identify the theoretical research that has been done on artificial intelligence (AI) and its applications (particularly in financial institutions [FIs]) and how it improves the customer experience. Every financial institution that wants to succeed in the fast-paced commercial world of today must focus on enhancing financial services and offering top-notch customer service. FIs now have the chance, thanks to the development of AI technology, to improve their customer service skills, unlike in the past. Through the use of chatbots, virtual assistants, tailored recommendations and real-time help, AI can completely transform customer service. FIs can offer round-the-clock assistance, minimise response times and manage a greater number of inquiries simultaneously by incorporating them into their customer service processes. These clever algorithms can replicate genuine language and respond quickly, just like in real-world human interactions. Financial organisations can offer customised product or service recommendations to their consumers by gaining insight into their particular tastes. These technologies are able to recognise possible issues or dissatisfactions before they become more serious by studying the conduct and sentiment of customers. This makes it possible for FIs to step in quickly and offer suitable solutions, enhancing client happiness and loyalty. virtual assistants and chatbots. Organisations can improve their customer service abilities and obtain a competitive edge in today's digital market by implementing AI technologies. This chapter thoroughly examines how the application of AI in financial services is transforming and improving the customer experience in detail.

From Digital Disruption to Dominance, 123–132

doi:10.1108/978-1-83549-608-420251005

Keywords: Artificial intelligence; artificial intelligence applications; financial services; financial industry; customer loyalty/experiences

1. Introduction

Artificial intelligence (AI) and robotics technological advancements are drastically altering the way services are provided (Belanche et al., 2020; Chebbi et al., 2024; Flavián et al., 2022). Automated technology is expected to eventually replace workers in tasks requiring mechanical, analytical, intuitive and even empathic intelligence, according to Huang and Rust (2021).

The science of AI is a recent development that unifies theory, methodology, technology and application systems by simulating human intellect through computer programmes and extending it to resemble human thought processes. By continuously modelling and investigating human behaviour, its fundamental goal is to become an ideal and fully developed intelligent machine. The field of applications for AI is growing, and after years of research, both the theory and technology are becoming more developed. It has since evolved into an integrated, multifunctional, application-oriented composite discipline, surpassing the level of simple human behaviour modelling. This technology is referred to as 'the hottest technology in the early 21st century', along with virtual reality and 3D printing technologies (Li et al., 2021).

AI has come a long way in the last 40 years in mimicking human cognitive processes and reasoning. The primary AI tools available in the past were restricted to sequential processing and extremely minimal knowledge and logic representation. Building a computer with the architecture and processing power to replicate the human brain and cognitive processes is the essence of a more advanced kind of AI. As a result, knowledge representations based on massive processing power, quick data retrieval and experience-based pattern recognition are all made possible. Artificial neural network (ANN) technology is also known as neural computing (Al-Gasaymeh et al., 2023; Alkhaldi et al., 2023; Li et al., 2021; Warwick, 2013).

According to Wirtz et al. (2018), task orientation, degree of anthropomorphism (from none to high) and manifestation (virtual or physical) are the factors that differentiate AI software that operates independently and learns over time from service robots. Due to economies of size and breadth, AI data and expertise are anticipated to become significant sources of competitive advantage for businesses, creating 'winners-take-all' marketplaces (Wirtz et al., 2018). As a sector driving internal and customer-oriented automation processes, the banking and finance industries have emerged as archetypal instances of the AI technology revolution globally (Caron, 2019).

The segment's primary goal in utilising AI is to provide proactive and customised customer services at a reduced cost. Other clear goals include managing and controlling back-end business processes to reduce human error and free up time for top management to work on more productive projects. However, despite being a critical sector of our economy, there is not much adoption of AI technology in this field (Kumari et al., 2024).

The structure of this chapter is as follows: The literature on AI ideas, applications in financial institutions (FIs) and strategies to improve the customer experience utilising AI in financial services is evaluated in the second section. A conclusion of the entire chapter is provided in the final section.

This chapter's objective is to

Find out what theoretical research has been done on AI, its applications (particularly in FIs) and how much it improves the experience of customers.

2. Literature Review

Financial organisations at all levels are facing growing pressure to improve their performance. Organisations must undergo a timely digital transition in order to achieve this. An organisation that anticipates disruption is managing the issue through digital transformation. Making the transition to new technologies necessary for the industry to be sustainable and productive (Ebert & Duarte, 2018).

AI is a new trend in technology that has advanced in today's society. A few AI applications have been put into practice, and AI is of great interest for pilot projects in highly data-driven businesses like the finance sector (Kumari et al., 2024). Banks and insurance firms are a prime example of this, as they are at the forefront of AI and provide automation, analysis and decision-making as means of managing financial and corporate processes. AI is used in the banking industry to identify and report abnormalities such as large account deposits and odd debit card usage, credit scoring, wealth and risk management, prevention of money laundering, fraud prevention and many other activities that support a bank's fraud department (Lin, 2020).

The companies need to reinvent to be more digital, data-driven and in the cloud; to have more variable cost structures, agile operations and automation and to create stronger capabilities in e-commerce and security. AI will be a key technology to find new contactless solutions across the financial industry (Builtin, 2019).

2.1 AI: A Comprehensive Overview

AI is becoming more and more common in the financial industry due to its rapid development. The expansion of fintech, the advancement of AI in the financial sector and the pressure on FIs to use these technologies to save costs, control risk, enhance service quality and boost profits are all accelerated by certain factors. Bayesian statistics, one of the machine learning algorithms, sprang to fame in the early 1960s and has remained in widespread usage in the financial Industry to this day (Al-Araj et al., 2022; Hatamlah et al., 2023; Xie, 2019).

Moreover, the reason that Bayesian theory has become popular in the financial area is its application in the auditing area. In the auditing field, judgements made by auditors used to rely on professional knowledge and experience, but different cases have different situations. Various uncertain factors need to be considered in the decision-making process of auditing. Thus, the Bayesian model reduces the auditor's emotional misjudgement and offers objective, logical probability to aid in the auditor's capacity to make more correct evaluations (Sorensen, 1969).

The initial phase of AI's collaboration with the financial sector is centred on using computer power to lessen the strain on financial professionals. In order to forecast market trends and offer individualised financial plans, the financial sector employed expert systems, or knowledge-based intelligence systems, up until the 1980s. Six elements make up a simple expert system (Xie, 2019).

(1) Knowledge base.
(2) Database.
(3) Inference engine.
(4) Capability for explanation.
(5) Information gathering.
(6) User interface.

A rule-based expert system was proposed by Hodgkinson and Walker (2003) to facilitate the decision-making process and assist financial intuitions in deciding whether to approve credit applications for cooperative credit loans. To support the ranking of listed businesses in the Taiwan stock market, Shue et al. (2009) developed an expert system with a domain knowledge base and an operational knowledge base. In order to assist middle-sized and small-sized businesses in resolving the issue of low funding preventing them from accessing competent data security analysis, Janulevičius and Goranin (2013) developed an expert system for risk management.

2.2 AI: Application in Banking

The major application of AI has been in the provision of diverse financial services since this industry has benefited from the technology's growing capabilities in recent years (Fernandez, 2019). Among these applications, the most well-known ones are as follows:

2.2.1 Alarm System

The financial system is more secure against bank and ATM robberies when AI is used instead of a traditional emergency button alarm system. There are three steps to this system's operation: In order to obtain the features, artificial vision first takes a picture for image processing. An ANN provides the warning message status and classifies the incident according to the discovered pattern. The output class is established based on how the neural network is classified. If the output is 1, then GSM technology should be used to send a warning message and sound the alarm (Ortiz et al., 2016).

2.2.2 Cloud Security

Security concerns are the primary cause of the alarmingly high failure rate of many cloud computing-related projects. Modelling cloud computing involves five steps: cloud service models, mobility and banking applications, cloud deployment models and cloud risk management models. In addition, risk planning, analysis, identification, prioritisation, evaluation, treatment, control and documentation are the eight components of risk management that make up good cloud computing. The cloud Delphi technique uses data collection to assign a probability of occurrence and develop a network analysis using Levenberg–Marquardt-based backpropagation. Following the construction of the network, the data are trained and then tested. An ANN is the final tool used to implement the prediction cloud security paradigm (Elzamly et al., 2017).

2.2.3 Phishing Websites

People are tricked by phishing websites into giving their usernames and passwords, which are then utilised for a variety of illicit activities. One AI method for identifying phishing websites is the data mining algorithm. Classifier and associative algorithms can also be used to anticipate these webpages. A collection of many indicators, including URL and domain identity, security and encryption, Java script and source code, page style and content, the web address bar and the human social component, make up the 27 key feature vectors. A number of methods were employed to identify the optimal approach, including PART, PRISM, JRip, C4.5, MCAR and CBA; MCAR surpassed all other techniques in terms of accuracy and speed. Finding a crucial attribute to accomplish this purpose is not always simple using this technique, however the fuzzy data mining algorithm is used to automatically identify phishing websites, especially e-banking websites (Aburrous et al., 2010).

2.2.4 Chatbot

Customers must get in touch with the officials in order to resolve any concerns or questions they may have regarding the goods or services offered by banking institutions. Nevertheless, this procedure takes a lot of time and is very monotonous. Numerous industries have profited from the development of AI-based banking technology, which is also successful in commercial settings. Furthermore, Watson – an IBM creation – is meant to respond to inquiries. It accomplishes this by utilising natural language processing (NLP) and machine learning methods, which aid in information retrieval and the representation of built-in domain knowledge. Most large, expanding banks now use these bots since they are helpful in providing improved customer service (Singh et al., 2018).

2.2.5 Intelligence and Augmented Reality

The newest technology is being used by a variety of industries to improve their operations, which is a huge benefit for company management. By providing more details, augmented reality helps people by broadening their perception and simplifying communication. It provides virtual assistance to mitigate difficult real-world issues. Numerous industries, including gaming, media and healthcare, have already implemented augmented reality to streamline current procedures. This application for business development can be used by industries with high operating costs and high levels of risk (Heng, 2015). Banking and financial organisations also employ augmented reality to analyse and illustrate consumer behaviour and provide the best advice to improve customers' spending habits. However, sophisticated systems are also put in place to enhance productivity and lessen physical labour. As an illustration, JP Morgan implemented a contract intelligence system that results in a 0.36 million hour reduction in worker activity (Dubey, 2019).

2.2.6 Mobile Banking

These days, mobile banking is very popular; the majority of individuals utilise mobile payments, and 65 out of 100 member groups use it. The majority of clients have favourable perceptions of online payment services, which draw them away from traditional card transactions and help to improve banking services by optimising income production. By collecting and analysing user-generated data, this user experience transformation makes it possible to provide each customer with superior service based on the patterns or insights found in the data (Dubey, 2019). According to Payne et al. (2018), banks can leverage the recent surge in client interest in AI-enabled mobile banking to expand their customer base.

The information above makes it clear that millions of consumers and banking industry workers benefit from AI in their banking experiences. Through cloud security, phishing detection and warning systems, AI streamlines a number of procedures that lessen the workload for staff members. However, other apps like chatbots, augmented reality and mobile banking are improving the consumer experience.

2.3 AI Applications in Financial Services: Customer Loyalty

The banking and insurance sectors of the finance industry are highly competitive, complex businesses that are under tremendous pressure to change in order to remain in the market. Maintaining customer loyalty in this context – which includes perceived value, commitment, trust and satisfaction – is crucial (Ansari & Riasi, 2016).

Redefining financial service operations with modern technology and a constant customer focus has already been demonstrated by data giants like Google, Facebook and Apple. However, traditional FS suppliers frequently fail to give their clients with sufficient flexibility and innovative strengths. Thus, AI is welcomed as a disruptive invention that can upend established financial markets. By utilising cutting-edge technologies, these market players avoid constructing upon outdated structures. AI has the potential to enhance client orientation, reduce expenses and quicken innovation by utilising lean and agile procedures. These businesses, which are primarily startup ventures, have spearheaded significant advancements in a variety of fields, including crowdfunding, wealth management, payments, and lending (Inn, 2016).

Maintaining and growing the relationship between bankers and customers is critical to retaining current clients and increasing client loyalty. If banking institutions meet the changing demands and expectations of their consumers, the customer relationship will be robust. Improved customer loyalty may result from luring clients with superior services offered at competitive costs. An ANN that is already in use by other businesses for the same reason can be used in the banking sector to forecast customer loyalty. Following data collection, factor analysis should be used to extract the important factors from all the available variables, preparing the data for additional modelling. In this prediction model, the ANN and feedforward backpropagation are both part of the algorithm. K subsets are derived from the data's classification during the dataset training process in K-fold cross-validation. After testing the dataset, the algorithm's performance may be assessed using the coefficient of efficiency and root mean square error. High accuracy can be achieved, as demonstrated by the ANN's prediction of customer loyalty (Kishada et al., 2016).

The adoption of AI is expected to provide enormous growth potential and expansion opportunities in the financial services industry. Following is a summary of a few of them (Chintalapati, 2021).

- Adoption of AI is expected to change the conventional framework for pricing strategy. Applications driven by AI will stand out from the competition, which will eventually increase user loyalty and engagement.
- There is greater promise in identifying the false-positives and false-negatives that ultimately result in operational efficiency across prominent AI analytical and reasoning activities like know-your-customer (KYC) and anti-money laundering (AML).
- Extreme automation and quicker adoption of customers' financial agendas are made possible by Personal Finance Management (PFM) and an open API-driven approach to customer communication and servicing. These factors ultimately contribute to the streamlining of customers' financial behaviour.
- FIs can increase the productivity of their operations by using AI to automate repetitive, human error-prone tasks like data entry, data collection, customer data verification and validation, errand and duplicate identification and removal, and many more.
- Applications running on AL are designed to periodically verify the financial parameters included in the regulatory reporting process. This enables the pertinent stakeholders to be alerted as soon as there is a deviation from the compliance requirements.

- More customer loyalty and retention: By using analytical reasoning as a phenomenon that intervenes, FIs can concentrate on continuously improving the performance and features of their products. Optimising customer engagement with more pertinent content also produces better customer experiences, which in turn increase customer loyalty and retention (Sternberg et al., 2018).
- Over time, market consolidation will result from the deployment of AI. Businesses that can work better together will decide to merge or come together to achieve greater business results. Reducing search effort and onboarding delays for end consumers is what niche players want to achieve by strengthening and consolidating their offerings and areas of expertise.

3. Conclusion

AI is reshaping the banking sector in the age of modern technology, and it is becoming more and more crucial for the sector to adopt AI technologies into its operations in order to remain viable in a cutthroat market. The purpose of this chapter is to list the theoretical studies that have been done on AI, its applications (particularly in FIs) and the degree to which it enhances customer experience, given its well-known significance. According to reputable journals, the researcher used research papers. They encompass a wide range of terms associated with the ideas behind AI applications, including chatbots, phishing sites, cloud security, alarm systems, mobile banking, and intelligence and augmented reality. And the extent to which these concepts impact the financial sector, especially financial services. One of the best academic search engines for finding journal article resources was Google Scholar, which was used extensively in this chapter. Many journal publishers use it as well because it is a sophisticated and user-friendly academic search engine. It enables scholars to increase the visibility and reach of publications and provide several pertinent search results in response to queries.

Based on the information covered, the researcher concludes that AI applications have great potential for advancement in FIs in the future. This is directly related to how quickly and sustainably the financial sector can overcome the obstacles resulting from its adoption of AI. Therefore, the researcher believes that in order to improve the position of FIs in the market in the digital future, professionals and academics should concentrate on the potential dangers that these institutions might encounter when utilising AI technology.

References

Aburrous, M., Hossain, M. A., Thabtah, F., & Dahal, K. (2010). Intelligent phishing detection system for e-banking using fuzzy data mining. *Journal of Expert Systems with Applications*, *37*(12), 7913–7921.

Al-Araj, R. E. E. M., Haddad, H. O. S. S. A. M., Shehadeh, M. A. H. A., Hasan, E., & Nawaiseh, M. Y. (2022). The effect of artificial intelligence on service quality and customer satisfaction in Jordanian banking sector. *WSEAS Transactions on Business and Economics*, *19*(12), 1929–1947.

Al-Gasaymeh, A. S., Almahadin, H. A., Shehadeh, M., Migdady, H., & Atta, A. A. B. (2023, March). Investigating the role of artificial intelligence in embedded finance on improving a nonfinancial customer experience. In *2023 International conference on business analytics for technology and security (ICBATS)*. March 7–8, 2023, Dubai, UAE (pp. 1–6). IEEE.

Alkhaldi, F., Shehadeh, M., Abu-AlSondos, I. A., & Almazaydeh, L. (2023, December). Artificial intelligence applications and roles in supply chain sustainability. In *2023 Asia conference on cognitive engineering and intelligent interaction (CEII)*, December 15–16, 2023, Hong Kong, China (pp. 120–124). IEEE.

Ansari, A., & Riasi, A. (2016). Modelling and evaluating customer loyalty using neural networks: Evidence from startup insurance companies. *Future Business Journal*, *2*(1), 15–30.

Belanche, D., Casalo, L. V., Flavian, C., & Schepers, J. (2020). Robots or frontline employees?: Exploring customers' attributions of responsibility and stability after service failure or success. *Journal of Service Management*, *31*(2), 267–289.

Builtin. (2019). *AI and the bottom line: 15 examples of artificial intelligence in finance*. https://builtin.com/artificial-intelligence/ai-finance-banking-applications-companies

Caron, M. S. (2019). The transformative effect of AI on the banking industry. *Banking & Finance Law Review*, *34*(2), 169–214.

Chebbi, T., Migdady, H., Hmedat, W., & Shehadeh, M. (2024). Another look at the price clustering behavior: Evidence from the Muscat stock exchange. *Review of Behavioral Finance*, *16*(5), 773–791.

Chintalapati, S. (2021). Early adopters to early majority—What's driving the artificial intelligence and machine learning powered transformation in financial services. *International Journal of Financial Research*, *12*(4), 43–51.

Dubey, V. (2019). FinTech innovations in digital banking. *International Journal of Engineering Research and Technology*, *8*(10), 597–601.

Ebert, C., & Duarte, C. H. C. (2018). Digital transformation. *IEEE Software*, *35*(4), 16–21.

Elzamly, A., Hussin, B., Naser, S. S. A., Shibutani, T., & Doheir, M. (2017). Predicting critical cloud computing security issues using artificial neural network (ANNs) algorithms in banking organizations. *International Journal of Information Technology and Electrical Engineering*, *6*(2), 40–45.

Fernandez, A. (2019). Artificial intelligence in financial services. *SSRN Electronic Journal*. https://doi.org/10.2139/ssrn.3366846

Flavián, C., Pérez-Rueda, A., Belanche, D., & Casaló, L. V. (2022). Intention to use analytical artificial intelligence (AI) in services – The effect of technology readiness and awareness. *Journal of Service Management*, *33*(2), 293–320.

Hatamlah, H., Allan, M., Abu-AlSondos, I., Shehadeh, M., & Allahham, M. (2023). The role of artificial intelligence in supply chain analytics during the pandemic. *Uncertain Supply Chain Management*, *11*(3), 1175–1186.

Heng, S. (2015). Augmented reality: Specialized applications are the key to this fast-growing market for Germany. *Deutsche Bank Research, Current Issues Sector Research*, 1–14.

Hodgkinson, L., & Walker, E. (2003). An expert system for credit evaluation and explanation. *Journal of Computing Sciences in Colleges*, *19*(1), 62–72.

Huang, M. H., & Rust, R. T. (2021). Engaged to a robot? The role of AI in service. *Journal of Service Research*, *24*(1), 30–41.

Inn, L. (2016). Fintech: Ecosystem and business models. *Advanced Science and Technology Letters*, 57–62.

Janulevičius, J., & Goranin, N. (2013). Expert system for data security risk management for SMEs. *Mokslas–Lietuvos ateitis/Science–Future of Lithuania*, *5*(2), 84–87.

Kishada, Z. M. E., Wahab, N. A., & Mustapha, A. (2016). Customer loyalty assessment in Malaysian Islamic banking using artificial intelligence. *Journal of Theoretical and Applied Information Technology*, *87*(1), 80–91.

Kumari, B., Kaur, J., & Swami, S. (2024). Adoption of artificial intelligence in financial services: A policy framework. *Journal of Science and Technology Policy Management*, *15*(2), 396–417.

Li, Y., Yi, J., Chen, H., & Peng, D. (2021). Theory and application of artificial intelligence in financial industry. *Data Science in Finance and Economics*, *1*(2), 96–116.

Lin, F. (2020). Research on the development of financial industry under the background of big data and artificial intelligence. In *5th International conference on financial innovation and economic development (ICFIED 2020)*, January 10–12, 2020, Sanya, China (pp. 1–4). Atlantis Press.

Ortiz, J., Marin, A., & Gualdron, O. (2016). Implementation of a banking system security in embedded systems using artificial intelligence. *Advances in Natural and Applied Sciences*, *10*(17), 95–101.

Payne, E. M., Peltier, J. W., & Barger, V. A. (2018). Mobile banking and AI-enabled mobile banking: The differential effects of technological and non-technological factors on digital natives' perceptions and behavior. *Journal of Research in Interactive Marketing*, *12*(3), 328–346.

Shue, L. Y., Chen, C. W., & Shiue, W. (2009). The development of an ontology-based expert system for corporate financial rating. *Expert Systems with Applications*, *36*(2), 2130–2142.

Singh, M., Singh, R., Pandey, A., & Kasture, P. (2018). Chat-bot for banking industry. In *International conference on communication, security and optimization of decision support systems (ICCSOD 2018)*, August 30–31, 2018, Bangkok, Thailand (pp. 247–249). IEEE.

Sorensen, J. E. (1969). Bayesian analysis in auditing. *The Accounting Review*, *44*(3), 555–561.

Sternberg, F., Pedersen, K. H., Ryelund, N. K., Mukkamala, R. R., & Vatrapu, R. (2018). Analysing customer engagement of Turkish airlines using big social data. In *2018 IEEE international congress on big data (BigData congress)*, July 2–7, 2018, Los Alamitos, California, USA (pp. 74–81). IEEE.

Warwick, K. (2013). *Artificial intelligence: The basics*. Routledge.

Wirtz, J., Patterson, P. G., Kunz, W. H., Gruber, T., Lu, V. N., Paluch, S., & Martins, A. (2018). Brave new world: Service robots in the frontline. *Journal of Service Management*, *29*(5), 907–931.

Xie, M. (2019, April). Development of artificial intelligence and effects on financial system. *Journal of Physics: Conference Series*, *1187*(3), 032084.

Chapter 6

Investigating the Role of AI Techniques in CCFD: A Quantitative Study in the Accounting and Finance Sector

Rawnaa Ibrahim[a,c] *and Israa Badr*[b]

[a]HSE University, Russia
[b]Ain Shams University, Egypt
[c]Egyptian Russian University, Egypt

Abstract

This study aims to investigate the practical utilisation of Artificial Intelligence (AI) techniques in combating credit card fraud (CCF) within the accounting and finance sectors. It will evaluate the efficacy of machine learning (ML), blockchain and fuzzy logic in detecting fraudulent transactions, aiming to provide valuable insights for professionals including fraud examiners, auditors, accountants, bankers and organisations. The research seeks to determine whether AI and ML methods yield beneficial outcomes in the realm of credit card fraud detection (CCFD). It will focus on applying AI and ML techniques in CCFD, incorporating interviews, cross-country questionnaires and a sample size of 403. The study endeavours to contribute to understanding the optimal mechanism for detecting CCF and its potential for widespread application.

Keywords: ML; blockchain; fuzzy logic; AI; CCFD

1. Introduction

The ongoing expansion of the internet and the introduction of modern technologies have resulted in a discernible rise in fraudulent behaviour in a number of business sectors (ACFE, 2020). Financial crimes and widespread fraudulent schemes, such as CCF, e-commerce fraud, financial statement fraud, insurance fraud, money laundering and asset misappropriation, have caused significant harm

From Digital Disruption to Dominance, 133–162

Published under exclusive licence by Emerald Publishing Limited
doi:10.1108/978-1-83549-608-420251006

to a number of businesses (PWC, 2020). Because of credit cards' convenience and adaptability to both online and offline purchases, they have become more popular as payment methods in businesses of all kinds (Beju & Făt, 2023). Credit card transactions are still susceptible to fraud, even with their widespread use. The 2020 Global Economic Crime and Theft Survey report reported a substantial financial impact, estimating a loss of approximately $11 billion in the United States from credit card theft in both the questioned year and the previous year, 2019. Globally, payment card fraud caused losses of approximately $28.65 billion (Abd El Naby et al., 2021). Bragg (2019) defines CCF as an unauthorised act that involves the use of a physical card or its details without the cardholder's knowledge.

There has been a spike in fraudulent activity in tandem with credit card transactions. Online fraud includes transactions made via mobile devices, the internet or e-commerce platforms, while offline fraud usually entails using stolen cards in person (Maharjan & Chuda, 2019). In traditional face-to-face transactions, commonly referred to as offline transactions, the physical handling of the card exposes it to potential theft. Conversely, online transactions require the disclosure of sensitive information such as the card number, expiration date and CVV. A variety of fraudulent activities, including the theft of account credentials, as well as internet-related schemes like website replication, card cloning and questionable merchant platforms, contribute to the increasing risk (Bansal & Garg, 2021).

Credit card holders often remain unaware when their card information is accessed or stolen, creating a challenging scenario where fraudulent transactions seamlessly blend with legitimate ones, making it difficult to differentiate between them (Yee et al., 2018). To address CCFD, Artificial Intelligence (AI) methods are required. Prominent credit card firms, such as American Express, MasterCard and Visa, have successfully integrated AI to identify and prevent fraudulent activities. Because of the variety of AI methodologies and algorithms, there is a lack of knowledge about the use of AI in CCFD, despite its proven success (Lim et al., 2021). AI enables computers to absorb knowledge from historical fraud trends and forensic accountants' experiences, allowing for the effective processing of massive datasets and the creation of complex algorithms (Bao et al., 2022). A wide range of sectors, including manufacturing, e-commerce, robotics, deep learning, machine learning (ML), cognitive computing, Internet of Things (IoT) and automation, can utilise AI due to its adaptability. Moreover, by validating and authenticating user identities, AI is essential to decreasing identity theft, which includes cases such as CCF (Dayyabu et al., 2023). Implementing systems for verification and processing that use deep learning or ML turns out to be a successful tactic for seeing suspicious patterns, stopping fraud before it starts and discovering irregularities in card transactions (Asha & Suresh Kumar, 2021). Since worldwide fraud rates are rising, prompt action is necessary to reduce the risks of financial loss, reputational harm and insolvency presented by fraudsters (Issa et al., 2016). A wide range of ML techniques are essential for both identifying fake cards and detecting fraud. The study's goal is to find out how well AI technologies, like ML, blockchain, fuzzy logic and the combined model of fuzzy logic systems and artificial neural network (ANN), can find

CCF in the finance and accounting fields. Moreover, the study addresses the underutilisation of fuzzy logic and recommends its integration with other AI approaches.

Ultimately, it seeks to overcome significant challenges in identifying fraudulent transactions in the credit card industry. The problem statement highlights the pervasive issue of CCF, affecting both online and offline transactions despite existing security measures. Businesses face substantial financial losses due to fraudulent activities. The study shows that to solve this problem effectively, we need advanced technological solutions like AI, ML, blockchain, fuzzy logic and the model that combines fuzzy logic systems and ANNs. It's important to look into AI methods like ML, blockchain, fuzzy logic and combined models like fuzzy logic systems with ANN because fraud is becoming more common in many business areas. Traditional fraud detection methods may struggle to cope with the complexity and scale of modern schemes. AI enables the analysis of large datasets, pattern identification and real-time anomaly detection, enhancing the ability to prevent and address fraudulent transactions effectively.

The subsequent sections of this study follow this structure: Section 2, Related Work, and Section 3: Diagram of Study Variables (Fig. 6.1). Section 4 elaborates on the research method, employing Statistical Package for the Social Sciences (SPSS). In Section 5, there is a discussion of data analysis using statistical methods. Finally, Section 6 of the study concludes by discussing the conclusions.

2. Literature Review

2.1 CCFD

Stojanović (2021) delved into the application of AI in combating cybercrime and detecting CCF. Building upon prior research, they proposed various AI methods for identifying CCF, with a focus on incorporating intelligent agents into transactions. This approach showcased a notable success rate in fraud detection while minimising false alarms, thereby boosting overall efficiency. By prioritising real-time fraud detection, their intelligent agent approach analysed customer behaviour patterns and flagged deviations as potential fraud indicators. Similarly, Amanze and Onukwugha (2018) introduced multi-agent techniques for fraud analysis and CCFD, leveraging a mathematical model for credit card identification. Their study assessed the agents' resilience to CCF over time and across varying rates of consumer fraud notifications. ML techniques continually evolve to streamline processes in our daily lives, albeit facing challenges in managing diverse and complex training datasets. Blockchain technology emerges as a promising solution, offering decentralised platforms to enhance data security. As highlighted by Bin Sulaiman et al. (2022), blockchains could serve as a medium for collecting data for CCFD, facilitating secure data exchange among banks and financial institutions.

2.2 ML

ML algorithms are essential for detecting CCF because of their ability to evaluate data, find complex patterns and predict credit card theft incidents. These algorithms cover both supervised and unsupervised learning strategies. A number of algorithms used in CCFD include RF, KNN, DT, SVM, LR, NB and TAN. Strong ML models include SVM, KNN, NB, DT, RF and TAN when it comes to detecting CCF. Data points are separated by SVM using optimal hyperplane delineation. According to Somvanshi et al. (2016), transactions are categorised by KNN according to how close they are to neighbouring instances (Shah, 2023). Class probabilities are estimated by NB using probabilistic learning (Jadhav & Channe, 2016): Decision trees are built by DT for feature concentric classification (Jadhav & Channe, 2016): Decision trees are combined by RF to reduce overfitting (Randhawa et al., 2018), and inter-feature correlations are captured by TAN by enriching NB with a tree-like dependency structure to capture inter-feature correlations (Yee et al., 2018). By offering a variety of techniques for identifying and blocking fraudulent transactions, these approaches improve the robustness of fraud detection systems. Algorithms for detecting CCF do have some benefits and drawbacks, however. A number of considerations should be made when choosing an algorithm for a particular application, including the size of the dataset, the feature space's complexity, the processing demands, the findings interpretability and the kind of fraud being addressed. Several academics have presented strategies for improving fraud prevention and detection after conducting a comprehensive analysis of CCFD using ML.

Prasad et al. (2023) have presented an ensemble approach for improving CCFD. The technique involves deep learning to reduce false negatives and identification mistakes, as well as refining model parameters and performance indicators. The research makes use of the SVM, LR, RF, DT and XGBoost. Examining several measures shows that DT performs best, with a 100% recall value. XGBoost, LR, RF and SVM follow with 85%, 74.49%, 75.9% and 69%, respectively. This all-encompassing method greatly improves CCFD systems by combining many classifier ensembles and carefully assessing each one's effectiveness. But the assessment parameters also highlight some of the model's operational constraints. LR, RF, KNN, AdaBoost and Bagging are among the techniques used by Sahithi et al. (2022) to create a weighted average ensemble method for CCFD. Their model, which used the European Credit Card Company dataset, outperformed baseline models including RF Bagging (98.91%), LR (98.90%), AdaBoost (97.91%), KNN (97.81%) and Bagging (95.37%) with an astounding accuracy of 99%. This study shows how well their ensemble model works in this crucial area of CCFD. However, the lack of information about the feature selection process hinders repeatability. Ashraf et al. carried out a comparison study in 2022 of many CCFD techniques, including SVM, ANN, Bayesian Network, KNN, Hidden Markov Model, Fuzzy Logic-Based System and Decision Trees. The authors used both the KDD dataset and the regular KDD CUP 99 Intrusion Dataset. They discovered that the accuracy of the following techniques varied: decision trees – 94.7%, KNN – 97.15%, Bayesian – 97.52%, SVM – 94.65%, ANN – 99.71%, KNN – 97.15%,

HMM – 95.2% and fuzzy logic-based systems – 97.93%. This thorough analysis examined many methods for identifying CCF. However, it is important to note that the dataset did not accurately represent financial activity.

In the context of CCFD, Naik and Kanikar (2019) evaluated and compared a number of ML algorithms, such as Naïve Bayes, J48, Logistic Regression and AdaBoost. They analysed a 1,000-item online dataset that included both fraudulent and non-fraudulent transactions as part of their technique. The results revealed high accuracy levels, with AdaBoost and Logistic Regression achieving 100% accuracy. J48 and Naïve Bayes also showed noteworthy accuracy of 69.93% and 83%, respectively. The findings demonstrate that several algorithms are capable of managing the many scenarios that arise while attempting to identify CCF. We may use this information to strengthen our fraud detection systems. It is important to note, however, that the dataset only included 1,000 credit card transaction records, which may not accurately reflect the variety of CC users. Karthik et al. (2022) presented an inventive CCFD model that uses ensemble learning strategies like boosting and bagging. This one-of-a-kind method creates a hybrid bagging and boosting ensemble classifier by combining the salient features of both approaches. The authors used AdaBoost to design features in the behavioural feature space. They used the area under the precision-recall (AUPR) curve to measure how well the model could predict. On the Brazilian bank dataset, it went from 58.03% to 69.97%, and on the UCSD-FICO dataset, it went from 54.66% to 69.40%. Nevertheless, the research does not provide a thorough analysis of the computational complexity or resource needs related to the suggested paradigm.

This section's literature analysis placed a strong emphasis on the need to keep on researching ML algorithms for CCFD. Therefore, we expect a positive correlation between ML approaches and CCFD.

H1. There is a positive nexus between ML approaches and CCFD.

2.3 Blockchain

Blockchain technology and architecture ensure the consistency and integrity of transaction logs by guaranteeing that every party involved in a transaction has a copy of the ledger. This eliminates the need for intermediaries, allowing communication parties to transact directly. Use cases in finance, such as provenance tracking across the entire process chain and back-end transaction processing, demonstrate this. By providing a peer-to-peer network and inherent anti-tampering protections, blockchain technology surpasses conventional fraud protection techniques that rely on multiple validators. This makes it a superior solution for sectors requiring fast and secure transmission of verifiable data and transactions. In industries like banking, where contracts, financial procedures and transactions are critical, blockchain can greatly enhance productivity by simplifying the management of large volumes of documents. Despite its decentralised design and challenges, blockchain technology offers exciting opportunities in the financial industry. It can lower fraud, facilitate quick and secure transactions and improve risk management in the global financial system.

The cryptography algorithms used in blockchains provide an extra layer of security for processing and storing transaction data, which is crucial given the frequent targeting of financial institutions by fraudsters. Moreover, the implementation of blockchain-enabled self-executing contracts has the potential to streamline operational procedures and significantly reduce the time and resources spent on contract administration by businesses. Scholars such as Sultana and Bertino (2012), Kherbouche et al. (2022), Liu et al. (2023), Zhao et al. (2012) have explored this topic, according to Chatterjee et al. (2023). Utilising federated learning (FL) and blockchain in the realm of CCFD offers a heightened level of security, transparency and cooperation in identifying and thwarting fraudulent activities. With FL, various entities can collectively train an ML model on their respective datasets without the need to disclose sensitive information to one another, thereby safeguarding privacy and data security. Through the implementation of FL, organisations can enhance the precision and efficacy of fraud detection models by leveraging a broader and more varied dataset for training purposes.

Bin Sulaiman et al. (2022) propose decentralised fraud detection as a viable FL-based blockchain approach for CCFD. This method involves utilising FL and blockchains to establish a decentralised system for fraud detection, which enhances privacy, transparency and security. However, the study noted that this approach requires substantial computational resources and meticulous handling of sensitive data. In this context, the study emphasised the importance of ongoing research to enhance the scalability and optimisation of both blockchain and FL technologies. Balagolla et al. (2021) proposed Smart Contracts for Fraud Detection as a feasible approach, involving the use of smart contracts on a blockchain to automate the fraud detection and prevention process. This approach offers advantages such as increased automation and efficiency. However, the study highlighted limitations due to smart contract technology's capabilities and the potential for errors or vulnerabilities. We emphasised the importance of continuous research to improve smart contract technology and its integration with ML algorithms in this area. According to Awan et al. (2019), FL with homomorphic encryption for fraud detection is a viable method within FL-based blockchain approaches for CCFD. This approach entails using FL with homomorphic encryption to improve privacy and security. However, the study pointed out drawbacks, including the potential for high computational costs and the need for specialised expertise. The study stressed the importance of ongoing research to optimise and scale homomorphic encryption for large-scale fraud detection systems.

Li et al. (2020) suggested blockchain-based fraud prevention as a viable FL-based blockchain approach for CCFD. This method involves using blockchains to prevent fraud by creating a tamper-proof record of transactions and ensuring compliance with regulations. This approach leads to improved security and compliance. However, it requires widespread adoption of blockchain-based fraud prevention systems and has potential privacy concerns. In this regard, the study underlined the need for continuing research to support the development and use of blockchain-based fraud prevention systems. Shayan et al. (2020) proposed distributed ledger (DL) for Fraud Analysis as a practical method within the FL-based blockchain for CCFD. This approach utilises distributed ledger technology (DLT) to track and analyse credit card transactions for fraud detection. It offers advantages such as increased transparency and traceability. However, the study noted limitations related to the need for careful management of sensitive data and potential privacy concerns. The study emphasised the importance of ongoing research aimed at optimising and scaling DLT for fraud analysis. Fan et al. (2023) suggested identity verification based on blockchain technology. This method uses blockchain technology to confirm credit card customers' identities and combat identity theft. It offers advantages such as enhanced client privacy and security. The study did point out several restrictions on the widespread use of blockchain technology-based identification systems, as well as certain privacy issues. The study underlined how crucial it is to continue doing research in order to implement blockchain-based identification solutions.

Qu et al. (2023) proposed a consortium blockchain as a fraud detection tool. This is one of the blockchain-based FL methods for CCFD. This method involves establishing a shared fraud detection system across multiple organisations through the use of a consortium blockchain. It offers benefits for better communication among multiple organisations. The research did identify limitations on the need for participation organisations to reach a consensus and on the cautious handling of sensitive material. The study emphasised how important it is to keep going with the research papers in order to use blockchain consortium solutions for fraud detection. Yazdinejad et al. (2022) assert that blockchain-based fraud reporting plays a crucial role. This is one of the blockchain-based FL methods for detecting CCF. This method uses blockchains to create a secure and transparent system for reporting and investigating suspected fraud. It offers benefits like improved transparency and traceability. The study emphasised how important it is to continue working on the research papers in order to use blockchain-based fraud reporting solutions.

Only a limited number of studies have delved into the implications of blockchain technology for the accounting and auditing sectors. According to Dai and Vasarhelyi (2017), the blockchain serves as an accounting information system by distributing transaction verification, storage and management among multiple nodes, thereby preventing unauthorised changes to data or records. This enables the real-time reporting of reliable accounting information to stakeholders at various aggregation levels based on their roles and requirements, thereby authenticating audit-related information. Faccia and Mosteanu (2019) suggest that blockchains can transition accounting from a double-entry to a triple-entry system, reducing error risks and detecting fraudulent transactions. Liu et al. (2019) classify blockchains into permissionless and permissioned forms and discuss their implications and challenges for auditors, emphasising the need for auditors to adapt to blockchain technology and actively contribute to its development. Brender and Gauthier (2018) assert that auditors must become more IT-oriented to ensure the proper set-up and deployment of blockchain technology, which inherently ensures the accuracy and completeness of transactions through encoded controls and automation. Additionally, the auditing industry needs to change in order to adapt to the blockchain-driven changes in the landscape, moving away from a focus on financial statements and towards testing accounting information systems and ensuring proper blockchain implementation. Additionally, attestation services may transition from backward-looking activities to forward-looking strategic analysis and advice based on big data. However, the readiness of audit teams to adapt to these changes remains a concern, prompting the need for upskilling and investment in technological capabilities. Despite theoretical discussions, empirical research on the impact of blockchains on the accounting and auditing professions remains limited. Brender et al. (2018) surveyed auditors in Switzerland and found that the profession is not fully prepared for blockchain's potential effects, necessitating a shift towards greater IT orientation and forward-looking practices, along with changes in auditor roles and responsibilities.

This section's literature analysis placed a strong emphasis on the need to keep investigating blockchain approaches for CCFD. Therefore, we expect a positive correlation between blockchain approaches and CCFD.

H2. There is a positive nexus between blockchain approaches and CCFD.

2.4 Fuzzy Logic

Razooqi et al. (2016) conducted a study utilising a fuzzy database to identify CCF by analysing users' behaviour and spending habits. Their goal was to make a model using fuzzy logic systems and ANN to see how well these AI methods could tell the difference between real and fake transactions. The findings demonstrated that both methods proved effective in detecting CCF. The accuracy rates of both models, however, showed that the ANN approach outperformed fuzzy logic. Specifically, the study revealed that the ANN method exhibited a 33% higher accuracy rate compared to fuzzy logic in identifying CCFD within the financial sector. Similarly, Saeed (2019) utilised authentic data from Sudanese financial institutions to develop unique intelligent type-2 fuzzy logic systems (FLSs) tailored for detecting debit card fraud. The study's findings point to a system that exhibits a high degree of accuracy in the banking sector's automated fraud detection. Using MATrix LABoratory (MATLAB), Behera and Panigrahi (2017) developed a two-stage fuzzy expert system for the identification of CCF. They started by processing incoming transactions using a pattern-matching method. This component consists of two modules: an address-matching module and a fuzzy clustering module. Based on how far the transaction deviates from the norm, each of these modules gives it a score. Their findings confirmed the efficacy of the fuzzy logic expert system in identifying CCF based on a comparison of its performance with other fraud detection systems. Askari and Hussain (2020) described a methodology for e-transaction fraud detection using intuitionistic fuzzy logic and the C4.5 decision tree. They looked at both derived and standard characteristics in their analysis of an online transaction dataset. In comparison to other investigations, their study showed that the fuzzy logic-based system produced a particularly high and efficient detection rate. Even though they are not the most effective method, experts still view fuzzy logic-based systems as one of the most suitable and affordable AI-based mechanisms for fraud detection in the financial industry. To detect fraudulent financial statements, Besuspariene and Niskanen (2023) developed a fuzzy model. The model makes use of 14 financial indicators, which are categorised into six input variables according to their relationship to accounting concepts like equity, liabilities, assets and income. Rather than evaluating financial statement fraud in its entirety, this method offers a more detailed view of possible fraud situations linked to financial statements. The approach used to create the model to identify fake financial statements was fuzzy logic. Using a decision tree, the authors evaluated the fuzzy logic model's output and got comparable results. Although the model was originally designed for micro and small businesses, it may also be used for medium-sized and big businesses. However, it might not be appropriate for tiny businesses that are inherently involved in the preparation of profit and loss statements. The suggested methodology seeks to decrease risk for small enterprises and perhaps improve corporate transparency for public authorities by aiding in the detection of fraudulent financial transactions.

Lau et al. (1999) demonstrated how complimentary neural networks and fuzzy modelling are in overcoming computing constraints by using them to operate a plastic injection moulding process. Alam et al. (2000) used fuzzy clustering and self-organising neural networks to successfully identify possibly failing banks, demonstrating the predictive value of these techniques for decision-makers. Using fuzzy clustering to classify bankruptcy, Lenard et al. (2000) distinguished excessive financial ratios as indicative of impending financial trouble. Lenard and Alam (2004) combined non-financial data with financial factors to create a fuzzy logic model for fraud detection and forecast accuracy. The fuzzy logic model combined non-financial data with financial statement variables for analysis, creating clusters for various statements that represented red flags in fraud identification. The model's total prediction accuracy was 86.7%. Nolan (1998) provided evidence of how expert fuzzy classification improves performance by effectively representing ambiguous concepts, expanding the operating range in poorly defined contexts and reducing the susceptibility to outliers. Ammar et al. (2000) used fuzzy set theory to address imprecision in assessed information and develop a multi-layer fuzzy rule-based system for ranking state financial management. With an emphasis on cost reduction via fraud detection, Pathak et al. (2005) proposed a fuzzy logic-based method enabling auditors to identify fraud in settled insurance claims. To handle ambiguous or fuzzy data, Fuzzy Association Rules (FAR) expands on conventional association rules. The main goal of classical association rule mining is to discover associations between items in datasets where objects are considered either present or absent. But in real-world situations, data could not always be clear-cut or binary; instead, it might include imprecision or ambiguity. Fuzzy association rules use fuzzy logic, which enables the representation of uncertainty and imprecision in data, to identify patterns in imprecise or fuzzy datasets. These rules express links between fuzzy sets instead of crisp ones, making it possible to find linkages even when the data are poorly defined.

Fuzzy association rules are especially helpful in fields like expert systems, natural language processing and decision-making systems where input is inherently imprecise or ambiguous. They provide a framework that is more adaptable for identifying significant patterns in this kind of data. The framework was developed by Dubois et al. (2006) and Sadgali et al. (2019). In fact, fuzzy logic addresses cognitive doubts by using language to express the degree of truth rather than merely binary true or false values. It enables a more complex portrayal of uncertainty, which is often present in natural language processing and human decision-making. Fuzzy logic allows for a spectrum of truth degrees, while conventional logic only allows for propositions to be true or false. Truth values in fuzzy logic may vary from entirely true to completely false. This makes it possible for fuzzy logic to represent the natural ambiguity and imprecision seen in a lot of real-world situations. Many domains where human thinking is necessary, such as expert systems, control systems and decision-making procedures, find applications for fuzzy logic. Allowing for uncertainty and imprecision contributes to the development of more resilient and flexible systems that more closely resemble human decision-making (Herrera-Viedma et al., 2020). This new method, which uses anomaly scores to describe a company's financial management, combines a genetic algorithm with fuzzy logic to potentially transform the detection of financial statement fraud. By harnessing the power of genetic algorithms, the system dynamically evolves a set of fuzzy rules or parameters tailored to maximise fraud detection efficacy while minimising false positives. Fuzzy logic, with its ability to model uncertainty and imprecision, provides a robust framework for defining rules that capture the nuanced nature of financial data and fraud indicators. Thanks to iterative optimisation guided by the genetic algorithm, the system skilfully adjusts to changing fraud patterns. This is a sophisticated and flexible answer to the hard problem of finding fraud in corporate financial statements (Hoogs et al., 2007).

A hybrid intelligent system that combines a fuzzy expert system is a state-of-the-art toolkit for financial diagnosis and analysis, helping businesses detect and resolve their financial problems. This novel method combines the best features of fuzzy logic and expert systems: the expert system uses heuristics and domain knowledge to direct the diagnostic process, while fuzzy logic allows the modelling of imprecise and uncertain financial data. Using a mix of different methods, the hybrid intelligent system can easily understand large amounts of complex financial data, finding patterns and outliers that could mean problems like missing information in financial statements, issues with cash flow or too much debt. This system learns and improves iteratively, becoming more and more skilled at identifying a variety of financial problems, providing insightful analysis to stakeholders and assisting in well-informed decision-making to reduce risks and maximise financial performance (Uthayakumar et al., 2020). In light of this section's literature analysis, we have developed the following hypothesis:

H3. There is a positive nexus between fuzzy logic approaches and CCFD.

3. Diagram of Study Variables

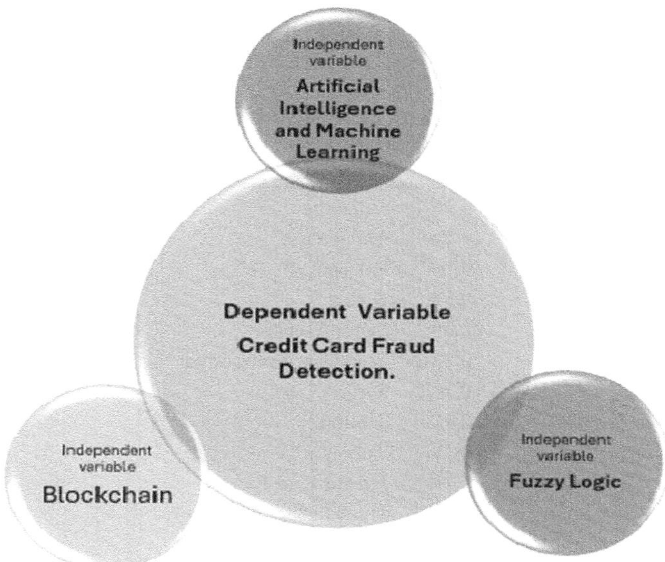

Fig. 6.1. Study Variables. *Source:* Developed by the authors.

4. Study Methodology

The study used an empirical methodology, employing the survey approach to collect primary data via the distribution of a uniform questionnaire. We sent and correctly filled out a total of 403 questionnaires. We used the SPSS to analyse the data using percentages, tables and chi-square methods. Furthermore, it's critical to keep in mind that a survey is a particular kind of research design. On the other hand, one way to get data is via an interview or a postal questionnaire. Despite the multitude of methods available for data collection, we have selected two primary methods for gathering questionnaire data:

(1) In-person interviews by Zoom.
(2) Phone conversations.

Several aspects impact the selection of an appropriate technique, including the availability of possible participants or respondents, the literacy levels of the respondents, the nature of the subject matter and the motivation level of the respondents.

4.1 Population Size

The researchers do a comparative analysis across many countries, yielding an undetermined population number. The following Table 6.1 presents the percentages of observations for each nation that participated in completing the questionnaires.

Table 6.1. Countries Involved in the Questionnaire.

Country	Observations	%	Country	Observations	%
Australia	3	0.7%	Lebanon	3	0.7%
Bahrain	2	0.5%	Malaysia	3	0.7%
Belgium	1	0.2%	Pakistan	3	0.7%
Brazil	2	0.5%	Russia	83	20.6%
Egypt	161	40.0%	Saudi Arabia	9	2.2%
England	3	0.7%	St Gallen, Switzerland	3	0.7%
France	3	0.7%	Syria	3	0.7%
Germany	8	2.0%	Tunisia	6	1.5%
Iran	3	0.7%	Turkey	3	0.7%
Ireland	3	0.7%	United Kingdom	69	17.1%
Jordan	6	1.5%	United states of America	3	0.7%
Kuwait	9	2.2%	Poland	11	2.7%
Total				403	100%

Source: Developed by the authors.

Table 6.1 depicts information on the percentages of countries that have expressed their views on the efficiency and effectiveness of AI tools – specifically, ML, blockchain and fuzzy logic for CCFD. Due to their status as the writers' respective countries, Egypt and Russia achieved a significantly high completion rate of 40% and 20.6%, respectively. The United Kingdom completed the survey with a participation rate of 17.1%. Subsequently, the remaining nations' involvement revealed almost the same proportion.

4.2 Sample Size

For conducting an empirical study, the authors will rely on a stratified random sample, which was calculated as follows:

To find out the total sample size, we will use the equation as follows:

$$n = \frac{Z^2 * P(1-P)}{d^2}$$

The variables in this formula are:

n = the sample size.

Z = the Z-score or a standard normal deviate corresponding when the confidence level 95% then $Z = 1.96$.

P = the estimated proportion of the study variable, it is equal to 0.50. 'With prevalence reported from the previous study.'

d = the margin of error when the confidence level 95% then $d = 5\%$.

$$n = \frac{Z^2 * P(1-P)}{d^2} = (1.96)2 * 0.5 * 0.5/(0.05)2 = 384.16$$

$\approx$ 384 Questionnaire.

Therefore, we should take a minimum of 384 samples. The study determined that a sample size of 384 and 403 respondents yielded accurate estimates that align with community rates at a 95% confidence level, with a margin of error ranging from 5%.

4.3 Analysing Characteristics of the Sample

By considering the valid replies obtained for statistical analysis, we can elucidate the sample categorisation. The researchers possess a characterisation of the sample, including occupation, years of experience and educational level. The subsequent figures and tables, presented below, further demonstrate this.

Table 6.2. The Distribution of Sample Items Is Based on Occupation.

Occupation		**Valid Questionnaire**	**Percent**
Valid	Academic Positions	170	42.2%
	Researcher	106	26.3%
	Auditors	36	8.9%
	Fraud examiners	18	4.5%
	Bankers	55	13.6%
	Forensic Accountant/Analyst	12	3.0%
	Others	6	1.5%
	Total	403	100%

Source: Developed by the authors.

As shown in Table 6.2, we selected a research sample of 403 respondents to mirror the distribution of questionnaires among the study participants. The subsequent analysis focuses on the contents of the questionnaires. To complete the study, we processed, analysed and entered the study sample information into the statistical programme. The table above shows that each study group's statistical analysis yielded a satisfactory rate, indicating the reliability of the results for testing the research hypotheses.

Table 6.3. The Categorisation of Sample Objects Is Based on Academic Achievements.

Education Level		**Frequency**	**Percent**
Valid	Bachelor's Degree	25	6.2%
	Master's Degree	33	8.2%
	PhD or equivalent	294	73%
	Others	51	12.7%
	Total	403	100%

Source: Developed by the authors.

As shown in Table 6.3, researchers found that the largest proportion recorded was obtaining a PhD degree, and their number was 294 respondents, equivalent to a proportion of 73%. The category of others pertains to professional and international qualifications, accounting for a total of 51 certifications 'per individual,' which corresponds to a proportion of 12.7%, followed by the total number of members of the 33 respondents with a Master degree, the equivalent ratio of 8.2%, and finally the total number of members of the 25 respondents with a Bachelor degree, the equivalent ratio of 6.2%. We can attribute this disparity to the heterogeneity of academic credentials within the study's sample.

Table 6.4. The Categorisation of Sample Objects Based on Years of Experience.

Experience		Frequency	Percent
Valid	Less than 5 years	41	10.2%
	From 6 to 10 years	82	20.3%
	More than 10 years	280	69.5%
	Total	403	100%

Source: Developed by the authors.

As shown in Table 6.4, the study sample and its level of experience have varied, as indicated in the previous table. The most experienced individuals registered for the class with more than 10 years of experience, representing 69.5%. The category with 6–10 years of experience follows, accounting for 20.3% of the sample. The category with less than 5 years of experience represents 10.2% of the sample. After carefully examining the survey forms, we conducted the data encoding process and subsequently inputted the responses into a computer system using SPSS.

5. Data Analysis and Results

The researchers employ statistical methods, reliability and validity tests, as well as the analysis and testing of data relevant to the study hypotheses.

5.1 The Statistical Methods Used

5.1.1 Statistics Reliability

The methods focus on assessing the reliability of survey-based data analysis results, specifically the consistency of respondents' answers and the potential for sharing the results with the community. This is accomplished by reliability coefficient tests and the honesty coefficient. We used the Cronbach's alpha coefficient (Cronbach alpha) to evaluate the stability of the coefficient within the community. A Cronbach's alpha value greater than 0.5 signifies internal consistency, reflecting the reliability of a set of questions designed to measure a single underlying construct.

5.1.2 Validity

To confirm the apparent scale's validity, writers first conduct tests and gather various perspectives from professors to improve the questionnaire's accuracy and objectivity.

5.1.3 Stability

We employed Cronbach's alpha test (reliability analysis) to ensure the dependability of the study tool. The researcher utilised Cronbach's alpha coefficient, a statistical method for assessing the reliability of survey data. This method examines the degree of consistency in respondents' answers and the potential for disseminating the results to the community.

5.2 The Reliability and Validity Test

Consistency and validity coefficient tests evaluate the reliability of questionnaire results, producing the following outcome.

Table 6.5. Summary Results of Cronbach's Coefficient Alpha for Study Sample.

Reliability Statistics	
Cronbach's Alpha	*N* of Items
0.972	30

Source: Developed by the authors.

In Table 6.5, the study found that the Cronbach's alpha coefficient yields a value of approximately 97.2%, indicating a high level of relative validity for the majority of the responses pertaining to the usage hypothesis.

This section presents the findings of the descriptive statistical analysis conducted on the data. The analysis includes the means and SD of all dimensions investigated in the study, as well as the paragraphs that comprise each dimension. It is crucial to include the study's scale in the presentation.

Table 6.6. Likert Scale 5-Points Scale.

Strongly Disagree	**Disagree**	**Neutral**	**Agree**	**Strongly Agree**
1	2	3	4	5

Source: Developed by the authors.

As shown in Table 6.6, the mean value of the items exceeds 3.5, which indicates a high degree of perception, suggesting agreement among the sample members on the item. However, if the mean is between 2.5 and 3.49, it indicates a medium level of perception. Conversely, if the mean is below 2.49, it suggests a low level of perception (Hawamdeh, 2007).

5.3 Analysis and Testing of Data Related to the Study Hypotheses

Ho. In the accounting and finance sectors, ML techniques have no impact on CCFD.

H1. In the accounting and finance sectors, ML techniques have a positive impact on CCFD.

The researchers of the study employed measures such as means, standard deviations and chi-square to determine the acceptance of the null hypothesis or alternative hypothesis, as presented in the subsequent tables.

Table 6.7. Descriptive Statistics.

Descriptive Statistics			
Questions	***N***	**Mean**	**Std. Deviation**
Group No. 1: The importance of ML in CCFD.			
Q1. AI is extensively utilised and plays a critical role in CCFD (Lim et al., 2021).	403	4.56	0.660
Q2. ML provides the system with the capability to learn from experience automatically without human intervention (Prasad et al., 2023).	403	4.49	0.793
Q3. ML seeks to predict future events with high accuracy by using different algorithmic models (Sadgali et al., 2019).	403	4.56	0.791
Q4. ML is very different than the conventional computation approaches, where systems are explicitly programed to calculate or solve a problem (Sahithi et al., 2022, April).	403	4.57	0.731
Q5. ML deals with the input data that are used to train a model, where the model learns different patterns in the input data and uses that knowledge to predict (Lim et al., 2021).	403	4.59	0.709
Q6. ML-driven fraud detection systems alleviate the challenge of manually checking all transactions, particularly in larger financial institutions (Bello et al., 2023).	403	4.57	0.721
Weighted Mean	4.5567		
Std. Deviation	0.65971		

Source: Developed by the authors.

Table 6.7 displays descriptive data that highlight the significant influence of ML on the identification of CCF. The data show that there is a high level of agreement about the importance of ML, with an average rating of 4.56. The capacity of ML to autonomously learn from past events, accurately forecast future events and set itself apart from conventional computer techniques by adjusting to data patterns rather than depending on explicit programming is acknowledged by respondents. Furthermore, the ability of ML to handle substantial amounts of transactions and minimise the need for human verifications in the field of fraud detection is much appreciated. The small standard deviation of 0.66 indicates a strong agreement on the crucial role of ML in improving CCFD.

Table 6.8. Chi-Square Table.

Group 1: The Importance of ML in CCFD.

Test Statistics

	Q1. AI is extensively utilised and plays a critical role in CCFD (Lim et al., 2021).	Q2. ML provides the system with the capability to learn from experience automatically without human intervention (Prasad et al., 2023).	Q3. ML seeks to predict future events with high accuracy by using different algorithmic models (Sadgali et al., 2019).	Q4. ML is very different than the conventional computation approaches, where systems are explicitly programmed to calculate or solve a problem (Sahithi et al., 2022, April).	Q5. ML deals with the input data that are used to train a model, where the model learns different patterns in the input data and uses that knowledge to predict (Lim et al., 2021).	Q6. The ML-driven fraud detection systems alleviate the challenge of manually checking all transactions, particularly in larger financial institutions (Bello et al., 2023).
Chi-Square	612.347[a]	555.027[a]	665.499[a]	645.548[a]	445.764[b]	430.816[b]
Df	4	4	4	4	3	3
Asymp. Sig.	0.000	0.000	0.000	0.000	0.000	0.000

[a]The questions labelled with "a" have a degrees of freedom (Df) value of 4.
[b]The questions labelled with "b" have a degrees of freedom (Df) value of 3.
Source: Developed by the authors.

The chi-square test findings for ML's relevance in CCFD are shown in Table 6.8. All p-values are 0.000, and the chi-square values for the questions range from 430.816 to 665.499, indicating substantial statistical significance. The results show that the respondents' opinions on the function of ML in CCFD are quite meaningful and not based on random chance. According to the findings, several factors are considered crucial for more effective fraud detection systems. Some of these benefits include the following: the ability to analyse training data, the predictive potential of ML, the extensive usage of AI and the reduction of the requirement for human transaction checks. The constant significance across all metrics, even if the value of F ranges from 3 to 4 depending on the issue, shows that there is an agreement on the efficacy of ML in CCFD.

Ho. The blockchain has no impact on CCFD.
H2. Blockchain has a positive impact on CCFD.

Table 6.9. Descriptive Statistical.

Group 2: Blockchain Has an Impact on CCFD.			
Q1. Blockchain is one of the emerging technologies for making the possibility of providing a decentralised platform that could result in providing enhanced security to the data (Liu et al., 2023).	403	4.57	0.738
Q2. Blockchain could be considered the medium of data collection for CCFD in how data are exchanged among banks and financial institutions securely (Bin Sulaiman et al., 2022).	403	4.52	0.793
Q3. Based on your knowledge or experience, FL and blockchain technologies enhance CCFD (Awan et al., 2019; Li et al., 2020).	403	4.43	0.826
Q4. Based on your knowledge or experience, using smart contracts on a blockchain and integrating them with ML algorithms can effectively automate fraud detection and prevention (Bello et al., 2024).	403	4.44	0.755
Q5. Based on your knowledge or experience, use DLT to track and analyse CC transactions for fraud detection (Balagolla et al., 2021).	403	4.41	0.821
Q6. Based on your knowledge or experience, use blockchain to create a secure and transparent system for reporting and investigating suspected fraud (Liu et al., 2023).	403	4.51	0.703
Q7. Based on your knowledge or experience, use blockchain to prevent fraud by creating a tamper-proof record of transactions and ensuring compliance with regulations (Mustyala, 2023).	403	4.33	1.042
Q8. Based on your knowledge or experience, how can consortium blockchain be used to create a shared fraud detection system among multiple organizations (Liu et al., 2023).	403	4.44	0.772
Q9. Based on your knowledge or experience, use blockchain and decentralised identity verification protocols to prevent identity theft and fraud (Balagolla et al., 2021).	403	4.50	0.710
Weighted Mean	4.4593		
Std. Deviation	0.68405		

Source: Developed by the authors.

Table 6.9 presents the results of descriptive statistics for Group 2, emphasising the strong influence of blockchain technology on CCFD. The descriptive statistics reveal a significant endorsement for the role of blockchain in improving security and transparency in data management, with a weighted mean rating of 4.46. Respondents agree that blockchain has the capacity to provide a decentralised platform for secure data exchange across financial organisations. Additionally, it may be used for the purpose of monitoring and analysing transactions, producing records that are impervious to manipulation and ensuring compliance with regulatory obligations. The integration of smart contracts with ML algorithms is regarded as a very effective approach for automating the detection of fraudulent actions. Moreover, the decentralised identity verification offered by blockchain technology is considered a helpful tool in avoiding occurrences of identity theft. Furthermore, the endorsement is given to the use of consortium blockchains for the purpose of implementing shared fraud detection systems that span across several organisations. The standard deviation of 0.68 indicates a significant degree of agreement about the usefulness of blockchain in CCFD.

Table 6.10 presents the chi-square test results for the impact of blockchain technology on CCFD. The chi-square values for each question range from 283.700 to 646.367, all with p-values of 0.000, indicating a high level of statistical significance. Respondents strongly support the perceived importance of blockchain technologies, including their provision of decentralised platforms, secure data exchange, integration of smart contracts with ML and creation of tamper-proof records. A strong consensus on blockchain's efficacy in improving fraud detection systems and avoiding fraud via safe and transparent techniques is confirmed by the constant importance across all questions, with degrees of freedom ranging between 3 and 4. Therefore, we reject the hypothesis that blockchain has no effect on CCFD in the accounting and financial sectors, and instead, we embrace the hypothesis that blockchain has a beneficial effect on CCFD in these sectors.

Table 6.10. Chi-Square.

Group 2: Blockchain Has an Impact on CCFD.

Test Statistics

	Q1. Blockchain is one of the emerging technologies for making the possibility of providing a decentralised platform that could result in providing enhanced security to the data (Liu et al., 2023).	Q2. Blockchain could be considered the medium of data collection for CCFD in how data are exchanged among banks and financial institutions securely (Bin Sulaiman et al., 2022).	Q3. Based on your knowledge or experience, FL and blockchain technologies enhance CCFD (Awan et al., 2019; Li et al., 2020).	Q4. Based on your knowledge or experience, use smart contracts on a blockchain and integrating them with ML algorithms can effectively automate fraud detection and prevention (Bello et al., 2024).	Q5. Based on your knowledge or experience, use distributed ledger technology to track and analyse credit card transactions for fraud detection (Balagolla et al., 2021).	Q6. Based on your knowledge or experience, use blockchain to create a secure and transparent system for reporting and investigating suspected fraud (Liu et al., 2023).	Q7. Based on your knowledge or experience, use blockchain to prevent fraud by creating a tamper-proof record of transactions and ensuring compliance with regulations (Mustyala, 2023).	Q8. Based on your knowledge or experience, the use of consortium blockchain to create a shared fraud detection system among multiple organisations (Liu et al., 2023).	Q9. Based on your knowledge or experience, use blockchain and decentralised identity verification protocols to prevent identity theft and fraud (Balagolla et al., 2021).
Chi-Square	646.367[a]	590.015[a]	310.777[b]	300.792[b]	460.437[a]	549.295[a]	283.700[b]	308.811[b]	351.412[b]
Df	4	4	3	3	4	4	3	3	3
Asymp. Sig.	0.000	0.000	0.000	0.000	0.000	0.000	0.000	0.000	0.000

[a]The questions labelled with “a” have a degrees of freedom (Df) value of 4.
[b]The questions labelled with “b” have a degrees of freedom (Df) value of 3.
Source: Developed by the authors.

Regarding the examining how fuzzy logic and CCFD relate to one another is the primary goal of the research. We used descriptive statistics and the chi-square test to look into the second hypothesis.

Ho. Fuzzy logic has no impact on CCFD.
H3. Fuzzy logic has a positive impact on CCFD.

Table 6.11. Descriptive Statistical.

Group 3: Fuzzy Logic Has an Impact on CCFD.			
Q1. Fuzzy logic represents cognitive uncertainties, measuring the intensity of the truth values for unquantifiable measures (Herrera-Viedma et al., 2020).	403	4.39	0.825
Q2. FAR can be found in the literature, such as a generalisation of association rules when initial data are fuzzy or if they have been previously processed to provide them with imprecision (Sam et al., 2023).	403	4.43	0.781
Q3. Using a fuzzy database to CCFD by monitoring users' behaviour and spending patterns (Darwish, 2020).	403	4.40	0.836
Q4. They aimed to build a model using fuzzy logic systems and ANN to compare the AI techniques that would correctly and accurately identify legitimate or fraudulent transactions (Saeed, 2019).	403	4.38	0.851
Q5. Fuzzy logic can indicate that both methods are effective in CCFD (Karthika & Senthilselvi, 2023).	403	4.36	0.860
Q6. Based on your knowledge or experience, the use of fuzzy logic can detect financial statement fraud (Saeed, 2019).	403	4.31	0.915
Q7. Based on your knowledge or experience, the use of fuzzy logic assesses the risk of managerial fraud (Ilori et al., 2024).	403	4.31	0.913
Q8. Based on your knowledge or experience, the hybrid intelligent system and a fuzzy expert system to diagnose financial problems in companies (Al, 2024).	403	4.36	0.879
Q9. A genetic algorithm based on fuzzy logic will be used to detect financial statement fraud based on anomaly scores as a metric for characterising corporate financial behaviour (Karthika & Senthilselvi, 2023).	403	4.35	0.881
Q10. Fuzzy logic uses fuzzy set theory to represent imprecision in evaluated information and judgement (Imeni, 2020).	403	4.42	0.810
Q11. Fuzzy logic and expert reasoning to develop clusters for different statements representing red flags in the detection of fraud (Sam et al., 2023).	403	4.36	0.890
Weighted Mean	4.3695		
Std. Deviation	0.80901		

Source: Developed by the authors.

Table 6.11 presents the descriptive data on the influence of fuzzy logic on CCFD, which uncover many noteworthy discoveries. The investigation shows that fuzzy logic is very skilled at dealing with cognitive uncertainty and imprecision in financial data, hence enhancing fraud detection skills. Literature confirms that fuzzy logic is capable of extending association rules to handle imprecise data and may aid in tracking user behaviour using fuzzy databases. The research suggests that combining fuzzy logic with ANN improves the precision of identifying

Table 6.12. Chi-Square.

Group 3: Fuzzy Logic Has an Impact on CCFD.

Test Statistics

	Q1. Fuzzy logic represents cognitive uncertainties, measuring the intensity of the truth values for un quantifiable measures (Herrera-Viedma et al., 2020).	Q2. FAR can be found in the literature, such as a generalisation of association rules when initial data are fuzzy or if they have been previously processed to provide them with imprecision (Sam et al., 2023).	Q3. Using a fuzzy database to detect credit card fraud by monitoring users' behaviour and spending patterns (Darwish, 2020).	Q4. They aimed to build a model using fuzzy logic systems and artificial neural networks to compare the AI techniques that would correctly and accurately identify legitimate or fraudulent transactions (Saeed, 2019).	Q5. Fuzzy logic can indicate that both methods are effective in credit card fraud detection (Karthika & Senthilselvi, 2023).	Q6. Based on your knowledge or experience, the use of fuzzy logic can detect financial statement fraud (Saeed, 2019).	Q7. Based on your knowledge or experience, the use of fuzzy logic assesses the risk of managerial fraud (Ilori et al., 2024).	Q8. Based on your knowledge or experience, the hybrid intelligent system and a fuzzy expert system to diagnose financial problems in companies (Al, 2024).	Q9. A genetic algorithm based on fuzzy logic will be used to detect financial statement fraud based on anomaly scores as a metric for characterising corporate financial behaviour (Karthika & Senthilselvi, 2023).	Q10. Fuzzy logic uses fuzzy set theory to represent imprecision in evaluated information and judgement (Imeni, 2020).	Q11.Fuzzy logic and expert reasoning to develop clusters for different statements representing red flags in the detection of fraud (Sam et al., 2023).
Chi-Square	447.558[a]	478.576[a]	472.993[a]	441.603[a]	427.310[a]	270.658[b]	261.427[b]	279.928[b]	270.955[b]	294.002[b]	288.285[b]
Df	4	4	4	4	4	3	3	3	3	3	3
Asymp. Sig.	0.000	0.000	0.000	0.000	0.000	0.000	0.000	0.000	0.000	0.000	0.000

[a]The questions labelled with "a" have a degrees of freedom (Df) value of 4.
[b]The questions labelled with "b" have a degrees of freedom (Df) value of 3.
Source: Developed by the authors.

fraudulent transactions. Additionally, it highlights the effectiveness of fuzzy approaches, such as genetic algorithms, in detecting financial statement fraud. The respondents generally agree on the usefulness of fuzzy logic for detecting both financial and managerial fraud, as well as its capacity to effectively handle imprecise information during evaluation. The weighted mean rating of 4.37 indicates a significant endorsement of the usefulness of fuzzy logic in CCFD. Additionally, the standard deviation of 0.81 demonstrates consistency in the replies.

The findings of the chi-square test for the influence of fuzzy logic on CCFD are shown in Table 6.12. There is a great degree of statistical significance since all *p*-values are 0.000 and the chi-square values for the questions vary from 261.427 to 478.576. The findings show that most respondents believe fuzzy logic may be used to identify fraud in a variety of situations, such as handling cognitive uncertainties, extending the usage of association rules, monitoring user behaviour and integrating with artificial neural networks. The results also demonstrate the use of fuzzy logic in characterising imprecise information, detecting financial and managerial wrongdoing and detecting fraud via the application of genetic algorithms. The questions exhibit high agreement about the impact of fuzzy logic in enhancing fraud detection systems, with degrees of freedom ranging from 3 to 4. Indicating that we accept the alternative hypothesis, *H3*: Fuzzy logic has a positive impact on CCFD in the accounting and finance industry, and reject *Ho*: Fuzzy logic has no impact on CCFD in the accounting and finance sector.

6. Main Findings and Discussion

The study employed various statistical methods, including reliability and validity tests, to analyse the data. We assessed reliability using the Cronbach's alpha coefficient, revealing a high value of approximately 97.2%, signifying a high level of consistency and relative validity in the responses. We ensured validity through extensive testing and feedback from professors to improve the questionnaire's accuracy and objectivity. The descriptive statistical analysis revealed that the mean values of items exceeded 3.5, indicating a high degree of agreement among respondents.

Our study examines the influence of ML on the CCFD in the accounting and finance industries. The aim is to assess the premise that ML has a beneficial impact. The data shown in Table 6.7 demonstrate a significant degree of consensus among participants, with an average rating of 4.56. This indicates the crucial importance of ML in detecting fraud. The data highlight the capacity of ML to independently acquire knowledge from previous events, accurately forecast future events and handle substantial transaction volumes without human involvement. The results of the chi-square test in Table 6.8 provide further validation for these findings, since they show significant statistical values for all questions. This suggests that ML is an important factor in improving CCFD. As a result, we can reject the null hypothesis (*Ho*) in favour of the alternative hypothesis (*H1*).

Similarly, a study has shown the influence of blockchain technology on fraud detection in CCFD, with the premise that blockchain has a favourable effect on fraud detection. The descriptive statistics shown in Table 6.9 provide compelling evidence for the positive impact of blockchain technology on enhancing security and transparency in data management. This view is credible because of the weighted mean rating of 4.46. Questionnaire respondents acknowledge blockchain technology's ability to create decentralised platforms, secure data transfers and immutable records. Furthermore, they emphasise the need for smart contracts and ML to efficiently automate the detection of fraudulent activity. The chi-square test findings shown in Table 6.10 provide substantial *p*-values, further proving that blockchain greatly improves CCFD. Therefore, we invalidate the null hypothesis (*Ho*) and validate the alternative hypothesis (*H2*), thereby validating the beneficial influence of blockchain on fraud detection in the accounting and financial industries.

Furthermore, the study delves into the nexus between fuzzy logic and CCFD, indicating that fuzzy logic enhances fraud detection. According to Table 6.11, fuzzy logic is a vital tool at dealing with cognitive ambiguity and imprecision in financial data, which makes it easier to spot fraudulent actions. The study highlights the effectiveness of genetic algorithms in detecting financial statement fraud and merging fuzzy logic with ANN in identifying fraudulent transactions. The statistically significant values provided by the chi-square test (Table 6.12) provide additional evidence that fuzzy logic is crucial in several facets of fraud detection. As a result, we can say that fuzzy logic positively affects CCFD in the accounting and financial sector, rejecting the null hypothesis (*Ho*) and accepting the alternative hypothesis (*H3*).

Overall, the findings indicate that AI techniques, including ML, blockchain and fuzzy logic, significantly enhance CCFD in the accounting and finance sectors. The high reliability and validity coefficients confirm the robustness of the questionnaire tool, and the strong agreement among respondents underscores the perceived effectiveness of these technologies. These insights can guide professionals in adopting advanced technologies to mitigate fraud risks and improve financial security.

The literature review reveals that various studies align with the findings of this study, which demonstrate the significant positive impact of AI techniques, including ML, blockchain and fuzzy logic, on CCFD in the accounting and finance sectors. Stojanović (2021) and Amanze and Onukwugha (2018) both emphasise the success of AI and multi-agent techniques in improving real-time fraud detection and resilience against fraud, which is corroborated by the study's high average scores and significant chi-square test results for AI's effectiveness in recognising patterns and predicting fraud. In the same way, Bin Sulaiman et al. (2022) talk about how blockchain technology could help improve data security. This is similar to what the study found, which is that blockchain helps a lot with secure fraud detection, as shown by the high agreement scores and chi-square test results. The study also agrees with previous research on ML algorithms, such as that by Somvanshi et al. (2016), Shah (2023), Jadhav and Channe (2016) and Randhawa et al. (2018). It shows that ML techniques like KNN, SVM, NB, DT, RF and TAN work well in CCFD, as shown by their strong agreement and high recall values. The study's results are in line with those of Prasad et al. (2023) and Sahithi et al. (2022), which looked at ensemble approaches and weighted average ensemble methods. These methods show that fraud detection is more accurate and effective.

Additionally, Ashraf et al. (2022) provide a comparative analysis supporting the diverse application of ML techniques in fraud detection, which aligns with the study's validation of various ML algorithms. The study's high reliability and validity coefficients further reinforce the perceived effectiveness of these advanced technologies, guiding professionals in mitigating fraud risks and enhancing financial security.

We can offer several possible explanations for the uncovered results include the advanced capabilities of AI techniques like ML, blockchain and fuzzy logic in analysing large datasets and detecting complex patterns, leading to more accurate fraud detection. The high quality and volume of data used for training these models likely enhanced their performance. Additionally, the integration of multiple AI methods might have created a synergistic effect, improving overall effectiveness. The strong agreement among respondents could be attributed to their expertise and familiarity with these technologies. Furthermore, the rigorous research design ensured robust data collection, and the growing adoption of AI in the financial sector, driven by regulatory and security needs, likely influenced the positive perceptions and outcomes observed in the study.

7. Conclusion and Final Marks

This study delves into the practical implementation of AI methodologies to tackle CCFD within the accounting and finance domains. It evaluates the efficacy of ML, blockchain and fuzzy logic in identifying and preventing fraudulent activities, providing valuable insights for industry professionals. While acknowledging AI's significant contributions, the research focuses on its application specifically in CCFD, employing interviews and cross-country questionnaires.

The study's novelty lies in its pursuit of identifying the most efficient mechanism for CCFD and assessing its global applicability. It understates the importance of these methodologies in combating CCF advocating for their wider adoption, particularly emphasising the underutilisation of fuzzy logic. The empirical phase of the study aimed to validate the theoretical findings by surveying stakeholders and formulating hypotheses to gauge the impact of ML, blockchain and fuzzy logic on CCFD. Through a standardised questionnaire distributed to 403 respondents, the study conducted statistical analyses, including chi-square tests using SPSS, to evaluate these hypotheses. The sample, drawn from a variety of countries, provided rich data with notable completion rates from Egypt and Russia. The study determined a sample size of 384 using random sampling, but the 403 responses received exceeded that. An analysis of respondents' characteristics, such as occupation and educational level, offered insights into their profiles. Reliability and validity tests, including Cronbach's alpha coefficient, confirmed the accuracy and consistency of the questionnaire data.

Descriptive statistics and chi-square tests showed high mean scores and significant values, demonstrating the positive impact of ML, blockchain and fuzzy logic on CCFD. Overall, this study furnishes valuable insights into the efficacy of AI techniques in combating CCF, offering actionable implications for stakeholders in the accounting and finance sectors.

References

Abd El Naby, A., Hemdan, E. E. D., & El-Sayed, A. (2021, July). Deep learning approach for credit card fraud detection. In *2021 International conference on electronic engineering (ICEEM)* (pp. 1–5). IEEE. https://ieeexplore.ieee.org/abstract/document/9480639

Al, B. A. M. A. R. (2024). Analyzing the impact of data visualization applications for diagnosing the health conditions through hesitant fuzzy-based hybrid medical expert system. *Ain Shams Engineering Journal*, *15*(5), 102705.

Alam, P., Booth, D., Lee, K., & Thordarson, T. (2000). The use of fuzzy clustering algorithm and self-organizing neural networks for identifying potentially failing banks: An experimental study. *Expert Systems with Applications*, *18*(3), 185–199. https://www.sciencedirect.com/science/article/abs/pii/S0957417499000615

Amanze, B. C., & Onukwugha, C. G. (2018). Credit card fraud detection system in Nigeria banks using adaptive data mining and intelligent agents: A review. *International Journal of Scientific and Technology Research*, *7*(7).

Ammar, S., Wright, R., & Selden, S. (2000). Ranking state financial management: A multilevel fuzzy rule-based system. *Decision Sciences*, *31*(2), 449–481.

Asha, R. B., & Suresh Kumar, K. R. (2021). Credit card fraud detection using artificial neural network. *Global Transitions Proceedings*, *2*(1), 35–41. https://www.sciencedirect.com/science/article/pii/S2666285X21000066

Ashraf, M., Abourezka, M. A., & Maghraby, F. A. (2022). A comparative analysis of credit card fraud detection using machine learning and deep learning techniques. In *Digital transformation technology: Proceedings of ITAF 2020* (pp. 267–282). Springer. https://link.springer.com/chapter/10.1007/978-981-16-2275-5_16

Askari, S. M. S., & Hussain, M. A. (2020). IFDTC4. 5: Intuitionistic fuzzy logic-based decision tree for E-transactional fraud detection. *Journal of Information Security and Applications*, *52*, 102469. https://www.sciencedirect.com/science/article/abs/pii/S2214212619307318

Association of Certified Fraud Examiners [ACFE]. (2020). *Report to the Nations*. https://acfepublic.s3-us-west-2.amazonaws.com/2020-Report-to-the-Nations.pdf

Awan, S., Li, F., Luo, B., & Liu, M. (2019, November). Poster: A reliable and accountable privacy-preserving federated learning framework using the blockchain. In *Proceedings of the 2019 ACM SIGSAC conference on computer and communications security* (pp. 2561–2563). https://dl.acm.org/doi/abs/10.1145/3319535.3363256

Balagolla, E. M. S. W., Fernando, W. P. C., Rathnayake, R. M. N. S., Wijesekera, M. J. M. R. P., Senarathne, A. N., & Abeywardhana, K. Y. (2021, April). Credit card fraud prevention using blockchain. In *2021 6th International conference for convergence in technology (I2CT)* (pp. 1–8). IEEE. https://ieeexplore.ieee.org/abstract/document/9418192

Bansal, A., & Garg, H. (2021). An efficient techniques for fraudulent detection in credit card dataset: A comprehensive study. *IOP Conference Series: Materials Science and Engineering*, *1116*(1). IOP Publishing. https://iopscience.iop.org/article/10.1088/1757-899X/1116/1/012181/meta

Bao, Y., Hilary, G., & Ke, B. (2022). Artificial intelligence and fraud detection. *Innovative Technology at the Interface of Finance and Operations*, *I*, 223–247. https://link.springer.com/chapter/10.1007/978-3-030-75729-8_8

Behera, T. K., & Panigrahi, S. (2017). Credit card fraud detection using a neuro-fuzzy expert system. In *Computational intelligence in data mining: Proceedings of the international conference on CIDM, 10–11 December 2016* (pp. 835–843). Springer. https://link.springer.com/chapter/10.1007/978-981-10-3874-7_79

Beju, D. G., & Făt, C. M. (2023). Frauds in banking system: Frauds with cards and their associated services. In *Economic and financial crime, sustainability and good governance* (pp. 31–52). Springer International Publishing.

Bello, H. O., Idemudia, C., & Iyelolu, T. V. (2024). Integrating machine learning and blockchain: Conceptual frameworks for real-time fraud detection and prevention. *World Journal of Advanced Research and Reviews, 23*(1), 056–068.

Bello, O. A., Ogundipe, A., Mohammed, D., Adebola, F., & Alonge, O. A. (2023). AI-driven approaches for real-time fraud detection in US financial transactions: Challenges and opportunities. *European Journal of Computer Science and Information Technology, 11*(6), 84–102.

Besuspariene, E., & Niskanen, V. A. (2023). Fuzzy model for detection of fraudulent financial statements: A case study of Lithuanian micro and small enterprises. *European Journal of Business Science and Technology, 9*(2), 165–185.

Bin Sulaiman, R., Schetinin, V., & Sant, P. (2022). Review of machine learning approach on credit card fraud detection. *Human-Centric Intelligent Systems, 2*(1–2), 55–68. https://link.springer.com/article/10.1007/s44230-022-00004-0

Bragg, S. M. (2019). *Fraud examination: Prevention, detection, and investigation* (2nd ed.). AccountingTools, Inc.

Brender, N., & Gauthier, M. (2018). Impacts de la Blockchain sur le métier d'auditeur. *Expert Focus, 92*(6/7), 444–448.

Brender, N., Gauthier, M., Morin, J. H., & Salihi, A. (2018). The potential impact of blockchain technology on audit practice. *Journal of Strategic Innovation and Sustainability, 14*(2). https://doi.org/10.33423/jsis.v14i2.1370

Chatterjee, P., Das, D., & Rawat, D. (2023). Securing financial transactions: Exploring the role of federated learning and blockchain in credit card fraud detection. *Authorea Preprints*. https://www.techrxiv.org/doi/full/10.36227/techrxiv.22683403.v1

Dai, J., & Vasarhelyi, M. A. (2017). Toward blockchain-based accounting and assurance. *Journal of Information Systems, 31*(3), 5–21. https://publications.aaahq.org/jis/article-abstract/31/3/5/1105/Toward-Blockchain-Based-Accounting-and-Assurance

Darwish, S. M. (2020). A bio-inspired credit card fraud detection model based on user behavior analysis suitable for business management in electronic banking. *Journal of Ambient Intelligence and Humanized Computing, 11*(11), 4873–4887.

Dayyabu, Y. Y., Arumugam, D., & Balasingam, S. (2023). The application of artificial intelligence techniques in credit card fraud detection: A quantitative study. *E3S Web of Conferences, 389*, 07023. EDP Sciences. https://www.e3s-conferences.org/articles/e3sconf/abs/2023/26/e3sconf_uesf2023_07023/e3sconf_uesf2023_07023.html

Dubois, D., Hüllermeier, E., & Prade, H. (2006). A systematic approach to the assessment of fuzzy association rules. *Data Mining and Knowledge Discovery, 13*, 167–192. https://link.springer.com/article/10.1007/s10618-005-0032-4

Faccia, A., & Mosteanu, N. R. (2019). Accounting and blockchain technology: From double-entry to triple-entry. *Business and Management Review, 10*(2), 108–116. https://cberuk.com/cdn/conference_proceedings/2019-07-12-18-10-20-PM.pdf

Fan, M., Zhang, Z., Li, Z., Sun, G., Yu, H., & Guizani, M. (2023). Blockchain-based decentralized and lightweight anonymous authentication for federated learning. In *IEEE transactions on vehicular technology*. https://ieeexplore.ieee.org/abstract/document/10097460

Hawamdeh, S. (2007). *Creating collaborative advantage through knowledge and innovation* (Vol. 5). World Scientific. https://doi.org/10.1142/6337

Herrera-Viedma, E., Palomares, I., Li, C. C., Cabrerizo, F. J., Dong, Y., Chiclana, F., & Herrera, F. (2020). Revisiting fuzzy and linguistic decision making: Scenarios and challenges for making wiser decisions in a better way. *IEEE Transactions on Systems, Man, and Cybernetics: Systems, 51*(1), 191–208. https://ieeexplore.ieee.org/abstract/document/9306916

Hoogs, B., Kiehl, T., Lacomb, C., & Senturk, D. (2007). A genetic algorithm approach to detecting temporal patterns indicative of financial statement fraud. *Intelligent Systems in Accounting, Finance and Management: International Journal, 15*(1–2), 41–56.

Ilori, O., Nwosu, N. T., & Naiho, H. N. N. (2024). Advanced data analytics in internal audits: A conceptual framework for comprehensive risk assessment and fraud detection. *Finance & Accounting Research Journal, 6*(6), 931–952.

Imeni, M. (2020). Fuzzy logic in accounting and auditing. *Journal of Fuzzy Extension and Applications, 1*(1), 66–72.

Issa, H., Sun, T., & Vasarhelyi, M. A. (2016). Research ideas for artificial intelligence in auditing: The formalization of audit and workforce supplementation. *Journal of Emerging Technologies in Accounting, 13*(2), 1–20. https://publications.aaahq.org/jeta/article-abstract/13/2/1/9209/Research-Ideas-for-Artificial-Intelligence-in

Jadhav, S. D., & Channe, H. P. (2016). Comparative study of K-NN, naive Bayes and decision tree classification techniques. *International Journal of Science and Research, 5*(1), 1842–1845.

Karthik, V. S. S., Mishra, A., & Reddy, U. S. (2022). Credit card fraud detection by modelling behaviour pattern using hybrid ensemble model. *Arabian Journal for Science and Engineering, 47*(2), 1987–1997. https://link.springer.com/article/10.1007/s13369-021-06147-9

Karthika, J., & Senthilselvi, A. (2023). Smart credit card fraud detection system based on dilated convolutional neural network with sampling technique. *Multimedia Tools and Applications, 82*(20), 31691–31708.

Kherbouche, M., Pisoni, G., & Molnár, B. (2022). Model to program and blockchain approaches for business processes and workflows in finance. *Applied System Innovation, 5*(1), 10. https://www.mdpi.com/2571-5577/5/1/10

Lau, H. C. W., Wong, T. T., & Pun, K. F. (1999). Neural-fuzzy modeling of plastic injection molding machine for intelligent control. *Expert Systems with Applications, 17*(1), 33–43. https://www.sciencedirect.com/science/article/abs/pii/S0957417499000196

Lenard, M. J., & Alam, P. (2004). The use of fuzzy logic and expert reasoning for knowledge management and discovery of financial reporting fraud. In *Organizational data mining: Leveraging enterprise data resources for optimal performance* (pp. 230–246). IGI Global. https://www.igi-global.com/chapter/organizational-data-mining/27919

Lenard, M. J., Alam, P., & Booth, D. (2000). An analysis of fuzzy clustering and a hybrid model for the auditor's going concern assessment. *Decision Sciences, 31*(4), 861–884.

Li, Y., Chen, C., Liu, N., Huang, H., Zheng, Z., & Yan, Q. (2020). A blockchain-based decentralized federated learning framework with committee consensus. *IEEE Network*, *35*(1), 234–241. https://ieeexplore.ieee.org/abstract/document/9293091

Lim, K. S., Lee, L. H., & Sim, Y. W. (2021). A review of machine learning algorithms for fraud detection in credit card transaction. *International Journal of Computer Science & Network Security*, *21*(9), 31–40. https://koreascience.kr/article/JAKO202129436693259.page

Liu, L., Li, Y., & Jiang, T. (2023). Optimal strategies for financing a three-level supply chain through blockchain platform finance. *International Journal of Production Research*, *61*(11), 3564–3581.

Liu, M., Wu, K., & Xu, J. J. (2019). How will blockchain technology impact auditing and accounting: Permissionless versus permissioned blockchain. *Current Issues in Auditing*, *13*(2), A19–A29.

Maharjan, A., & Chuda, P. (2019). Comparative analysis of algorithms for credit card fraud detection. In *KEC conference*. https://old.kecnepal.com/wp-content/uploads/2020/01/Paper_36.pdf

Mustyala, A. (2023). Leveraging blockchain for fraud risk reduction in Fintech: Infrastructure setup and migration strategies. *EPH-International Journal of Science and Engineering*, *9*(2), 1–10.

Naik, H., & Kanikar, P. (2019). Credit card fraud detection based on machine learning algorithms. *International Journal of Computer Applications*, *182*(44), 8–12.

Nolan, J. R. (1998). An expert fuzzy classification system for supporting the grading of student writing samples. *Expert Systems with Applications*, *15*(1), 59–68. https://www.sciencedirect.com/science/article/abs/pii/S0957417498000116

Pathak, J., Vidyarthi, N., & Summers, S. L. (2005). A fuzzy-based algorithm for auditors to detect elements of fraud in settled insurance claims. *Managerial Auditing Journal*, *20*(6), 632–644. https://www.emerald.com/insight/content/doi/10.1108/02686900510606119/full/html

Prasad, P. Y., Chowdarv, A. S., Bavitha, C., Mounisha, E., & Reethika, C. (2023, April). A comparison study of fraud detection in usage of credit cards using machine learning. In *2023 7th International conference on trends in electronics and informatics (ICOEI)* (pp. 1204–1209). IEEE. https://ieeexplore.ieee.org/abstract/document/10125838

PricewaterhouseCoopers. (2020). *PwC's Global Economic Crime and Fraud Survey 2020*. https://www.pwc.com/ua/en/survey/2020/economic-crime-survey.html

Qu, Y., Uddin, M. P., Gan, C., Xiang, Y., Gao, L., & Yearwood, J. (2022). Blockchain-enabled federated learning: A survey. *ACM Computing Surveys*, *55*(4), 1–35. https://dl.acm.org/doi/abs/10.1145/3524104

Randhawa, K., Loo, C. K., Seera, M., Lim, C. P., & Nandi, A. K. (2018). Credit card fraud detection using AdaBoost and majority voting. *IEEE Access*, *6*, 14277–14284. https://ieeexplore.ieee.org/abstract/document/8292883

Razooqi, T., Khurana, P., Raahemifar, K., & Abhari, A. (2016, April). Credit card fraud detection using fuzzy logic and neural network. In *Proceedings of the 19th communications & networking symposium* (pp. 1–5).

Sadgali, I., Sael, N., & Benabbou, F. (2019). Performance of machine learning techniques in the detection of financial frauds. *Procedia Computer Science*, *148*, 45–54.

Saeed, S. K. (2019). A fraud-detection fuzzy logic based system for the Sudanese financial sector. *Journal of Engineering and Computer Science*, *20*(1), 17–30.

Sahithi, G. L., Roshmi, V., Sameera, Y. V., & Pradeepini, G. (2022, April). Credit card fraud detection using ensemble methods in machine learning. In *2022 6th International conference on trends in electronics and informatics (ICOEI)* (pp. 1237–1241). IEEE. https://ieeexplore.ieee.org/document/9776955

Sam, U., Moses, G., & Olajide, T. (2023). *Credit card fraud detection using machine learning algorithms*. https://www.researchgate.net/publication/376482000_Credit_Card_Fraud_Detection_Using_Machine_Learning_Algorithms

Shah, R. (2023). *Introduction to k-nearest neighbors (kNN) algorithm*. https://ai.plainenglish.io/introduction-to-knearest-neighbors-knn-algorithm-e8617a448fa8. Accessed on November 20, 2023.

Shayan, M., Fung, C., Yoon, C. J., & Beschastnikh, I. (2020). Biscotti: A blockchain system for private and secure federated learning. *IEEE Transactions on Parallel and Distributed Systems*, *32*(7), 1513–1525. https://ieeexplore.ieee.org/abstract/document/9292450

Somvanshi, M., Chavan, P., Tambade, S., & Shinde, S. V. (2016, August). A review of machine learning techniques using decision tree and support vector machine. In *2016 International conference on computing communication control and automation (ICCUBEA)* (pp. 1–7). IEEE. https://ieeexplore.ieee.org/abstract/document/7860040

Stojanović, B., Božić, J., Hofer-Schmitz, K., Nahrgang, K., Weber, A., Badii, A., Sundaram, M., Jordan, E., & Runevic, J. (2021). Follow the trail: Machine learning for fraud detection in Fintech applications. *Sensors*, *21*(5), 1594. https://doi.org/10.3390/s21051594

Sultana, S., & Bertino, E. (2012). A comprehensive model for provenance. In *Advances in conceptual modeling: ER 2012 workshops CMS, ECDM-NoCoDA, MoDIC, MORE-BI, RIGiM, SeCoGIS, WISM, Florence, Italy, October 15-18, 2012. Proceedings 31* (pp. 121–130). Springer. https://link.springer.com/chapter/10.1007/978-3-642-33999-8_15

Uthayakumar, J., Metawa, N., Shankar, K., & Lakshmanaprabu, S. K. (2020). Intelligent hybrid model for financial crisis prediction using machine learning techniques. *Information Systems and E-Business Management*, *18*, 617–645. https://link.springer.com/article/10.1007/s10257-018-0388-9

Yazdinejad, A., Dehghantanha, A., Parizi, R. M., Hammoudeh, M., Karimipour, H., & Srivastava, G. (2022). Block hunter: Federated learning for cyber threat hunting in blockchain-based IIoT networks. *IEEE Transactions on Industrial Informatics*, *18*(11), 8356–8366. https://ieeexplore.ieee.org/abstract/document/9759988

Yee, O. S., Sagadevan, S., & Malim, N. H. A. H. (2018). Credit card fraud detection using machine learning as data mining technique. *Journal of Telecommunication, Electronic and Computer Engineering*, *10*(1–4), 23–27. https://jtec.utem.edu.my/jtec/article/view/3571

Zhao, J., Simmhan, Y., & Prasanna, V. (2012). On presenting apropos provenance for situation awareness and data forensics. In *Provenance and annotation of data and processes: 4th international provenance and annotation workshop, IPAW 2012, Santa Barbara, CA, USA, June 19–21, 2012, revised selected papers 4* (pp. 250–253). Springer. https://link.springer.com/chapter/10.1007/978-3-642-34222-6_30

Chapter 7

Determinants of Financial Inclusion in Nigeria: The Monetary Policy and Banking Sector Factors

Peterson K. Ozili

Central Bank of Nigeria, Nigeria

Abstract

This study investigates the determinants of financial inclusion in Nigeria. The study extends the empirical debate on the determinants of financial inclusion by focusing on the monetary policy and banking sector factors that influence the level of financial inclusion in Nigeria. The study employs the two-stage least squares regression method to estimate the determinants of financial inclusion in Nigeria during the 2007–2021 period. The results show that the central bank monetary policy rate, the savings deposit rate and the loan to deposit ratio of banks are significant determinants of financial inclusion in Nigeria. Specifically, an increase in the central bank interest rate decreases the level of financial inclusion, an increase in the savings deposit rate increases the level of financial inclusion and an increase in the loan-to-deposit ratio decreases the level of financial inclusion. These determinants are robust to alternative estimation using the quantile regression method. There is further evidence that the interbank lending rate, inflation rate and the nominal interest rate are also determinants of financial inclusion in Nigeria based on the two-stage least squares estimation.

Keywords: Financial inclusion; determinants; monetary policy; index; inflation; central bank; Nigeria; interest rate; savings; interbank lending

1. Introduction

Financial inclusion is a process that brings everyone into the formal financial system so that everyone can have access to available formal financial services

From Digital Disruption to Dominance, 163–186

Published under exclusive licence by Emerald Publishing Limited
doi:10.1108/978-1-83549-608-420251007

which they can use to improve their welfare (Barajas et al., 2020; Ozili, 2024). A World Bank 2021 Global Findex report shows that 1.7 billion people are unbanked or excluded from the formal financial system, and a large majority of these people are in developing countries (Demirgüç-Kunt et al., 2022). This has led policymakers in developing countries to embrace financial inclusion as a top policy priority.

Despite financial inclusion being a top priority in developing countries, there are heated debates about the determinants of financial inclusion, with many studies suggesting that the determinants are mostly microeconomic factors and demand-side factors (Barik & Lenka, 2022; Fahmy & Ghoneim, 2023; Giday, 2023). Others argue that the determinants are mostly macroeconomic and supply side factors (Gebrehiwot & Makina, 2019; Markose et al., 2022; Matsebula & Sheefeni, 2022). The different perspectives or debates arise due to the multi-dimensional nature of financial inclusion and the unique challenges each country face on the path to financial inclusion (Fernández-Olit et al., 2020; Ozili, 2021b; Prabhakar, 2019).

Majority of the single country studies in the literature suggest that most of the determinants of financial inclusion are country specific. This is also true for Nigeria as existing studies suggest that financial literacy, gender, income, age, internet usage, access to credit and the level of poverty are some determinants of financial inclusion in Nigeria (see Adetunji & David-West, 2019; David et al., 2018; Ene et al., 2019; Eze & Markjackson, 2020; Ozili, 2021a). Despite this evidence documented in the literature, the current reality of financial inclusion in Nigeria remains very challenging.

Nigeria's level of banked-based financial inclusion is still very low despite the efforts of the government to accelerate financial inclusion since 2012 when the central bank issued the National Financial Inclusion Strategy and the revised version of the Strategy in 2018. In 2023, Nigeria recorded a 52% level of bank-based financial inclusion according to the 2023 Access to Finance EFInA report. This means that only 52% of Nigerians have a formal bank account. This indicates that only 110.9 million people have a bank account in Nigeria, and 102.1 million people are unbanked out of a population of 213 million people. This huge number of unbanked people is a cause for serious concern for the monetary authority in Nigeria, and it has led the monetary authority to announce that it would look inwards and undertake a critical evaluation of the existing monetary policy framework and the structural factors in the banking sector to determine which aspects of the current monetary policy framework and banking sector factors are beneficial and detrimental to financial inclusion in Nigeria.

This calls for the need to re-examine the determinants of financial inclusion in Nigeria with a particular focus on the monetary policy factors and the banking sector factors that affect the level of financial inclusion in Nigeria. Although existing studies have examined some determinants of financial inclusion in Nigeria (David et al., 2018; Ene et al., 2019; Eze & Markjackson, 2020), such studies did not extensively examine the monetary policy factors and banking sector factors that determine the level of financial inclusion in Nigeria. Existing studies did not consider the role of central bank interest rate or the interbank lending rate in influencing the level of financial inclusion in Nigeria, considering the fact that changes in interest rate can make financial services become more expensive and can discourage unbanked Nigerians from joining the formal financial sector.

This study contributes to the financial inclusion determinants literature (e.g. Fernández-Olit et al., 2020; Gebrehiwot & Makina, 2019; Markose et al., 2022; Matsebula & Sheefeni, 2022; Ozili, 2021b; Prabhakar, 2019). It extends the literature by focusing on the monetary policy factors that may influence the level of financial inclusion and to determine the effect in the context of a developing country. The present study also contributes to the literature that examines the banking factors that aid or inhibit progress towards financial inclusion. The present study shows that the savings deposit rate, the loan to deposit ratio and the interbank lending rate are crucial banking sector factors affecting the level of financial inclusion in Nigeria. This study is the first to document this evidence in the context of Nigeria. The present study also contributes to the methodological literature on financial inclusion. The present study contributes to the methodological literature by employing sophisticated methods such as the quantile regression method to ensure that the results are robust and that the insights gained from the analysis are reliable.

The rest of the study is organised as follows: Section 2 presents the contextual framework and literature review. Section 3 presents the research methodology. Section 4 presents the empirical results while the conclusion of the study is reported in Section 5.

2. Contextual Framework and Literature Review

2.1 Contextual Framework

The Central Bank of Nigeria (CBN) is the monetary authority in Nigeria, and it is also responsible for increasing the level of financial inclusion in Nigeria. The CBN uses the agent banking network, microfinance institutions, bank branch expansion, automated teller machines (ATMs), mobile money operators, payment service banks, payment service providers, super agents and bank verification number (BVN) registration to promote financial inclusion in Nigeria (NFIS, 2018). CBN has made some progress in increasing financial inclusion in Nigeria. The COVID-19 pandemic also accelerated digital financial inclusion in Nigeria as many consumers and businesses had to shift from cash payments to digital payments which led to a spike in digital financial inclusion in Nigeria (Wezel and Ree, 2023). The 2021 Global Findex data confirm the growing trend in financial inclusion and digital payments in Nigeria.[1] The Global Findex data in Fig. 7.1 show that account ownership of any type increased to 45% in 2021 from 30% in 2011. Access to formal credit increased to 6% in 2021 from 2% in 2011. The use of digital payments declined to 34% in 2021 from 37% in 2011. Meanwhile, data

[1]The World Bank 2021 Global Findex data reports financial inclusion indicators that are comparable across countries.

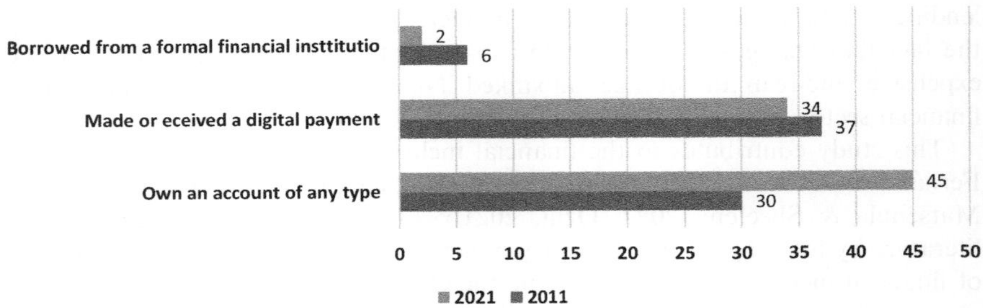

Fig. 7.1. Global Findex Data (Nigeria). *Source:* World Bank Global Findex 2021.

from EFInA report a higher level of financial inclusion that is significantly different from the data reported in the World Bank's Global Findex data, and the difference is due to differences in the definition of financial inclusion. EFInA data report a 74% level of formal inclusion in 2023 (see Fig. 7.2), indicating that 165.6 million people are formally included while 58.2 million people are formally excluded out of a population of 213.4 million people. The increase to 74% in 2023 from 56% in 2020 is due to the marginal growth in the banked population and major gains in the adoption of formal non-bank digital payment channels. Of the 74% level of formal inclusion, 52% are formally banked, 12% own a non-bank account and 10% are informally included. In terms of demographics (see Fig. 7.3), people who are formally employed (99%), informally employed (68%), business owners (56%), educated (68%), rich (71%), live in urban areas (64%) and men (58) have a higher level of financial inclusion compared to adults who are women (47%), live in rural areas (38%), poor (27%), uneducated (16%) and farmers (36%). In terms of regional spread, the Northern states recorded high levels of financial exclusion with the North-East states having exclusion levels that are

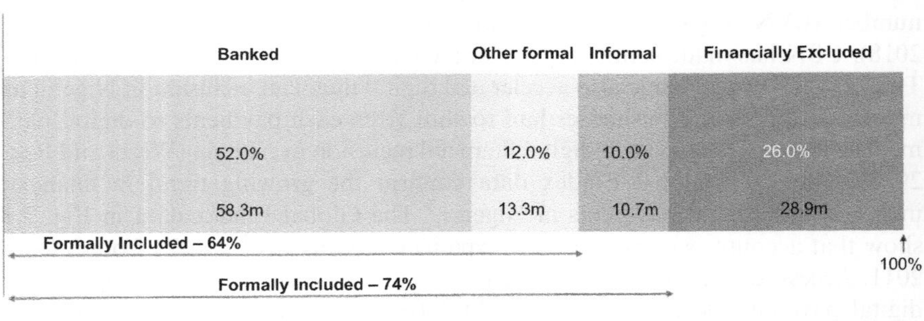

Fig. 7.2. 2023 Level of Financial Inclusion. *Source:* EFInA Access to Financial Services in Nigeria 2023.

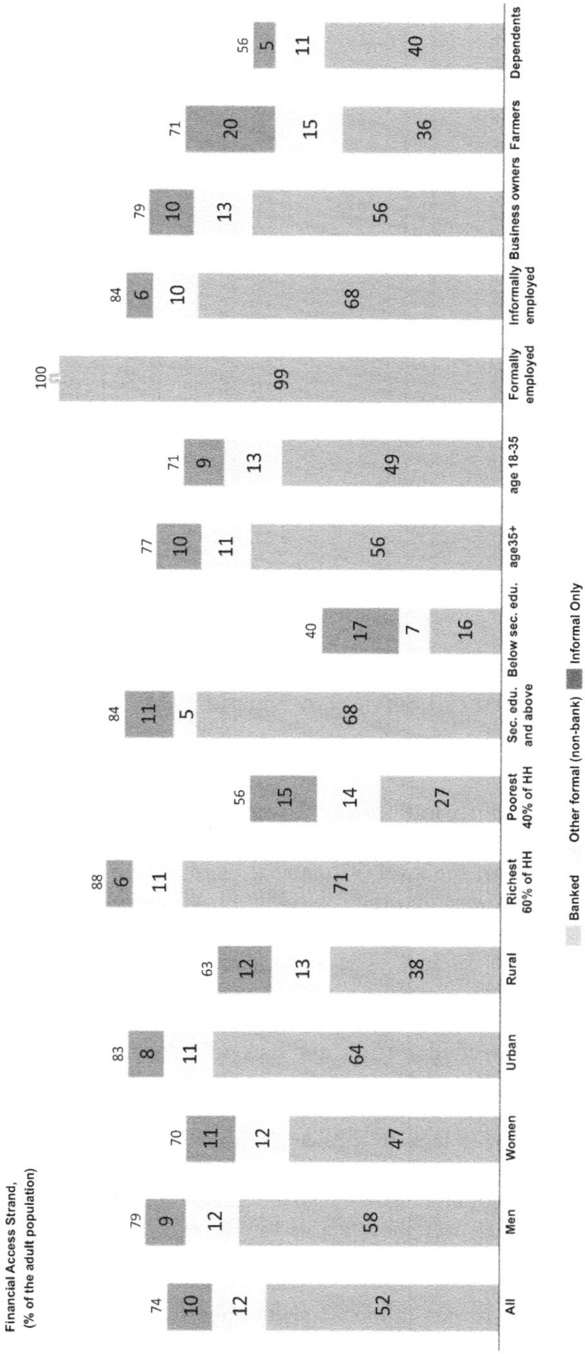

Fig. 7.3. Demographic Characteristics. *Source:* EFinA Access to Financial Services in Nigeria 2023.

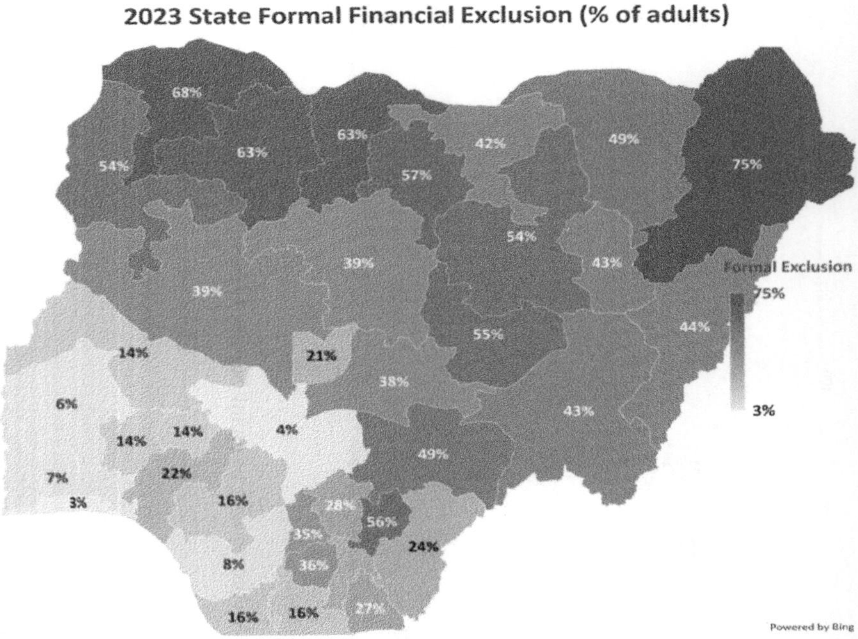

Fig. 7.4. Financial Inclusion Mapping Across Nigeria. *Source:* EFinA Access to Financial Services in Nigeria 2023.

above the national average, particularly in Borno state where the level of financial exclusion is 75% as shown in Fig. 7.4.

Despite the progress made so far, the level of financial inclusion in Nigeria is still low compared to the global average and the sub-Saharan African average, as shown in Fig. 7.5. Many factors are contributing to the low level of financial inclusion in Nigeria according to EFInA. The most cited factors are little/insufficient funds, followed by irregular income, high cost of financial services, long distance to a financial institution and limited access to financial access points especially in rural areas. The less cited factors are lack of adequate support infrastructure such as lack of internet connectivity, poor access to roads, lack of identity and poor electricity infrastructure while for communities with internet and electricity access, the challenge is lack of mobile devices.[2] For rural households that have mobile phones, the major challenge is often language barrier when mobile applications are configured in English language. For those who understand English language, the barrier they face is low financial literacy and

[2]Data from 2020 A2F shows that ownership of mobile phones (mostly feature phones) amongst the excluded was about 71%.

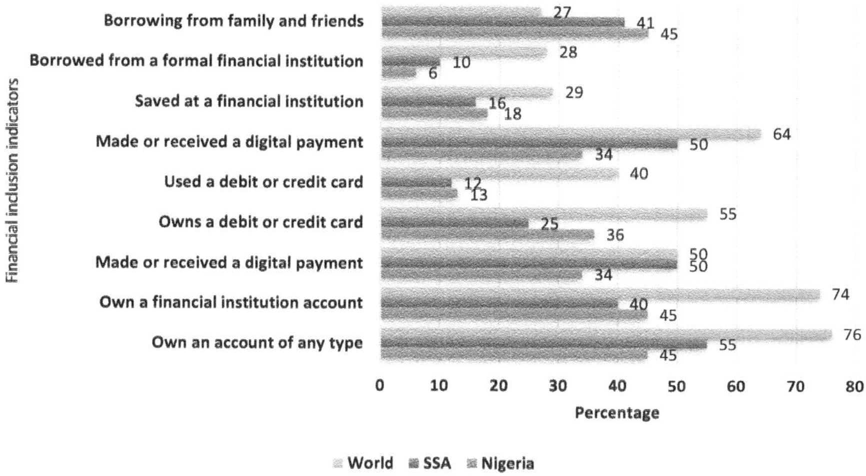

Fig. 7.5. Financial Inclusion in Nigeria, Sub-Saharan Africa and the World. *Source:* World Bank Global Findex 2021.

little understanding of mobile financial apps. For individuals who would like to open formal accounts, one hurdle they face is the difficulty of obtaining a BVN/NIN identification number due to not having sufficient documentation.[3] Given these challenges, the central bank continues to increase its monetary policy interest rate to combat high inflation. Increasing interest rate in times of high inflation can be detrimental to bank-led financial inclusion because it can decrease the level of financial inclusion in Nigeria. Therefore, it is important to understand and investigate how certain monetary policy actions of the central bank and bank-specific factors hinder or accelerate progress towards financial inclusion in Nigeria.

2.2 Literature Review

The literature categorises the determinants of financial inclusion into the demand side determinants and the supply side determinants of financial inclusion. The demand side determinants include age, education level, income, race, gender, marital status, etc. (see, for example, Barik & Lenka, 2022; Fahmy & Ghoneim, 2023; Giday, 2023). The supply side determinants include bank branches, ATMs, mobile money services, bank account ownership, etc. (see, for example, Adil & Jalil, 2020; Barik & Lenka, 2022; Markose et al., 2022). Financial inclusion determinants may also be classified into the micro-determinants and

[3]BVN – Bank verification number; NIN – National Identification Number.

macro-determinants of financial inclusion. The micro-determinants of financial inclusion include internet usage, mobile phone ownership, digital literacy, informal finance, etc. (see, for example, Ezzahid & Elouaourti, 2021; Ghosh & Vinod, 2017; Tinta et al., 2022). The macro-determinants of financial inclusion include inflation, monetary policy, economic growth, financial development, etc. (see, for example, Dabla-Norris et al., 2021; Gebrehiwot & Makina, 2019; Vo et al., 2019). The present study is positioned within the literature that examines the supply-side determinants and the macro-determinants of financial inclusion.

The literature has extensively examined the effect of financial inclusion on monetary policy, but very little research has been done on the effect of monetary policy on financial inclusion. For instance, Lapukeni (2015) examines the effect of financial inclusion on inflation. The author used inflation as a measure of monetary policy effectiveness. The author used granger causality tests and found some causality between financial inclusion and inflation. Jungo et al. (2022) examined the impact of financial inclusion on monetary policy in Sub-Saharan Africa (SSA) countries and in Latin America and the Caribbean (LAC) countries. They found that monetary policy accelerates financial inclusion in both regions. They also found that there is reverse causality between financial inclusion and monetary policy in both SSA and LAC countries. They further found that financial inclusion increases the effectiveness of monetary policy in SSA countries while financial inclusion improves the efficiency of monetary policy in LAC countries. Lenka and Bairwa (2016) examined the impact of financial inclusion on monetary policy (measured in terms of inflation) in the South Asian Association for Regional Cooperation (SAARC) countries from 2004 to 2013. The authors used principal component analysis (PCA) to construct a financial inclusion Index, and found that financial inclusion, exchange rate and interest rate have a negative effect on inflation in SAARC countries. Mbutor and Uba (2013) examined the impact of financial inclusion on monetary policy in Nigeria. They argue that higher financial inclusion would improve the effectiveness of monetary policy through the opening of more bank branches. However, they found a result that did not support their argument. They found a negative relationship between financial inclusion and monetary policy. Ait Lahcen and Gomis-Porqueras (2021) proposed a monetary model with endogenous credit market participation to study the effect of financial inclusion on inequality and welfare. They found that monetary policy has distributional consequences for financial inclusion and that a direct transfer to bank account holders will yield the highest welfare benefits for credit market participants. Anarfo et al. (2019) assessed the relationship between monetary policy and financial inclusion in 48 sub-Saharan African economies from 1990 to 2014. They found a bi-causal relationship between monetary policy and financial inclusion, implying that monetary policy affects financial inclusion, and financial inclusion is also influenced by monetary policy.

Some studies have emerged focusing on Nigeria. A substantial part of this literature focuses on the demand-side determinants of financial inclusion in Nigeria. For example, Adetunji and David-West (2019) used survey data of more than 22,000 respondents in Nigeria to investigate the determinants of financial inclusion in Nigeria. They found that financial literacy is a positive determinant of financial inclusion because financial literacy influences people's savings patterns with formal and informal financial institutions. Similarly, Abdu et al. (2015) assessed the demand-side determinants of financial inclusion in Nigeria using the 2011 Global Findex dataset. They assessed the determinants from a socio-economic and demographic context and found that youthful age, better education and high income are positive determinants of financial inclusion while old age, being female and having low income are associated with financial exclusion. Ozili (2021a) also examined the determinants of financial inclusion in Nigeria using a descriptive analysis and showed that formal borrowing and savings are significant determinants of financial inclusion. Other Nigerian studies considered some monetary aggregates as determinants of financial inclusion. For example, Eze and Markjackson (2020) examined the financial inclusion determinants in Nigeria using data spanning from 2000 to 2018 and using the ordinary least square technique. They found that domestic credit to private sector, rural deposits to loans ratio and the lending interest rate have a significant positive impact on financial inclusion. David et al. (2018) examined the determinants of financial inclusion in Nigeria from 1990 to 2016 and using time series data. They included some monetary aggregate variables into their model and found that GDP per capita, broad money, credit and internet usage have a significant positive effect on financial inclusion in Nigeria. Ene et al. (2019) examined some determinants of financial inclusion in Nigeria in year 2011 and found that ATMs have an insignificant effect on financial inclusion while point-of-sale devices have a significant impact on financial inclusion in Nigeria.

While the above studies examined the determinants of financial inclusion from the demand-side factors. These studies did not extensively examine the monetary policy factors and bank-specific factors that determine the level of financial inclusion in Nigeria. Moreover, the existing studies that examine the effect of financial inclusion on monetary policy did not use the central bank interest rate or the interbank lending rate as indicators of monetary policy rather they used only the inflation rate which may be difficult for central banks to control. The present study fills these gaps in the literature by focusing on the case of Nigeria and using multiple indicators of monetary policy to identify the salient monetary policy factors alongside other bank-specific factors that drive the level of financial inclusion in Nigeria.

3. Research Methodology

3.1 The Sample

The study used Nigerian data collected from the World Bank's Global Financial Development Indicators (GFDI) and the World Development Indicators (WDI). The collected data span from 2007 to 2021 which is a 15-year period. Ten variables were used for the study (see Table 7.1 for description of the variables). The first three variables were used to develop a composite index of financial inclusion while the other seven variables are the determinants of financial inclusion for this study.

Table 7.1. Description of the Variables.

Symbol	Variable Name	Description	Source
ATT	ATMs per 100,000 adults	Number of ATMs per 100,000 adults.	GFDI
AOT	Bank accounts per 1,000 adults	Number of depositors with commercial banks per 1,000 adults.	GFDI
BRR	Bank branches per 100,000 adults	Number of commercial bank branches per 100,000 adults.	GFDI
FID	Financial inclusion index	The index is derived from the principal component analysis of the three financial inclusion variables (i.e. ATT, AOT and BRR).	Author
EFF	Bank cost to income ratio	Bank operating expenses divided by sum of net-interest and operating incomes.	GFDI
LDR	Bank credit to bank deposit ratio	Deposit money bank total credit divided by total deposits.	GFDI
INF	Inflation rate	Inflation as measured by the annual growth rate of the GDP implicit deflator.	WDI
MPR	Monetary policy rate	Central bank's reference interest rate. The rate on which all other rates are anchored.	CBN
NIR	Nominal interest rate	Interest rate that takes into account the prevailing inflation rate.	WDI
SD	Savings deposit rate	The interest rate that is paid on the deposits in savings account in a bank.	CBN
IBR	Interbank lending rate	The interest rate at which banks lend from each other overnight.	CBN

Source: World Bank and Central Bank of Nigeria Statistics.

3.2 Descriptive Statistics and Correlation

Table 7.2 shows that, on average, Nigeria had a double-digit monetary policy rate of 11.2% while the interbank lending rate is also a double-digit rate at 11.6% over the period examined. In contrast, the average annual savings deposit rate is very low at 2.9% and is too low to attract new depositors to bring their savings to the formal financial system. The average nominal interest rate is higher than the average annual inflation rate which suggests that loans will be costly for borrowers. The loan-to-deposit ratio and the efficiency ratio are high and above 50% which indicates that Nigerian banks do not give out many loans from the deposits

Table 7.2. Descriptive Statistics.

Statistic	FID	MPR	SD	NIR	INF	LDR	EFF	IBR
Mean	−0.264	11.243	2.945	15.757	8.234	72.618	78.137	11.586
Median	−0.265	12.000	3.224	16.172	9.543	71.895	61.369	11.862
Maximum	−0.252	14.000	4.129	18.866	16.342	103.355	202.041	22.954
Minimum	−0.277	6.083	1.433	11.358	0.686	53.887	51.148	4.016
Std. Dev.	0.006	2.419	0.921	1.759	3.818	16.086	47.038	4.413
Skewness	0.002	−0.795	−0.338	−0.904	−0.099	0.689	2.143	0.662
Observations	14	15	15	15	15	15	15	15

Source: Author's computation.

they receive and they are less cost efficient. In terms of the correlation among the variables, Table 7.3 shows that the MPR variable is significant and positively correlated with the FID variable. This result indicates that the monetary policy rate is positively correlated with financial inclusion in Nigeria. In contrast, the NIR and LDR variables are significant and negatively correlated with the FID variable. This result indicates that the nominal interest rate and the loan-to-deposit ratio are inversely correlated with financial inclusion in Nigeria. Meanwhile, the SD, INF, EFF and IBR variables have an insignificant correlation with the FID variable.

3.3 Model Specification, Estimation Procedure and Variable Justification

The model used to estimate the determinants of financial inclusion is similar to the model used in previous single-country studies such as Bozkurt et al. (2018), Eldomiaty et al. (2020) and Rashdan and Eissa (2020). The baseline model, in Eq. (1), estimates the financial inclusion index as a function of bank cost to income ratio, bank total credit to bank total deposit ratio, inflation rate, monetary policy rate, savings deposit rate, nominal interest rate and interbank lending rate.

$$\begin{aligned}(\mathrm{FID})_{i,t} = {} & \beta_0 + \beta_1 \mathrm{MPR}_{i,t} + \beta_2 \mathrm{SD}_{i,t} + \beta_3 \mathrm{NIR}_{i,t} + \beta_4 \mathrm{INF}_{i,t} \\ & + \beta_5 \mathrm{LDR}_{2i,t} + \beta_6 \mathrm{EFF}_{i,t} + \beta_7 \mathrm{IBR}_{i,t} + \epsilon_{i,t} \ldots\ldots\ldots \end{aligned} \quad (1)$$

FID = financial inclusion index, EFF = bank cost to income ratio, LDR = bank credit to bank deposit ratio, INF = inflation rate. MPR = monetary policy rate, NIR = nominal interest rate, SD = savings deposit rate, IBR = interbank lending rate where i, t represents country and year. $\epsilon_{i,t}$ is the error term.

The two-stage least squares method is the method used to estimate the model. The two-stage least squares regression method addresses potential endogeneity issues especially where the independent variables are correlated with the error term (Angrist & Imbens, 1995; Sheikhi et al., 2022). In an additional analysis, a robustness test was conducted using the quantile regression method which addresses outliers in the data and the potential for non-linearity with the predictor variables (Koenker, 2005). In the quantile regression estimations, the quantile was set at the 0.5 quantile (or 50th percentile). This means that 50% of the data points are less than the value of the median.

Regarding the variable justification, the financial inclusion index is the dependent variable. Many studies in the literature used a financial inclusion index due to the multi-dimensional nature of the financial inclusion indicators (Sethy, 2015; Yadav et al., 2021; Yorulmaz, 2018). INF is the inflation rate variable. The literature suggests that high inflation can make basic financial services become expensive for banked adults to afford, and it has the potential to discourage unbanked adults from joining the formal sector if basic financial services are too costly (Neaime & Gaysset, 2018). Therefore, a negative relationship between the INF and FID variables is anticipated. The EFF variable is the cost-to-income ratio of banks. It is commonly referred to as the efficiency ratio of banks. Banks with a high cost to income ratio will reduce their cost by decreasing their non-core

Table 7.3. Correlation Matrix for the Dependent and Independent Variables.

Variables	FID	MPR	SD	NIR	INF	LDR	EFF	IBR
FID	1.000							
	–							
MPR	0.546**	1.000						
	(0.04)	–						
SD	0.151	0.608**	1.000					
	(0.61)	(0.02)	–					
NIR	−0.624**	−0.296	0.206	1.000				
	(0.02)	(0.30)	(0.47)	–				
INF	0.224	−0.064	−0.097	−0.210	1.000			
	(0.44)	(0.82)	(0.73)	(0.47)	–			
LDR	−0.761***	−0.336	0.270	0.435	−0.259	1.000		
	(0.00)	(0.23)	(0.35)	(0.11)	(0.37)	–		
EFF	−0.361	−0.838***	−0.275	0.515**	0.064	0.284	1.000	
	(0.21)	(0.00)	(0.33)	(0.05)	(0.82)	(0.32)	–	
IBR	−0.069	0.482*	0.298	0.183	−0.119	0.244	−0.440	1.000
	(0.81)	(0.08)	(0.29)	(0.52)	(0.68)	(0.40)	(0.11)	–

Source: Author's computation.

Note: ***, ** and * represent statistical significance at the 1%, 5% and 10% levels.

banking activities, which includes financial inclusion activities (Demirgüç-Kunt & Klapper, 2013). The decrease in financial inclusion activities may occur through the closure of some bank branches or the withdrawal of ATM machines in some locations, all of which will decrease the level of financial inclusion. Therefore, a negative relationship between the cost-to-income ratio and the level of financial inclusion is anticipated. The LDR variable is also a potential determinant of financial inclusion. It is the loan to deposit ratio of banks. A high LDR ratio suggests that banks are extending more credit to borrowers from the deposits they receive which is beneficial for financial inclusion as it will increase access to credit. Therefore, a positive relationship is anticipated between the LDR and FID variables. The MPR variable is the central bank monetary policy rate or the central bank interest rate. When the central bank raises the MPR, financial institutions will respond by raising all interest rates because the MPR is the interest rate on which all other interest rates are anchored on. The increase in the MPR rate will lead to the tightening of financing conditions, it will make loans become more expensive, and it will lead to a decrease in loan supply (Ozili, 2023). It will reduce access to formal credit and will be detrimental to financial inclusion. Therefore, a negative relationship between the MPR and FID variable is anticipated. The SD variable is the savings deposit rate. A high interest rate paid on savings will motivate unbanked adults to bring their money to banks in the form of savings deposit so that they can take advantage of the attractive savings deposit rate (Bharadwaj & Suri, 2020). Therefore, a positive relationship between the SD and FID variables is anticipated. The IBR variable is the interest rate at which banks lend to themselves overnight. A high overnight lending rate will increase the cost of bank liquidity. Banks can mitigate this effect by accelerating their efforts to attract depositors to bring their deposit to banks so that the deposits can be a source of cheap liquidity for banks. Bank's effort to attract depositors, as a strategy to counter a high interbank rate, will lead to higher financial inclusion as it will lead to new depositors bringing their monies into banks. Therefore, a negative relationship between the IBR and FID variables is anticipated. The NIR variable is the nominal (market) interest rate. When the nominal rate increases, loans become expensive, borrowers will pay a premium to borrow via high interest rates. It will reduce access to credit, and it will be a setback for financial inclusion as many households will not be able to access and afford formal credit due to a high nominal interest rate (Heng et al., 2021; Ozili, 2023). Therefore, a negative relationship between the NIR and FID variables is anticipated.

4. Empirical Results

4.1 Baseline Result

This section presents the baseline empirical result for the determinants of financial inclusion in Nigeria. The two-stage least squares result is reported in Table 7.4.

The MPR variable is significant and negatively related to the FID variable. This result indicates that the monetary policy rate has a negative effect on financial inclusion in Nigeria.

Table 7.4. Two-Stage Least Squares Regression for the Determinants of Financial Inclusion (FID).

Variables	Coefficient	*t*-Statistic	Prob. Value
MPR	−0.014***	−7.38	0.000
SD	0.023***	6.11	0.000
NIR	−0.005***	−2.84	0.004
INF	−0.001*	−1.74	0.081
LDR	−0.001***	−6.41	0.000
EFF	−0.0002	−1.53	0.127
IBR	0.002***	3.21	0.000
J-statistic	6.837		
Prob(*J*-statistic)	0.008		

Source: Author's computation.

Note: *** and * represent statistical significance at the 1% and 10% levels.

The result implies that a high monetary policy rate would tighten financing conditions in the banking sector and motivate banks to reduce credit to formal borrowers. It will make access to formal credit more difficult for households and adversely affect financial inclusion. The result supports the findings of Ozili (2023) who show that monetary policy has a negative impact on financial inclusion in emerging markets. In terms of economic significance, the MPR coefficient is not economically significant because a unit increase in the monetary policy rate leads to a 0.01% decrease in financial inclusion.

The SD variable is significant and positively related to the FID variable. This result indicates that the saving deposit rate has a positive effect on financial inclusion in Nigeria. The result implies that a high savings deposit rate will attract adults to bring their monies into the banking system so that they can receive interest on their savings deposit, thereby increasing financial inclusion. The result is consistent with Chummun and Ojah (2016) who argue that aggregate savings, and the desire to increase savings, can enable financial inclusion in African economies. In terms of economic significance, the SD coefficient is not economically significant because a unit increase in the savings deposit rate leads to a 0.023% increase in financial inclusion.

The NIR variable is significant and negatively related to the FID variable. The result indicates that the nominal interest rate has a negative effect on financial inclusion in Nigeria. The result implies that a high nominal interest rate will constrain access to credit by making loans become expensive, thereby discouraging individuals from accessing formal credit. This will have a detrimental impact on financial inclusion as unbanked adults will avoid joining the formal financial sector if formal credit is too costly. This result is consistent with Uddin et al. (2017) and Heng et al. (2021) who show that high inflation is injurious in financial inclusion. In terms of economic significance, the NIR coefficient is not economically significant because a unit increase in the nominal interest rate leads to a 0.005% decrease in financial inclusion.

The INF variable is significant and negatively related to the FID variable. This result indicates that an inflation rate has a negative effect on financial inclusion in Nigeria. The result implies that a high inflation rate makes financial services become costly and unaffordable for Nigerians, and it will discourage unbanked individuals from joining the financial sector, thereby becoming a setback for financial inclusion in Nigeria. This result is consistent with Evans (2016) who found that inflation has a significant effect on financial inclusion in Nigeria. In terms of economic significance, the INF coefficient is not economically significant because a unit increase in the inflation rate leads to a 0.001% decrease in financial inclusion.

The LDR variable is significant and negatively related to the FID variable. This result indicates that the loan-to-deposit rate has a negative effect on financial inclusion in Nigeria. The result implies that a high loan to deposit ratio is detrimental for financial inclusion in Nigeria. In terms of economic significance, the LDR coefficient is not economically significant because a unit increase in the loan to deposit ratio leads to a 0.001% decrease in financial inclusion.

The IBR variable is significant and positively related to the FID variable. This result indicates that the inter-bank lending rate has a positive effect on financial inclusion in Nigeria. The result implies that a high interbank lending rate will lead to increase in financial inclusion because a high interbank lending rate means that it will be costly for banks to borrow among themselves. Therefore, banks will increase their own efforts to attract a large number of depositors in order to receive cheap liquidity, in form of customer deposits, which will reduce the need to borrow from other banks. Their efforts to attract depositors will lead to higher financial inclusion for new depositors. In terms of economic significance, the IBR coefficient is not economically significant. A unit increase in the interbank lending rate leads to a 0.002% increase in financial inclusion. The EFF variable is positive but insignificant in relation to the FID variable. The positive coefficient, although not significant, suggests that bank efficiency does not have a significant effect on financial inclusion in Nigeria.

4.2 Sensitivity/Robustness Tests

4.2.1 Quantile Regression Estimation

In this section, the results are re-estimated using the quantile regression estimation technique to address the issue of outliers in the data. The quantile regression estimates are robust against outliers in the dataset, and it is a suitable estimator to use when there is the potential for non-linearity in the relationship between the dependent and independent variables as well as when the data are non-normally distributed (Huang et al., 2017; Koenker, 2017). The quantile regression result for the determinants of financial inclusion in Nigeria is reported in Table 7.5. The MPR variable remains negatively significant in relation to the

Table 7.5. Quantile Regression Estimation for the Determinants of Financial Inclusion (FID).

Variables	Coefficient	*t*-Statistic	Prob. Value
MPR	−0.015***	−4.25	0.004
SD	0.019**	2.83	0.025
NIR	−0.003	−0.600	0.567
INF	−0.001	−0.82	0.439
LDR	−0.001***	−4.19	0.004
EFF	−0.0003	−1.19	0.272
IBR	0.002	1.657	0.142
Adjusted R^2	65.96		

Note: *** and ** represent statistical significance at the 1% and 5% levels.

FID variable. This indicates that the result is robust, and it confirms that monetary policy rate has a negative effect on financial inclusion in Nigeria. The SD variable also remains positively significant in relation to the FID variable in Table 7.5. This indicates that the result is robust, and it confirms that the savings deposit rate has a positive effect on financial inclusion in Nigeria. The NIR variable is insignificant in relation to the FID variable. This indicates that the result in Table 7.5 is not robust with the earlier result obtained in Table 7.4. The INF variable is also insignificant in relation to the FID variable. This indicates that the result in Table 7.5 is not robust with the earlier result in Table 7.4. The LDR variable is also negatively significant in relation to the FID variable. This indicates that the loan-to-deposit rate has a negative effect on financial inclusion in Nigeria. The result in Table 7.5 is robust with the earlier result in Table 7.4. The EFF variable is insignificant in relation to the FID variable. This indicates that the result in Table 7.5 is not robust with the earlier result obtained in Table 7.4. Also, the IBR variable is insignificant in relation to the FID variable. This indicates that the result in Table 7.5 is not robust with the earlier result obtained in Table 7.4.

4.2.2 Granger Causality Test

Before conducting the Granger causality test, it is important to first conduct a unit root test to check the stationarity of the time series data for the seven variables to avoid obtaining spurious causation. We use the Augmented Dickey–Fuller (ADF) unit root test to check for stationarity in the time series data for the three variables. The ADF unit root test is reported in Table 7.6. The ADF test in Table 7.6 shows that the time series data for the NIR and INF variables have *p*-values which are less than 5%. This indicates that the time series data for the NIR and INF variables do not have a unit root and are therefore stationary. As a result, we

Table 7.6. Summary of Augmented Dickey-Fuller (ADF) Unit Root Test for the Variables.

Time Series Data	***t*-Statistic**	***p*-Value**	**Decision Rule: (If $p > 0.5$, Data Has Unit Root and Is Non-stationary)**	**Remark**
FID	−0.805	0.7836	$p > 0.05$; the data has a unit root	Data is non-stationary
MPR	−1.554	0.4761	$p > 0.05$; the data has a unit root	Data is non-stationary
SD	−1.971	0.294	$p > 0.05$; the data has a unit root	Data is non-stationary
NIR	1.156	0.995	$p > 0.05$; the data has a unit root	Data is non-stationary
INF	−3.309	0.038	$p < 0.05$; the data does not have a unit root	Data is stationary
LDR	−3.540	0.026	$p < 0.05$; the data does not have a unit root	Data is stationary
EFF	−2.160	0.227	$p > 0.05$; the data has a unit root	Data is non-stationary
IBR	−2.782	0.086	$p > 0.05$; the data has a unit root	Data is non-stationary

Source: Author's computation.

will not take the first difference of the time series data for these variables before conducting the Granger causality test. In contrast, the time series data for the FID, MPR, SD, NIR, EFF and IBR variables have p-values which are greater than 5%. This indicates that the time series data for these variables have a unit root and are therefore non-stationary. As a result, we will take the first difference of the time series data for these variables before conducting the Granger causality test. The Granger causality test in Table 7.7 reports a p-value which is less than 0.05 for the MPR, SD, NIR, INF, LDR, EFF and IBR variables, indicating that there is no uni-directional or bi-directional causality between financial inclusion and its determinants.

5. Conclusion

Financial inclusion can contribute immensely to human well-being and economic development in Nigeria if appropriate financial inclusion strategies are developed and implemented. Presently, the CBN and deposit money banks are collaborating to accelerate financial inclusion in Nigeria. The current reality in Nigeria is that certain monetary policy actions of the central bank and bank-specific factors may help to accelerate or hinder progress towards greater financial inclusion. My curiosity on this issue led me to investigate the monetary policy and bank-specific factors that affect financial inclusion in Nigeria. Data were analysed for 15 years from 2007 to 2021. The results showed that the central bank monetary policy rate, the savings deposit rate and the loan to deposit ratio of banks are significant determinants of financial inclusion in Nigeria. These determinants are robust to alternative estimation using the quantile regression method. There is some evidence that the interbank lending rate, inflation rate and the nominal interest rate are also determinants of financial inclusion in Nigeria based on the two-stage least squares estimation.

Based on these findings, it is recommended that the monetary authority, or the CBN, should accelerate financial inclusion for the entire population by taking monetary policy actions that are not injurious or too burdensome on banks so that banks can be motivated to increase access and use of banking services for members of the population. This can be done by decreasing the monetary policy rate and decreasing the nominal interest rate so that the financial services offered by banks will be affordable to everyone, thereby attracting members of the population to join the formal financial sector. The central bank should also require banks to raise the savings deposit rate to attract unbanked adults who are willing to bring their money into the formal financial system.

The findings stress the importance of fine-tuning monetary policies to ensure that it does not place obstacles for banks and lead to the exclusion of many people from the formal financial system. It is also recommended that the central bank should increase its effort to reduce the rate of inflation as it was shown in the study that inflation adversely affects financial inclusion. The central bank should use an effective inflation targeting framework to reduce inflation so that financial services will become cheaper and easily accessible to the population. This will

Table 7.7. Pairwise Granger Causality Tests.

Lags: 2				
Null Hypothesis:	**Obs**	***F*-Statistic**	**Prob.**	**Decision Rule**
D(MPR) does not Granger cause D(FID)	11	0.15567	0.8592	Prob> 5%; No granger causality
D(FID) does not Granger cause D(MPR)		0.79429	0.4943	Prob> 5%; No granger causality
D(SD) does not Granger cause D(FID)	11	1.67512	0.2642	Prob> 5%; No granger causality
D(FID) does not Granger cause D(SD)		2.26248	0.1853	Prob> 5%; No granger causality
D(NIR) does not Granger cause D(FID)	11	4.90637	0.0546	Prob> 5%; No granger causality
D(FID) does not Granger cause D(NIR)		4.77356	0.0575	Prob> 5%; No granger causality
INF does not Granger cause D(FID)	11	1.36020	0.3257	Prob> 5%; No granger causality
D(FID) does not Granger cause INF		0.04645	0.9550	Prob> 5%; No granger causality
LDR does not Granger cause D(FID)	11	0.22694	0.8035	Prob> 5%; No granger causality
D(FID) does not Granger cause LDR		0.23342	0.7987	Prob> 5%; No granger causality
D(EFF) does not Granger cause D(FID)	11	0.06896	0.9341	Prob> 5%; No granger causality
D(FID) does not Granger cause D(EFF)		1.08572	0.3959	Prob> 5%; No granger causality
D(IBR) does not Granger cause D(FID)	11	0.80877	0.4887	Prob> 5%; No granger causality
D(FID) does not Granger cause D(IBR)		0.69416	0.5356	Prob> 5%; No granger causality
D(NIR) does not Granger cause D(MPR)	12	3.57605	0.0851	Prob> 5%; No granger causality
D(MPR) does not Granger cause D(NIR)		3.00877	0.1140	Prob> 5%; No granger causality

Source: Author's computation.

encourage more people to join the formal financial sector. Finally, it is recommended that the central bank and deposit money banks should collaborate and develop a progressive approach that would increase banks' capacity to accelerate financial inclusion in Nigeria. Such progressive approach may include opening more bank branches, providing more ATMs and opening more bank accounts.

The study has few limitations. The study used country-level industry data to investigate the determinants of financial inclusion in Nigeria and these data offered some interesting insights. The study did not use bank-level data of the 33 deposit money banks in Nigeria. Using bank-level data may provide additional insights. Another limitation of the study is the 15-year sample period. The sample period could be longer. The short period examined in the study was due to data unavailability.

This research presents plentiful opportunities for future research. For example, future studies can assess the fiscal policy factors affecting financial inclusion to determine whether factors such as government social welfare transfers, unemployment compensation payments and tax payments can lead to higher financial inclusion in Nigeria. Further research can also examine other macro financial determinants of financial inclusion such as aggregate tax rate, private credit to GDP ratio and the level of financial stability, among others. There is also a need to compare the determinants of financial inclusion in Nigeria with that of other emerging economies such as Brazil and Argentia. Such studies would provide insights on the areas where Nigeria is doing better or poorly in comparison with emerging economies.

References

Abdu, M., Buba, A., Adamu, I., & Muhammad, T. (2015). Drivers of financial inclusion and gender gap in Nigeria. *Empirical Econometrics and Quantitative Economics Letters*, *4*(4), 186–199.

Adetunji, O. M., & David-West, O. (2019). The relative impact of income and financial literacy on financial inclusion in Nigeria. *Journal of International Development*, *31*(4), 312–335.

Adil, F., & Jalil, A. (2020). Determining the financial inclusion output of banking sector of Pakistan—Supply-side analysis. *Economies*, *8*(2), 42.

Ait Lahcen, M., & Gomis-Porqueras, P. (2021). A model of endogenous financial inclusion: Implications for inequality and monetary policy. *Journal of Money, Credit, and Banking*, *53*(5), 1175–1209.

Anarfo, E. B., Abor, J. Y., Osei, K. A., & Gyeke-Dako, A. (2019). Monetary policy and financial inclusion in sub-Sahara Africa: A panel VAR approach. *Journal of African Business*, *20*(4), 549–572.

Angrist, J. D., & Imbens, G. W. (1995). Two-stage least squares estimation of average causal effects in models with variable treatment intensity. *Journal of the American Statistical Association*, 431–442.

Barajas, A., Beck, T., Belhaj, M., & Naceur, S. B. (2020). *Financial inclusion: What have we learned so far? What do we have to learn?* IMF Working Papers, 2020(157).

Barik, R., & Lenka, S. K. (2022). Demand-side and supply-side determinants of financial inclusion in Indian states: Evidence from post-liberalization period. *Emerging Economy Studies*, *8*(1), 7–25.

Bharadwaj, P., & Suri, T. (2020, May). Improving financial inclusion through digital savings and credit. In *AEA Papers and Proceedings* (Vol. 110, pp. 584–588). American Economic Association.

Bozkurt, İ., Karakuş, R., & Yildiz, M. (2018). Spatial determinants of financial inclusion over time. *Journal of International Development*, *30*(8), 1474–1504.

Chummun, B. Z., & Ojah, K. (2016). Aggregate savings and financial inclusion: Lessons for developing African economies. *Africagrowth Agenda*, *2016*(07), 4–9.

Dabla-Norris, E., Ji, Y., Townsend, R. M., & Unsal, D. F. (2021). Distinguishing constraints on financial inclusion and their impact on GDP, TFP, and the distribution of income. *Journal of Monetary Economics*, *117*, 1–18.

David, O. O., Oluseyi, A. S., & Emmanuel, A. (2018). Empirical analysis of the determinants of financial inclusion in Nigeria: 1990-2016. *Journal of Finance and Economics*, *6*(1), 19–25.

Demirgüç-Kunt, A., & Klapper, L. (2013). Measuring financial inclusion: Explaining variation in use of financial services across and within countries. *Brookings Papers on Economic Activity*, *2013*(1), 279–340.

Demirgüç-Kunt, A., Klapper, L., Singer, D., & Ansar, S. (2022). *The Global Findex Database 2021: Financial inclusion, digital payments, and resilience in the age of COVID-19*. World Bank Publications.

Eldomiaty, T., Hammam, R., & El Bakry, R. (2020). Institutional determinants of financial inclusion: Evidence from world economies. *International Journal of Development Issues*, *19*(2), 217–228.

Ene, E. E., Abba, G. O., & Fatokun, G. F. (2019). The impact of electronic banking on financial inclusion in Nigeria. *American Journal of Industrial and Business Management*, *9*(6), 1409–1422.

Evans, O. (2016). *Determinants of financial inclusion in Africa: A dynamic panel data approach*. MPRA.

Eze, G. P., & Markjackson, D. (2020). Determinants of financial inclusion in Nigeria. *Journal of Economics and Finance*, *11*(1), 14–22.

Ezzahid, E., & Elouaourti, Z. (2021). Financial inclusion, mobile banking, informal finance, and financial exclusion: Micro-level evidence from Morocco. *International Journal of Social Economics*, *48*(7), 1060–1086.

Fahmy, M., & Ghoneim, H. (2023). Financial inclusion demand-side determinants: Analysis from Egypt. *Management & Sustainability: An Arab Review*, *2*(3), 255–284.

Fernández-Olit, B., Martín Martín, J. M., & Porras González, E. (2020). Systematized literature review on financial inclusion and exclusion in developed countries. *International Journal of Bank Marketing*, *38*(3), 600–626.

Gebrehiwot, K. G., & Makina, D. (2019). Macroeconomic determinants of financial inclusion: Evidence using dynamic panel data analysis. In D. Makina (Ed.), *Extending financial inclusion in Africa* (pp. 167–191). Academic Press.

Ghosh, S., & Vinod, D. (2017). What constrains financial inclusion for women? Evidence from Indian micro data. *World Development*, *92*, 60–81.

Giday, H. G. (2023). Financial inclusion and its demand-side determinants: Evidence from Ethiopia. *Cogent Economics & Finance*, *11*(1), 2186031.

Heng, D., Chea, S., & Heng, B. (2021). *Impacts of interest rate cap on financial inclusion in Cambodia*. International Monetary Fund.

Huang, Q., Zhang, H., Chen, J., & He, M. J. J. B. B. (2017). Quantile regression models and their applications: A review. *Journal of Biometrics & Biostatistics*, *8*(3), 1–6.

Jungo, J., Madaleno, M., & Botelho, A. (2022). The relationship between financial inclusion and monetary policy: A comparative study of countries in sub-Saharan Africa and Latin America and the Caribbean. *Journal of African Business*, *23*(3), 794–815.

Koenker, R. (2005). *Quantile regression*. Cambridge University Press.

Koenker, R. (2017). Quantile regression: 40 years on. *Annual Review of Economics*, *9*, 155–176.

Lapukeni, A. F. (2015). The impact of financial inclusion on monetary policy effectiveness: The case of Malawi. *International Journal of Monetary Economics and Finance*, *8*(4), 360–384.

Lenka, S. K., & Bairwa, A. K. (2016). Does financial inclusion affect monetary policy in SAARC countries? *Cogent Economics & Finance*, *4*(1), 1127011.

Markose, S., Arun, T., & Ozili, P. (2022). Financial inclusion, at what cost? Quantification of economic viability of a supply side roll out. *The European Journal of Finance*, *28*(1), 3–29.

Matsebula, V., & Sheefeni, J. (2022). Financial inclusion and macroeconomic stability in South Africa. *International Journal of Economics and Financial Issues*, *12*(4), 56.

Mbutor, M. O., & Uba, I. A. (2013). The impact of financial inclusion on monetary policy in Nigeria. *Journal of Economics and International Finance*, *5*(8), 318–326.

Neaime, S., & Gaysset, I. (2018). Financial inclusion and stability in MENA: Evidence from poverty and inequality. *Finance Research Letters*, *24*, 230–237.

NFIS. (2018). *National financial inclusion strategy (Revised)*. Central Bank of Nigeria.

Ozili, P. K. (2021a). Financial inclusion in Nigeria: Determinants, challenges, and achievements. In E. Özen, S. Grima, & R. D. Gonzi (Eds.), *New challenges for future sustainability and wellbeing (Emerald studies in finance, insurance, and risk management)* (pp. 377–395). Emerald Publishing Limited. https://doi.org/10.1108/978-1-80043-968-920211020

Ozili, P. K. (2021b). Financial inclusion research around the world: A review. *Forum for Social Economics*, *50*(4), 457–479.

Ozili, P. K. (2023). Impact of monetary policy on financial inclusion in emerging markets. *Journal of Risk and Financial Management*, *16*(7), 303.

Ozili, P. K. (2024). Vulnerable group theory of financial inclusion. *Perspectives on Global Development & Technology*, *22*(5–6), 396–414.

Prabhakar, R. (2019). Financial inclusion: A tale of two literature. *Social Policy and Society*, *18*(1), 37–50.

Rashdan, A., & Eissa, N. (2020). The determinants of financial inclusion in Egypt. *International Journal of Financial Research*, *11*(1).

Sethy, S. K. (2015). Developing a financial inclusion index and inclusive growth in India: Issues and challenges. *Indian Economic Journal*, *63*(2), 283–311.

Sheikhi, A., Bahador, F., & Arashi, M. (2022). On a generalization of the test of endogeneity in a two stage least squares estimation. *Journal of Applied Statistics*, *49*(3), 709–721.

Tinta, A. A., Ouédraogo, I. M., & Al-Hassan, R. M. (2022). The micro determinants of financial inclusion and financial resilience in Africa. *African Development Review*, *34*(2), 293–306.

Uddin, A., Chowdhury, M. A. F., & Islam, M. N. (2017). Determinants of financial inclusion in Bangladesh: Dynamic GMM & quantile regression approach. *The Journal of Developing Areas*, *51*(2), 221–237.

Vo, A. T., Van, L. T. H., Vo, D. H., & McAleer, M. (2019). Financial inclusion and macroeconomic stability in emerging and frontier markets. *Annals of Financial Economics*, *14*(02), 1950008.

Wezel, T., & Ree, M. J. J. (2023). *Nigeria—Fostering financial inclusion through digital financial services*. International Monetary Fund.

Yadav, V., Singh, B. P., & Velan, N. (2021). Multidimensional financial inclusion index for Indian states. *Journal of Public Affairs*, *21*(3), e2238.

Yorulmaz, R. (2018). An analysis of constructing global financial inclusion indices. *Borsa Istanbul Review*, *18*(3), 248–258.

Chapter 8

Financial Inclusion Redefined: The Malaysian Experience With Crowdfunding and Fintech

Ibrahim Alnafrah[a,d], *Sulaiman Mouselli*[b] *and Nedaa Shhadah*[c]

[a]Ural Federal University, Russia
[b]Arab International University, Syria
[c]Higher Institute of Business Administration, Syria
[d]Middle East University, Jordan

Abstract

This study investigates the impact of crowdfunding on financial inclusion in Malaysia, focusing on equity crowdfunding (ECF) and peer-to-peer (P2P) financing. Using monthly data from January 2019 to May 2023, we construct a financial inclusion index and employ autoregressive distributed lag (ARDL) and wavelet coherence methodologies to analyse short-term, long-term and time-frequency relationships. Our findings reveal that P2P financing and broad market price significantly enhance financial inclusion in the long run while ECF and initial public offerings (IPOs) have a modest positive impact. The results of short-term dynamics indicate complex relationships, with immediate positive effects from ECF and IPOs, but initial adjustments required for P2P financing. Additionally, wavelet analysis demonstrates varying cyclical behaviours and temporal relationships between crowdfunding activities and financial inclusion, particularly influenced by economic shocks such as the COVID-19 pandemic. These results provide valuable insights for policymakers and Fintech innovators in leveraging crowdfunding to promote financial inclusion in emerging economies.

Keywords: Crowdfunding; financial inclusion; Fintech; equity crowdfunding; peer-to-peer (P2P) lending; Malaysia

From Digital Disruption to Dominance, 187–208

Published under exclusive licence by Emerald Publishing Limited
doi:10.1108/978-1-83549-608-420251008

1. Introduction

Financial inclusion has emerged as a central point for the achievement of the Sustainable Development Goals (SDGs) and gained wide interest from politicians and researchers alike. The many advantages of Fintech in enhancing efficiency and reducing costs introduce it as a potential promotor to financial inclusion (Ajouz et al., 2023; Alkhwaldi et al., 2022; Arner et al., 2020; Hasan et al., 2023). While it is not seen as a goal itself, financial inclusion is considered an enabler for at least eight of the seventeen SDGs. Among the various Fintech innovations, crowdfunding stands out as a disruptive force that democratises access to capital by allowing funds to be solicited from a large number of individuals and institutions. It capitalises on digital revolution by offering web-based platforms that make investing and borrowing widely available and affordable. Crowdfunding comes in four main forms that range from equity to debt and from reward (non-monetary rewards, products or services) to donation (no monetary or material reward) (Beier & Wagner, 2015; Burtch et al., 2013) in addition to many other forms such as community-based crowdfunding, segregated client model, notary model and guaranteed return model (Abdul Halim, 2024).

Malaysia, as the first country in the ASEAN region to implement crowdfunding legislation (Cheah, 2015), presents an interesting case study for examining the relationship between crowdfunding and financial inclusion. The country has shown consistent progress in its Global Financial Inclusion Index, moving from 20th to 18th position and scoring 52.8 points in 2023 compared to 49.6 points in 2022 (Principal Financial Services, 2023). This improvement is largely attributed to government and employer support, manifested through better online connectivity and increased volume of real-time transactions. According to the Securities Commission Malaysia (2024), the total funds raised through equity crowdfunding (ECF) and peer-to-peer (P2P) crowdfunding grow by 29% to RM2.2 billion in 2023 from RM1.7 billion in 2022 with 11 ECF and P2P approved platform operators in 2023. P2P crowdfunding is the favourite model with total funds raised of RM2.09 billion while ECF has only secured RM126.28 million in 2023 (Securities Commission Malaysia, 2024).

Despite the growing body of literature on the positive impact of Fintech on financial inclusion, there is a lack of empirical evidence specifically addressing the role of crowdfunding. Most existing studies either focus on theoretical aspects or use aggregate indicators of Fintech, failing to isolate the effects of specific crowdfunding types (Abdul Halim, 2024; Cevik, 2024; Jenik et al., 2017; Katseli & Boufounou, 2020; Slimani & Ziky, 2021). This gap in the literature is mainly due to the lack of long-term data series on both crowdfunding and financial inclusion indicators which makes statistical tests and inferences challenging. Hence, there is no established empirical proven evidence on the impact of crowdfunding on financial inclusion and not on Malaysia. Thus, this paper attempts to fill this gap by investigating the impact of two main components of crowdfunding, ECF and P2P, on financial inclusion in Malaysia.

In light of this context, our study aims to address the following research questions.

RQ1. What is the impact of crowdfunding, specifically ECF and P2P, on financial inclusion in Malaysia?
RQ2. How do the effects of ECF and P2P crowdfunding on financial inclusion differ from each other?
RQ3. What are the short- and long-term relationships between crowdfunding and financial inclusion in Malaysia?
RQ4. How do the cyclical behaviour, temporal evolution and time-frequency dependencies of crowdfunding and financial inclusion variables interact across different scales?

By addressing these research questions, this study aims to provide a comprehensive understanding of the relationship between crowdfunding and financial inclusion in Malaysia. Our analysis will not only shed light on the overall impact of crowdfunding but also offer insights into the specific roles of ECF and P2P models in promoting financial inclusion. Furthermore, by examining both short- and long-term relationships, as well as cyclical behaviours and time-frequency dependencies, we aim to provide a nuanced perspective on how these financial innovations interact with financial inclusion over time and across different scales. Thus, the contribution of this chapter is threefold. First, it does not only examine the impact of crowdfunding on financial inclusion but also compares between the effect of two distinguished types of crowdfunding on such impact, which gives further insights on the dynamics of different types of crowdfunding on financial inclusion. Second, our study constructs monthly financial inclusion index for Malaysia to validate the potential impact of crowdfunding on financial inclusion. Third, we use a plethora of econometric methods that range from ARDL, wavelet spectrum method and wavelet coherence approach to analyse both short- and long-term relationships between our examined variables, as well as the cyclical behaviour, temporal evolution and time-frequency dependencies of these variables across different scales.

The rest of this chapter is organised as follows. Section 2 reviews the literature on the relationship between crowdfunding and financial inclusion. In the first part of Section 3, we explain our data in terms of variables' definition, and we provide descriptive statistics and the correlation matrix of variables under investigation. In the second part of Section 3, we discuss the empirical models that will be applied in our study. Section 4 illustrates the results from applying the empirical tests and discusses their implications. Section 5 concludes and provides recommendations.

2. Literature Review

There is a wealth of literature on the positivity of Fintech on financial inclusion. The relatively lower operating costs associated with Fintech accommodate clients' needs at reduced costs in comparison with traditional financial services (Demirgüc-Kunt et al., 2015, 2018; Emuron et al., 2024). Fintech stimulates competition between financial institutions to offer services at lower costs, which enhances financial inclusion (Chauvet & Jacolin, 2017; Owen & Pereira, 2018). Fintech introduces services and products that support financial decision-making and stimulate savings without the need to pay unnecessary high fees (Ajouz et al., 2024; Auboin & Marchetti, 2018, pp. 1–13; Claessens et al., 2018; Karlan et al., 2014; Moses et al., 2021). Fintech provides tools that assist MSMEs in tax planning, manage financial flows and bridges the credit gap (Alkhazaleh et al., 2023; Auboin & Marchetti, 2018, pp. 1–13; Gosavi, 2018; Ighobor, 2015; Karlan et al., 2014; Modibbo et al., 2021; Moses et al., 2021; Rehman et al., 2023; Thomas, 2023).

Fintech allows to circumvent financial intermediation (Ali et al., 2021; World Bank, 2019) and physical presence to service the needs of isolated communities via the internet and mobile phones (Diniz et al., 2012; Joia & dos Santos, 2019). Fintech reduces bureaucracy and red tapes and provide alternatives to unattractive clients for traditional banks (Allen et al., 2016; Diniz et al., 2012; Oliveira, 2018). Fintech facilitates negotiation between services providers and clients through online matching and auction (Lusardi & Mitchell, 2011, 2014). Finally, Fintech offers comprehensive and accurate tools for risk refinement and assessment which enables better evaluation of risk and consequently offering credit with less unnecessary required guarantees (Frame et al., 2001; Gai et al., 2018; Gomber et al., 2018; Liberti & Petersen, 2019; Owen & Pereira, 2018; Siddik & Kabiraj, 2018).

On the flip side of the coin, a limited number of studies argue against any positive impact of Fintech on financial inclusion (CGAP, 2018; Della Peruta, 2017; Michael et al., 2022). For example, Michael et al. (2022) argue that the impact of Fintech is U-shape similar to those of any other innovations. They claim that little Fintech probably helps but too much will hurt sustainable development because resources will move from helping the poor to support rich customers who save and buy online easily. Moreover, they argue that Fintech just substitutes traditional financial services without having impact on financial inclusion. Della Peruta (2017) argues that mobile money services require a relatively inclusive banking system and cannot substitute it. Furthermore, it is documented that the growth of digital credit in East Africa through credit providers has manifested in more debt and default rates particularly among the poor, younger people and rural residents (CGAP, 2018). Moreover, Demir et al. (2022) found that Fintech reduces inequality in high-income countries but increases it in low-income countries.

The empirical evidence on the impact of crowdfunding on financial inclusion is rather mixed. Maskara et al. (2021) documented a positive impact of P2P lending platforms on financial inclusion in the United Stated but argue that such impact was asymmetric between rural and urban communities. That is, while P2P lending platforms enhance financial inclusion of residents in rural areas which lack traditional institutions, they provide an alternative to residents of urban communities with fewer fringe banks. In the same context, Chung et al. (2023) examined the dynamic interplay between two Fintech products, P2P lending and cryptocurrency markets. They found a positive association between the growth in cryptocurrency market and P2P lending requests especially from good credit rating borrowers with cryptocurrencies technical knowledge who intend to borrow for investment purposes. Hence, they concluded that cryptocurrency market provides economic gains to P2P lending market at least in the short run. However, they warned that the beneficiaries of such gains are mere creditworthy and tech-savvy investors which may provoke inequality in access to financial services.

Cevik (2024) investigated the relationship between digital lending, digital capital raising and financial inclusion in a panel of 84 countries. He found that digital lending negatively affected financial inclusion while digital capital raising has an insignificant impact on financial inclusion. He also reported an insignificant impact of Fintech on financial inclusion for the full sample, which turned to be positive and significant for the developing countries subsample. However, this study combined all types of digital lending together and all types of digital capital raising together and did not investigate the impact of P2P and ECF on financial inclusion alone.

Despite the substantial body of research highlighting the positive effects of Fintech on financial inclusion, several critical gaps remain, particularly concerning crowdfunding's nuanced impact. While existing literature has explored various aspects of Fintech's contribution to financial inclusion, there is limited detailed analysis focusing on specific crowdfunding models, particularly ECF and P2P lending. This study aims to address this gap by investigating the impact of these two distinct types of crowdfunding on financial inclusion in Malaysia (*RQ1*). Although studies have documented the general effects of Fintech, there is a lack of comprehensive comparative analysis between ECF and P2P models and how their impacts differ (*RQ2*).

Furthermore, the existing research often overlooks the dynamic nature of these impacts. Our study will explore both short- and long-term relationships between crowdfunding activities and financial inclusion, offering a more granular understanding of their interactions over different temporal scales (*RQ3*). Additionally, while the literature has touched upon Fintech's cyclical behaviours and time-frequency dependencies, there is a need for deeper analysis into how these elements interact with financial inclusion across various scales (*RQ4*).

Addressing these gaps, this study aims to provide a comprehensive examination of ECF and P2P lending's impact on financial inclusion in Malaysia. By focusing on the distinct effects of these crowdfunding models, analysing both immediate and extended-term impacts and exploring cyclical and time-frequency aspects, this research seeks to fill the existing voids in the literature. It will offer valuable insights into how different crowdfunding strategies can be optimised to enhance financial inclusion, thus guiding future research and policy-making in this rapidly evolving field.

3. Data and Methodology

3.1 Data

To investigate the role of Fintech in financial inclusion in Malaysia, we constructed a time series dataset with monthly data from January 2019 to May 2023. Our variables include Equity Crowdfunding (Equity) to capture innovative capital-raising methods accessible to a broad audience and Peer to Peer Financing (Peer) to illustrate alternative financing avenues outside traditional banking systems. The Broad Market Price (bmp) reflects overall market performance, providing a benchmark for economic activity while the Initial Public Offer (IPO) captures capital market activity relevant to both investors and new enterprises. To generate the Financial Inclusion (FI) variable, we used data from Credit Card (CC) and Debit Card (DC) usage, which indicate consumer access to credit and personal funds, respectively. Additionally, Internet Banking (IB) and Mobile Banking (MB) are critical indicators of technological adoption in financial services, facilitating remote access to banking. ATM usage reflects the availability and accessibility of basic banking services. We first scaled these variables and then averaged them to create the FI variable, opting not to apply principal component analysis (PCA) to avoid losing variances in all variables and ensure full representation of all FI-related variables. These measures collectively provide a comprehensive overview of how Fintech innovations influence financial inclusion in Malaysia. Table 8.1 provides a comprehensive list of all variables used in this study, along with their definitions and respective sources.

Table 8.1. Variables, Definition and Data Sources.

Variable	Code	Definition	Source
Equity crowdfunding	Equity	A method of raising capital through the collective effort of a large number of individual investors via online platforms.	The Securities Commission Malaysia (SC)
Peer to peer financing	Peer	A type of financing that enables individuals to obtain loans directly from other individuals, bypassing traditional financial institutions.	The Securities Commission Malaysia (SC)
Broad market price	bmp	The average price level of a broad market index, representing the overall performance of a market or sector.	World Federation of Exchange
Initial public offer	IPO	The process by which a private company offers shares to the public for the first time to raise capital.	Bursa Malaysia
Financial inclusion	FI	The availability and equality of opportunities to access financial services, promoting economic stability and growth.	World Bank

Table 8.1. *(Continued)*

Variable	Code	Definition	Source
Credit card	CC	A payment card issued by financial institutions that allows cardholders to borrow funds for purchases with the promise to repay them.	Bank Negara Malaysia
Debit card	DC	A payment card that deducts money directly from a consumer's checking account to pay for a purchase.	Bank Negara Malaysia
Internet banking	IB	A system that enables customers of a bank to conduct a range of financial transactions through the bank's website.	Bank Negara Malaysia
Mobile banking	MB	A service provided by a financial institution that allows its customers to conduct financial transactions remotely using a mobile device.	Bank Negara Malaysia
ATM	ATM	Automated teller machine, an electronic banking outlet that allows customers to complete basic transactions without the aid of a branch representative or teller.	Bank Negara Malaysia

All variables are transformed to represent the first difference in their natural logarithmic form to reduce the impact of extreme values and facilitate a more meaningful interpretation of the data. The descriptive statistics are reported in Table 8.2. As shown in Table 8.2, the equity variable exhibits relatively high variability compared to the other variables, as indicated by its larger standard deviation (0.714). Notably, the results of skewness and kurtosis indicate the potential presence of asymmetry and leptokurtosis. Specifically, equity has a high skewness (4.438) and kurtosis (28.344), suggesting a significant right tail and extreme values. Similarly, peer shows negative skewness (−0.447) and high kurtosis (5.403), indicating potential left tail risks. The IPO variable also exhibits substantial variability with a standard deviation of 3.162, skewness of −0.248, and kurtosis of 2.928, reflecting some asymmetry and moderate peakness. Additionally, FI displays more moderate skewness and kurtosis, although FI has

Table 8.2. Descriptive Statistics.

	Equity	Peer	IPO	bmp	FI
Mean	0.112	0.018	0.001	−0.001	0.036
Median	0.083	0.004	0.001	−0.001	0.014
Max	4.484	0.384	6.000	0.034	0.647
Min	−0.771	−0.391	−8.000	−0.055	−0.678
Std. Dev.	0.714	0.130	3.162	0.017	0.281
Skewness	4.438	−0.447	−0.248	−0.359	−0.100
Kurtosis	28.344	5.403	2.928	4.123	3.045
Obs.	52	52	52	52	52

Note: Authors calculations.

skewness values of −0.100, and kurtosis value of 3.045, indicating moderate tails and outliers. These results suggest high volatility in certain variables, particularly in equity and IPO, and indicate potential asymmetric behaviour and extreme value risks across the dataset. These results underscore the necessity of applying advanced econometric techniques to adequately capture the dynamic and potentially non-linear relationships among these variables (Alnafrah, 2024). The returns dynamics of the variables are shown in Fig. 8.1.

Table 8.3 presents the results of the correlation analysis among the variables. The findings reveal a positive correlation between FI and both Peer and Equity, suggesting that movements in financial indicators are aligned with changes in peer and equity metrics. Conversely, the variance inflation factor (VIF) test results exhibit values less than 3 for all variables, indicating the absence of multicollinearity among the independent variables. This implies that each independent variable contributes unique information to the model without redundancy, ensuring reliable and interpretable regression estimates where 'FI' is the dependent variable.

3.2 Empirical Models

This study employs two primary methodologies to investigate the role of Fintech in improving financial inclusion in Malaysia: The ARDL model and wavelet coherence analysis. The study utilises monthly data, with Financial Inclusion (FI) as the dependent variable and Equity, Peer, IPO and bmp as independent variables.

3.2.1 ARDL

The ARDL model, introduced by Pesaran et al. (2001), is employed to examine the long- and short-run relationships between financial inclusion and the selected

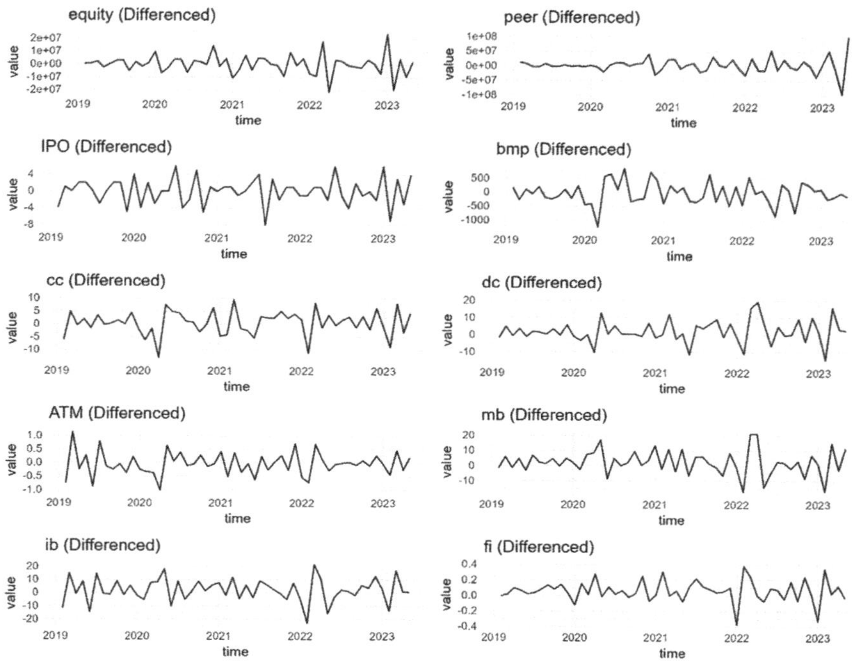

Fig. 8.1. Returns Dynamics of the Variables.

Table 8.3. Correlation Matrix.

	FI	Peer	IPO	bmp	Equity	VIF
FI	1					
Peer	0.897	1				1.088
IPO	0.051	0.115	1			1.149
bmp	−0.366	−0.229	−0.081	1		1.076
Equity	0.474	0.445	0.126	0.091	1	1.153

Note: Authors calculations.

Fintech indicators. This approach is particularly suitable for our analysis due to its ability to handle variables with different orders of integration and its efficiency in small sample sizes (Pesaran & Shin, 1999).

The ARDL model for our study can be expressed as follows:

$$\Delta \mathrm{FI}_t = \alpha_0 + \sum_{i=1}^{p} \beta_i \Delta \mathrm{FI}_{t-i} + \sum_{i=0}^{q_1} \gamma_i \Delta \mathrm{Equity}_{t-i} + \sum_{i=0}^{q_2} \delta_i \Delta \mathrm{Peer}_{t-i} + \sum_{i=0}^{q_3} \theta_i \Delta \mathrm{IPO}_{t-i} + \sum_{i=0}^{q_4} \lambda_i \Delta \mathrm{bmp}_{t-i} + \phi_1 \mathrm{FI}_{t-1} + \phi_2 \mathrm{Equity}_{t-1} + \phi_3 \mathrm{Peer}_{t-1} + \phi_4 \mathrm{IPO}_{t-1} + \phi_5 \mathrm{bmp}_{t-1} + \epsilon_t \quad (1)$$

Where:

FI_t is the financial inclusion index at time t.

Equity, Peer, IPO, and bmp are the independent variables at time t.

Δ denotes the first difference operator.

α_0 is the intercept.

β_i, γ_i, δ_i, θ_i and λ_i are the short-run coefficients.

ϕ_1, ϕ_2, ϕ_3, ϕ_4 and ϕ_5 are the long-run coefficients.

p and q_1 to q_4 are the optimal lag lengths.

ϵ_t is the error term.

The ARDL approach involves several steps. First, we select the optimal lag length using information criteria (e.g. AIC; SIC). Second, bounds test is applied to check for cointegration (Pesaran et al., 2001). Third, we estimate the long- and short-run coefficients if cointegration is confirmed. Finally, diagnostic tests are performed to ensure model validity.

3.2.2 Wavelet Coherence Analysis

To complement the ARDL analysis and capture the time-frequency dependencies between financial inclusion and Fintech indicators, we employ wavelet coherence analysis. This technique, based on the continuous wavelet transform (CWT), allows for the examination of co-movement and lead–lag relationships across different time scales (Grinsted et al., 2004).

The continuous wavelet transform of a time series $x(t)$ is defined as follows:

$$W_x(u,s) = \int_{-\infty}^{\infty} x(t) \frac{1}{\sqrt{s}} \psi^* \left(\frac{t-u}{s} \right) dt \tag{2}$$

Where:

$W_x(u,s)$ is the wavelet coefficient.

u is the location parameter.

s is the scale parameter.

ψ^* is the complex conjugate of the mother wavelet function.

The wavelet coherence between two time series $x(t)$ and $y(t)$ is then calculated as follows:

$$R^2(u,s) = \frac{\left| S\left(s^{-1} W_{xy}(u,s)\right) \right|^2}{S\left(s^{-1} \left| W_x(u,s) \right|^2\right) \cdot S\left(s^{-1} \left| W_y(u,s) \right|^2\right)} \tag{3}$$

Where:

$R^2(u,s)$ is the wavelet coherence.

S is a smoothing operator in both time and scale.

$W_{xy}(u,s)$ is the cross-wavelet transform of $x(t)$ and $y(t)$.

The wavelet coherence analysis will be conducted for each pair of variables (FI with Equity, Peer, IPO and bmp) to investigate the strength of co-movement between financial inclusion and each Fintech indicator and the lead–lag relationships across different time scales. By combining the ARDL and wavelet coherence methodologies, this study aims to provide a comprehensive understanding of both the long- and short-run relationships between Fintech indicators and financial inclusion, as well as their time-frequency dynamics in the Malaysian context.

4. Results and Discussion

4.1 Test Results of Unit Root Test

The stationarity of variables under study is an essential issue because when the series is non-stationary, the problem of spurious regression can occur. In this case, it can lead to incorrect results and misinterpretation. To avoid this problem, the variables must be stationary. Table 8.4 presents the results of the Augmented Dickey–Fuller (ADF) unit root test performed to assess the stationarity of the variables considered in this study. The results show that all variables except for IPO are not stationary at $I(0)$ level while at the $I(1)$, after taking the first difference, all variables become stationary. Accordingly, since the variables are stationary at mixed levels, we applied the ARDL method.

Table 8.4. Results of ADF Unit Root Test.

	$I(0)$		$I(1)$	
Variable	**Test Stat.**	***p*-Value**	**Test Stat.**	***p*-Value**
Equity	−1.744	0.677	−7.374	0.011***
Peer	−2.356	0.431	−3.752	0.029**
IPO	−3.431	0.061*	−5.162	0.000***
bmp	−2.238	0.479	−4.594	0.000***
FI	−2.543	0.356	−5.996	0.000***

Note(s): ***,** and* denote stationarity at 1%, 5% and 10% significance level, respectively. According to Hanna–Quinn Information Criterion and Schwartz Information Criterion, 1 lag is determined as the appropriate lag length.

4.2 ARDL Model Results

Table 8.5 shows the results of the ARDL model. The results reveal that in the long run, P2P financing and broad market price have a substantial positive impact on financial inclusion. Specifically, the long-run coefficient for P2P financing (2.452) suggests that an increase in P2P financing significantly enhances financial inclusion. This indicates that as more individuals and businesses engage in P2P financing, more people are likely to gain access to financial services. Similarly, the broad market price coefficient (4.573) implies that a favourable market environment also promotes financial inclusion, possibly through increased investor confidence and market stability that encourages more people to engage with financial markets. Additionally, the results also show that ECF and initial public offerings (IPOs) also positively influence financial inclusion, albeit to a lesser extent. The coefficient for ECF (0.011)

Table 8.5. ARDL Results.

	Financial Inclusion (3.1.3.1.1)	
	Coefficient	**S.E**
Short term		
ECT	−2.891***	0.325
Δ_{FI}	1.121***	0.239
$\Delta_{lnEquity}$	0.108*	0.056
Δ_{lnPeer}	−1.334***	0.2891
Δ_{IPO}	0.013**	0.006
Δ_{lnbmp}	−0.431	1.289
Constant	0.024*	0.028
Long term		
L_{FI}	2.891***	0.122
L_{Equity}	0.011**	0.108
L_{Peer}	2.452***	0.116
L_{IPO}	0.019**	0.023
L_{bmp}	4.573***	0.1882
Adjusted R^2	0.83	

Note: ***, ** and * indicate significance at the level of 1%, 5% and 10%.

indicates a modest positive relationship, suggesting that increasing ECF activities slightly boosts financial inclusion. Similarly, the IPO coefficient (0.019) also shows a positive impact, meaning that a more active IPO market can contribute to higher levels of financial inclusion through providing more investment opportunities and facilitating capital access for businesses that can offer financial services.

The results also show that in the short run, the dynamics are more complex. The coefficients indicate that short-term changes in P2P financing, ECF and previous levels of financial inclusion significantly influence current financial inclusion. For example, the negative coefficient for lagged P2P financing (−1.334) suggests that a sudden increase in P2P financing might initially reduce financial inclusion before its benefits are realised in the long term. This is due to market adjustments and the time required for individuals to adopt and trust new financial technologies. This may also be due to the substitutive nature of P2P to conventional banking where increase in P2P activities could result in cash withdrawals from banks (Ishak & Rahman, 2021).

Conversely, the positive coefficient for ECF (0.108) in the short run implies that immediate increases in ECF positively impact financial inclusion. Moreover, the significant positive short-run coefficient for lagged financial inclusion (1.1214) highlights the inertia in financial inclusion levels. This means that past improvements in financial inclusion continue to influence current levels, reinforcing the idea that financial inclusion builds on itself over time. Additionally, the positive coefficient for the immediate change in IPOs (0.013) suggests that IPO activities can quickly enhance financial inclusion through increased investor participation and market liquidity. Furthermore, the error correction term is negative and highly significant, suggesting that any short-term deviations from this long-run equilibrium are corrected over time, ensuring that the financial inclusion levels revert to their equilibrium path after a disturbance.

The results of the ARDL bounds test and error correction model (ECM) shown in Table 8.6 provide substantial insights into the impact of Fintech on financial inclusion. By examining the long- and short-run dynamics, we can understand how different facets of Fintech innovation influence financial inclusion over time. Additionally, the cointegration test confirms a long-run relationship between the variables, indicating that ECF, P2P financing, broad market price and IPOs are jointly associated with financial inclusion in the long term.

The diagnostic plots of the ARDL model, shown in Fig. 8.2, indicate the stability of the model over time. The Recursive CUSUM test (top left) and Recursive CUSUM of squares test (top right) both display that their respective black lines remain well within the 5% significance limits represented by the red dashed lines, suggesting that there is no structural instability in the parameters of the model over time. Similarly, the Recursive MOSUM test (bottom left) demonstrates that the moving sum of recursive residuals also stays within the red limits, further confirming the model's stability. Therefore, these diagnostic tests provide evidence that our model maintains consistent parameter estimates and variance stability throughout the sample period.

Table 8.6. Post Estimation Tests.

Test	**Value**	***p*-Value**
Breusch–Godfrey test for the autocorrelation	1.229	0.276
Box-Ljung test	0.698	0.4.3
Studentised Breusch-Pagan test	16.019	0.312
Shapiro-Wilk normality test	0.988	0.879
RESET test	0.151	0.699
Pesaran et al. (2001) cointegration test	$I(0)$	$I(1)$
10% critical value	2.868	3.782
5% critical value	3.358	4.365
1% critical value	4.455	5.615
F-statistic = 10.040		

Note: Authors calculations.

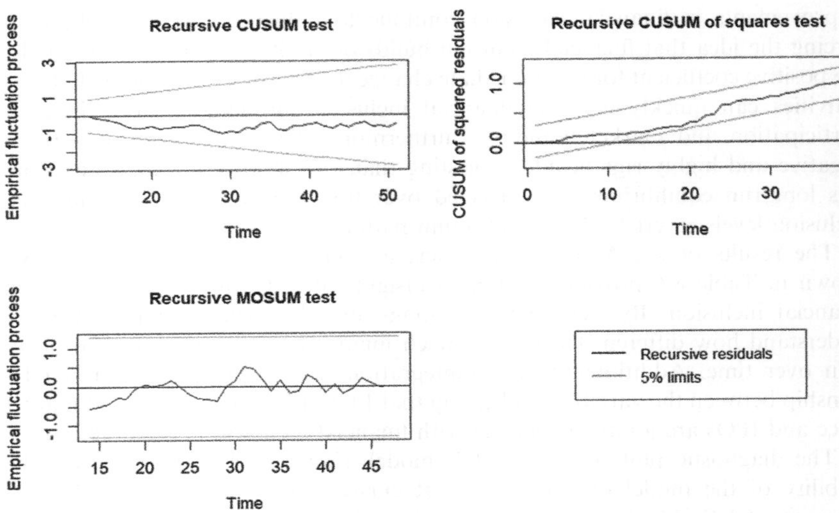

Fig. 8.2. ARDL Stability Test (Recursive CUSUM).

4.3 Wavelet Spectrum Results

The wavelet power spectrum analysis of P2P lending transactions, IPO, bmp and FI reveals significant insights into the cyclical behaviour and temporal evolution of these variables. Fig. 8.3 indicates strong short-term volatilities, particularly around 3–4 months, which are prominent from mid-2019 to early 2020, reflecting quarterly financial cycles, investor behaviour and market responses to various economic policies. Notably, the onset of the COVID-19 pandemic in early 2020 likely contributed to heightened volatility and increased oscillations in these variables as investors reacted to unprecedented economic uncertainties. Additionally, a moderate power observed also in medium to longer-term periods, notably around 6–8 months during mid to late 2020, suggests semi-annual or annual fluctuations driven by broader economic trends, including the initial economic recovery phases post-lockdowns. Towards late 2020 and into 2021, the effects of global inflation shocks and economic stimulus measures influenced these patterns, reflecting the interplay between recovery efforts and market adjustments. These findings imply that financial inclusion, financial market activities of companies and P2P lending transactions are influenced by both short-term economic shocks and longer-term recovery trends, providing valuable insights for investors, policymakers and market analysts in understanding the cyclical nature of this financial activity amidst significant global events. As for ECF, the results reveal notable patterns in its cyclical behaviour. Fig. 8.3 shows high power concentration in short-term periods (3–4 months) indicates significant volatility, especially during early 2020, likely due to the COVID-19 pandemic. Moreover, medium to longer-term periods (6–8 months) also show moderate power,

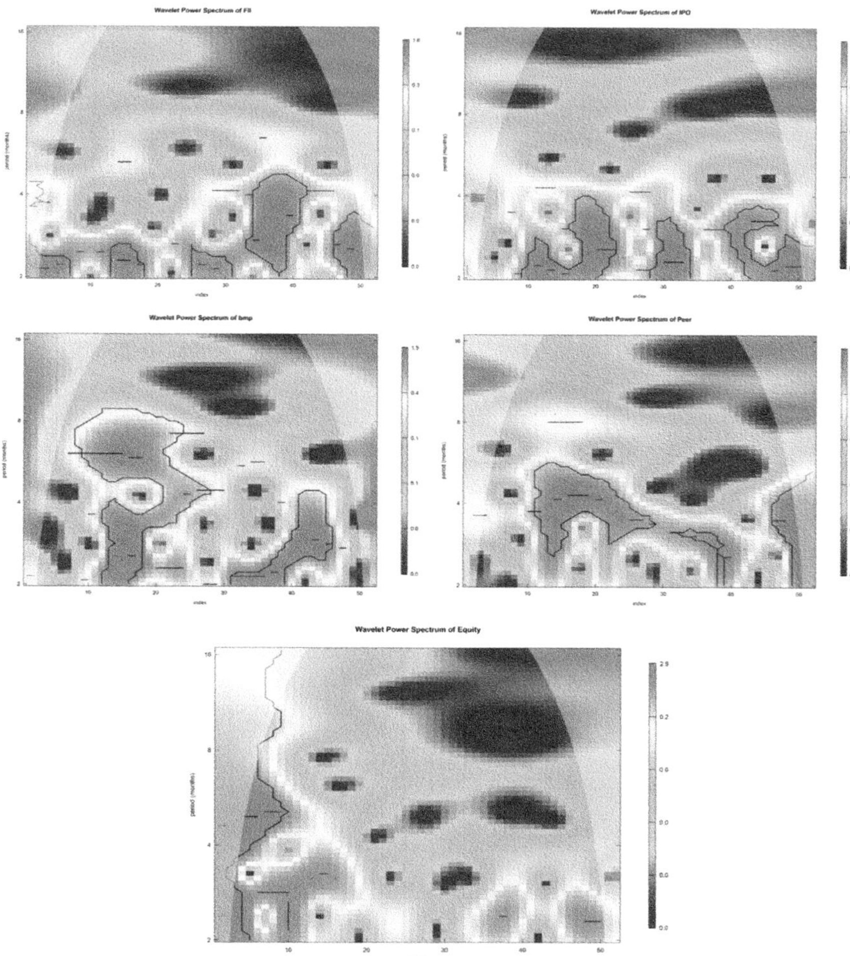

Fig. 8.3. Wavelet Spectrum of the Variables.

reflecting the impacts of the global economic recovery and inflation shocks post-pandemic. These fluctuations highlight the dynamic nature of ECF, influenced by immediate economic disruptions and longer-term market adjustments.

4.4 Wavelet Coherence Results

The results of the wavelet coherence, shown in Fig. 8.4, between ECF and financial inclusion (FI) from January 2019 to May 2023 provides insights into their temporal relationship across different scales. High coherence regions,

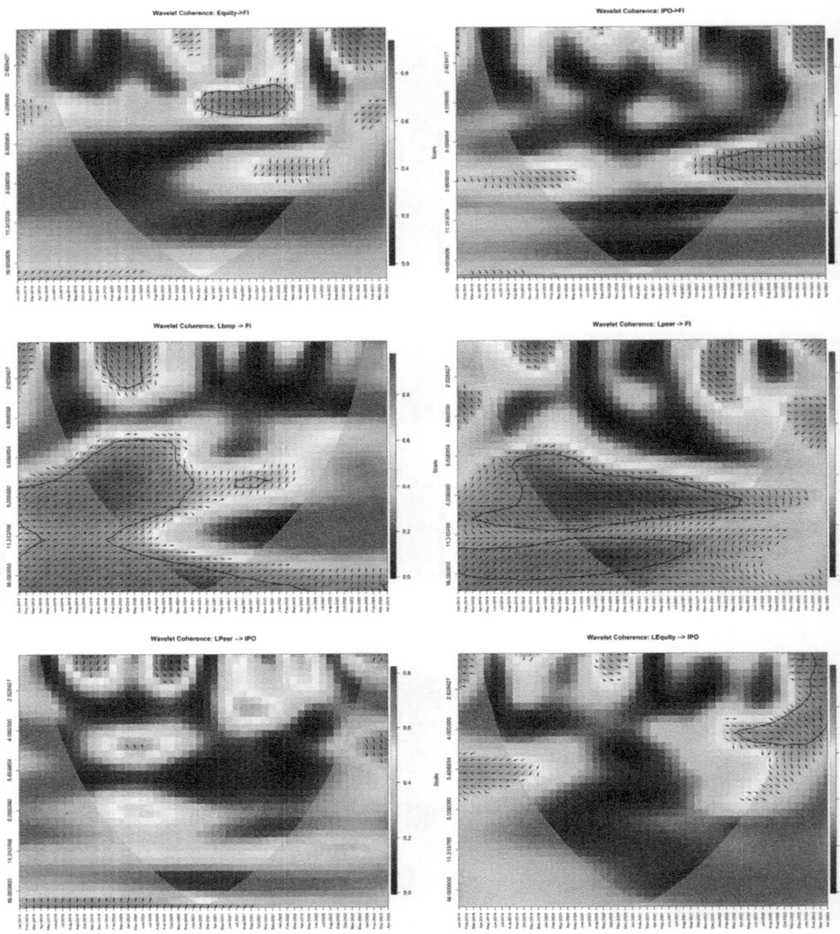

Fig. 8.4. Wavelet Coherence Results.

especially around the medium-term scales (approximately 6–12 months), suggest a strong correlation between Equity and FI during these periods. Notably, the significant coherence around mid-2021 could be attributed to post-pandemic economic adjustments, where increased ECF activities might have coincided with efforts to enhance financial inclusion. The arrows pointing predominantly right and upward in high coherence areas indicate a positive phase relationship, where changes in ECF precede similar changes in financial inclusion. This pattern underscores the interconnectedness of these two variables, highlighting how shifts in crowdfunding dynamics can influence financial inclusion initiatives and vice versa. Understanding this relationship is crucial for policymakers and stakeholders aiming to leverage ECF as a tool for improving financial inclusion.

As for the dynamic relationship between FI and Peer, the results reveal complex dynamics over various timeframes. The results show significant areas of high coherence (regions with black arrows) at different periods, especially between early 2019 and late 2020. These zones suggest strong interactions between P2P lending and financial inclusion during these times. The arrows within the plot indicate the phase difference between the two series. Arrows pointing to the right imply that the series are in phase while arrows pointing to the left indicate that they are out of phase. In areas of high coherence, the arrows generally point to the right and upward, suggesting that changes in P2P lending tend to lead changes in financial inclusion. The period during and immediately following the COVID-19 crisis (2020) shows particularly strong coherence. This indicates that P2P lending had a significant role in financial inclusion during the pandemic, possibly as an alternative financial resource during economic uncertainty. As the economy began to recover from COVID-19 (post-2021), there are still areas of high coherence but at longer periods, suggesting a sustained relationship between P2P lending and financial inclusion during the recovery phase. Furthermore, the area at a scale between 2 and 5 months, particularly towards the end of 2022 and the beginning of 2023, shows arrows pointing from right to left. This indicates an inverse relationship between peer and FI in this period and scale range. This suggests that during this time frame, movements in financial inclusion are leading the changes in P2P lending rather than the other way around. This reflects changes in economic and regulatory conditions affecting financial inclusion and subsequently impacting P2P lending activities.

5. Conclusion and Implications

We investigate the impact of crowdfunding on financial inclusion and compare between the effect of two distinguished types of crowdfunding on financial inclusion, which gives further insights into the dynamics of different types of crowdfunding on financial inclusion. To this end, we construct monthly financial inclusion index for Malaysia to validate the potential impact of crowdfunding on financial inclusion and a plethora of statistical methods that ranges from ARDL, wavelet spectrum method and wavelet coherence approach to analyse not only the short- and long-term relationships between our examined variables but also to gain further insights into the cyclical behaviour, temporal evolution and temporal relationship of these variables across different scales.

The implications of ARDL findings are profound for policymakers and financial technology innovators. The long-run positive impact of P2P financing and broad market price on financial inclusion underscores the importance of fostering a supportive environment for these Fintech activities. Therefore, policymakers should consider regulations that facilitate P2P financing and maintain market stability to ensure sustained improvements in financial inclusion. On the other hand, the short-run dynamics indicate that while immediate benefits can be gained from ECF and IPO activities, there may be initial market adjustments required for P2P financing.

For Fintech companies, the results highlight the importance of focusing on long-term strategies to enhance financial inclusion. To this end, innovations in P2P financing and efforts to maintain a stable market environment should be prioritised to achieve sustained financial inclusion. Additionally, continuous engagement in ECF and IPOs can provide immediate boosts to financial inclusion, aiding in the quicker adoption of financial services by previously underserved populations.

The results from wavelet spectrum indicate that financial inclusion, financial market activities of companies and P2P lending transactions are influenced by both short-term economic shocks and longer-term recovery trends, providing valuable insights for investors, policymakers and market analysts in understanding the cyclical nature of this financial activity amidst significant global events. As for ECF, the results reveal notable patterns in its cyclical behaviour with high power concentration in short-term periods which indicates significant volatility, especially during early 2020, likely due to the COVID-19 pandemic. Moreover, medium to longer-term periods also show moderate power, reflecting the impacts of the global economic recovery and inflation shocks post-pandemic. These fluctuations highlight the dynamic nature of ECF, influenced by immediate economic disruptions and longer-term market adjustments.

Finally, the results of the wavelet coherence analysis between Fintech financing tools and IPOs reveal that ECF plays a more prominent role than P2P lending in the long term. This suggests that Fintech tools focused on investments and tangible projects contribute more significantly to financial inclusion in the Malaysian economy, thereby highlighting the need for supportive policies, investor education, balanced regulations and an emphasis on real projects to enhance financial accessibility and stimulate growth.

The findings of this study have several key policy implications for enhancing financial inclusion through crowdfunding. Policymakers should focus on creating a regulatory environment that supports the growth and stability of both ECF and P2P lending platforms. For ECF, which shows significant long-term benefits, policies should encourage investment in tangible projects and provide clear guidelines to protect investors while fostering innovation. This can be achieved through targeted incentives for ECF platforms and streamlined processes for startups seeking to raise capital. Simultaneously, for P2P lending, which demonstrates immediate impacts but requires initial market adjustments, regulations should aim to ensure transparency, risk management and consumer protection. Implementing frameworks that mitigate risks and provide safeguards against financial volatility will enhance trust and stability in P2P markets. Additionally, integrating financial literacy programs that educate both investors and borrowers about the opportunities and risks associated with these crowdfunding models can facilitate more informed participation. Lastly, as the study highlights the cyclical nature of crowdfunding impacts, it is crucial for policymakers to be adaptable and responsive to economic shocks, ensuring that policies remain robust and effective during periods of financial instability. By addressing these areas, policymakers can better leverage crowdfunding to promote inclusive financial growth and contribute to sustainable economic development.

References

Ajouz, M., Abuamria, F., Al Zeer, I., Salahat, M., Shehadeh, M., Binsaddig, R., Al-Sartawi, A., & Al-Ramahi, N. M. (2023). Navigating the uncharted: The shaping of FinTech ecosystems in emerging markets. *Cuadernos de Economía, 46*(132), 189–201.

Abdul Halim, M. D. (2024). Does crowdfunding contribute to digital financial inclusion? *Research in Globalization*, 100238.

Ajouz, M., Shehadeh, M., Jabarin, R., Sharar, S. A., Jawabra, S., & Salman, W. (2024, February). Is FinTech catalyst or constraint for banking performance? In *2024 2nd International conference on cyber resilience (ICCR)* (pp. 1–5). IEEE.

Ali, I., Modibbo, U. M., Chauhan, J., & Meraj, M. (2021). An integrated multi-objective optimization modelling for sustainable development goals of India. *Environment, Development and Sustainability, 23*, 3811–3831.

Alkhazaleh, A., Assaf, A., Shehada, M., Almustafa, E., & Allahham, M. (2023). Analysis of the impact of fintech firms' lending on the expansion of service base companies in Jordan. *Information Sciences Letters, 12*(8), 2891–2902.

Alkhwaldi, A. F., Alharasis, E. E., Shehadeh, M., Abu-AlSondos, I. A., Oudat, M. S., & Bani Atta, A. A. (2022). Towards an understanding of FinTech users' adoption: Intention and e-loyalty post-COVID-19 from a developing country perspective. *Sustainability, 14*(19), 12616.

Allen, F., Demirguc-Kunt, A., Klapper, L., & Peria, M. S. M. (2016). The foundations of financial inclusion: Understanding ownership and use of formal accounts. *Journal of Financial Intermediation, 27*, 1–30.

Alnafrah, I. (2024). ESG practices mitigating geopolitical risks: Implications for sustainable environmental management. *Journal of Environmental Management, 358*, 120923. https://doi.org/10.1016/j.jenvman.2024.120923

Arner, D. W., Buckley, R. P., Zetzsche, D. A., & Veidt, R. (2020). Sustainability, FinTech and financial inclusion. *European Business Organization Law Review, 21*, 7–35.

Auboin, M., & Marchetti, J. (2018). *The contribution of digitalization to inclusive trade*. ICTSD Global Platform on Digital Trade.

Beier, M., & Wagner, K. (2015). Crowdfunding success: A perspective from social media and e-commerce. In *Thirty sixth international conference on information systems (ICIS), Fort Worth, Texas*.

Burtch, G., Ghose, A., & Wattal, S. (2013). An empirical examination of the antecedents and consequences of contribution patterns in crowd-funded markets. *Information Systems Research, 24*(3), 499–519. https://doi.org/10.1287/isre.1120.0468

Cevik, S. (2024). *Promise (un) kept? Fintech and financial inclusion*. IMF Working Paperm WP/24/131. International Monetary Fund.

CGAP. (2018). *It's time to slow digital credit's growth in East Africa, CGAP blog series digital credit: Borrower experiences and emerging risks*. https://www.cgap.org/blog/its-time-slow-digital-credits-growth-east-africa. Accessed on July 27, 2024.

Chauvet, L., & Jacolin, L. (2017). Financial inclusion, bank concentration, and firm performance. *World Development, 97*, 1–13.

Cheah, C. (2015, July 1). Malaysia first in ASEAN to have crowdfunding laws. *Star*. https://www.thestar.com.my/News/Nation/2015/07/01/crowdfunding-laws-malaysia/

Chung, S., Kim, K., Lee, C. H., & Oh, W. (2023). Interdependence between online peer-to-peer lending and cryptocurrency markets and its effects on financial inclusion. *Production and Operations Management*, *32*(6), 1939–1957.

Claessens, S., Frost, J., Turner, G., & Zhu, F. (2018, September). Fintech credit markets around the world: Size, drivers and policy issues. *BIS Quarterly Review*. https://www.bis.org/publ/qtrpdf/r_qt1809e.htm

Della Peruta, M. (2017). Adoption of mobile money and financial inclusion: A macroeconomic approach through cluster analysis. *Economics of Innovation and New Technology*, *27*(2), 154–173.

Demir, A., Pesqué-Cela, V., Altunbas, Y., & Murinde, V. (2022). Fintech, financial inclusion and income inequality: A quantile regression approach. *The European Journal of Finance*, *28*(1), 86–107.

Demirgüc-Kunt, A., Klapper, L., Singer, D., Ansar, S., & Hess, J. R. (2018). *The Global Findex Database 2017*. http://documents.worldbank.org/curated/en/332881525873182837/The-Global-Findex-Database-2017-Measuring-Financial-Inclusion-and-the-Fintech-Revolution. Accessed on July 26, 2024.

Demirgüc-Kunt, A., Klapper, L., Singer, D., & Van Oudheusden, P. (2015). *The Global Findex Database 2014: Measuring financial inclusion around the world*. https://papers.ssrn.com/sol3/papers.cfm?abstract_id=2594973#. Accessed on July 26, 2024.

Diniz, E., Birochi, R., & Pozzebon, M. (2012). Triggers and barriers to financial inclusion: The use of ICT-based branchless banking in an Amazon county. *Electronic Commerce Research and Applications*, *11*(5), 484–494.

Emuron, A., van der Nest, D. P., & Coffie, C. P. K. (2024). FinTech and financial development: The role of traditional financial institutions. *African Journal of Economic and Management Studies*.

Frame, W. S., Srinivasan, A., & Woosley, L. (2001). The effect of credit scoring on small-business lending. *Journal of Money, Credit, and Banking*, 813–825.

Gai, K., Qiu, M., & Sun, X. (2018). A survey on FinTech. *Journal of Network and Computer Applications*, *103*, 262–273.

Gomber, P., Kauffman, R. J., Parker, C., & Weber, B. W. (2018). On the fintech revolution: Interpreting the forces of innovation, disruption, and transformation in financial services. *Journal of Management Information Systems*, *35*(1), 220–265.

Gosavi, A. (2018). Can mobile money help firms mitigate the problem of access to finance in Eastern sub-Saharan Africa? *Journal of African Business*, *19*(3), 343–360.

Grinsted, A., Moore, J. C., & Jevrejeva, S. (2004). NPG - Application of the cross wavelet transform and wavelet coherence to geophysical time series. *Nonlinear Processes in Geophysics*, *11*, 561–566. https://doi.org/10.5194/npg-11-561-2004

Hasan, M., Noor, T., Gao, J., Usman, M., & Abedin, M. Z. (2023). Rural consumers' financial literacy and access to FinTech services. *Journal of the Knowledge Economy*, *14*(2), 780–804.

Ighobor, K. (2015). Sustainable Development Goals are in sync with Africa's priorities. *Africa Renewal*, *29*(3), 3–5.

Ishak, M. S. I., & Rahman, M. H. (2021). Equity-based Islamic crowdfunding in Malaysia: A potential application for Mudharabah. *Qualitative Research in Financial Markets*, *13*(2), 183–198. https://doi.org/10.1108/QRFM-03-2020-0024

Jenik, I., Lyman, T., & Nava, A. (2017). *Crowdfunding and financial inclusion* CGAP (Consultative Group to Assist the Poor) working paper, 41.

Joia, L. A., & dos Santos, R. P. (2019). ICT-equipped bank boat and the financial inclusion of the riverine population of Marajó Island in the Brazilian Amazon. *Information Systems Journal*, *29*(4), 842–887.

Karlan, D., Osei, R., Osei-Akoto, I., & Udry, C. (2014). Agricultural decisions after relaxing credit and risk constraints. *Quarterly Journal of Economics*, *129*(2), 597–652.

Katseli, L., & Boufounou, P. (2020). Crowdfunding: An innovative instrument for development finance and financial inclusion. In *Recent advances and applications in alternative investments*. IGI Global.

Liberti, J. M., & Petersen, M. A. (2019). Information: Hard and soft. *Review of Corporate Finance Studies*, *8*(1), 1–41.

Lusardi, A., & Mitchell, O. S. (2011). Financial literacy around the world: An overview. *Journal of Pension Economics and Finance*, *10*(4), 497–508.

Lusardi, A., & Mitchell, O. S. (2014). The economic importance of financial literacy: Theory and evidence. *American Economic Journal: Journal of Economic Literature*, *52*(1), 5–44.

Maskara, P. K., Kuvvet, E., & Chen, G. (2021). The role of P2P platforms in enhancing financial inclusion in the United States: An analysis of peer-to-peer lending across the rural–urban divide. *Financial Management*, *50*(3), 747–774.

Michael, B., Koroleska, N., Tai, A., & Wong, D. W. H. (2022). A critical look at using financial technology policy to promote the sustainable development goals. *Sustainable Development*, *30*(6), 1911–1920.

Modibbo, U. M., Ali, I., & Ahmed, A. (2021). Multi-objective optimization modelling for analysing sustainable development goals of Nigeria: Agenda 2030. *Environment, Development and Sustainability*, *23*(6), 9529–9563.

Moses, D., Asukwo, A. E., Yusuf, M. A., & Ibanga, I. J. (2021). Achieving sustainable development goals 2016-2030 in Nigeria through female enrolment into electrical/electronics engineering trade in technical colleges of Adamawa state. *Journal of Advanced Research in Economics and Administrative Sciences*, *2*(1).

Oliveira, D. S. C. D. (2018). *Fintechs e inclusão financeira: o caso da implementação de uma plataforma digital de pagamentos em favelas do Rio de Janeiro e São Paulo*. (Unpublished doctoral dissertation).

Owen, A. L., & Pereira, J. M. (2018). Bank concentration, competition, and financial inclusion. *Review of Development Finance*, *8*(1), 1–17.

Pesaran, M. H., & Shin, Y. (1999). An autoregressive distributed-lag modelling approach to cointegration analysis. In S. Strøm (Ed.), *Econometrics and economic theory in the 20th century: The Ragnar Frisch centennial symposium* (pp. 371–413). Cambridge University Press.

Pesaran, M. H., Shin, Y., & Smith, R. J. (2001). Bounds testing approaches to the analysis of level relationships. *Journal of Applied Econometrics*, *16*, 289–326.

Principal Financial Services. (2023). *Global Financial Inclusion Index 2023*. Principal Financial Group.

Rehman, S. U., Al-Shaikh, M., Washington, P. B., Lee, E., Song, Z., Abu-AlSondos, I. A., Shehadeh, M., & Allahham, M. (2023). FinTech adoption in SMEs and bank credit supplies: A study on manufacturing SMEs. *Economies*, *11*(8), 213.

Securities Commission Malaysia. (2024). *Securities Commission Malaysia Annual Report 2023*. https://www.sc.com.my/resources/publications-and-research/sc-annual-report-2023

Siddik, M. N. A., & Kabiraj, S. (2018). Does financial inclusion induce financial stability? Evidence from cross-country analysis. *Australasian Accounting, Business and Finance Journal*, *12*(1), 34–46.

Slimani, A., & Ziky, M. (2021). Crowdfunding and financial inclusion: A systematic literature review and a conceptual framework. *International Journal of Business and Economy*, *3*(4), 25–37.

Thomas, N. M. (2023). Modeling key enablers influencing FinTechs offering SME credit services: A multi-stakeholder perspective. *Electronic Markets*, *33*(1), 18.

World Bank. (2019). *Impact bonds and maximizing finance for development*. The World Bank. https://documents1.worldbank.org/curated/ar/585221565076840397/pdf/Impact-Bonds-Maximizing-Finance-for-Development.pdf. Accessed on July 26, 2024.

Part 3

The Future of FinTech: Sustainability and Challenges

Chapter 9

Impact of Financial Technology (FinTech) on Sustainable Growth: Key Factors, Practical Cases and Empirical Review

Imene Guermazi

Institute of Higher Commercial Studies, Sfax, Tunisia

Abstract

This paper aims to investigate the impact of FinTech on sustainable growth. First, we delve into the evolution of FinTech solutions and the key factors that shape their influence on sustainability. We highlight how FinTech fosters environmental, social and economic sustainability (ESG) within the financial sector. Additionally, we provide practical examples of FinTech firms contributing to the promotion of ESG factors, the enhancement of renewable energies and the reduction of energy costs. Furthermore, we review empirical studies that confirm the significant and positive impact of FinTech on various aspects such as financial inclusion, green finance, women's empowerment, renewable energy adoption, ESG considerations and environmental protection. These insights have substantial implications for all stakeholders involved. By harnessing adherence to FinTech solutions and promoting FinTech innovations, efficiency and sustainable practices, stakeholders can actively contribute to building a more resilient, inclusive and sustainable global economy.

Keywords: FinTech; sustainable growth; ESG; financial inclusion; green finance; women's empowerment

1. Introduction

FinTech is an ideal term representing technological progress in the financial industry; it has been created by the fusion of finance and technology. The concept of FinTech is a melting pot of varied projects based on digital platforms, data analytics,

From Digital Disruption to Dominance, 211–224

doi:10.1108/978-1-83549-608-420251010

automation and blockchain technologies for changing traditional financial services. These changes have gone beyond the borders of the banking sector and created new thought in other sectors as well. They engendered more efficient and accessible financial operations and have led to greater financial inclusion, risk management and more investment opportunities for individuals and businesses globally.

FinTech expansion also impacted sustainable growth, enhancing not only economic growth but environmental stewardship, social responsibility and ethical considerations. Financial services and technology can be more beneficial when they embody responsible financial practices, transparent governance, inclusive financial services and investments that yield positive impacts on both society and the planet.

In this paper, we attempt to map the role of FinTech in sustainable development and assess how FinTech can contribute to sustainable development goals. In other words, we argue that FinTech, when applied, can drive inclusive growth, increase efficiency and foster innovation, enhancing sustainable development.

This chapter has many theoretical and practical implications. First, we describe the evolution of FinTech over the years. Second, we analyse the key FinTech factors driving sustainable growth. Third, we review practical cases of FinTech applications enhancing sustainability. Fourth, we review empirical evidence of FinTech's impact on sustainable growth.

We structure these contributions as follows: In Section 2, we define FinTech and present its evolution. In Sections 3 and 4, we discuss key factors deriving the impact on the financial industry and sustainable growth. Section 5 presents practical cases while Section 6 documents empirical studies.

2. FinTech and Its Evolution Over Time

FinTech, short for Financial Technology, entails the use of technology to create and innovate financial services (Ajouz et al., 2023; Pandey et al., 2023). These comprise digital banking, payment systems, investment platforms, blockchains and the Internet of Things (Ahmed et al., 2006; Alkhazaleh et al., 2023; Palmaccio et al., 2021; Son & Jang, 2023; Wang et al., 2021). Developments in this area can be traced back to the early days of electronic trading systems in the 1970s and 1980s. This laid the foundation for automated trading and financial markets. However, the term gained prominent usage in the 21st century due to the rapid increase in internet accessibility, mobile devices and other digital platforms. Key milestones in the evolution of FinTech include

- Online Banking: The 1990s marked a shift from the traditional form of banking to online banking, enabling customers to access their banking remotely. This made them avoid endless queues, leading to convenience, time and cost savings for both banks and customers.
- Payment Systems: The development of electronic payment systems, such as credit/debit cards, online payment gateways and mobile wallets, revolutionised transaction and money management.

- Peer-to-Peer Lending: P2P lending platforms were first introduced in the mid-2000s. These have disrupted traditional lending models, connecting borrowers with individual investors, thereby surpassing traditional financial intermediaries.
- Blockchain Technology and Cryptocurrencies: The invention of blockchain technology in 2009 and the introduction of Bitcoin thereafter paved the way for decentralised digital currencies and many innovations related to digital assets, smart contracts and secure transactions.
- Robo-Advisors and WealthTech: The appearance of robo-advisors and automated investment platforms in the last half of the 2000s and during the early 21st century enabled the democratisation of investment management services, making them accessible and affordable for all retail investors.

Overall, FinTech evolved from simple electronic banking to a varied technology/service ecosystem, redefining the financial industry and driving digital transformation across the world.

3. Role of FinTech in Transforming Traditional Financial Services

FinTech has disrupted traditional financial services, resulting in very significant changes in most of the segments of financial services (Alkhwaldi et al., 2022; Takeda & Ito, 2021). Some of these significant impacts are as follows:

- Improved customer experience: FinTech solutions have made financial services more accessible, more user-friendly and more customisable. People have been able to do transactions, invest and manage their bank accounts easily through digital platforms and mobile apps.
- Efficiency and cost savings: FinTech mechanisms, digitisation and streamlined processes have disrupted operational costs and made institutions more efficient, faster in transaction times and better in scalability.
- Product diversity and innovation: FinTech has led to the emergence of new offerings like robo-advisors, digital lending platforms, crowdfunding, P2P payments and micro-investing.
- Financial inclusion: Through access to affordable and accessible financial solutions, FinTech has promoted financial inclusion for underserved populations, unbanked individuals and small businesses. Globally, mobile banking, digital wallets and microfinance platforms have allowed more people to access financial services.
- Disintermediation and Competition: FinTech revolutionised the conventional models of banking and finance, offering better and more agile customer-focused solutions.
- Risk management and compliance: FinTech innovations include advanced risk management tools, real-time analytics and compliance solutions that help institutions navigate regulatory challenges and risks and execute more robust cybersecurity measures.

4. Impact of FinTech on Sustainable Growth

The goal of sustainable growth is to achieve a balance between the need to reduce harmful effects on ecosystems and communities and economic and industrial growth. FinTech can serve this goal by key factors easing the acquisition of the requisite knowledge for informing strategic planning, decision-making processes and strategy development. Financial value interacts with social/environmental value, with mutual reinforcement of financial and social goals (Ajouz et al., 2024; Carè et al., 2023; Shehadeh, 2024).

4.1 FinTech Key Factors Driving Sustainable Growth

Several key factors contribute to driving sustainable growth in the financial industry, aligning with broader economic, social and environmental objectives (Lin et al., 2023). These factors are as follows:

- Sustainable investment platforms (Devine et al., 2022): FinTechs have created trading platforms that use sustainable criteria to select and evaluate investments. This facilitates access for investors to sustainable portfolios and monitoring of the environmental and social consequences of their investment decisions. Accordingly, it also channels money into socially and environmentally positive impact investments, lowering carbon emissions and promoting green infrastructure.
- Environmental drivers (Zhe et al., 2024): Financial technologies engender superior investments in renewable energies, environmentally friendly technologies and projects that reduce climate change risks. Increasing digital transactions removes paper-based procedures, which reduces deforestation and carbon emissions from paper production.
- Social factors: Sustainable finance is growingly considering significant social issues related to poverty reduction and increased access to education, health and social equity. Machine learning techniques and artificial intelligence allow for the processing of vast amounts of data, thereby helping poverty reduction and supporting sustainable economic growth (Raghavendra et al., 2023).
- Blockchain and traceability (Shahzad et al., 2023): Blockchain technology can confirm the origin and sustainability of goods, advancing transparency and corporate responsibility through the supply chain.
- Governance and Transparency (Dicuonzo et al., 2024): Financial sector development drivers related to good governance and transparency, including good governance as well as transparency; quality risk management systems, ethical business, adherence to regulatory requirements and stakeholder engagement, provide both trust and stability for the long run and create value.
- Technology and Innovation (Lin et al., 2023): Incorporating technology – FinTech solutions, artificial intelligence, blockchain and digital platforms – may provide a boost to innovation and efficiency in financial services. Technological factors enable new business models, better delivery of services and products, improved customer experience and support for sustainable finance activities.

- Innovation (Gomber et al., 2018): FinTech innovations about the delivery of products/services, business strategies and process implementations to remain competitive, solve emerging challenges and take advantage of opportunities for sustainable value creation.
- Efficiency: Effective use of technology and automation combined with workflow reduction and cost-effectiveness of practices enhances profitability, resilience and accountability for the environment (Gu et al., 2021; Jin & Han, 2018).
- Energy efficiency and emissions reduction: Energy management based on blockchain solutions enables real-time monitoring of energy consumption. This increases efficiency and lowers carbon footprint (Petri et al., 2020; Tao et al., 2022).

4.2 Practical Effects of FinTech Applications

4.2.1 Peer-to-Peer Lending Platforms (Deng et al., 2019)

P2P lending platforms are online platforms that provide channels for individuals or businesses to lend directly to each other, cutting out intermediary banks. In the lending environment, FinTech makes such platforms more efficient and inclusive; hence, it plays a crucial role in sustainable growth in several ways.

- Financial inclusion: P2P lending enables access to credit for those people and small businesses that traditional banks have underserved. It, therefore, advances financial inclusion and supports economic growth by empowering individuals and entrepreneurs to invest in sustainable initiatives.
- Cost reduction: One of the most significant benefits of P2P lending platforms is the avoidance of traditional banking infrastructure and intermediaries. This will help borrowers offer lower interest rates and fees. This enables businesses and individuals to allocate resources more efficiently to sustainable projects.
- Green and Sustainable Project Funding: Among P2P lending platforms are those interested in funding only green or sustainable projects. This type of platform connects investors wishing to support initiatives of environmental dimensions, with borrowers interested in raising capital for projects in sustainable agriculture, eco-friendly businesses and renewable energy.

4.2.2 Robo-Advisors for Sustainable Investing (Faradynawati & Söderberg, 2022)

Robo-advisors are automated investment platforms that use algorithms to provide investment advice and manage portfolios. If deployed in the arena of sustainable investments, robots have many benefits for investors and contribute towards several ways of sustainable growth.

- ESG inclusion: The investment decisions of robo-advisors may involve factors from environmental, social and governance perspectives.
- Diversification: The diversification of robo-advisors' investments in various asset classes and sectors reduces their risk and, by the way, supports sustainable investments such as clean technology and renewable energy.

- Accessibility: Compared to full-service wealth management, robo-advisors are less expensive and demand smaller investment amounts.

4.2.3 Sustainable Investing Platforms (Devine et al., 2022)

Sustainable investing platforms link investors to opportunities involving social and environmental impact as well as financial returns. They use FinTech capabilities to afford efficiency, transparency and measurement of the impact on investment activities. They optimise technology for tracking and measuring the environmental and social effects of investments. This transparency equips investors with a reliable, measurable outcome of their investment decisions.

4.3 FinTech Firms Practical Cases

4.3.1 M-KOPA Solar Kenya (Majale et al., 2024)

M-KOPA Solar is a FinTech company that sells, with mobile payment plans, pay-as-you-go solar home systems for off-grid households in Kenya. This model has substantially promoted sustainability by

- Not consuming fossil fuels in its generation of energy.
- Providing clean and renewable energy to rural and disadvantaged areas.
- Saving energy costs of, which increased the revenues and livelihoods of households and provide opportunities for productive activities.

4.3.2 Truvalue Labs USA (Erhemjamts et al., 2024)

Truvalue Labs is a FinTech startup in the United States focusing on the analysis of ESG data. Their AI-powered platform monitors and analyses large sets of data concerning the ESG performance of companies in real-time. This data-driven model will assist investors and businesses in making informed decisions regarding sustainable investments and practices. Truvalue Labs' platform contributes to sustainability by

- Encouraging companies to improve their ESG performance and transparency.
- Helping investors recognise and support companies that have robust sustainability practices.
- Facilitating the integration of ESG factors into investment decisions, thus capitalising on the sustainability opportunity.

4.3.3 Ant Forest by Ant Group China (Mi et al., 2021)

Ant Forest is an application initiated by Ant Group, one of the largest FinTech companies in China. It enables an individual to behave in an environmentally friendly way, using public transportation, saving energy and reducing their carbon footprint at the individual level. Every time these things are done in a day, the individual earns virtual 'green energy points' that can be redeemed for planting real trees in designated forest areas. Ant Forest promotes sustainability by

- Raising awareness and incentivising sustainable behaviour by a very large number of users.
- Making reforestation and environmental conservation possible through planting trees.
- Visualising how FinTech can gamify sustainability and engage people to work together to achieve environmental ends.

4.3.4 Lendahand (Gooch et al., 2020)

Lendahand is a fintech platform from the Netherlands that offers impact investments in emerging markets. The platform connects investors directly to sustainable and social impact projects within fields like renewable energy, agriculture and small business development to fund those projects for the betterment of positive social and environmental outcomes. Through Lendahand, sustainability is promoted in the following ways:

- Investment capital flows into projects in developing regions, which contribute to the growth of the economy and the empowerment of social actors.
- Investors supporting renewable energy projects and job creation, thereby reducing poverty and addressing investment gaps and driving positive change within neglected communities.

These specific FinTech applications showcase how technology can be harnessed to promote sustainable growth in finance and investment, encouraging a more environmentally and socially responsible approach to economic development.

5. Empirical Literature

A first part of studies investigated the impact of FinTech on green growth or Sustainable Development Goals (SDGs) globally. Yu and Li (2024) performed a two-way fixed effects model on data from 270 Chinese cities during 2006–2021. They showed the regulating mechanism of FinTech's sustainable development effect by measuring marketisation levels and green technology developments. Wei et al. (2024) used the novel MMQR technique to investigate the effects of FinTech, green finance, natural resources and green growth on environmental sustainability in BRICS countries. The results show a positive correlation between FinTech and green finance project enhancement. Moreover, FinTech has a substantial impact on sustainable development, following a particular U-shaped pattern that contributes to reducing resource restrictions. Chen et al. (2024) observed the World Development Indicator from 2000 to 2022 and employed the quantile autoregressive distributed lag (QARDL) model to account for the asymmetric impacts of FinTech and green growth on sustainable economic growth. They found evidence of long-run associations between the variables. Specifically, the lagged value of green growth has a positive and significant impact on sustainable economic growth, whereas FinTech positively and significatively influences sustainable economic growth. Kashif et al. (2024) encompassed data from 89 countries and employed a two-stage least-square regression approach with the instrumental variables and a two-step generalised method of moments. Their founding provided evidence that FinTech exerts a significant favourable influence on sustainable finance. Carè et al. (2023) employed multiple-case study methodology and grounded theory to investigate the contribution of FinTech companies to reaching SDGs. They provided evidence that the contribution of FinTechs to SDGs rises when they collaborate with other companies.

Other authors examined the effects of FinTech on resource extraction. Cao et al. (2021) and Miller et al. (2023) stated that FinTech enables ethical mineral sourcing using blockchain-based supply chain tracing. Ul-Durar et al. (2024) demonstrated the potential mitigating role of FinTech on resource extraction sustainability in 27 countries from the Asian OBOR group. Radulescu et al. (2024) performed deep learning-based FinTech to explore sustainability challenges in mineral extraction through a quantised deep learning approach for mineral identification during mining. Nilashi et al. (2024) used an in-depth Strengths, Weaknesses, Opportunities and Threats analysis to show that FinTech improves sustainable mineral management and promotes SDGs. Murshed (2024) suggested that ecological deficits are first widened and then eventually reduced by FinTech funding. In addition, there is an inverted U-shaped imbalance in the FinTech financing–ecological nexus.

A third part of the papers explored the influence of FinTech on environmental protection and renewable energies. Nenavath and Mishra (2023) showed that FinTech enhances the significant effect of green finance on the finance structure and environmental quality protection. Jiang (2023) studied the impact of FinTech on the sustainable development of renewable Chinese energy enterprises during 2009–2020 using mechanism tests. The findings reveal that FinTech promotes the sustainable development of renewable energy enterprises by improving investment efficiency. Firdousi et al. (2023) collected a panel dataset of 26 Morgan Stanley Capital International in developing countries from 2011 to 2021 and performed pooled ordinary least squares and robust fixed effects. Their results provided evidence that FinTech development discourages carbon emissions and boosts renewable energy resource consumption. Wang et al. (2024) documented that Fintech reduces carbon emissions via alleviating financing constraints, improving energy efficiency and promoting green innovation. Amaliah et al. (2024) confirmed that digital financial inclusion, proxied by automated teller machines and debit, significantly and positively impacts GDP growth and exerts a significant positive moderating effect on CO_2 emissions. Liu et al. (2024) suggest that FinTech reduces financing constraints and promotes green technological advances and, by the way, the green transformation of high-carbon enterprises across the board.

Other authors focused on the correlation between FinTech and bank sustainability effectiveness. Hidayat-ur-Rehman and Hossain (2024) underscored the direct and significant influence of FinTech adoption on bank sustainable performance. Notably, competitiveness and green finance play a mediating role and bridge the gap between sustainable and performance FinTech adoption. Salah Mahdi et al. (2023) suggested that FinTech development promotes banks' involvement in corporate social responsibility (CSR) strategies, but decreases banks' financial stability. Additionally, the results showed that FinTech positively moderates the impact of CSR on financial stability.

Another stream of literature examined the impact of FinTech on women's empowerment. Esmaeilpour Moghadam and Karami (2023) showed that the association between FinTech and women's empowerment is positive and significant in countries with low levels of gender discrimination. However, this relationship is irrelevant in countries classified as having high gender discrimination. Sidana et al. (2023) provided evidence that FinTech has increased women's financial literacy and security, empowered them to make financial decisions and promoted professional development. Therefore, FinTech has the potential to eliminate gender disparities and financial fragility at the macro-level, allowing women to fully engage in the economy while also contributing to long-term gender parity and economic progress.

Additionally, some studies investigated the impact of FinTech on environmental, social and governance (ESG). Ding et al. (2024) analysed the impact of FinTech development on firm ESG performance in a sample of Chinese listed companies. They suggested that FinTech development boosts corporate ESG practices through the easing of financial constraints. Du et al. (2022) found that regional FinTech expansion considerably influences Chinese firms' ESG performance and improves external governance. El Khoury et al. (2023) used dynamic conditional correlation, time-varying parameter vector autoregression and generalised autoregressive conditional heteroskedasticity to explore the impact of the Russia–Ukraine war on the spillover dynamics of FinTech, Morgan Stanley Capital International, renewable energy, ESG and gold. The results suggest that ESG and FinTech are net transmitters in developed countries, whereas renewable energy and gold are net receivers. Dicuonzo et al. (2024) demonstrated that FinTech in 180 listed banks enhances substantially ESG performance.

Further authors explored the interplay between FinTech, green finance and sustainable growth. Udeagha and Muchapondwa (2023) explored the combined effects of financial technology and green finance in accomplishing the region's carbon neutrality goals during 1990–2020 in BRICS economies. The findings reveal that green finance, FinTech and energy innovation promote environmental sustainability. Nenavath and Mishra (2023) analysed Indian data from 2010 to 2021 using the panel regression method and a two-step generalised model of moments. Their results showed that FinTech improves the substantial influence of green finance in the financial framework and environmental quality preservation while having no effect on the relationship between green finance and economic efficiency.

Finally, a few papers found a negative impact of FinTech on sustainable growth. Najaf et al. (2023) found evidence of the superior stock performance and sustainability of non-FinTech companies compared to FinTech companies.

Yasmeen et al. (2024) used the Panel Method of Moments Quantile Regression to analyse the interplay between financial technology and mineral extraction in the context of eliminating energy deprivation in the BRICS economies from 2004 to 2021. Their findings showed that FinTech, with mineral reduction, increases resource competition and raises energy poverty.

As shown by this review, most studies showed that FinTech plays a core role in driving various dimensions of sustainability: financial inclusion, green finance, women's empowerment, renewable energy, ESG considerations and environmental protection. Therefore, FinTech has the potential to act as a catalyst for sustainable development by positively influencing various areas such as financial access, environmental conservation, social equity and responsible investment practices. However, limited literature has conducted cross-country comparisons regarding this correlation. This underscores the importance of ongoing comparative research across countries to identify the factors that strengthen this relationship and foster its impact in regions where this correlation is less prominent.

6. Conclusion

This paper studied the relationship between FinTech and sustainability. We describe the progression over time and the key factors linking FinTech to sustainable growth. Further, we review practical cases and empirical studies highlighting this association. This analysis underscores that FinTech innovations have remarkably impacted all sustainable dimensions. Integration of FinTech has enhanced efficiencies, cost savings, green growth, transparency, environmental protection and new energies, among many others.

These insights have many implications. Financial institutions can improve their operational efficiency and reduce their costs through the use of FinTech solutions harnessing sustainable practices such as digital payment, paperless processes and green financing. By embracing sustainability as a core principle, FinTech stakeholders can contribute meaningfully to a more resilient, inclusive and sustainable global economy. Additionally, regulators and policymakers can take into consideration the positive influence that FinTech plays on sustainability when developing regulatory frameworks. This will include green investment incentives, encouragement of ESG reporting and the promotion of sustainable finance. Regarding consumers, they greatly benefit in terms of transparency, cost reduction and environmentally friendly practices, such as digital banking, which helps to eliminate paper usage and green investment platforms, which create opportunities for sustainable investment.

To reinforce this influence, we recommend policymakers first enhance education and awareness among stakeholders, such as consumers, businesses and organisations, regarding the significance of FinTech integration for sustainability achievement. Second, they should collaborate with financial institutions and FinTech to leverage FinTech's potential for sustainable growth. Additionally, they should be continuously assessing and improving regulatory efficiency in enforcing responsible practices in FinTech towards promoting green investments and sustainable innovation. Moreover, international cooperation, partnership and knowledge-sharing initiatives towards furthering the utilisation of FinTech would help enhance sustainable growth globally.

References

Ahmed, K., Hossain, M., & Adams, M. B. (2006). The effects of board composition and board size on the informativeness of annual accounting earnings. *Corporate Governance: An International Review*, *14*(5), 418–431.

Ajouz, M., Abuamria, F., Al Zeer, I., Salahat, M., Shehadeh, M., Binsaddig, R., AL-sartawi, A., & Al-Ramahi, N. M. (2023). Navigating the uncharted: The shaping of FinTech ecosystems in emerging markets. *Cuadernos de Economía*, *46*(132), 189–201.

Ajouz, M., Abuamria, F., Shehadeh, M., Abu-AlSondos, I. A., Aldulaimi, S. H., & Abdeldayem, M. (2024, January). Exploring the cascade: How buy-now-pay-later platforms fuel impulse buying tendency and the subsequent impact on sustainability. In *2024 ASU international conference in emerging technologies for sustainability and intelligent systems (ICETSIS)* (pp. 1–5). IEEE.

Alkhazaleh, A., Assaf, A., Shehada, M., Almustafa, E., & Allahham, M. (2023). Analysis of the impact of fintech firms' lending on the expansion of service base companies in Jordan. *Information Sciences Letters*, *12*(8), 2891–2902.

Alkhwaldi, A. F., Alharasis, E. E., Shehadeh, M., Abu-AlSondos, I. A., Oudat, M. S., & Bani Atta, A. A. (2022). Towards an understanding of FinTech users' adoption: Intention and e-loyalty post-COVID-19 from a developing country perspective. *Sustainability*, *14*(19), 12616.

Amaliah, I., Ali, Q., Sudrajad, Q., Rusgianto, S., Nu'man, H., & Aspiranti, T. (2024). Does digital financial inclusion forecast sustainable economic growth? Evidence from an emerging economy. *Journal of Open Innovation: Technology, Market, and Complexity*, *10*(2), 100262.

Cao, S., Powell, W., Foth, M., Natanelov, V., Miller, T., & Dulleck, U. (2021). Strengthening consumer trust in beef supply chain traceability with a blockchain-based human-machine reconcile mechanism. *Computers and Electronics in Agriculture*, *180*, 105886.

Carè, R., Boitan, I. A., & Fatima, R. (2023). How do FinTech companies contribute to the achievement of SDGs? Insights from case studies. *Research in International Business and Finance*, *66*, 102072.

Chen, L., Ma, R., Li, J., & Zhou, F. (2024). Revolutionizing sustainable economic growth in China: Harnessing natural resources, green development, and FinTech for a greener future. *Resources Policy*, *92*, 104944.

Deng, X., Huang, Z., & Cheng, X. (2019). FinTech and sustainable development: Evidence from China based on P2P data. *Sustainability*, *11*, 6434.

Devine, A., Sanderford, A., & Wang, C. (2022). Sustainability and private equity real estate returns. *The Journal of Real Estate Finance and Economics*, 1–27.

Dicuonzo, G., Palmaccio, M., & Shini, M. (2024). ESG, governance variables and FinTech: An empirical analysis. *Research in International Business and Finance*, *69*, 102205.

Ding, J., Li, L., & Zhao, J. (2024). How does FinTech prompt corporations toward ESG sustainable development? Evidence from China. *Energy Economics*, *131*, 107387.

Du, P., Huang, S., Hong, Y., & Wu, W. (2022). Can FinTech improve corporate environmental, social, and governance performance?—A study based on the dual path of internal financing constraints and external fiscal incentives. *Frontiers in Environmental Science*, *10*, 1061454.

El Khoury, R., Nasrallah, N., Hussainey, K., & Assaf, R. (2023). Spillover analysis across FinTech, ESG, and renewable energy indices before and during the Russia–Ukraine war: International evidence. *Journal of International Financial Management & Accounting*, *34*(2), 279–317.

Erhemjamts, O., Huang, K., & Tehranian, H. (2024). Climate risk, ESG performance, and ESG sentiment in US commercial banks. *Global Finance Journal*, *59*.

Esmaeilpour Moghadam, H., & Karami, A. (2023). Financial inclusion through FinTech and women's financial empowerment. *International Journal of Social Economics*, *50*(8), 1038–1059.

Faradynawati, I. A. A., & Söderberg, I.-L. (2022). Sustainable investment preferences among robo-advisor clients. *Sustainability*, *14*.

Firdousi, S. F., Afzal, A., & Amir, B. (2023). Nexus between FinTech, renewable energy resource consumption, and carbon emissions. *Environmental Science & Pollution Research*, *30*, 84686–84704.

Gomber, P., Kauffman, R. J., Parker, C., & Weber, B. W. (2018). On the FinTech revolution: Interpreting the forces of innovation, disruption, and transformation in financial services. *Journal of Management Information Systems*, *35*(1), 220–265.

Gooch, D., Kelly, R., Stiver, A., van der Linden, J., Petre, M., Richards, M., Klis-Davies, A., MacKinnon, J., Macpherson, R., & Walton, C. (2020). The benefits and challenges of using crowdfunding to facilitate community-led projects in the context of digital civics. *International Journal of Human-Computer Studies*, *134*, 33–43.

Gu, W., Wang, J., Hua, X., & Liu, Z. (2021). Entrepreneurship and high-quality economic development: Based on the triple bottom line of sustainable development. *The International Entrepreneurship and Management Journal*, *17*, 1–27.

Hidayat-ur-Rehman, I., & Hossain, M. N. (2024). The impacts of FinTech adoption, green finance and competitiveness on banks' sustainable performance: Digital transformation as moderator. *Asia-Pacific Journal of Business Administration*. ahead-of-print. https://doi.org/10.1108/APJBA-10-2023-0497

Jiang, B. (2023). Does FinTech promote the sustainable development of renewable energy enterprises? *Environmental Science and Pollution Research*, *30*, 65141–65148.

Jin, J., & Han, L. (2018). Assessment of Chinese green funds: Performance and industry allocation. *Journal of Cleaner Production*, *171*, 1084–1093.

Kashif, M., Pinglu, C., Ullah, S., & Mubasher, Z. (2024). Evaluating the influence of financial technology (FinTech) on sustainable finance: A comprehensive global analysis. *Financial Markets and Portfolio Management*, *38*, 123–155.

Lin, Y., Lu, Z., & Wang, Y. (2023). The impact of environmental, social, and governance (ESG) practices on investment efficiency in China: Does digital transformation matter? *Research in International Business and Finance*, *66*, 102050.

Liu, J., Kang, X., & Wang, W. (2024). FinTech's impact on green total factor productivity of high carbon enterprises. *Emerging Markets Finance and Trade*, *60*(4), 744–768.

Majale, C., Opinde, G., & Nygaard, I. (2024). Bringing light, connectivity and waste to local communities: A study of the post-consumption value chain for off-grid solar devices in Kenya. *Energy Research and Social Science*, *112*, 103516.

Mi, L., Xu, T., Sun, Y., Zhao, J., Lv, T., Gan, X., Shang, K., & Qiao, L. (2021). Playing Ant Forest to promote online green behavior: A new perspective on uses and gratifications. *Journal of Environmental Management*, *278*(2), 111544.

Miller, T., Cao, S., Foth, M., Boyen, X., & Warwick Powell, W. (2023). An asset-backed decentralised finance instrument for food supply chains – A case study from the livestock export industry. *Computers in Industry*, *147*, 103863.

Murshed, M. (2024). The role of FinTech financing in correcting ecological problems caused by mineral resources: Testing the novel ecological deficit hypothesis. *Resources Policy*, *88*, 104439.

Najaf, K., Haj Khalifa, A., Obaid, S. M., Rashidi, A. A., & Ataya, A. (2023). Does sustainability matter for FinTech firms? Evidence from United States firms. *Competitiveness Review*, *33*(1), 161–180.

Nenavath, S., & Mishra, S. (2023). Impact of green finance and FinTech on sustainable economic growth: Empirical evidence from India. *Heliyon*, *9*(5), e16301.

Nilashi, N., Abumalloh, R., Keng-Boon, O., Tan, G., Cham, T., & Aw, E. (2024). Unlocking sustainable resource management: A comprehensive SWOT and thematic analysis of FinTech with a focus on mineral management. *Resources Policy*, *92*.

Palmaccio, M., Dicuonzo, G., & Belyaeva, Z. S. (2021). The internet of things and corporate business models: A systematic literature review. *Journal of Business Research*, *131*, 610–618.

Pandey, D. K., Hassan, M. K., Kumari, V., Zaied, Y. B., & Rai, V. K. (2023). Mapping the landscape of FinTech in banking and finance: A bibliometric review. *Research in International Business and Finance*, 102116.

Petri, I., Barati, M., Rezgui, Y., & F. Rana, O. (2020). Blockchain for energy sharing and trading in distributed prosumer communities. *Computers in Industry*, *123*, 103282.

Radulescu, M., Dalal, S., Lilhore, U., K., & Saimiya, S. (2024). Optimizing mineral identification for sustainable resource extraction through hybrid deep learning enabled FinTech model. *Resources Policy*, *89*, 104692.

Raghavendra, A. H., Majhi, S. G., Mukherjee, A., & Bala, P. K. (2023). Role of artificial intelligence (AI) in poverty alleviation: A bibliometric analysis. *VINE Journal of Information and Knowledge Management Systems*. ahead-of-print. https://doi.org/10.1108/VJIKMS-05-2023-0104

Salah Mahdi, I. B., Bouaziz, M., & Boujelbène Abbes, M. (2023). The moderating effect of FinTech on the relationship between CSR and banks' financial stability: Baron and Kenny's approach analysis. *EuroMed Journal of Business*. ahead-of-print. https://doi.org/10.1108/EMJB-03-2023-0082

Shahzad, U., Asl, M. G., & Tedeschi, M. (2023). Is there any market state-dependent contribution from Blockchain-enabled solutions to ESG investments? Evidence from conventional and Islamic ESG stocks. *International Review of Economics & Finance*, *86*, 139–154.

Shehadeh, M. (2024). Digital transformation: A catalyst for sustainable business practices. In *Technological innovations for business, education and sustainability* (pp. 29–45). Emerald Publishing Limited.

Sidana, A., Goel, R., & Rehman, M. (2023). A study of stimulating sustainable women empowerment through FinTech applications. In Q. T. Islam, R. Goel, & T. Singh (Eds.), *Fostering sustainable businesses in emerging economies* (pp. 207–221). Emerald Publishing Limited.

Son, B., & Jang, H. (2023). Economics of blockchain-based securities settlement. *Research in International Business and Finance*, *64*, 101842.

Takeda, A., & Ito, Y. (2021). A review of FinTech research. *International Journal of Technology Management*, *86*(1), 67–88.

Tao, R., Su, C. W., Naqvi, B., & Rizvi, S. K. A. (2022). Can FinTech development pave the way for a transition towards low-carbon economy: A global perspective. *Technological Forecasting and Social Change*, *174*, 121278.

Udeagha, M. C., & Muchapondwa, E. (2023). Green finance, FinTech, and environmental sustainability: Fresh policy insights from the BRICS nations. *The International Journal of Sustainable Development and World Ecology*, *30*(6), 633–649.

Ul-Durar, S., De Sisto, M., Arshed, N., Naveed, S., & Farooqi, M. (2024). FinTech adoption in achieving ecologically sustainable mineral management in Asian OBOR countries – A cross-section and time autoregressive robust analysis. *Resources Policy*, *91*.

Wang, C., Wang, L., Zhao, S., Yang, C., & Albitar, K. (2024). The impact of FinTech on corporate carbon emissions: Towards green and sustainable development. *Business Strategy and the Environment*, *33*(6), 5776–5796.

Wang, Y., Xiuping, S., & Zhang, Q. (2021). Can FinTech improve the efficiency of commercial banks?—An analysis based on big data. *Research in International Business and Finance*, *55*, 101338.

Wei, H., Yue, G., & Khan, N. (2024). Uncovering the impact of FinTech, natural resources, green finance and green growth on environment sustainability in BRICS: An MMQR analysis. *Resources Policy*, *89*.

Yasmeen, R., Huang, H., & Shah, W. (2024). Assessing the significance of FinTech and mineral resource depletion in combating energy poverty: Empirical insights from BRICS economies. *Resources Policy*, *89*, 104691.

Yu, R., & Li, J. (2024). Does FinTech influence sustainable development under natural resource constraints: Insights from 270 Chinese cities. *Resources Policy*, *91*, 104924.

Zhe, D., Su, N., Zhu, X., Mahmoud, H., & Akhtar, T. (2024). Non-linear relationship between FinTech, natural resources, green innovation and environmental sustainability: Evidence from panel smooth transition regression model. *Resources Policy*, *91*, 104902.

Chapter 10

Exploring Cutting-Edge Algorithms in FinTech: Leveraging Machine Learning and Artificial Intelligence for Achieving Sustainability

Maha Shehadeh

Al-Ahliyya Amman University, Jordan; Bangor University, UK

Abstract

This chapter explores the intersection of cutting-edge algorithms in the financial technology (FinTech) sector, with a particular focus on the application of machine learning (ML) and artificial intelligence (AI) to enhance sustainability and ethical finance practices. The transformative capabilities of ML and AI are examined through their roles in revolutionising financial services by increasing operational efficiency, improving decision-making processes and enhancing risk management strategies. Specific applications discussed include fraud detection, anomaly detection in financial statements, robo-advisory services, prediction of customer deposits, combating money laundering, sentiment analysis, loan eligibility prediction, stock price prediction and the automation of routine tasks through chatbots. Additionally, the chapter addresses the crucial role of AI and ML in supporting green finance initiatives, reducing carbon footprints and promoting financial inclusion, thereby contributing to sustainable economic development. The detailed exploration provides insights into how these advanced technologies are key in shaping the future of the financial industry towards more sustainable outcomes.

Keywords: FinTech; machine learning; carbon footprint reduction; artificial intelligence (AI); financial inclusion; sustainability

From Digital Disruption to Dominance, 225–244

doi:10.1108/978-1-83549-608-420251011

1. Concepts of Financial Technology, Artificial Intelligence and Machine Learning

1.1 Definition of FinTech

FinTech, a term that merges 'financial' and 'technology', signifies the technological innovations in finance that are revolutionising the delivery of services by financial institutions and altering the way consumers and businesses engage with them. These companies leverage technology to move away from traditional practices, in financial services, aiming to transform how services are delivered through advanced communication technologies, the internet and automated information processing (Arner et al., 2016; Chen, 2016; Fortnum et al., 2017; Gabor & Brooks, 2020; Szpringer, 2016).

According to Christensen's theory of disruptive innovation (2003), FinTech companies fall into two categories: 'Sustainable FinTechs', which are established financial service providers using IT to maintain their market positions through incremental improvements, and 'Disruptive FinTechs', which are new or startup companies challenging the status quo by introducing novel products and services (Chiu, 2016; McWaters et al., 2015). These enterprises promise increased flexibility, security, efficiency and opportunities compared to traditional financial services (Gomber et al., 2017). As a result, FinTech startups and even major IT companies are making inroads into the financial industry, becoming popular and attracting customers traditionally served by established providers.

This shift towards digital finance is part of a broader digital transformation trend affecting all aspects of financial operations. Digital transformation in the financial sector represents a fundamental change in how organisations conduct business, engage with customers and streamline their operations. By integrating digital technologies such as AI, blockchain and big data analytics into their core functions, financial institutions can enhance service delivery, improve data management and offer personalised customer experiences. This digital-first approach not only meets the rising expectations of tech-savvy consumers but also ensures robust security measures and compliance with evolving regulatory standards (Shehadeh, 2024; Shehadeh, Alshurafat, & Arabiat, 2024, Shehadeh, Hussainey, et al., 2024).

Despite the financial industry traditionally being an early adopter and heavy user of new IT solutions, the emergence of innovative business models and new competitors has significantly impacted the industry's dynamics. In a fast-changing economic environment and faced with stringent and costly regulatory demands, traditional players in banking and financial services are undergoing a significant change with the advent of digital finance (Gomber et al., 2017). As a result, FinTech startups and even major IT companies are making inroads into the financial industry, becoming popular and attracting customers traditionally served by established providers. According to McKinsey, FinTech companies provide essential financial services including money storage, saving, borrowing, investing, transferring, paying and securing finances. The range of these companies includes startups, growth companies, banks and cross-sector firms, with examples like Venmo, Zelle, Robinhood and Coinbase (McKinsey & Company, 2023).

1.2 The Impact and Importance of FinTech in Modern Financial Services

FinTech has become an essential component of the modern financial landscape, significantly impacting the payment ecosystem since around 2010. For example, Square, founded in 2009, enabled small businesses to accept credit card payments via mobile devices, showing FinTech's role in enhancing financial accessibility and convenience. Today, FinTech influences all financial sectors, including those traditionally resistant to digital disruption (Ajouz et al., 2023; 2024; Alkhwaldi et al., 2022; Alkhazaleh et al., 2023; Rehman et al., 2023).

The adoption of FinTech has been rapid and widespread. According to McKinsey, by 2021, nearly half of US consumers had used a FinTech product, mainly for peer-to-peer payments and non-bank money transfers. Venture capital funding in the sector increased sharply from $19.4 billion in 2015 to $33.3 billion in 2020 (McKinsey & Company, 2023). This surge shows significant growth and interest in FinTech solutions across various financial domains.

However, a market correction in 2022 slowed the sector's growth, resulting in decreased values and decreased venture capital funding. As a result, FinTech companies have shifted their focus from rapid expansion to sustainable and profitable growth. Traditional banks have capitalised on this by developing their own FinTech-driven digital services, increasing competition for client deposits and balances.

Despite recent challenges, FinTech remains essential to the current digital change of banking and e-commerce, particularly in developing regions. According to McKinsey, 73% of global banking interactions currently occur through digital channels, indicating a continuous demand for FinTech solutions, especially from B2B firms. FinTech companies must navigate evolving regulations and ensure they have the necessary resources for compliance (Williams, 2024).

1.3 Artificial Intelligence and Machine Learning

In this section, we aim to focus on elucidating and reviewing the fundamental concepts foundational to contemporary technologies like artificial intelligence (AI) and machine learning (ML).

1.3.1 Artificial Intelligence (AI)

AI is leading the charge in technological advancements, causing significant changes across multiple industries, including finance. AI involves replicating human cognitive abilities through machines, particularly computer systems. These functions include learning; acquiring knowledge; understanding the application of this knowledge; reasoning; applying learnt rules to derive broad or specific conclusions and self-correcting.

There are different categories of AI, such as narrow or weak AI, which is engineered and trained to perform specific tasks like operating voice assistants or running image recognition software. On the other hand, strong or general AI, which would possess the ability to perform any intellectual task that a human can, offers broader capabilities. However, this type of AI is still largely theoretical at this stage.

1.3.2 Machine Learning (ML)

ML technologies form the foundational pillar of modern tech progress. As an essential part of AI, ML enables systems to independently adapt and learn from their environment. These systems process and understand large datasets, leveraging this information to enhance their functionality and decision-making capabilities. This technological progression allows industrial structures to improve their efficiency, making informed decisions based on continuously analysed data. ML employs algorithms that focus on iterative learning, data analysis, pattern recognition and making decisions based on these identified patterns, as described by Tatsat et al. (2020). Additionally, the importance of ML stems from its continuous adaptability and learning from new data. This continuous learning process ensures that its decision-making accuracy is consistently honed, leading to significant advances across various fields including science, technology and business.

1.3.2.1 Types of Machine Learning. As detailed by Yao et al. (2018), ML techniques can be differentiated based on the data and goals applied during the training phase and can be segmented into various core types, as shown in Fig. 10.1.

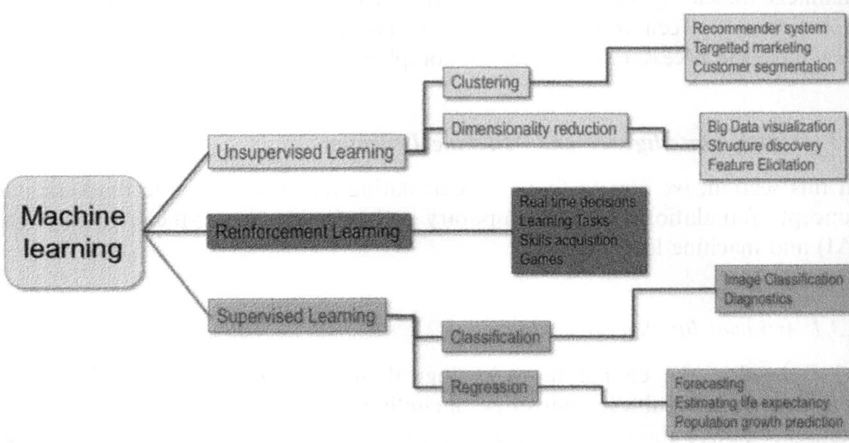

Fig. 10.1. Types of Machine Learning. *Source:* Seccia et al. (2021).

1.3.2.1.1 Supervised Learning. Consider this as having a teacher–student relationship. The student, provided with a series of problems along with their solutions, learns over time to address new challenges independently. Similarly, in supervised learning, systems are educated using labelled data, which serves as a reference, allowing the system to create rules for general application. This method is mainly used for tasks like classification and predicting numerical values.

1.3.2.1.2 Unsupervised Learning. Imagine giving someone a jigsaw puzzle without showing them the completed picture. They would sort the pieces based on colour or shape to assemble the image. Unsupervised learning follows a similar concept; it processes data to discover latent patterns or structures without any predefined labels, particularly effective in clustering and exploratory data analysis.

1.3.2.1.3 Semi-Supervised Learning. This approach blends supervised and unsupervised learning methodologies. In this scenario, the system is equipped with some labelled data along with a larger volume of unlabelled data. It's similar to partially solved jigsaw puzzles where the learner uses the connected pieces to figure out where the remaining pieces fit.

1.3.2.1.4 Reinforcement Learning. Imagine a video game where characters adapt their tactics with each action, learning from successes and failures. Reinforcement learning applies this principle to machines. It involves a cyclic process of experimentation, feedback and strategy adjustment to achieve the best possible results.

ML plays a key role in pushing technological developments and solving complex problems that were previously impossible with conventional approaches. Leveraging these technologies across various sectors is a critical step towards fostering a more innovative and efficient future.

2. How FinTech Companies Use AI, Machine Learning and Deep Learning

FinTech companies are leveraging AI, ML and deep learning (DL) technologies to drive innovation and development in the financial services sector. These cutting-edge technologies, known for their accuracy and speed, offer intelligent solutions to complex and multifaceted challenges. This section will explore how FinTech companies use these technologies to analyse big data, enhance data security, develop personalised financial services and improve decision-making processes and risk management. Additionally, we will examine the role of these technologies in promoting sustainability within the financial service industry.

2.1 Fraud Detection

As e-commerce becomes increasingly integrated into everyday life, the use of credit cards as the primary method for transactions has significantly increased. This rise has coincided with a notable increase in credit card fraud incidents, exploiting vulnerabilities in current security protocols (Lucas et al., 2020; Zhang et al., 2019).

Traditional security infrastructures, often static and linear, are inadequate for the dynamic and intricate nature of contemporary financial crimes.

AI and ML are the cornerstones of combating these sophisticated fraudulent threats within the FinTech sector. They not only offer significant computational capabilities but also provide an adaptive and intelligent approach to process complex, non-linear and extensive data in real time. This results in predictive insights and analyses that greatly surpass traditional fraud detection systems (Abdallah et al., 2016; Bolton & Hand, 2002).

In practice, AI and ML use specially developed algorithms to detect and react to patterns indicative of fraudulent activities within large datasets. These algorithms are dynamic, continually learning and adapting to new fraud techniques. Their development is essential for finding even minor anomalies in transaction data, enabling rapid responses, shortening the time to address threats and reducing potential damage.

Further enhancing these capabilities, DL, a specialised subset of ML, uses neural networks (NNs) designed for processing transaction data. These networks are particularly adept at managing sequential data, which allows them to discover complex patterns and behaviours typical of advanced fraud schemes. For example, recurrent neural networks (RNN) and long short-term memory (LSTM) networks are highly effective in analysing sequences of transactions, proving essential for identifying potential fraud (Abdel-Hamid et al., 2014; Zhang et al., 2019).

Within the framework of credit card transactions, each transaction provides a wealth of data points. DL algorithms carefully examine these points, examining transaction behaviours, merchant categories, spending habits and other pertinent variables. They quickly identify unusual patterns and inconsistencies, generating immediate alerts for further investigation or immediate intervention.

2.2 Identifying Anomalies Within Banking Financial Statements

In the financial services sector, especially when analysing complex financial statements, ML algorithms represent a cutting-edge solution for detecting, scrutinising and addressing anomalies. These algorithms excel in navigating through vast, unstructured datasets, providing insights and highlighting inconsistencies that manual inspections often overlook (Perols, 2011). This shift towards ML from traditional methods has been well-documented by researchers such as Rezaee (2005) and Albrecht et al. (2015), who detailed how ML aids in the identification, analysis and correction of anomalies within financial statements. These mechanisms are notably superior in managing large and complex data sets.

The capability of ML to detect anomalies, whether they are accidental errors or potential indicators of fraud, is further emphasised by Green and Choi (1997) and Lin et al. (2003). Their research underscores the efficiency of ML in carefully examining financial data to find inconsistencies that might otherwise remain hidden.

2.3 Robo-Advisory Services

In today's financial landscape, robo-advisory services stand out as a revolutionary innovation, combining cutting-edge technology with complex investment strategies. FinTech companies are at the forefront of highlighting these services by employing complex algorithms to provide personalised financial advice, as detailed by Abraham et al. (2019). These algorithms effectively process extensive and diverse data, devising investment strategies that align with the specific goals and risk profiles of individual clients.

Supporting this perspective, research by Lopez-Garcia et al. (2015) and Woodyard and Grable (2018) points to the efficiency, cost-effectiveness and speed of robo-advisors. These features enhance the investment process, making it easier and more accurate to navigate the financial markets.

Moreover, Phoon and Koh (2017) emphasise the critical role of quantitative data and algorithms in the success of robo-advisory services. These elements make robo-advisors highly attractive to investors seeking reliable, innovative and personalised investment options. The clear, analytical and unbiased nature of robo-advisory services underscores their growing popularity and adoption among investors, reflecting the significant impact of FinTech companies in this domain.

2.4 Predicting Customer Deposits

The application of ML for predictive modelling of customer deposits represents a significant technological leap within the FinTech sector. This advancement aids FinTech companies in understanding the complexities of financial behaviours and economic indicators, thereby enhancing financial stability and service delivery (Banke & Yitayaw, 2022; Derbali, 2022).

ML is especially effective in analysing intricate, multi-dimensional data sets, enabling FinTech companies to predict customer deposit patterns with increased accuracy and efficiency (Leo et al., 2019). By employing algorithms such as multiple linear regression (MLR) and artificial neural networks (ANNs), these companies can systematically analyse historical data, macroeconomic factors and financial reports to forecast future deposit trends.

Customer deposits are vital for the financial health of any banking institution, and their dynamic nature requires sophisticated analysis that ML can provide. Advanced algorithms, like ANNs, are especially adept at managing the diverse variables that influence deposit behaviours, offering essential insights for liquidity management, risk reduction and service enhancement. The ability of ANNs to handle complex, non-linear relationships within large datasets enables FinTech companies to effectively forecast deposit trends, aligning their strategic planning with anticipated future patterns (Muslim et al., 2020).

2.5 Combating Money Laundering

Addressing money laundering within the expansive realm of cryptocurrency necessitates innovative approaches that transcend traditional anti-money laundering (AML) methods. The decentralised nature and anonymity provided by cryptocurrencies create major challenges for traditional AML efforts (Canhoto, 2021; Lorenz et al., 2020). In response, ML, particularly supervised learning, has emerged as an essential tool, enabling FinTech companies to analyse large datasets and identify potential money laundering activities.

However, the implementation of ML-based AML strategies in the cryptocurrency sector is not without challenges. A significant concern is the 'black box' phenomenon, where the decision-making process of many ML models lacks transparency, complicating compliance with regulatory standards (Jullum et al., 2020). The main challenge is developing models that not only effectively identify suspicious activities but also conform to the transparency standards required by regulatory bodies.

FinTech companies use various ML algorithms, including logistic regression, random forests, support vector machines and decision trees, to find illegal transactions. Each algorithm offers specific advantages and limitations (Alarab et al., 2020; Chen, 2018). For example, decision trees provide a clear, interpretable model but can be prone to biases while support vector machines excel at managing diverse variables but may struggle with very large datasets.

To effectively combat cryptocurrency money laundering, FinTech companies must adopt a balanced approach. This strategy should focus on optimising detection accuracy, ensuring model transparency and adhering to regulatory standards. Moreover, as highlighted by Pettersson Ruiz and Angelis (2022), a comprehensive strategy that includes continuous research, collaboration among various stakeholders and regulatory updates is critical for effectively addressing the challenges posed by cryptocurrency-based money laundering.

2.6 Sentiment Analysis

Text classification (TC) is an essential branch of ML that focuses on assigning predefined labels to text, streamlining the management and analysis of data. This function is invaluable, especially in managing the unstructured data that abounds in the business and financial sectors – a common scenario in the burgeoning field of financial technology (FinTech), where large volumes of such data are generated.

One of the primary applications of TC in FinTech is sentiment analysis. Companies use algorithms such as Naive Bayes, logistic regression and support vector machines to interpret customer reviews and feedback. These algorithms carefully analyse text to find the underlying sentiments – be they positive, negative or neutral. This analysis is essential for FinTech companies looking to enhance their offerings, products and customer engagement strategies (Al-Araj et al., 2022; Hartmann et al., 2019). By understanding the subtleties of customer sentiments, these companies can actively address issues and improve positive customer interactions.

In the financial sector, particularly within FinTech, TC is essential for real-time data analysis. Techniques like Random Forest and Gradient Boosting are used to sift through and categorise large datasets, including financial news and investor feedback (Zhao et al., 2020). For instance, a FinTech investment firm might employ TC to automatically classify news articles regarding specific stocks or market sectors. The categorised data are then analysed to gather insights into market sentiments, trends and possible investment opportunities or risks.

Imagine a scenario where a FinTech institution employs an LSTM neural network to categorise and analyse real-time news feeds. This method allows the institution to quickly identify market sentiments and trends, enabling quick responses to market changes, optimising investment strategies and reducing risks.

TC exceeds its function as a simple technological tool; within FinTech, it becomes a strategic asset that transforms unstructured textual data into actionable insights. Its application in decoding sentiments and delivering real-time insights into customer feedback and market conditions not only improves the timeliness and relevance of business responses but also informs strategic decision-making, aligning with the latest trends, sentiments and market expectations. This integration highlights the vital role of TC in reinforcing the analytical capabilities of FinTech companies, driving innovation and precision in financial services.

2.7 Loan Eligibility Prediction

The integration of AI and ML into financial lending has revolutionised the process, delivering exceptional accuracy and speed to the evaluation of loan eligibility. Traditional methods of assessing borrowers' creditworthiness are being steadily refined or replaced by advanced AI and ML models, which help a faster and more detailed loan approval process, applicable even in the specific context of Islamic banking (Rawate & Tijare, 2017).

Neural networks (NNs), including specialised types such as radial basis NNs and decision trees, are at the forefront of this transformation. These models significantly enhance the accuracy of credit-risk assessments, crucial in the complex and vital task of loan approval. This process, which involves a thorough analysis of applicants' financial integrity, benefits greatly from the capabilities of AI and ML technologies (Hamid & Ahmed, 2016; Iqbal et al., 2021).

One of the most innovative advancements in this field is the SBCO-based deep neuro fuzzy network classifier. This model integrates Swarm Search and Bee Colony Optimisation techniques, significantly improving the accuracy and reliability of predicting loan eligibility. Such advancements underscore a significant shift in how financial institutions make lending decisions, showing the powerful impact of AI and ML in transforming traditional financial practices (Odeh et al., 2011; Singh & Ru, 2023).

2.8 Stock Price Prediction

The COVID-19 pandemic has significantly changed the global financial landscape, prompting a significant reevaluation of the analytical tools and methodologies traditionally used for market analysis and stock price prediction (Hatamlah et al., 2023). During this period, the role of machine learning and DL technologies, particularly LSTM and K-Nearest Neighbours (KNN), has become increasingly important (Alkhatib et al., 2013; Chebbi et al., 2024; Li et al., 2017).

The pandemic induced heightened market volatility worldwide, spotlighting the essential role of technological innovations like AI and machine learning in stock market forecasting. KNN, in particular, has shown strong abilities in forecasting stock prices, demonstrating better performance compared to other models such as LSTM and the ARIMA time series model (Borovkova & Tsiamas, 2019; Fischer & Krauss, 2018).

The studies mentioned highlight the adaptability and efficacy of machine and DL technologies. These algorithms excel in handling complex numerical relationships and delivering accurate, practical forecasts. As a result, a wide array of stakeholders, including investors, analysts and policymakers, have increased their dependence on these predictive models, especially during times of market instability (Moghar & Hamiche, 2020; Khattak et al., 2021).

The flexibility of LSTM and KNN has been especially valuable in adapting to rapidly changing data during the pandemic. These models have proven instrumental in interpreting current market dynamics and forecasting future trends, playing an essential role in strategic decision-making. The comprehensive and dynamic analyses enabled by these technologies provide stakeholders with robust, data-driven insights, following strict analytical standards (Lachaab & Omri, 2024; Li et al., 2017; Selvin et al., 2017).

2.9 Automation and Chatbots

Automation has emerged as a particularly advantageous innovation for the finance sector, greatly reducing the burden of repetitive, low-value tasks. By automating routine processes, it frees up human employees to concentrate on more strategic, high-value activities, leading to considerable time and cost savings (Tatsat et al., 2020).

The incorporation of ML and AI into automation technologies further enhances employee support. Algorithms such as decision trees, NNs and support vector machines are essential in analysing complex data, assisting finance teams in making informed decisions. In some cases, these algorithms can even recommend optimal actions, which employees can then validate and execute.

Furthermore, AI and automation, enhanced by advanced algorithms like Random Forest and Gradient Boosting, excel at identifying and correcting errors within financial operations. This capability decreases the time needed to find and fix errors, as a result increasing the efficiency of human teams, speeding up reporting processes and improving the accuracy of financial records (Tatsat et al., 2020).

AI chatbots, powered by natural language processing (NLP) and ML , are becoming increasingly vital in customer support within finance and banking. The rising popularity of live chat software in the finance industry underscores the growing importance of chatbots as the next evolutionary step in customer service. These chatbots often employ algorithms like LSTM to enhance customer interactions and service delivery (Adams et al., 2023). This technological progression not only optimises customer service but also integrates seamlessly into the digital transformation strategies of financial institutions.

2.10 Human Resource Management (HRM)

The integration of AI into human resource management (HRM) represents a significant evolution, transforming traditional HR methods and decisions. AI excels in real-time data analysis, predictive analytics and task automation, significantly enhancing the speed and quality of HR operations (Pereira et al., 2023). These advancements not only optimise HR processes but also improve the workplace experience, fostering higher engagement and productivity among employees.

However, the rapid adoption of AI in HRM comes with its set of ethical challenges, particularly concerning decision-making algorithms (Duggan et al., 2020). The complex and often opaque nature of AI systems requires a detailed examination of their ethical implications. Developing ethical guidelines and frameworks is essential to ensure that AI's application in HRM is transparent, fair and accountable. Addressing these ethical concerns is fundamental to maintaining trust and integrity in AI-enhanced HR practices, ensuring they positively affect both the organisational culture and employee well-being (Charlwood & Guenole, 2022; Hermann, 2022).

In the realm of recruitment, AI significantly streamlines the hiring process, efficiently sorting through large pools of applicants and assessing candidates based on various criteria. Despite these advantages, ethical issues such as fairness, bias and transparency arise. It is vital to critically evaluate the ethical aspects of algorithmic decisions to avoid unintended biases and ensure the recruitment process is fair and just (Prikshat et al., 2022). This thorough examination is crucial to maintain ethical standards and ensure that AI tools in HRM benefit the organisation without compromising ethical values.

3. Leveraging Machine Learning and Artificial Intelligence in FinTech to Advance Sustainable Development Goals

FinTech has greatly developed with the integration of ML and AI. This section explores how these technologies contribute to achieving the United Nations Sustainable Development Goals (SDGs), focusing on poverty alleviation, economic growth, sustainable infrastructure, reduced inequalities, sustainable cities, climate action and global partnerships.

3.1 Financial Inclusion and Poverty Reduction (SDG 1)

AI-driven solutions in FinTech have increased accessibility to financial services, essential for poverty reduction. Mobile banking applications, employing AI to function in regions with limited connectivity, significantly enhance financial inclusion (Alkhaldi et al., 2023; Kelikume, 2021).

FinTech significantly contributes to financial inclusion by providing access to financial services to populations typically underserved by traditional banks. Digital platforms help various financial activities such as micro-lending, crowd-funding and basic banking services, which are accessible via smartphones and computers. This inclusivity not only supports economic growth in developing regions but also promotes equality in financial access. Technologies like mobile money have been particularly transformative in regions with low banking penetration, offering services that range from transfers to savings in a secure environment (Al-Gasaymeh et al., 2023; Ediagbonya & Tioluwani, 2023).

3.2 Economic Growth and Employment (SDG 8)

FinTech innovations have been key in driving economic growth and job creation, directly contributing to SDG 8. These advancements streamline financial services, reduce operational costs and improve financial accessibility through automation and AI integration, enhancing service reliability and efficiency (Hoang et al., 2022).

The impact of FinTech on economic growth and employment has been significant, as evidenced by two key studies. Ben Romdhane et al. (2024) found that active FinTech use in Asian countries reduces inflation and unemployment, emphasising the need to promote digital transactions. Song and Appiah-Otoo (2022) revealed that FinTech and its components – third-party payment, credit and insurance – positively impact China's economic growth, with the eastern regions and Zhejiang province benefiting most. Their research highlighted a bidirectional causality between FinTech and economic growth, underscoring its role in economic development.

Moreover, AI-driven analytics enhance financial decision-making and responsiveness to market demands, boosting customer satisfaction. While automation may displace some traditional roles, it creates new opportunities in tech-driven sectors, requiring skills in software development, data analysis and system maintenance. As FinTech companies expand, they hire for roles like customer support, compliance and cybersecurity, contributing to job creation. Additionally, FinTech enables new business models, providing essential financial services to underserved populations and stimulating entrepreneurial activities.

3.3 Resilient Infrastructure and Innovation (SDG 9)

FinTech companies play a key role in driving innovation and sustainability in the financial sector. By leveraging AI and ML technologies, these companies offer innovative financial solutions that enhance operational efficiency and promote financial inclusion. For instance, advanced AI-powered risk assessment tools enable more secure financial operations, reducing losses and increasing trust in the financial system. Digital lending services and mobile banking applications expand access to financial services for underserved communities, contributing to economic and social sustainability. Additionally, these technological innovations more effective asset and risk management, allowing companies to make informed investment decisions that support sustainable growth. Through this integrated approach, FinTech companies significantly contribute to building a robust and resilient financial ecosystem capable of adapting to future challenges and supporting long-term sustainable development (Farahani et al., 2022).

3.4 Reducing Inequality (SDG 10)

Financial technology, or FinTech, is increasingly recognised as a vital tool in advancing financial inclusion, which is crucial for reducing income inequality as detailed in the United Nations' SDG 10. FinTech offers innovative solutions that bypass traditional barriers to financial services such as high costs, documentation requirements and physical distance, which disproportionately affect underserved and rural populations. By leveraging mobile technology, FinTech enables access to financial services for nearly 1.7 billion adults who are currently excluded from formal financial systems (Demir et al., 2022). This technological integration into financial services not only broadens the base of individuals who can participate in the economy but also promotes equitable economic growth by facilitating more evenly distributed financial resources. As a result, FinTech stands out as a key driver in the quest to bridge economic disparities and foster comprehensive economic development (Li et al., 2023). These efforts are essential to achieving greater economic equality and ensuring that financial benefits are accessible to all segments of society, ultimately contributing to the broader goals of SDG 10.

3.5 Climate Action Through Corporate Carbon Reduction and Green Innovation (SDG 13)

FinTech significantly enhances green innovations and corporate strategies aimed at reducing carbon footprints. By providing more accessible and efficient funding opportunities, FinTech enables startups and businesses focused on environmental sustainability to overcome the usual financial barriers associated with high-risk, innovative projects (Wang et al., 2024). This expands the investment base and supports risk diversification, which is crucial for supporting ventures that traditional financial institutions often avoid due to their uncertainty (Guang-Wen and Siddik, 2023; Yan et al., 2022).

Moreover, FinTech tools use big data to capture consumer preferences for green products, directing companies towards innovations that align with market demands (Nguyen et al., 2020). This not only fosters technological innovations such as carbon capture and energy-saving technologies but also enhances green management practices within corporations (Wang et al., 2012). These innovations are instrumental in reducing corporate carbon emissions directly and indirectly.

Additionally, the role of green policy innovations cannot be understated. Market-based environmental policies like carbon trading and stringent environmental regulations catalyse corporate actions towards carbon reduction (Zhang et al., 2017; Zhu & Niu, 2024) FinTech's integration with these policy tools helps streamline and enforce compliance, thereby promoting sustainable corporate practices.

3.6 Enhancing Global Partnerships (SDG 17)

ML and AI facilitate effective partnerships by integrating diverse data streams, enabling comprehensive monitoring and evaluation of SDG progress across different sectors and stakeholders (Danladi et al., 2023; OECD, 2021).

The adoption of AI and ML in FinTech not only propels technological advancements and operational efficiencies but also aligns financial sector capabilities with sustainable development objectives. This collaboration is crucial for achieving a more equitable and sustainable global society.

4. Conclusion

To conclude this chapter, it is crucial to recognise the transformative role of ML and AI within the FinTech sector. These technologies significantly enhance operational efficiency, decision-making capabilities and risk management. They also strongly support green finance initiatives, help reduce carbon footprints and promote financial inclusion, thereby contributing significantly to the achievement of SDGs.

However, while recognising these advancements, we must not overlook the ethical considerations and privacy concerns associated with AI and ML. The rapid adoption of these technologies raises significant issues regarding data security, user privacy and the potential for bias in algorithmic decision-making. Ensuring transparency and fairness in AI algorithms is essential to prevent discrimination and maintain public trust.

Moreover, the rise in automation driven by AI could have socioeconomic impacts, such as job displacement in certain sectors. Therefore, it is crucial to approach the integration of these technologies with a strategy that includes robust regulatory frameworks to protect ethical standards and privacy while also promoting an environment where innovation thrives.

Ultimately, maintaining a balanced perspective is essential. By addressing these challenges head-on and ensuring ethical deployment of AI and ML, the FinTech industry can not only innovate and grow but also lead by example in the responsible use of transformative technologies. This balanced approach will enable the sector to sustain its contributions to economic development while ensuring fairness, privacy and inclusivity.

References

Abdallah, A., Maarof, M. A., & Zainal, A. (2016). Fraud detection system: A survey. *Journal of Network and Computer Applications, 68*, 90–113.

Abdel-Hamid, O., Mohamed, A. R., Jiang, H., Deng, L., Penn, G., & Yu, D. (2014). Convolutional neural networks for speech recognition. *IEEE/ACM Transactions on Audio, Speech, and Language Processing, 22*(10), 1533–1545.

Abraham, F., Schmukler, S. L., & Tessada, J. (2019). *Robo-advisors: Investing through machines*. World Bank Policy Research Working Paper, (134881).

Adams, H., Thames, B., Wagner, M. C., Montier, D., Clark, T., Ash, S., & Southard, M. (2023). Operators need to know how to communicate with customers. *Opflow, 49*(9), 20–24.

Ajouz, M., Abuamria, F., Al Zeer, I., Salahat, M., Shehadeh, M., Binsaddig, R., Al-Sartawi, A., & Al-Ramahi, N. M. (2023). Navigating the uncharted: The shaping of FinTech ecosystems in emerging markets. *Cuadernos de Economía, 46*(132), 189–201.

Ajouz, M., Shehadeh, M., Jabarin, R., Sharar, S. A., Jawabra, S., & Salman, W. (2024, February). Is FinTech catalyst or constraint for banking performance? In *2024 2nd International conference on cyber resilience (ICCR)* (pp. 1–5). IEEE.

Al-Araj, R. E. E. M., Haddad, H. O. S. S. A. M., Shehadeh, M. A. H. A., Hasan, E., & Nawaiseh, M. Y. (2022). The effect of artificial intelligence on service quality and customer satisfaction in Jordanian banking sector. *WSEAS Transactions on Business and Economics, 19*(12), 1929–1947.

Al-Gasaymeh, A. S., Almahadin, H. A., Shehadeh, M., Migdady, H., & Atta, A. A. B. (2023, March). Investigating the role of artificial intelligence in embedded finance on improving a nonfinancial customer experience. In *2023 International conference on business analytics for technology and security (ICBATS)* (pp. 1–6). IEEE.

Alkhatib, K., Najadat, H., Hmeidi, I., & Shatnawi, M. K. A. (2013). Stock price prediction using k-nearest neighbor (kNN) algorithm. *International Journal of Business, Humanities and Technology, 3*(3), 32–44.

Alarab, I., Prakoonwit, S., & Nacer, M. (2020). Comparative analysis using supervised learning methods for anti-money laundering in bitcoin data. In *Proceedings of the 5th International conference on machine learning technologies (ICMLT 2020)* (pp. 11–17). ACM. https://doi.org/10.1145/3409073.3409078

Albrecht, C., Holland, D., Malagueño, R., Dolan, S., & Tzafrir, S. (2015). The role of power in financial statement fraud schemes. *Journal of Business Ethics, 131*(4), 803–813. https://doi.org/10.1007/s10551-013-2019-1

Alkhaldi, F., Shehadeh, M., Abu-AlSondos, I. A., & Almazaydeh, L. (2023, December). Artificial intelligence applications and roles in supply chain sustainability. In *2023 Asia conference on cognitive engineering and intelligent interaction (CEII)* (pp. 120–124). IEEE.

Alkhazaleh, A., Assaf, A., Shehada, M., Almustafa, E., & Allahham, M. (2023). Analysis of the impact of fintech firms' lending on the expansion of service base companies in Jordan. *Information Sciences Letters, 12*(8), 2891–2902.

Alkhwaldi, A. F., Alharasis, E. E., Shehadeh, M., Abu-AlSondos, I. A., Oudat, M. S., & Bani Atta, A. A. (2022). Towards an understanding of FinTech users' adoption:

Intention and e-loyalty post-COVID-19 from a developing country perspective. *Sustainability*, *14*(19), 12616.
Arner, D. W., Barberis, J., & Buckley, R. P. (2016). 150 years of Fintech: An evolutionary analysis. *JASSA*, *3*, 22–29.
Banke, N. K., & Yitayaw, M. K. (2022). Deposit mobilization and its determinants: Evidence from commercial banks in Ethiopia. *Future Business Journal*, *8*(1), 1–10.
Ben Romdhane, Y., Kammoun, S., & Loukil, S. (2024). The impact of Fintech on inflation and unemployment: The case of Asia. *Arab Gulf Journal of Scientific Research*, *42*(1), 161–181.
Bolton, R. J., & Hand, D. J. (2002). Statistical fraud detection: A review. *Statistical Science*, *17*(3), 235–249.
Borovkova, S., & Tsiamas, I. (2019). An ensemble of LSTM neural networks for high-frequency stock market classification. *Journal of Forecasting*, *38*(6), 600–619.
Canhoto, A. (2021). Leveraging machine learning in the global fight against money laundering and terrorism financing: An affordances perspective. *Journal of Business Research*, *131*, 441–452.
Charlwood, A., & Guenole, N. (2022). Can HR adapt to the paradoxes of artificial intelligence? *Human Resource Management Journal*. https://doi.org/10.1111/1748-8583.12433
Chebbi, T., Migdady, H., Hmedat, W., & Shehadeh, M. (2024). Another look at the price clustering behavior: Evidence from the Muscat stock exchange. *Review of Behavioral Finance*, *16*(5), 773–791. https://doi.org/10.1108/RBF-02-2023-0053
Chen, L. (2016). From fintech to finlife: The case of fintech development in China. *China Economic Journal*, *9*(3), 225–239.
Chen, R. Y. (2018). A traceability chain algorithm for artificial neural networks using T–S fuzzy cognitive maps in blockchain. *Future Generation Computer Systems*, *80*, 198–210.
Chiu, I. H. (2016). Fintech and disruptive business models in financial products, intermediation and markets-policy implications for financial regulators. *Journal of Technology Law and Policy*, *21*, 55.
Danladi, S., Prasad, M. S. V., Modibbo, U. M., Ahmadi, S. A., & Ghasemi, P. (2023). Attaining sustainable development goals through financial inclusion: Exploring collaborative approaches to Fintech adoption in developing economies. *Sustainability*, *15*(17), 13039.
Demir, A., Pesqué-Cela, V., Altunbas, Y., & Murinde, V. (2022). Fintech, financial inclusion and income inequality: A quantile regression approach. *The European Journal of Finance*, *28*(1), 86–107.
Derbali, A. M. S. (2022). The factors determining the profitability of Tunisian banks (March 5, 2022). *SSRN*. https://ssrn.com/abstract54050611
Duggan, J., Sherman, U., Carbery, R., & McDonnell, A. (2020). Algorithmic management and app-work in the gig economy: A research agenda for employment relations and HRM. *Human Resource Management Journal*, *30*(1), 114–132.
Ediagbonya, V., & Tioluwani, C. (2023). The role of fintech in driving financial inclusion in developing and emerging markets: Issues, challenges and prospects. *Technological Sustainability*, *2*(1), 100–119.
Farahani, M. S., Esfahani, A., Moghaddam, M. N. F., & Ramezani, A. (2022). The impact of Fintech and artificial intelligence on COVID 19 and sustainable

development goals. *International Journal of Innovation in Management, Economics and Social Sciences*, *2*(3), 14–31.

Fischer, T., & Krauss, C. (2018). Deep learning with long short-term memory networks for financial market predictions. *European Journal of Operational Research*, *270*(2), 654–669.

Fortnum, D., Pollari, I., Mead, W., Hughes, B., & Speier, A. (2017). *The pulse of fintech Q1 2017: Global analysis of investment in fintech*. KPMG.

Gabor, D., & Brooks, S. (2020). The digital revolution in financial inclusion: International development in the fintech era. In *Material cultures of financialisation* (pp. 69–82). Routledge.

Gomber, P., Koch, J. A., & Siering, M. (2017). Digital finance and FinTech: Current research and future research directions. *Journal of Business Economics*, *87*, 537–580.

Green, B., & Choi, H. (1997). Assessing the risk of management fraud through neural network technology. *Auditing: A Journal of Practice & Theory*, *16*(1), 14–28.

Guang-Wen, Z., & Siddik, A. B. (2023). The effect of Fintech adoption on green finance and environmental performance of banking institutions during the COVID-19 pandemic: The role of green innovation. *Environmental Science and Pollution Research*, *30*(10), 25959–25971.

Hamid, A. J., & Ahmed, T. M. (2016). Developing prediction model of loan risk in banks using data mining. *Machine Learning and Applications: International Journal*, *3*(1), 1–9.

Hartmann, J., Huppertz, J., Schamp, C., & Heitmann, M. (2019). Comparing automated text classification methods. *International Journal of Research in Marketing*, *36*(1), 20–38.

Hatamlah, H., Allan, M., Abu-AlSondos, I., Shehadeh, M., & Allahham, M. (2023). The role of artificial intelligence in supply chain analytics during the pandemic. *Uncertain Supply Chain Management*, *11*(3), 1175–1186.

Hermann, E. (2022). Leveraging artificial intelligence in marketing for social good—An ethical perspective. *Journal of Business Ethics*, *179*(1), 43–61.

Khattak, M. A., Ali, M., Hamid, B. A., & Islam, M. U. (2021). Competition, diversification, and stability in the Indonesian banking system. *Bulletin of Monetary Economics and Banking*, *24*, 59–88.

Hoang, T. G., Nguyen, G. N. T., & Le, D. A. (2022). Developments in financial technologies for achieving the sustainable development goals (SDGs): FinTech and SDGs. In U. Akkucuk (Ed.), *Disruptive technologies and eco-innovation for sustainable development* (pp. 1–19). IGI Global. https://doi.org/10.4018/978-1-7998-8900-7.ch001

Iqbal, K., Munawar, H. S., Inam, H., & Qayyum, S. (2021). Promoting customer loyalty and satisfaction in financial institutions through technology integration: The roles of service quality, awareness, and perceptions. *Sustainability*, *13*(23), 12951.

Jullum, M., Løland, A., Huseby, R., Ånonsen, G., & Lorentzen, J. (2020). Detecting money laundering transactions with machine learning. *Journal of Money Laundering Control*, *23*(1), 173–186.

Kelikume, I. (2021). Digital financial inclusion, informal economy and poverty reduction in Africa. *Journal of Enterprising Communities: People and Places in the Global Economy*, *15*(4), 626–640.

Lachaab, M., & Omri, A. (2024). Machine and deep learning-based stock price prediction during the COVID-19 pandemic: The case of CAC 40 index. *EuroMed Journal of Business*, *19*(4), 781–797. https://doi.org/10.1108/EMJB-05-2022-0104

Leo, M., Sharma, S. S., & Maddulety, K. (2019). Machine learning in banking risk management: A literature review. *Risks*, *7*, 29.

Li, C., Razzaq, A., Ozturk, I., & Sharif, A. (2023). Natural resources, financial technologies, and digitalization: The role of institutional quality and human capital in selected OECD economies. *Resources Policy*, *81*, 103362.

Li, J., Bu, H., & Wu, J. (2017, June). Sentiment-aware stock market prediction: A deep learning method. In *2017 International conference on service systems and service management* (pp. 1–6). IEEE.

Lin, J., Hwang, M., & Becker, J. (2003). A fuzzy neural network for assessing the risk of fraudulent financial reporting. *Managerial Auditing Journal*, *18*(8), 657–665.

Lopez-Garcia, P., Onieva, E., Osaba, E., Masegosa, A. D., & Perallos, A. (2015). A hybrid method for short-term traffic congestion forecasting using genetic algorithms and cross entropy. *IEEE Transactions on Intelligent Transportation Systems*, *17*(2), 557–569.

Lorenz, J., Silva, M. I., Aparício, D., Ascensão, J. T., & Bizarro, P. (2020). Machine learning methods to detect money laundering in the Bitcoin blockchain in the presence of label scarcity. In Proceedings of the *First ACM International Conference on AI in Finance (ICAIF '20)*, Article No. 23. October 15–16, 2020. New York, NY, USA (pp. 1–8). ACM. https://doi.org/10.1145/3383455.3422549

Lucas, Y., Portier, P. E., Laporte, L., He-Guelton, L., Caelen, O., Granitzer, M., & Calabretto, S. (2020). Towards automated feature engineering for credit card fraud detection using multi-perspective HMMs. *Future Generation Computer Systems*, *102*, 393–402.

McKinsey and Company. (2023, October 24). Fintechs: A new paradigm of growth. https://www.mckinsey.com/industries/financial-services/our-insights/fintechs-a-new-paradigm-of-growth

McWaters, R. J., Bruno, G., Lee, A., & Blake, M. (2015, June). *The future of financial services: How disruptive innovations are reshaping the way financial services are structured, provisioned and consumed* (Vol. 125, pp. 1–178). World Economic Forum.

Moghar, A., & Hamiche, M. (2020). Stock market prediction using LSTM recurrent neural network. *Procedia Computer Science*, *170*, 1168–1173.

Muslim, M. A., Darsil, Y., Alamsyah, A., & Mustaqim, T. (2020). Bank prediction for prospective long-term deposit investors using machine learning light GBM and SMOTE. *Journal of Physics: Conference Series*, *1918*(1), 1–6.

Nguyen, H. M., Onofrei, G., Truong, D., & Lockrey, S. (2020). Customer green orientation and process innovation alignment: A configuration approach in the global manufacturing industry. *Business Strategy and the Environment*, *29*(6), 2498–2513.

Odeh, O., Koduru, P., Featherstone, A., Das, S., & Welch, S. M. (2011). A multi-objective approach for the prediction of loan defaults. *Expert Systems with Applications*, *38*(7), 8850–8857.

OECD. (2021). *Perspectives on global development 2021: From protest to progress?* OECD Publishing. https://doi.org/10.1787/405e4c32-en

Pereira, V., Hadjielias, E., Christofi, M., & Vrontis, D. (2023). A systematic literature review on the impact of artificial intelligence on workplace outcomes: A multi-process perspective. *Human Resource Management Review*, *33*(1), 100857.

Perols, J. (2011). Financial statement fraud detection: An analysis of statistical and machine learning algorithms. *Auditing: A Journal of Practice & Theory*, *30*(2), 19–50.

Pettersson Ruiz, E., & Angelis, J. (2022). Combating money laundering with machine learning–applicability of supervised-learning algorithms at cryptocurrency exchanges. *Journal of Money Laundering Control*, *25*(4), 766–778.

Phoon, K., & Koh, F. (2017). Robo-advisors and wealth management. *Journal of Alternative Investments*, *20*(3), 79–94.

Prikshat, V., Patel, P., Varma, A., & Ishizaka, A. (2022). A multi-stakeholder ethical framework for AI-augmented HRM. *International Journal of Manpower*, *43*(1), 226–250.

Rawate, K. R., & Tijare, P. A. (2017). Review on prediction system for bank loan credibility. *International Journal of Advance Engineering and Research Development*, *4*(12), 860–867.

Rehman, S. U., Al-Shaikh, M., Washington, P. B., Lee, E., Song, Z., Abu-AlSondos, I. A., Shehadeh, M., & Allahham, M. (2023). FinTech adoption in SMEs and bank credit supplies: A study on manufacturing SMEs. *Economies*, *11*(8), 213. https://doi.org/10.3390/economies11080213

Rezaee, Z. (2005). Causes, consequences, and deterrence of financial statement fraud. *Critical Perspectives on Accounting*, *16*(3), 277–298.

Seccia, R., Romano, S., Salvetti, M., Crisanti, A., Palagi, L., & Grassi, F. (2021). Machine learning use for prognostic purposes in multiple sclerosis. *Life*, *11*(2), 122.

Selvin, S., Vinayakumar, R., Gopalakrishnan, E. A., Menon, V. K., & Soman, K. P. (2017). Stock price prediction using LSTM, RNN and CNN-sliding window model. In *2017 International conference on advances in computing, communications and informatics* (pp. 1643–1647). ICACCI.

Shehadeh, M. (2024). Digital transformation: A catalyst for sustainable business practices. In A. Hamdan (Ed.), *Technological innovations for business, education and sustainability. Technological innovation and sustainability for business competitive advantage* (pp. 29–45). Emerald Publishing Limited. https://doi.org/10.1108/978-1-83753-106-620241003

Shehadeh, M., Alshurafat, H., & Arabiat, O. (2024). Inverting the paradigm: Digital transformation's impact on firm performance and the counterintuitive role of gender. *Competitiveness Review (Ahead-of-print)*. https://doi.org/10.1108/CR-11-2023-0299

Shehadeh, M., Hussainey, K., Alhadab, M., & Kilani, Q. (2024). Corporate narrative reporting on Industry 4.0 technologies: Do the COVID-19 pandemic and governance structure matter? *Review of Accounting and Finance*, *23*(5), 687–714. https://doi.org/10.1108/RAF-11-2023-0362

Singh, S., & Ru, J. (2023). Goals of sustainable infrastructure, industry, and innovation: A review and future agenda for research. *Environmental Science and Pollution Research*, *30*(11), 28446–28458.

Song, N., & Appiah-Otoo, I. (2022). The impact of fintech on economic growth: Evidence from China. *Sustainability*, *14*(10), 6211.

Szpringer, W. (2016). FinTech-new phenomena in the financial services market. *E-MENTOR*, *2*, 56–69. https://doi.org/10.15219/em64.1240
Tatsat, H., Puri, S., & Lookabaugh, B. (2020). *Machine learning and data science blueprints for finance*. O'Reilly Media.
Wang, C. A., Wang, L., Zhao, S., Yang, C., & Albitar, K. (2024). The impact of Fintech on corporate carbon emissions: Towards green and sustainable development. *Business Strategy and the Environment*, *33*(6), 5776–5796. https://doi.org/10.1002/bse.3778
Wang, Z., Yang, Z., Zhang, Y., & Yin, J. (2012). Energy technology patents– CO2 emissions nexus: An empirical analysis from China. *Energy Policy*, *42*, 248–260. https://doi.org/10.1016/j.enpol.2011.11.082
Williams, E. (2024). *Fintech, financial inclusion, and the future of finance*. Harvard Business School. https://www.hks.harvard.edu/centers/mrcbg/programs/growthpolicy/fintech-financial-inclusion-and-future-finance
Woodyard, A. S., & Grable, J. E. (2018). Insights into the users of robo-advisory firms. *Journal of Financial Service Professionals*, *72*(5).
Yan, C., Siddik, A. B., Yong, L., Dong, Q., Zheng, G. W., & Rahman, M. N. (2022). A two-staged SEM-artificial neural network approach to analyze the impact of FinTech adoption on the sustainability performance of banking firms: The mediating effect of green finance and innovation. *Systems*, *10*(5), 148.
Yao, M., Zhou, A., & Jia, M. (2018). *Applied artificial intelligence: A handbook for business leaders*. Topbots Inc.
Zhang, F., Liu, G., Li, Z., Yan, C., & Jiang, C. (2019). GMM-based undersampling and its application for credit card fraud detection. In Proceedings of the *2019 International Joint Conference on Neural Networks (IJCNN)*. July 14–19, 2019. Budapest, Hungary (pp. 1–8). IEEE. https://doi.org/10.1109/IJCNN.2019.8852415
Zhang, Y. J., Peng, Y. L., Ma, C. Q., & Shen, B. (2017). Can environmental innovation facilitate carbon emissions reduction? Evidence from China. *Energy Policy*, *100*, 18–28. https://doi.org/10.1016/j.enpol.2023.113476
Zhao, W., Zhang, G., Yuan, G., Liu, J., Shan, H., & Zhang, S. (2020). The study on the text classification for financial news based on partial information. *IEEE Access*, *8*, 100426–100437.
Zhu, X., & Niu, X. (2024). Impact of fintech, mineral resources extraction, and globalization on social inequality: Exploring the role of technology innovation in G10 economies. *Resources Policy*, *89*, 104606.

Chapter 11

Leveraging FinTech Innovations for Sustainable and Social Finance: A Comprehensive Analysis of Their Contributions to Social Impact Investment

Faeyz Abuamria and Mousa Ajouz

Palestine Ahliya University, Palestine

Abstract

The financial sector has recently undergone alterations and moved towards sustainability and social justice at the instigation of technological innovations and increased consideration of environmental and societal matters. This piece investigates how significant FinTech changes have been in relation to social impact investment and sustainable finance. Using technologies like blockchain, artificial intelligence (AI) or mobile payment systems, amongst others, FinTech has made it possible for more people to access financial services than ever before, leading to greater inclusion of marginalised populations into small-scale enterprises, rendering financial services available to even the lowliest citizens. The focus on fostering such inclusion mirrors social finance principles that promote economic self-reliance and decrease disparities among the populace. Additionally, through real-time data provision and analytics tools available for FinTech, informed decisions when investing become feasible, thereby ensuring that efficient capital allocation considers measurable social and environmental costs. However, even with such advances, challenges still inhibit FinTech from realising its full potential in terms of social impact investing, such as digital divide regulatory variations and data protection concerns. This paper examines how FinTech affects social impact investment using case studies, market trends and policy frameworks to further sustainable development and social equity.

Keywords: FinTech; innovations; sustainability; social finance; social impact investment; sustainable finance

From Digital Disruption to Dominance, 245–264

doi:10.1108/978-1-83549-608-420251012

1. Introduction

Since the credit crisis hit, the banking sector has experienced significant transformations, becoming more socially just and sustainable oriented. Social finance entails an investment approach that places greater importance on societal outcomes than returns while sustainable finance describes the usual types of investing. The advancement of green finance within the banking industry has fostered a new trend towards environmentally friendly business practices among companies (Mejia-Escobar et al., 2020; Secinaro et al., 2020). This trend has encouraged the emergence of a booming sustainable and social finance industry that attracts private capital, which bridges the gap between the two sectors by integrating environmental and social objectives into investment decisions made by the financial sector itself.

Traditional financial institutions have been revolutionised by technological breakthroughs such as blockchain, AI, mobile banking and P2P lending platforms, which have extended access to financial services to people who are poor and reduced transaction charges (AlMomani & Alomari, 2021; Taherdoost, 2023). Modern financial technology makes financial markets more accessible, efficient and user-friendly. For instance, big data analytics and AI facilitate the measurement of social returns for investors while digital services or mobile banking increase economic activities in underserved regions (Chueca Vergara & Ferruz Agudo, 2021; Cumming et al., 2023; Stolz & Lai, 2020).

FinTech innovations have significantly changed social impact investing by empowering social finance with greater transparency, efficiency and accessibility (Alkhazaleh et al., 2023; Alkhwaldi et al., 2022; Rehman et al., 2023). Blockchain technology or AI has democratised access to financial services since they are under-served small enterprises and poor populations that could not be included in the mainstream financial system (Demirgüç-Kunt et al., 2022). It promotes economic empowerment, hence reducing inequality, which aligns with social finance objectives (Ajouz et al., 2024; Shehadeh, 2024; Zhang, 2022). Likewise, FinTech provides an analytical ability through real-time records necessitating intelligent choices about investments within projects with appreciable social and environmental returns on investment (Arner et al., 2017). This consequently results in building confidence and enhancing more prominent capital inflows into social impact projects through bringing accountability as well as transparency in the use of funds (Arner et al., 2017). Taken as a whole, FinTech acts as one of the critical enablers of social impact investing, supporting sustainable and socially beneficial results due to the paramount role it plays in enhancing accessibility, transparency and efficiency.

Some gaps exist, though, despite these developments that hinder FinTech from maximising its impact on social impact investing. One such critical gap is the digital divide; the absence of technology and internet penetration rates in remote areas, for instance, rigs the expansion capacity of FinTech solutions, thus limiting the entry point for those who would require greater assistance from social finance (Demirgüç-Kunt et al., 2022). Similarly, regulatory challenges and a lack of standardisation in operations lead to inconsistencies and uncertainties that could scare away potential investors, making it difficult for social impact projects to scale up (Degerli, 2019). Still, privacy concerns on data and security are notable because they increase cybersecurity risks due to the increased use of digital platforms, which may reduce trustworthiness in FinTech (Mustapha et al., 2023). Lastly, incorporating AI and blockchain technologies into existing banking systems demands sizeable investments and expertise that are not easy for small entities intending to employ (Arner et al., 2017). Addressing these gaps will enable FinTech to achieve its optimal potential towards advancing social impact investing alongside attaining Sustainable Development Goals (SDGs).

This chapter seeks to elucidate the different ways in which social impact investing has been influenced by FinTech technologies, using case studies, market trends and regulatory frameworks (Macchiavello & Siri, 2022). It also examines new financial technology for socially impact investing and socially responsible investing (SRI) strategies by investigating innovative financial products introduced by social finance while emphasising the role of FinTech in encouraging socially minded entrepreneurs within various dispositions that have been supported by empirical evidence.

2. Theoretical Foundations

2.1 FinTech: An Overview

FinTech is the use of digital technology to improve financial services to optimise efficiency and decrease costs; it is also aimed at making it more accessible. It aims to increase the efficiency of financial services provision, reduce costs and make banking services more accessible at any time for customers' convenience (Harsono & Suprapti, 2024). It is based on different theoretical domains, such as disruptive innovation theory, which explains how new technologies can disrupt existing businesses by providing better ways to do things more cheaply and conveniently. Also, transaction cost theory shows that financial technology (FinTech) brings down transaction costs, leading to an efficient market (Kou et al., 2021; Lee et al., 2021). Diffusion of innovation theory helps understand how FinTech solutions gain acceptance due to factors like relative advantage, compatibility, complexity, trialability and observability (Chuc et al., 2021).

FinTech is used in a narrow sense to mean technology-driven innovation in finance where information and communication technologies platforms are utilised during designing production distribution of financial products (AlMomani & Alomari, 2021; Elia et al., 2023; Giglio, 2021). Consequently, as digitalisation continues to advance, it represents a host of finance technologies that are being more closely integrated into the financial system and impacting virtually every aspect of the industry. This has been evident in lending money, borrowing cash or saving for future transactions (Suryono et al., 2020).

The FinTech ecosystem comprises various stakeholders such as talent, demand, policy and capital (Ajouz et al., 2023). Unlike unproven constructs, this ecosystem offers a platform for developing new ideas within certain limits before trying them out in real life (Hendrikse et al., 2020). At the heart of this ecosystem are FinTech startups that leverage technologies, including blockchain, AI and big data analytics, to develop groundbreaking financial products and services. Mutual coordination of these actors is instrumental in accelerating innovation processes within financial domains, enabling transparent, safe transactions as well as enhancing access to poorer population groups through inclusive products/services design (Chuc et al., 2021; Chueca Vergara & Ferruz Agudo, 2021).

2.2 Sustainable Finance

Sustainable finance combines all sectors of the financial industry and links the activities of investors with the United Nations SDGs. This encompasses different kinds of financial products, such as Green Bonds, Social Bonds and ESG Investment Funds, which aim to support projects that promote a sustainable tomorrow (Chuc et al., 2021; Thompson, 2023). The major aim is to ensure just economic development while at the same time minimising environmental degradation, hence establishing a basis for the financial sector to contribute positively to society and the earth.

This paper argues that both regulatory frameworks and historical developments have played a significant role in influencing sustainable finance. Arising from the principles of socially responsible investing in the 1960s and 1970s, sustainable finance increased after global environmental awareness during the late 1990s and early 2000s. International agreements like the Kyoto Protocol and the Paris Agreement have dramatically enhanced this growth, which has embraced sustainable development while combating climate change (Falcone, 2020). Integrating sustainable finance with FinTech innovations is pertinent, considering that they simplify processes and promote fairer accessibility to such investments.

Key stakeholders of sustainable finance encompass social purpose businesses financed through mechanisms like social impact bonds alongside green bonds (Rizzello & Kabli, 2020). Additionally, new products are introduced by FinTech innovations such as GT Capital Environmental Score, MSCI ESG ratings and the SDG Index that manages ESG-related information through data. Besides this, donation-based crowdfunding platforms (e.g. JustGiving; GoFundMe) and loan-based ones such as Zopa and Funding Circle have sprung up to allow supporters to contribute money for social impact projects (Gafni et al., 2021). Processes are faster, more choices are available, and services are cheaper than traditional financial instruments due to these developments (Jarvis & Han, 2021; Xu, 2022). Thus, integrating these innovations makes sustainable finance supportive of a more inclusive and environmentally oriented financial system.

2.3 Social Finance

Social finance usually combines financial techniques with social goals for increased financial returns and social benefits. A variety of players would take part in figuring this out; these include governments, investors, philanthropists and charities mainly targeting long-term investments for economic, social or environmental gains (Kuanova et al., 2021; Palakurti, 2023). This has enabled contributions to entities involved in inclusive finance, like healthcare and employment creation, while also addressing those organisations engaged in business for social impact, with financial exclusion being its main engine. For example, Medically Home uses social-impact investments to develop viable solutions to issues faced by society as a whole. SRI and social impact investment are designed to solve societal problems directly by applying ESG criteria as well as new financial models (Lanteri, 2024; Nguyen et al., 2021).

Social enterprises, impact investing and microfinance are the main concepts in social finance. Social enterprises impact healthcare, sustainable development and education by prioritising environmental and social issues and financial performance (Pinheiro et al., 2021). Impact investing seeks to create positive social and financial returns while gaining popularity among investors pursuing double motives (Gutterman, 2020). Microfinance loans are small amounts given to people without access to traditional banks in order for them to start enterprises and improve their economic conditions in poor places (Adnan & Kumar, 2021). FinTech, crowdfunding and blockchain are among the latest trends aimed at improving social finance; their effect has included a reduction of costs associated with impact investments as well as microfinancing, thus making it possible to access more people (Chen, 2024; Chuc et al., 2021).

2.4 Social Impact Investing

It is astonishing how fast social impact investments have been growing recently. A historical high was set last year when $502 billion worth of transactions were undertaken, representing a 42.4% increment from the previous year (Newmark & Pena, 2023). This kind of investment means directing money to entities like businesses, organisations or funds so that they generate financial returns and have measurable positive social and environmental consequences. This approach combines traditional profit-making motives and altruism, aiming to meet enduring social problems (Bengo et al., 2021; Yaşar, 2021).

Social impact investing is important because it facilitates financing for initiatives that aim to solve some of the significant problems in society, like poverty reduction through access to better healthcare services or quality education provision, thus enabling investors to participate in solving global issues. Social impact investing supports fair growth with universal accessibility and sustainable water use under the SDGs, consequently acting as an engine for worldwide advancement. Besides, it fosters creativity within financial markets through the introduction of novel financial instruments and investment strategies like social impact bonds, green bonds and impact funds, which target objective social outcomes (Harvie et al., 2021; Lazzarini et al., 2021; Wendt, 2021).

Various advantages come with social impact investments. First, they enable people to see the actual effects resulting from the money they put in and then measure them against specific societal/environmental goals, thus ensuring accountability and real benefits for communities and ecosystems. In contrast to traditional belief systems in which socially driven capital does not entail higher returns, numerous impact investments have been offering commercially attractive terms, allowing people to build different portfolios that achieve both economic and societal goals simultaneously. Second, social impact investments can attract a wide range of investors, including consumers, organisations priding themselves on social responsibility, and philanthropic organisations; in this case, vast sums of money are driven towards projects with real effects on society. Additionally, firms adopt within their corporate cultures enhanced reputation, gaining the confidence and trust of all involved parties, e.g. clients, workers and authorities, which helps them enjoy increased loyalty from their customers, thus ensuring the long-term existence of their establishments (Agrawal & Hockerts, 2021; Camilleri, 2021; Phillips & Johnson, 2021).

3. FinTech's Role in Sustainable Finance

People often disregard FinTech's possible role in driving sustainable practices forward even though it has significantly contributed to social inclusiveness and social influence investment. The digital transformation within the financial sector enhances these efforts by optimising processes and leveraging technology to support more sustainable economic practices (Shehadeh, 2024; Shehadeh, Alshurafat, et al., 2024; Shehadeh, Hussainey, et al., 2024). Reformation of investment banks' behaviours and comprehension of international financial infrastructure are the main drivers behind sustainable finance growth, especially amid environmental and societal turning points that we face. When traditional finance, culprits are underpinning the status quo, transitioning from carbon-intensive projects to new markets in search of a competitive edge. New customers define the leading European banks as essential for sustainable financing. This switch must be made if we want sustainable financing. Green bonds are financial assets seeking to raise funds for environmentally friendly projects like renewable energy or sustainable agriculture, which have experienced significant expansion. Green bond sales in 2020 surpassed 1 trillion dollars due to global interest in sustainability by businesspeople willing to take risks and government support (Gupta & Kumar, 2024). This sits at the heart of the transformational power of blockchain technology in this market through its provision for transparency and traceability, ensuring it is highly efficient and instilling confidence among investors (Sannikova, 2024; Schmidt & González, 2020). This represents an example of blockchain technology transforming transactions, such as reducing settlement times from days to hours, thereby improving trust among contributors while minimising misuse as Spain's BBVA bank did when they issued their inaugural green bond using blockchain technology in 2018. The presence of green bond investments in blockchain improves human life quality by providing better environmental conditions. Therefore, it makes sense when advanced digital technologies, such as blockchain network systems, are integrated with bond trading platforms and gaining popularity.

Crowdfunding platforms are vital in financing sustainable projects alongside environment-related social actions. They enable any individual or organisation to collect small donations from many people, thus broadening finance access for innovative projects with notable impact on the world (Kukurba et al., 2021). For instance, the 'Ocean Cleanup' initiative received over two million dollars from a Kickstarter campaign for developing technologies to remove garbage from oceans and fight pollution there (Breznitz & Noonan, 2020). The site encourages eco-friendly solutions like solar gadgets and other green products using collective wisdom plus financial muscle, which can effectively tackle global challenges (Corsini & Frey, 2023; Thanuskodi, 2022). It democratises finance accessibility, allowing Kiwi investors to contribute towards sustainable development through cause-oriented investments that foster innovation for future generations. This joint endeavour promotes the creation and eventual launch of new technologies or projects that might have been impossible with conventional financing levels.

Digital payment systems, particularly mobile payment technology and blockchain advance sustainable development by supporting non-profit activities, widening financial inclusion and fostering economic growth. Point donations facilitated by mobile payment technologies allow for easy access to small donations to charitable causes. For example, following the East Japan Earthquake, there has been an increase in credit cards incorporated with donation features; for instance, in Japan, donors can give without physical contact but just through a system scan (Mai & Nguyen, 2024; Sirisawat et al., 2022). Blockchain ensures security and efficiency while other transactions remain visible with trust between donors; hence, funds are utilised as intended. Digital payment systems like M-PESA (a mobile phone-based money transfer service) have been developed in Kenya to facilitate financial inclusion among the unbanked population. Smart Money in the Philippines helps rural people access banking services (Moonde, 2023; Torrent-Sellens et al., 2021). On the other hand, this mix fosters growth and sustainability by promoting economic activity, ensuring proper utilisation of resources and job creation and ultimately contributing to sustainable development over time.

An illustration would be provided by wealthy societies such as Harvard and Yale Universities that have established endowment funds through socially responsible investing and impact investment. For example, Harvard could reduce carbon emissions worldwide by investing in green estate or sustainable agriculture. Yale may opt for affordable healthcare services meant for remote communities where people cannot access them, leading to improvements in individual health outcomes and returns from investments made (Yale, 2024). Harvard's $41 billion endowment fund aims at having a net-zero greenhouse gas emissions portfolio by 205, investing in sustainable agriculture, green real estate and high-ESG-rated companies; ESG stands for environment social and governance (Rosenberg, 2021). For instance, one strategy embraced by Harvard is purchasing shares of renewable energy companies that can contribute towards declining CO_2 emissions worldwide performance indices. Yale's $31 billion investment portfolio mainly addresses ESG issues by supporting social businesses focusing on reducing poverty levels while enhancing education standards and healthcare delivery systems (Yale, 2024). On this basis, Yale could invest in low-cost health services found mostly within disadvantaged areas to elevate general health status regarding financial gains.

Transparency alongside efficiency has been substantially enhanced by FinTech advancements in social and impact investments, including blockchain records on how funds are utilised, yielding social benefits. For example, by using blockchain technology, one can verify that money meant for constructing a school in developing nations was indeed used for that purpose. Digital service delivery like M-PESA (Kenyan mobile purse) offers avenues for savings, loans and money transfer, which promote financial inclusion and economic growth when extended to remote areas without banks.

Best practices in advancing sustainable and social finance include ensuring transparency and accountability through blockchain, deploying mobile money systems for underserved populations, digitising prepaid utility metering and partnering with traditional financial institutions and regulators to develop new solutions (Chen et al., 2021; Kozlov, 2021; Xu et al., 2021). For example, a partnership between a mobile money service and a traditional bank can offer a wider range of financial products in rural areas, enhancing financial inclusion and sustainability.

4. FinTech's Role in Social Finance

FinTech plays a transformative role in social finance by ensuring that the financially excluded are included. That social and environmental benefit is measured in tangible ways, tied to several SDGs. The sector is developing at an immense speed, with numerous ground-breaking advances that expand on traditional FinTech applications.

One of these innovations is DeFi through AMM integration. DeFi leverages blockchain technology to create open-source financial products that are not restricted to anyone because of a lack of bank or financial institution services (Bartoletti et al., 2022). These products are transparent, as all transactions are publicly recorded in real time on the ledger of the blockchain network. AMMs employ smart contracts to automate trade in cryptocurrencies or other digital assets. Instead of matching buyers with sellers manually, AMMs use mathematical formulas to execute trades using liquidity pools comprised of funds put into them by users, which they do from their wallets without taking them out. This way, it increases liquidity and cuts down on transaction costs by removing a middle person who makes a profit without adding any value to the transaction process. Thus, Balancer is a platform for decentralised peer-to-peer (P2P) trading, making finance inclusive for low-income people through democratising access to money markets.

Regenerative Finance (ReFi) combines FinTech systems with sustainability goals to create financial systems supporting environmental and social welfare (Lei et al., 2024). Performance should be calculated based on environmental and social returns when developing financial products within ReFi platforms by including ESGs. For example, Flow Carbon develops blockchain carbon credit marketplaces. This allows companies emitting huge amounts of carbon to buy and sell single credits, thereby encouraging reduction across the board since it shifts the burden from one company or individual on Earth to collective major culprits. Using blockchain will result in less fraud or double counting, promoting integrity among stakeholders. Lastly, it will promote clean energy projects, which will help reduce carbon footprint, hence saving nature and conserving biodiversity in the long run. Finally, social equity is part of its investment criteria.

Self-sovereign identity (SSI) systems allow people to claim ownership over their digital identities to securely and privately access financial services (Buttar et al., 2024). SSI differs from traditional identity management systems, where centralised entities control our identities by enabling individuals themselves to manage them via blockchain. A blockchain-based system creates different verifiable credentials stored in tamper-proof ledgers. The idea here is that people own and share their data without an intermediary trusting it, based on credit scores, which include sorry and support. A Refugees International example could be she receives certified credentials from an aid Agency and then uses them to open a bank account at Job Centre Plus on the Sovereign network. In addition, SSI may be seen to promote inclusive identity platforms that correspond to goals such as 'ensure inclusive and quality education for all and promote lifelong learning'; 'promote sustained, inclusive and sustainable economic growth, full productive employment', which are goals four and eight under SDGs.

Programmable money is a digital currency that uses computer code to set out rules and conditions of use, like those in the social effect bond. The contracts are programed to be executed automatically when the criteria are met, which avoids intermediaries and increases transparency while reducing the risk of corruption. Programmable money in social finance ensures that money goes where it is needed most. All funds, for example, assigned for educational purposes, should be directed towards education. This includes intelligent social impact investing or impact bonds where money would only be released when particular predefined outcomes such as improved schooling facilities within certain areas, not just anywhere or else low crime rates have been attained with the help from such contract agreements hence deterring idleness among youths. Singapore's Monetary Authority has experimented using Project Ubin as a case study on the potential of programmable money where they used it for disaster relief purposes thus ensuring that funds' intended objectives would always be met (Singh, 2024).

Mobile technology and data analytics have enabled microfinance platforms to provide financial services to the unbanked, which support SDG 1 (No Poverty) and SDG 8 (Decent Work and Economic Growth) (Parikh & Singh, 2018). User-friendly apps provide access to financial services in even some of the most remote locations using mobile technology (Ajouz & Abuamria, 2022). Therefore, tailored financial products are made possible through data analysis and the assessment of risks. From Blockchain to AI, fraud can be reduced through transparent and secure transactions. Tala, which operates in Kenya, Mexico and the Philippines, is one of the most notable examples (Parikh & Singh, 2018). It is a small venture capital-backed FinTech company that uses mobile technology and machine learning to provide micro-loans to the unbanked. Moreover, it is noteworthy that Tala analyses creditworthiness based on smartphone data and gives instant loans.

On the other hand, P2P lending platforms bypass traditional banking intermediaries to enable individuals and small organisations to access capital (Duarte et al., 2024). By leveraging crowdsourcing and digital technology, these platforms can pair borrowers with lenders more effectively than any other mode. Investing in DeFi and intelligent contract technologies further enhances this kind of effectiveness while blockchains safeguard the integrity through accountability; for instance, Funding Circle offers advanced analytics on their site, which practically matches borrowers to lenders who are more suited to them, thus providing faster access for those who seek funds quickly in a more dependable manner. This process aligns with Goal 9 of the SDGs by encouraging creativity and supporting sustainable industrialisation; therefore, a small-scale entrepreneur may benefit from quick money through Funding Circle, allowing them to expand their business and contribute to economic growth.

Various metrics can be used to evaluate the impact of FinTech innovations on social finance, such as increased financial inclusion, better credit availability, and stability for marginalised communities. Using FinTech, Tala has increased access to finance within its operational regions. In contrast, Grameen Bank has increased loan repayment rates and improved the livelihoods of its borrowers through the same method. Small businesses received extensive loan disbursements using Funding Circle, thus revealing the global potential of FinTech in its alignment with social finance principles. To a large extent, practical usage of technology promotes holistic progress in economies as it removes diversity barriers among societies; as a result, it is common sense to 'follow the market' because price is the preeminent feature of money; thus, technical analysis should be used when making financial decisions prior to growth or profit prospect assumptions. The practices are seen as ending social exclusion and promoting equality.

Consequently, financial technology experts prioritise the user experience to facilitate ease of use for people who need to be tech-savvy. This expands the reach and impact of FinTech initiatives through engagement with local financial institutions, government agencies or intergovernmental bodies, especially the World Bank. For instance, financing a project does not consist only of providing the necessary funds but also of supplying advice and expertise inevitably leading to development; still, another point would be that, therefore, firms must understand the financial obligations put across by regulators towards them and what repercussions these have on their business models and strategies; finally, success rests on understanding that these technologies are just tools to further strengthening upon what already exists this has been well illustrated on a platform. Consequently, they represent a shift from traditional models to ones that promote broad-based participation among poor individuals without targeting specific activities.

Innovations in FinTech have significantly impacted philanthropy, development finance and social responsibility, among others. Despite facing various challenges, particularly in regulation and consumer protection issues, financial technology firms have made notable contributions to societal development by creating value for the segments of society that were generally underserved or overlooked by the mainstream banking system. Initiating ideals for microfinance, which can be seen as a means of empowering people with low incomes economically since it involves loan beneficiaries who have little or no access to the formal banking sector, thereby excluding themselves from access aimed at supporting individuals without them having to present collateral securities before being considered eligible, hence limiting its extent at all times to the impoverished people. These social enterprises operate like typical businesses to gain profit.

5. FinTech's Contribution to Social Impact Investing

Social finance and its transformative role in FinTech has become a key player in the social finance revolution through advancing financial inclusion. It generates direct measurement for social and environmental impacts and contributes to several SDGs. Groundbreaking innovations occur daily in this field, which stretches conventional FinTech applications' limits.

Impact Investing Revolution with Advanced AI Analytics: These groundbreaking innovations use advanced AI analytics to revolutionise social impact investing by enabling more informed decision-making through comprehensive data analysis (Adeoye et al., 2024). The systems are powered by machine learning algorithms that process large datasets, including social media posts, sentiments, environmental impact updates and community feedback, hence providing on-the-go guidance on such aspects of investment as their social and environmental performance. For example, Impact Alpha employs AI to accumulate and analyse different aspects of impact investment, offering traders real-time information concerning how their funds are used to promote socially responsible investments. This invention supports SDGs: SDG 9 – Industry, Innovation and Infrastructure; SDG 17 – Partnership for Goals.

Decentralised autonomous organisations (DAOs) are the latest in social impact investments facelifts. They are based on blockchain technology, which enables decentralised governance (Bellavitis et al., 2023). This allows a group of investors to manage social projects collectively and fund them transparently and democratically. Using smart contracts like Giveth ensures that only agreed-upon milestones will attract disbursement, thus highlighting accountability issues while maintaining trust among participants through transparent transactions. For instance, the Giveth Foundation employs such structures as DAO when financing social good initiatives so that the donors can have their say over financial matters alongside assurance that their contributions are in harmony with community values or objectives. It endorses Sustainable Development Goal 16 (Peace, Justice, and Strong Institutions) by promoting inclusive decision-making and transparency.

Tokenisation is an innovative approach to impact investing that involves turning concrete projects like affordable housing developments and renewable energy into digital tokens on blockchains (Tian et al., 2022). Conversion of assets into digital tokens for subsequent exchange on digital exchanges increases asset liquidity on the one hand and easier access to them on the other hand. It enables investors to own small sections of large projects, which are more affordable than general ownership and increases the number of stakeholders in such projects. The most notable example is the Renewable Energy Token (RET), where investments in clean energy projects are tokenised, making them more liquid and accessible (Ali et al., 2024). This introduces us to SDG 7 and 13, i.e. affordable and clean energy, respectively.

The effectiveness of social impact investing can be enhanced through AI-powered impact analytics, DAOs and tokenisation through better measurement mechanisms, transparency and easy access. By so doing, they will enable such platforms as Impact Alpha to predict the various effects that will accompany such predictions more accurately. DAOs employed by Giveth stick to decentralised governance, which makes it possible for all stakeholders to take part in fund allocation processes based on its democratic principles while, at the same time, information is shared freely among the participants as compared to traditional models such as companies who do not disclose much about what they fund from time to time. On its part, the RET initiative uses tokenisation, thereby enhancing liquidity and accessibility to projects for fractional ownership, thus ensuring funding in projects that may otherwise have been ignored altogether. In conclusion, these innovations have collectively made impact investing more effective and fairer.

Real-time data streams should be integrated into impact measurement frameworks using IoT devices, satellite images and real-time reporting tools. This allows investors to quickly understand how their investments impact nature and society, thus improving responsiveness and effectiveness. Building vital ecosystems around impact investing can deepen collaboration and innovation. Initiatives such as the Global Impact Investment Network (GIIN) facilitate knowledge sharing and enable co-investment opportunities, reducing costs in terms of time-consuming paperwork involved in transactions related to these ventures.

Another potential future direction is extending blockchain technology to monitor the supply chain's social and environmental footprints, offering additional layers of transparency and accountability. Corporations ensure sustainable and ethical practices by placing every single step on a blockchain, thereby stimulating capital growth in socially responsible ventures. Governments can incentivise companies involved in socially responsible investing activities through tax exemptions or grants that encourage them to look for financing despite high entrance barriers.

How could we create a more simplified approach to unlock the future of impact investing? Such tools enable real-time reactions related to environmental and social investments. In what ways do we come up with a strong and cohesive ecosystem for social impact investing? Sometimes, they need some particular preferences in the use of financial instruments from their country, unlike private enterprise alone but as parts of the world aiming at achieving SDGs, thereby satisfying public demands and markets to join hands with NGO's examples would be UGIIN which helps coordinate services among its members so that the population can have access to them together as well as practicing uniform measurement standards.

6. Challenges and Future Directions

FinTech's fast growth leaves behind its regulatory framework, posing compliance challenges on social finance and social impact investment. Blockchain, cryptocurrencies and P2P lending are some innovative things that regulatory authorities globally want to be aware of in order to promote green finance. However, this creates obstacles for FinTech who want to expand their operations beyond borders since the rules may not be consistent. Hence, there is a need for standard laws that take care of innovativeness and the interest of the consumer at large. Thus, the Payment Services Directive II (PSD2) of the European Union intends to foster competition and innovation while guaranteeing customer protection and associated security measures. Nevertheless, social and financial institutions involved in such areas may still struggle to comply because they are constantly subjected to different interpretations and implementations across countries. Despite others, for FinTech to (social impact investment and social finance are some of the areas of critical ethical concerns within FinTech concerning matters about the privacy of data as well as algorithms that favour affluent urban communities based upon their biased decisions, which may even have seen some women denied microloans as opposed to men who received them without any hitches whatsoever).

Given that AI and machine learning oversee simplicity, they have caused people to ask themselves whether trust will still exist in case social impact investments remain as they are today. Therefore, another illustrative scenario arises whereby algorithmic biases lead to discrimination against some sections of society through the provision of some women with loans. In contrast, others were denied this just because they were female. When we talk about transparency, it could mean its opposite lack of transparency, which would result in trust issues. To deal with these fears, there is a need for implementing stringent controls at the leadership level so that there can be no secrecy within any process done through AI because someone will question it if such happens. Ensuring accountability involves putting vital corporate programs on place aids eyeing these risks as well the same time bridging digital division matters ensure that poor areas benefit from technology advances without enlarging existing division lines inclusive finance initiatives.

6.1 Technological Challenges

In FinTech, cybersecurity and data privacy are primary concerns, particularly in social finance and social impact investing, given the increasing rate and intricacy of cyberattacks. There are significant challenges in protecting sensitive financial information from getting into the wrong hands (breaches), breaching privacy policies and safeguarding data during transactions (integrity). Advanced encryption methods, multiple-factor authentication and continuous monitoring systems contribute to improved measures for security enhancement (improve cybersecurity). For instance, GDPR (General et al.) imposes strict requirements on how personal information can be used by companies, including collecting it or storing it on servers located outside Europe; hence, it may not always be possible to abide by this rule easily without interfering user's experience primarily where social impact investing platforms are facilitated. The fusion, compatibility or adaptability (due to newness) of different FinTech solutions result in several significant technological challenges.

Consequently, there is a movement towards consolidation since different ways may make sense, especially as the ecosystem continues expanding. These include, among others, transposing old into new forms and setting up platforms that can be reached from different regions without changing contents. Consequently, through openly programed interfaces, open banking initiatives envisage solving these dilemmas with a dream of creating one sizeable, interlinked finance world. Realising such a microscope comprises continuous cooperation, including banks, tech companies and rule makers who must work as one to encourage broader adoption of standard lending terms and methods in digital money so that smaller initiatives started up earlier cannot be scaled now.

6.2 Future Trends and Opportunities

Emerging technologies such as blockchain, AI and quantum computing are poised to reshape the landscape of social finance and social impact investing. Blockchain technology offers the potential for secure, transparent and tamper-proof financial transactions, revolutionising impact measurement and reporting areas. For example, blockchain can ensure that investments in social projects are tracked and reported transparently, building trust among investors.

AI and machine learning can enhance risk assessment, fraud detection and impact analysis, enabling more efficient and effective social finance initiatives. For instance, AI can analyse vast amounts of data to identify the most impactful social projects or to detect fraudulent activities in real time, ensuring that funds are used effectively.

Quantum computing, though still in its nascent stages, holds promise for solving complex financial problems at unprecedented speeds, potentially transforming fields such as cryptography and financial modelling for sustainable finance. This could lead to more sophisticated models for assessing the impact of social investments and better strategies for managing financial risks associated with these investments.

Sustainable and social finance is gaining traction as investors increasingly seek to align their portfolios with their values. Integrating ESG criteria into investment decisions is becoming mainstream, driven by regulatory pressures and growing awareness of climate risks. FinTech innovations can facilitate this transition by providing impact measurement, reporting, and verification tools. Platforms like Ethic and OpenInvest offer personalised ESG investment options, enabling investors to make informed decisions that support SDGs.

There are ample opportunities for further research and innovation in FinTech related to social finance and social impact investing. Areas such as decentralised finance (DeFi), RegTech (regulatory technology) and InsurTech (insurance technology) are ripe for exploration. DeFi leverages blockchain to create decentralised financial systems, democratising access to financial services and supporting inclusive social finance. RegTech solutions can enhance compliance and risk management through automated processes and real-time monitoring, which is crucial for maintaining the integrity of social impact investments. InsurTech innovations can improve the efficiency and accessibility of insurance services through digital platforms and data-driven underwriting, supporting resilience in communities. Additionally, research into the ethical implications of FinTech, including algorithmic bias and data privacy, is crucial to ensure that technological advancements benefit society as a whole and contribute to SDGs.

7. Conclusion

This comprehensive analysis has highlighted the transformative role of FinTech innovations in advancing sustainable and social finance, particularly through the lens of social impact investing. By leveraging technologies such as blockchain, AI and mobile payment systems, FinTech has significantly enhanced the accessibility, efficiency and transparency of financial services. These advancements have democratised access to financial markets, allowing underserved populations and small businesses to participate, thereby promoting economic empowerment and reducing inequality.

FinTech innovations have facilitated more informed investment decisions through real-time data and analytics, ensuring efficient capital allocation to projects that deliver measurable social and environmental benefits. The transparency and accountability provided by blockchain technology have further assured investors of the effective use of their funds, increasing trust and encouraging more significant investments in social impact projects.

Despite these advancements, several challenges hinder the full potential of FinTech in social impact investing. The digital divide remains a critical issue, limiting the reach of FinTech solutions in underdeveloped regions. Regulatory inconsistencies and the lack of standardised frameworks create uncertainties that can deter investors and limit the scalability of social impact projects. Additionally, data privacy and security concerns pose significant risks, as the increased reliance on digital platforms heightens the potential for cyber threats. The integration of advanced technologies such as AI and blockchain into traditional financial systems requires substantial investment and expertise, which can be a barrier for smaller organisations.

Addressing these challenges is crucial for FinTech to realise its full potential in driving social impact investing and achieving SDGs. This involves fostering a more inclusive technological ecosystem, harmonising regulatory frameworks and ensuring robust data privacy and security measures. Additionally, ongoing research and innovation in areas such as DeFi, RegTech and InsurTech are essential to continue evolving the FinTech landscape.

The future of FinTech in social finance looks promising, with emerging technologies poised to further reshape the landscape. Blockchain technology, AI and quantum computing offer new possibilities for secure, transparent and efficient financial transactions, risk assessment and impact analysis. The integration of these technologies can enhance the effectiveness and equity of social finance initiatives, ultimately driving greater social and environmental progress.

In conclusion, FinTech stands as a critical enabler of sustainable and socially responsible finance, offering tools and innovations that align financial objectives with broader societal goals. By continuing to address existing challenges and embracing future technological advancements, FinTech can significantly contribute to the global agenda of achieving sustainable development and social justice.

References

Adeoye, O. B., Okoye, C. C., Ofodile, O. C., Odeyemi, O., Addy, W. A., & Ajayi-Nifise, A. O. (2024). Artificial Intelligence in ESG investing: Enhancing portfolio management and performance. *International Journal of Science and Research Archive*, *11*(1), 2194–2205.

Adnan, S. A., & Kumar, P. (2021). Role of microfinance in economic development. *Adhyayan: A Journal of Management Sciences*, *11*(2), 22–30.

Agrawal, A., & Hockerts, K. (2021). Impact investing: Review and research agenda. *Journal of Small Business and Entrepreneurship*, *33*(2), 153–181.

Ajouz, M., & Abuamria, F. (2022). Does mobile payment promote financial inclusion among Palestinians women: A quantitative approach through structural equation modeling. *Journal of Islamic Finance*, *10*(2), 67–78.

Ajouz, M., Abuamria, F., Al Zeer, I., Salahat, M., Shehadeh, M., Binsaddig, R., Al-Sartawi, A., & Al-Ramahi, N. M. (2023). Navigating the uncharted: The shaping of FinTech ecosystems in emerging markets. *Cuadernos de Economía*, *46*(132), 189–201.

Ajouz, M., Abuamria, F., Shehadeh, M., Abu-AlSondos, I. A., Aldulaimi, S. H., & Abdeldayem, M. (2024, January). Exploring the cascade: How buy-now-pay-later platforms fuel impulse buying tendency and the subsequent impact on sustainability. In *2024 ASU international conference in emerging technologies for sustainability and intelligent systems (ICETSIS)* (pp. 1–5). IEEE.

Ali, S., Umar, M., Naveed, M., & Shan, S. (2024). Assessing the impact of renewable energy tokens on BRICS stock markets: A new diversification approach. *Energy Economics*, *134*, 107523.

Alkhazaleh, A., Assaf, A., Shehada, M., Almustafa, E., & Allahham, M. (2023). Analysis of the impact of fintech firms' lending on the expansion of service base companies in Jordan. *Information Sciences Letters*, *12*(8), 2891–2902.

Alkhwaldi, A. F., Alharasis, E. E., Shehadeh, M., Abu-AlSondos, I. A., Oudat, M. S., & Bani Atta, A. A. (2022). Towards an understanding of FinTech users' adoption: Intention and e-loyalty post-COVID-19 from a developing country perspective. *Sustainability*, *14*(19), 12616.

AlMomani, A. A., & Alomari, K. F. (2021). Financial technology (FinTech) and its role in supporting the financial and banking services sector. *International Journal of Academic Research in Business and Social Sciences*, *11*(8), 1793–1802.

Arner, D. W., Zetzsche, D. A., Buckley, R. P., & Barberis, J. N. (2017). FinTech and RegTech: Enabling innovation while preserving financial stability. *Georgetown Journal of International Affairs*, *18*(3), 47–58.

Bartoletti, M., Chiang, J. H. Y., & Lluch-Lafuente, A. (2022). A theory of automated market makers in DeFi. *Logical Methods in Computer Science*, *18*(4).

Bellavitis, C., Fisch, C., & Momtaz, P. P. (2023). The rise of decentralized autonomous organizations (DAOs): A first empirical glimpse. *Venture Capital*, *25*(2), 187–203.

Bengo, I., Borrello, A., & Chiodo, V. (2021). Preserving the integrity of social impact investing: Towards a distinctive implementation strategy. *Sustainability*, *13*(5), 2852.

Breznitz, S. M., & Noonan, D. S. (2020). Crowdfunding in a not-so-flat world. *Journal of Economic Geography*, *20*(4), 1069–1092.

Buttar, A. M., Shahid, M. A., Arshad, M. N., & Akbar, M. A. (2024). Decentralized identity management using blockchain technology: Challenges and solutions. In S. M. Idrees & M. Nowostawski (Eds.), *Blockchain transformations. Signals and communication technology*. Springer.

Camilleri, M. A. (2021). The market for socially responsible investing: A review of the developments. *Social Responsibility Journal*, *17*(3), 412–428.

Chen, Q. (2024). FinTech innovation in micro and small business financing. *International Journal of Global Economics and Management*, *2*(1), 284–290.

Chen, Y., Jermias, J., & Nazari, J. A. (2021). The effects of reporting frameworks and a company's financial position on managers' willingness to invest in corporate social responsibility projects. *Accounting and Finance*, *61*(2), 3385–3425.

Chuc, A. A. M., Atayah, A. A., & Özer, S. Q. (2021). Impact of financial technology (FinTech) on financial performance of micro finance institutions in Bahrain. *Sustainability*, *13*(2), 1183–1207.

Chueca Vergara, C., & Ferruz Agudo, L. (2021). Fintech and sustainability: Do they affect each other? *Sustainability*, *13*(13), 7012.

Corsini, F., & Frey, M. (2023). Exploring the development of environmentally sustainable products through reward-based crowdfunding. *Electronic Commerce Research*, *23*(2), 1183–1207.

Cumming, D., Johan, S., & Reardon, R. (2023). Global fintech trends and their impact on international business: A review. *Multinational Business Review*, *31*(3), 413–436.

Degerli, K. (2019). Regulatory challenges and solutions for fintech in Turkey. *Procedia Computer Science*, *158*, 929–937.

Demirgüç-Kunt, A., Klapper, L., Singer, D., & Ansar, S. (2022). *The Global Findex Database 2021: Financial inclusion, digital payments, and resilience in the age of COVID-19*. World Bank Publications.

Duarte, J., Siegel, S., & Young, L. (2024). The evolution of P2P lending. In F. Allen & M. Qian (Eds.), *Research handbook on alternative finance* (pp. 181–212). Edward Elgar Publishing.

Elia, G., Stefanelli, V., & Ferilli, G. B. (2023). Investigating the role of Fintech in the banking industry: What do we know? *European Journal of Innovation Management*, *26*(5), 1365–1393.

Falcone, P. M. (2020). Environmental regulation and green investments: The role of green finance. *International Journal of Green Economics*, *14*(2), 159–173.

Gafni, H., Hudon, M., & Périlleux, A. (2021). Business or basic needs? The impact of loan purpose on social crowdfunding platforms. *Journal of Business Ethics*, *173*, 777–793.

Giglio, F. (2021). Fintech: A literature review. *European Research Studies Journal, 24*(2B), 600–627.

Gupta, V., & Kumar, A. (2024). Green bonds: Accelerating green finance towards sustainable economic development. In R. Sharma, G. Rana, & S. Agarwal (Eds.), *Green innovations for industrial development and business sustainability* (pp. 127–145). CRC Press.

Gutterman, A. (2020). *What is impact investing*. https://ssrn.com/abstract=3823837

Harsono, I., & Suprapti, I. A. P. (2024). The role of fintech in transforming traditional financial services. *Accounting Studies and Tax Journal (COUNT), 1*(1), 81–91.

Harvie, D., Lightfoot, G., Lilley, S., & Weir, K. (2021). Social investment innovation and the 'social turn' of neoliberal finance. *Critical Perspectives on Accounting, 79*, 102248.

Hendrikse, R., Van Meeteren, M., & Bassens, D. (2020). Strategic couplingbetween finance, technology and the state: Cultivating a Fintech ecosystem for incumbent finance. *Environment and Planning A: Economy and Space, 52*(8), 1516–1538.

Jarvis, R., & Han, H. (2021). FinTech innovation: Review and future research directions. *International Journal of Banking, Finance and Insurance Technologies, 1*(1), 79–102.

Kou, G., Olgu Akdeniz, Ö., Dinçer, H., & Yüksel, S. (2021). Fintech investments in European banks: A hybrid IT2 fuzzy multidimensional decision-making approach. *Financial Innovation, 7*(1), 39.

Kozlov, D. (2021). The strategies of internalizing the negative externalities in the company's sustainable development. *Virtual Economics, 4*(3), 7–19.

Kuanova, L. A., Sagiyeva, R., & Shirazi, N. S. (2021). Islamic social finance: A literature review and future research directions. *Journal of Islamic Accounting and Business Research, 12*(5), 707–728.

Kukurba, M., Waszkiewicz, A. E., Salwin, M., & Kraslawski, A. (2021). Co-created values in crowdfunding for sustainable development of enterprises. *Sustainability, 13*(16), 8767.

Lanteri, A. (2024). *Financial social innovations: A new framework to understand the social innovations disrupting the world of finance, from crowdfunding to bitcoin.* Taylor & Francis.

Lazzarini, S. G., Cabral, S., Pongeluppe, L. S., Ferreira, L. C. D. M., & Rotondaro, A. (2021). The best of both worlds? Impact investors and their role in the financial versus social performance debate. In O. M. Lehner (Ed.), *A research agenda for social finance* (pp. 99–125). Edward Elgar Publishing.

Lee, C. C., Li, X., Yu, C. H., & Zhao, J. (2021). Does fintech innovation improve bank efficiency? Evidence from China's banking industry. *International Review of Economics & Finance, 74*, 468–483.

Lei, H., Xue, M., & Ye, J. (2024). The nexus between ReFi, carbon, fossil energy, and clean energy assets: Quantile time-frequency connectedness and portfolio implications. *Energy Economics, 132*, 107456.

Macchiavello, E., & Siri, M. (2022). Sustainable finance and fintech: Can technology contribute to achieving environmental goals? A preliminary assessment of 'green fintech'and 'sustainable digital finance'. *European Company and Financial Law Review, 19*(1), 128–174.

Mai, X. T., & Nguyen, T. (2024). Switching behaviors in peer-to-peer mobile payment applications: The role of sociability. *Journal of Systems and Information Technology*, *26*(1), 1–30.

Mejia-Escobar, J. C., González-Ruiz, J. D., & Duque-Grisales, E. (2020). Sustainable financial products in the Latin America banking industry: Current status and insights. *Sustainability*, *12*(14), 5648.

Moonde, C. (2023). *Secure mobile payment system based on Blockchain technology for higher learning institutions* Unpublished doctoral thesis. The University of Zambia.

Mustapha, I., Vaicondam, Y., Jahanzeb, A., Usmanovich, B. A., & Yusof, S. H. B. (2023). Cybersecurity challenges and solutions in the fintech mobile app ecosystem. *International Journal of Interactive Mobile Technologies*, *17*(22), 100–116.

Newmark, T. E., & Pena, M. A. (2023). *Impact investing for a sustainable planet: Insights from EcoEnterprises Fund.* Taylor & Francis.

Nguyen, L., Tran, S., & Ho, T. (2021). Fintech credit, bank regulations and bank performance: A cross-country analysis. *Asia-Pacific Journal of Business Administration*, *14*(4), 445–466.

Palakurti, N. R. (2023). The future of finance: Opportunities and challenges in financial network analytics for systemic risk management and investment analysis. *International Journal of Interdisciplinary Finance Insights*, *2*(2), 1–20.

Parikh, P., & Singh, P. (2018). Need for developing intelligent interfaces for big data analytics in the microfinance industry. In V. Aggarwal, V. Bhatnagar, & D. Mishra (Eds.), *Big data analytics. Advances in intelligent systems and computing*. Springer.

Phillips, S. D., & Johnson, B. (2021). Inching to impact: The demand side of social impact investing. *Journal of Business Ethics*, *168*(3), 615–629.

Pinheiro, P., Daniel, A., & Moreira, A. (2021). Social enterprise performance: The role of market and social entrepreneurship orientations. *Voluntas: International Journal of Voluntary and Nonprofit Organizations*, *32*(1), 45–60.

Rehman, S. U., Al-Shaikh, M., Washington, P. B., Lee, E., Song, Z., Abu-AlSondos, I. A., Shehadeh, M., & Allahham, M. (2023). FinTech adoption in SMEs and bank credit supplies: A study on manufacturing SMEs. *Economies*, *11*(8), 213.

Rizzello, A., & Kabli, A. (2020). Sustainable financial partnerships for the SDGs: The case of social impact bonds. *Sustainability*, *12*(13), 5362.

Rosenberg, J. S. (2021, June). Harvard endowment valued at $41.9 billion, up 2.4 percent. *Harvard Magazine*. Www.Harvardmagazine.Com/2020/09/Harvard-Endowment-41-9-Billion-on-7-3-Percent-Investment-Return. Accessed on June 18, 2016.

Sannikova, L. V. (2024). Green finance in the EU and Russia: Legal frameworks and opportunities of digitalisation. In L. V. Sannikova (Ed.), *Digital technologies and distributed registries for sustainable development: Legal challenges* (Vol. 64, pp. 97–109). Law, Governance and Technology Series. Springer.

Schmidt, W. C., & González, A. (2020). Fintech and Tokenization: A legislative study in Argentina and Spain about the application of Blockchain in the field of properties. *Advances in Distributed Computing and Artificial Intelligence Journal*, *9*(1), 1–120.

Secinaro, S., Calandra, D., Petricean, D., & Chmet, F. (2020). Social finance and banking research as a driver for sustainable development: A bibliometric analysis. *Sustainability*, *13*(1), 330.

Shehadeh, M. (2024). Digital transformation: A catalyst for sustainable business practices. In A. Hamdan (Ed.), *Technological innovations for business, education and sustainability (Technological innovation and sustainability for business competitive advantage)* (pp. 29–45). Emerald Publishing Limited.

Shehadeh, M., Alshurafat, H., & Arabiat, O. (2024). Inverting the paradigm: Digital transformation's impact on firm performance and the counterintuitive role of gender. *Competitiveness Review: An International Business Journal*. (ahead-of-print).

Shehadeh, M., Hussainey, K., Alhadab, M., & Kilani, Q. (2024). Corporate narrative reporting on Industry 4.0 technologies: Do the COVID-19 pandemic and governance structure matter? *Review of Accounting and Finance*, *23*(5), 687–714.

Singh, S. (2024). Blockchain technology: Enabling the rise of digital currencies. In G. Kaur, P. Lekhi, & S. Popli (Eds.), *Exploring central bank digital currencies: Concepts, frameworks, models, and challenges* (pp. 33–41). IGI Global.

Sirisawat, S., Chatjuthamard, P., Kiattisin, S., & Treepongkaruna, S. (2022). The future of digital donation crowdfunding. *PLoS One*, *17*(11), e0275898.

Stolz, D., & Lai, K. P. (2020). Impact investing, social enterprise and global development. In P. Mader, D. Mertens, & N. van der Zwan (Eds.), *The Routledge international handbook of financialization* (pp. 288–300). Routledge.

Suryono, R. R., Budi, I., & Purwandari, B. (2020). Challenges and trends of financial technology (Fintech): A systematic literature review. *Information*, *11*(12), 590.

Taherdoost, H. (2023). Fintech: Emerging trends and the future of finance. In A. N. Turi (Ed.), *Financial technologies and DeFi. Financial innovation and technology*. Springer.

Thanuskodi, S. (2022). Sustainable development of libraries: Some possibilities. *Special Education*, *1*(43), 7332.

Thompson, S. (2023). *Green and sustainable finance: Principles and practice in banking, investment and insurance* (Vol. 7). Kogan Page Publishers.

Tian, Y., Wang, C., Asutosh, A., Woo, J., & Adriaens, P. (2022). *Blockchain-enabled tokenization for sustainable and inclusive infrastructure investment. arXiv preprint arXiv:2208.04709*.

Torrent-Sellens, J., Salazar-Concha, C., Ficapal-Cusí, P., & Saigí-Rubió, F. (2021). Using digital platforms to promote blood donation: Motivational and preliminary evidence from Latin America and Spain. *International Journal of Environmental Research and Public Health*, *18*(8), 4270.

Wendt, K. (2021). Social stock exchanges: Democratization of capital investing for impact. In K. Wendt (Ed.), *Green and social economy finance* (pp. 290–327). CRC Press.

Xu, J. (2022). FinTech innovation and strategy. In J. Xu (Ed.), *The future and FinTech: ABCDI and beyond* (pp. 1–36). World Scientific.

Xu, X. C., Gu, X. W., Qing, W. A. N. G., Zhao, Y. Q., & Wang, Z. K. (2021). Open pit limit optimization considering economic profit, ecological costs and social benefits. *Transactions of Nonferrous Metals Society of China*, *31*(12), 3847–3861.

Yale. (2024, June). *Overview of Yale's endowment*. Yale University. Www.Yale.Edu/Funding-Yale-Home/Overview-Yales-Endowment. Accessed on June 18, 2016.

Yaşar, B. (2021). Impact investing: A review of the current state and opportunities for development. *Istanbul Business Research*, *50*(1), 177–196.

Zhang, J. (2022). FinTech and green finance: The case of Ant Forest in China. In *2021 International conference on public art and human development (ICPAHD 2021)* (pp. 657–661). Atlantis Press.

Chapter 12

The Impact of Artificial Intelligence on Audit Quality to Achieve Business Sustainability

Moamen A. Shazly[a], *khaled AbdElAlim*[b] *and Hesham Zakaria*[c]

[a]Arab Open University, Egypt
[b]May University in Cairo, Egypt
[c]Higher Institute of Administrative Sciences, Egypt

Abstract

The chapter examines the impact of artificial intelligence (AI) on audit quality to achieve business sustainable practices, trying to find that using AI as a substitute for human intelligence affects auditors' capability and experience, and it also affects audit process, starting from audit planning to the issuance of reporting to improve business sustainability. Based on the literature review about AI and audit quality, the chapter findings showed that AI adoption is a necessary requirement for auditors due to time constraints, accuracy requirements and job speed requirements. The impact of AI on audit quality is profound and multifaceted. By leveraging the capabilities of AI, auditors can enhance the accuracy, efficiency and objectivity of their work.

To guarantee that the application of AI benefits the auditing profession and the public it serves, it is imperative to solve the obstacles that come with it. AI has the ability to greatly improve audit quality, but its deployment needs to be closely monitored to prevent any early problems. With appropriate training, data and governance, AI can enhance the efficiency and effectiveness of audits, leading to more accurate and reliable financial reporting, which directly achieve business sustainability through enhancing financial reporting quality, investors' confidence, corporate governance and mitigation of agency conflicts.

Keywords: Artificial intelligence; external auditors; audit process; audit quality; business sustainability

From Digital Disruption to Dominance, 265–277

doi:10.1108/978-1-83549-608-420251013

1. Introduction

Artificial intelligence (AI) is a replacement for human intelligence. It is created by combining hardware and software to solve complicated business problems in a way that mimics the thinking, learning, clarifying and step-by-step recognition of a human expert. AI uses machine intelligence rather than human intellect and utilises expert systems in place of human experts. AI facilitates decision-making for managers by streamlining complicated choice elements and supplying more accurate information (Askary et al., 2018).

It is an emerging technology, and it aims to mimic the human judgements and cognitive skills, with competitive advantages for adopters (Munoko et al., 2020). Also, AI can be characterised as machine intelligence. According to computer science, a flexible, rational agent that senses its surroundings and acts to improve its odds of success in reaching a goal is the epitome of an 'intelligent' machine (Adiloglu & Gungor, 2019) The Organization for Economic Co-operation and Development (OECD) defines AI as a machine-based system that can make predictions, suggestions or judgements influencing actual or virtual environments for a certain set of human-specified objectives (Noordin et al., 2022).

These days, the concept of AI's utility is crucial to both academic and business practice. The advent of the technological revolution brings about changes like industry restructuring. AI is changing how businesses, governments, organisations and individuals operate (Issa et al., 2016).

There are two most cited definitions for the audit quality, De Angelo who defines audit quality as the joint probability that auditors both discover a breach in the client's accounting system and report the breach and De Fond and Zhang who define higher audit quality as greater assurance of high financial reporting quality (Rajgopal et al., 2021). Researchers suggest that audit quality is defined as the probability that the auditor will detect a breach and report it. If auditors do not remain independent, they will be less likely to report irregularities, thereby impairing audit quality (Tepalagul & Lin, 2015).

When competent and impartial individuals carry out audit tests and the techniques they employ yield pertinent and dependable data, the audit quality at the input level is enhanced. Higher audit quality is produced when the members of engagement team decide which particular tests to conduct and how best to assess the evidence gathered from those tests to create the audit report (Francis, 2011).

Sustainable business practices are rapidly gaining traction and becoming as a major trend, especially in the industrialised west. There's an easy explanation for that. The world community is currently dealing with a wide range of social and environmental issues, including gender inequality social inequality, unequal wealth distribution, failing economies, war and conflict, lack of education, widespread poverty, climate change, loss of habitat, extinction of species and ecological loss. If more sustainable business practices are adopted by the private sector, many of these issues can be resolved. Particularly in developing and less developed nations, these issues are severe (Chungyalpa, 2019).

The chapter discuses AI and its impact on audit quality in order to achieve business sustainability, tying to understand the use of AI as a substitute of human intelligence and how it affects the auditors' capabilities and experience, the overall audit process, starting from audit planning till the issuance of the audit report, to improve business sustainable practices.

2. Artificial Intelligence (AI)

AI is defined as a branch of science and computer engineering concerned with the development of intelligent machines or computers capable of thinking, learning and working independently. AI helps to analyse large amounts of data, recognise patterns and make decisions on its own. Organisations can use AI in a variety of ways. In order to facilitate decision-making, it can streamline the data analysis and document review processes. AI can also be used to provide customised reports that are tailored to the needs of the company (Noordin et al., 2022).

AI algorithms can complement other recent technologies, which determine data that can be inspected by AI (e.g. images from drones) or specific applications for AI algorithms (e.g. robotic process automation) (Fedyk et al., 2022).

According to Dheeriya & Singhvi (2021), basic tasks like information retrieval from contracts, leases and invoices can be readily completed with AI. The National Association of Corporate states that although they view AI as the top business enabler that will likely benefit their firms in the upcoming year, they also rank it as one of the biggest technology disruptors.

Noordin et al. (2022) recommended that firms which choose to employ AI in their operations should be aware of the risks that AI poses to financial data. AI may be able to recognise sensitive information that should be kept private from outside parties as it develops its ability to recognise data patterns. This information might be used to perpetrate other crimes or to influence financial institutions if it ended up in the wrong hands.

The authors can conclude that many industries have seen significant changes as a result of AI. AI adoption is a necessary requirement for auditors due to time constraints, accuracy requirements and job speed requirements.

3. Audit Quality

For instance, the legal view of auditing provides two types of audit quality that contrast each other: 'audit failure' and 'non-audit failure'. An audit failure happens in the case of lack of auditor independence or if the auditor independence is present, but the auditor incorrectly issues an unqualified audit report due to failure to accumulate sufficient competent evidence as necessitated by auditing standards. Conversely, a 'good audit', also known as a non-failure audit, is one in which the auditor adheres to auditing standards and provides an accurate judgement regarding the financial statements of the client while assuming a manageable amount of audit risk (Francis, 2011).

Hosseinniakani et al. (2014) outline the various audit quality elements, including auditor standards like professional competence, technical ability, independence and liability, as well as auditor specifications like size, industry expertise, auditor tenure, audit fees, non-audit services and auditor reputation.

Another common definition of audit quality is that it is a process that an auditor goes through to evaluate a financial statement's risk level of a material misstatement. In other words, an auditor inspects whether a financial statement has been fairly documented to ensure that there are no material misstatements and to ensure a strong internal control (Brown et al., 2016).

Actual quality and perceived quality have been presented as important issues in audit quality definition. Actual audit quality can be defined as the probability of reducing the risk of reporting a material misstatement in the financial statement (Harber & Marx, 2020).

The authors can infer from the literature review that there are (direct) measurements for audit quality, which are related to characteristics of external auditor includes (knowledge and educational level, experience, industry expertise and reputation), and there are (indirect) measurements for audit quality, which are related to audit process includes (audit planning, internal control evaluation and risk assessment, audit evidence and reporting) (see Fig. 12.1).

- *Knowledge and Educational Level of External Auditors*

  An essential function of external auditors is to guarantee the dependability and correctness of financial reporting. Their knowledge and educational level are essential to their ability to perform their duties effectively. Alsughayer (2021) had shown that auditors with higher levels of education and knowledge are more likely to detect financial misstatements. This is a result of their enhanced comprehension of accounting principles and auditing practices, as well as their capacity to assess financial data critically.

  Additionally, higher educated auditors are more likely to be up to date on the latest advancements in accounting and auditing, which can help them keep ahead of the curve and spot possible potential risks (Barr-Pulliam et al., 2023).

Fig. 12.1. Audit Quality Measurements Related to External Auditor.
Source: by the authors.

- *Experience of External Auditors*
  Experience is an important attribute that the auditor has. The professional experience is the power which can be obtained by the practice over time from past experiences and direct feedback and the general knowledge, which lead to accomplish the task with high quality. The auditor's experience contributes significantly to the judgements made by the auditor. Experience can also affect the auditor's predictive and detection ability against fraud to affect opinion taken by the auditor (Merdekawati, 2022).
- *Industry Expertise of the External Auditor*
  Auditors who have specialised in a particular field are called specialist auditors, for instance, those usually offer clients higher-quality services at reduced expenses.

  Currently, there is a rising need for specialised auditors who are differentiated in the industries and companies they work for. By getting to know their customers' distinctive characteristics better, auditors aim to increase their level of competence in a given industry. So, having knowledge of the industry may present great chances to carry out thorough audits on several businesses with comparable needs. The specialism of the audit industry is intimately related to the calibre of financial information reported by a corporation. Auditors are better able to apply auditing procedures to find fraud and raise the audit quality when they concentrate on a single industry (Alharasis et al., 2023).
- *Reputation of the External Auditor*
  The auditor's reputation is demonstrated by public confidence in the auditor through his performance (see Fig. 12.2). The auditors are responsible for keeping public trust and bound in honour of the auditors themselves and public accountant firms where they work by giving opinions that are appropriate to the company's state (Kutha & Susan, 2021; Suwarno et al., 2020).

Fig. 12.2. Audit Quality Measurements Related to Audit Process.
Source: by the authors.

- *Audit Planning*
  Since it will decide the audit's efficiency and effectiveness, the audit planning process is the most important one. The auditor must comprehend the company's accounting system, business operations and important internal controls in order to prepare the audit of the financial statements. They must also assess potential fraudulent activity, establish the degree of materiality and conduct analytical test procedures. Ultimately, the auditor must create a systematic audit programme (Apandi et al., 2022).
- *Internal Control Evaluation and Risk Assessment*
  The International Auditing and Assurance Standards Board (IAASB) has issued a number of standards on internal control evaluation and risk assessment, including ISA 315 (Revised 2019): Identifying and Assessing the Risks of Material Misstatement through Understanding the Entity and Its Environment, and ISA 330 (Revised 2019): Responding to Assessed Risks of Material Misstatement. These standards provide guidance to auditors on how to perform these important procedures.

  Evaluating an organisation's internal controls over financial reporting is known as internal control evaluation. This aids the auditor in assessing how much trust the company's financial statements can be trusted. Determining and evaluating the likelihood of a major mistake in the financial statements is known as risk assessment. This aids in the auditor's planning and resource allocation for the audit.
- *Audit Evidence*
  Audit evidence is an important element in the nature of the audit process where its importance in the accreditation of the auditor based on the composition of his professional opinion is not contrary to the international audit standards on the one hand and the legislation adopted on the other hand (Mohammed et al., 2021).
- *Reporting*
  According to International Standard on Auditing (ISA) 700: Forming an Opinion and Reporting on Financial Statements the auditor's report should be clear, concise and informative (IAASB, 2015). It must also be impartial and devoid of prejudice. When choosing the report's content, the auditor should apply professional judgement, keeping in mind the particulars of the audit as well as the requirements of the financial statement users.

  One of the most important things external auditors do is report. It entails informing the proper parties such as the company's management, shareholders and regulatory bodies of the audit's findings. In addition to disclosing any significant misstatements found during the audit, the auditor's report offers an assessment on the financial statements' fairness.

4. Impact of AI on Audit Quality

Albitar et al. (2020) mentioned that using cybersecurity and AI are improving the internal control by protecting information from threats on the internet. AI reduces human errors increases accuracy and protects firms against unknown threats and learns its patterns while cyber security protects firms' information against known cyber threats. Audit quality gives a guide for auditors on the things that should be regarded in relation to the effect of social distancing measures on audit quality.

Albawwat & Frijat (2021) explained the perceived ease of use, usefulness and contribution to the audit quality of different AI's types. The results indicate that auditors perceive assisted and augmented AI systems as ease of use in auditing while perceiving autonomous AI systems as complicated to use.

Fedyk et al. (2022) examined how AI affected the effectiveness and quality of audits for the biggest audit companies, as well as which audit companies employed AI personnel and how well they performed. The findings demonstrated how AI lowers costs, enhances audit quality and eventually replaces human auditors.

Yebi and Cudjoe (2022) investigated how AI is affecting the audit process, audit quality and the abilities and competencies of auditors. The findings demonstrated that AI has significantly impacted the abilities and competences of auditors, with many respondents confirming that IT skills are now among the essential competencies required of auditors. AI has also had a favourable impact on audit quality and process.

Noordin et al. (2022) described the opinions of external auditors regarding the application of AI in various United Arab Emirates (UAE)-based audit firms. The findings demonstrated that local and foreign audit firms' perceptions of AI's contribution to audit quality differed not significantly. Regarding the audit quality, all audit firms – local and foreign – perceive the same contributions.

The authors can infer from the literature review, there is a negative impact of AI on external auditors and positive impact on the audit process as follows.

The impact of AI on external auditors presents challenges (see Fig. 12.3) such as the need for auditors to develop new skills, knowledge and training to effectively utilise AI technologies. Moreover, the growing reliance on AI prompts questions about potential biases and highlights the necessity of strong control and

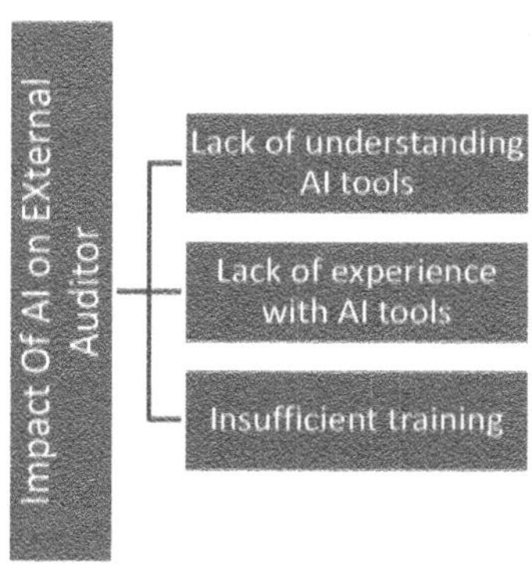

Fig. 12.3. Impact of AI on External Auditor. *Source:* by the authors.

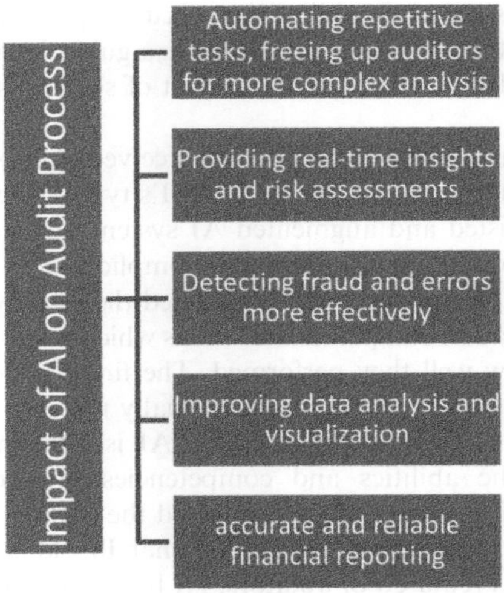

Fig. 12.4. Impact of AI on Audit Process. *Source:* by the authors.

oversight frameworks to guarantee the moral and appropriate application of AI in auditing.

The audit process is being profoundly impacted by AI, which is changing how auditors carry out their duties and provide their services. Automation of different audit procedures, increased productivity and improved accuracy and consistency of audit processes are all being achieved with AI-powered tools and methodologies.

One of the most significant impacts of AI on auditing is the automation of data analysis and testing (see Fig. 12.4). Large datasets can be swiftly and effectively analysed by AI algorithms, which can also spot trends and anomalies that could point to fraud or mistakes. This can greatly cut down on the time and work needed for manual review, freeing up auditors to work on more difficult and valuable jobs. AI is also being utilised to improve planning and risk assessment. AI systems are able to examine past data and spot trends and patterns that could point to possible potential risks. With the aid of these data, auditors may create more successful audit techniques and gain a deeper understanding of the client's business.

5. Business Sustainability

It is necessary to define the term 'sustainable business practices' and look at the guiding ideals and concepts of the term. The term 'sustainable business practices' is not well understood. To a multitude of diverse individuals, it can signify many things. Most people agree that a sustainable business is one that is both environmentally friendly and socially and economically responsible (KPMG, 2020). In other words the business is financially sound and self-reliant, tries to improve the social impact (championing equal opportunity, human rights and caring for the community) of its actions on key stakeholders (employees, customers, government and society) and ensures that its activities (production to consumption of its goods and services) do not adversely impact the environment (Chungyalpa, 2019).

Today, the trend is for companies to align their core business objectives and activities with social and developmental goals. For example, companies are leveraging their supply chain and production process to use raw materials and supplies from local suppliers and suppliers with responsibly sourced raw materials. In this way, they contribute towards developmental goals. The following are benefits associated with sustainable business practice (Whelan & Fink, 2016):

- Getting into new markets.
- Simplifying procedures, cutting expenses and raising general organisational effectiveness.
- Comparing and evaluating sustainability performance in light of regulations, standards codes and voluntary efforts.
- Evaluating performance within and between sectors and organisations.
- Reversing and controlling detrimental effects on the environment, society and government.
- Fulfiling the demands and expectations of important stakeholders on businesses' responsible, moral and ethical behaviour.
- Developing a positive reputation, goodwill and loyalty for the brand.
- Secure national and local government favours by aligning company objectives with development objectives thus engaging more explicitly with the development agenda.
- Deliver better solutions and achieve higher valuations and higher margins through close collaboration with local NGOs and donors.
- Emphasise and stress the link between financial and non-financial performance.
- Align companies with current trends concerning environment and social concerns and ensure long-term management strategic and policy success.
- Streamline processes, reduce costs and improve efficiency.
- Enable external stakeholders to understand the organisation's true value and tangible and intangible assets.

(Nobanee & Ali, 2021) The business sector has swiftly embraced sustainability throughout the last five years, with the proliferation of assets and benchmarks focused on sustainability issues. With the rise of capitalism and indexes that concentrate on sustainable issues throughout the preceding five years, the investing community has rapidly embraced sustainability. Cooperative securities and exchange-traded funds that specify in their registration or other documentation that they select assets according to environmental economic and regulatory factors are examples of sustainable investing.

In 2020, both their number and AUM (assets under management) increased. The financial data-driven decision-making process become a foundation of how each successful, long-lasting firm runs as more corporate leaders acquire accessibility to access to actual financial information and quick, reliable financial data.

6. Impact of AI on Audit Quality to Achieve Business Sustainability

As mentioned before, the authors conclude that there are five key points represented the impact of AI on audit quality:

(1) Automating repetitive tasks, freeing up auditors for more complex analysis.
(2) Providing real-time insights and risk assessments.
(3) Detecting fraud and errors more effectively.
(4) Improving data analysis and visualisation.
(5) Accurate and reliable financial reporting.

The impact of AI on audit quality associated with several benefits that contribute to business sustainability and business sustainable practice presented in Fig. 12.5 as follows.

- *Enhanced Financial Reporting Quality*
  A high-quality audit helps ensure the accuracy and reliability of financial statements. The probability of financial statements that are misstated is inversely correlated with higher audit quality. This is especially critical for companies trying to keep the confidence of creditors investors and other stakeholders because sound financial reporting is essential for capital allocation and decision-making (Alsughayer, 2021).
- *Improved Investor Confidence*
  Investor trust in a company's financial information can be increased by conducting high-quality audits. Reputable audit companies' clients have higher

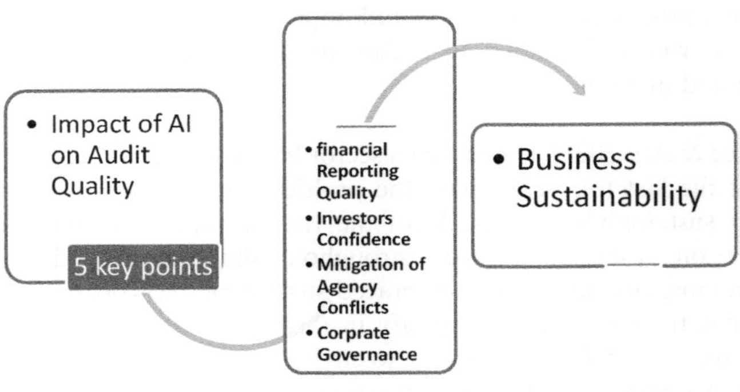

Fig. 12.5. Impact of AI on Audit Quality to Achieve Business Sustainability. *Source:* by the authors.

stock prices in the formative years, which may indicate that superior audit quality modifies investor attitudes and lessens information asymmetry (Owen Brown & Popova, 2019).

- *Mitigation of Agency Conflicts*
  Management and shareholder agency conflicts might be lessened with the aid of efficient audits. A lower probability of earnings management is linked to higher audit quality, and this is important since it guarantees that managers behave in the best interests of shareholders. Good audits can synchronise management incentives with shareholder interests by offering independent assurance on financial statements (Bawuah, 2024; Imbrogiano & Nichols, 2021).
- *Improved Corporate Governance*
  Corporate governance procedures are critical to the long-term viability of businesses, and they are intimately related to audit quality. Good audits support good corporate governance by offering an unbiased evaluation of risk management procedures and internal controls. There are positive correlations between different governance methods, including board independence and the existence of an audit committee, and audit quality (Alqadasi & Abidin, 2018; Hassan et al., 2021; Zaman et al., 2021).

References

Adiloglu, B., & Gungor, N. (2019). The impact of digitalization on the audit profession: A review of Turkish independent audit firms. *Journal of Business Economics and Finance*, *8*(4), 209–214.

Albawwat, I., & Frijat, Y. (2021). An analysis of auditors' perceptions towards artificial intelligence and its contribution to audit quality. *Accounting*, *7*(4), 755–762.

Albitar, K., Gerged, A. M., Kikhia, H., & Hussainey, K. (2020). Auditing in times of social distancing: The effect of COVID-19 on auditing quality. *International Journal of Accounting & Information Management*, *29*(1), 169–178.

Alharasis, E. E., Alidarous, M., & Jamaani, F. (2023). Auditor industry expertise and external audit prices: Empirical evidence from Amman Stock Exchange-listed companies. *Asian Journal of Accounting Research*, *8*(1), 94–107.

Alqadasi, A., & Abidin, S. (2018). The effectiveness of internal corporate governance and audit quality: The role of ownership concentration - Malaysian evidence. *Corporate Governance*, *18*(3). https://doi.org/10.1108/CG-02-2017-0043

Alsughayer, S. A. (2021). Impact of auditor competence, integrity, and ethics on audit quality in Saudi Arabia. *Open Journal of Accounting*, *10*(4, October), 125–140. https://doi.org/10.4236/ojacct.2021.104011

Apandi, R. N. N., Sofia, A., & Zulhaimi, H. (2022, July). Good audit planning practices in the digital era. In *6th global conference on business, management, and entrepreneurship (GCBME 2021)* (pp. 72–80). Atlantis Press.

Askary, S., Abu-Ghazaleh, N., & Tahat, Y. A. (2018, October). Artificial intelligence and reliability of accounting information. In *Conference on e-business, e-services and e-society* (pp. 315–324). Springer.

Barr-Pulliam, D., Calvin, C. G., Eulerich, M., & Maghakyan, A. (2023). Audit evidence, technology, and judgment: A review of the literature in response to ED-500. *Journal of International Financial Management & Accounting*, *35*, 36–67.

Bawuah, I. (2024). Audit committee effectiveness, audit quality and earnings management: Evidence from Ghana. *Cogent Business & Management*, *11*(1), 1–22. https://doi.org/10.1080/23311975.2024.2315318

Brown, V. L., Gissel, J. L., & Neely, D. G. (2016). Audit quality indicators: Perceptions of junior-level auditors. *Managerial Auditing Journal*, *31*, 949–980.

Chungyalpa, W. C. (2019). Understanding business sustainability: The what, the why and the how of sustainable business practices. *Indian Journal of Sustainable Development*, *5*(1 & 2), 24–37.

Dheeriya, P., & Singhvi, M. (2021). A conceptual framework for replacing audit committees with artificial intelligence infused bot. *EDPACS*, *63*(3), 1–18.

Fedyk, A., Hodson, J., Khimich, N., & Fedyk, T. (2022). Is artificial intelligence improving the audit process? *Review of Accounting Studies*, *27*(3), 938–985.

Francis, J. R. (2011). A framework for understanding and researching audit quality. *Auditing: A Journal of Practice & Theory*, *30*(2), 125–152.

Harber, M., & Marx, B. (2020). Audit quality and independence concerns in the South African audit industry: Contrasting views. *South African Journal of Accounting Research*, *34*(1), 1–23.

Hassan, N. A., Hanim, S., Zailani, M., & Hasan, H. A. (2021). A meta-analysis of integrated internal audit management effectiveness towards business sustainability. *Journal of Social Sciences & Humanities*, *29*(2), 233–252.

Hosseinniakani, S. M., Inacio, H., & Mota, R. (2014). A review on audit quality factors. *International Journal of Academic Research in Accounting, Finance and Management Sciences*, *4*(2), 243–254.

IAASB. (2015, December 4). *Hand book of international quality control, auditing, review, other assurance and related services pronouncements*. IAASB.

Imbrogiano, J.-P., & Nichols, E. (2021). How to serve sustainability performance in businesses? An appetizing recipe to link practices to performance in business sustainability research. *Business Strategy and the Environment*, *30*(4), 1497–2240.

Issa, H., Sun, T., & Vasarhelyi, M. A. (2016). Research ideas for artificial intelligence in auditing: The formalization of audit and workforce supplementation. *Journal of Emerging Technologies in Accounting*, *13*(2), pp1–20.

KPMG. (2020). *Business briefing series: 20 issues on building a sustainable business*. https://www.slideshare.net/slideshow/20-issues-building-a-sustainable-business/10265228. Accessed on March 5.

Kutha, N. M., & Susan, M. (2021). Institutional ownership, external auditor reputation, financial leverage, and earnings management. *Journal of Economics and Business*, *4*(1), 93–99.

Merdekawati, E. (2022). The effect of audit experience and audit risk on audit judgment with auditor's perceptions of the code of ethics of public accountants as moderating variables. In *E3S web of conferences* (Vol. 348, p. 00004). EDP Sciences.

Mohammed, S., Al-Arouda, S. F., & Mustafa, L. (2021). The effect of artificial intelligence technologies on audit evidence. *Journal of Accounting*, *7*, 281–288.

Munoko, I., Brown-Liburd, H. L., & Vasarhelyi, M. (2020). The ethical implications of using artificial intelligence in auditing. *Journal of Business Ethics*, *167*(2), 209–234.

Nobanee, H., & Ali, R. (2021). *The importance of sustainable practices*. https://www.researchgate.net/publication/355096830

Noordin, N. A., Hussainey, K., & Hayek, A. F. (2022). The use of artificial intelligence and audit quality: An analysis from the perspectives of external auditors in the UAE. *Journal of Risk and Financial Management*, *15*(8), 339.

Owen Brown, J., & Popova, V. K. (2019). How do investors respond to disclosure of audit quality indicators? *Auditing: A Journal of Practice & Theory*, *38*(4), 31–53. https://doi.org/10.2308/ajpt-52417

Rajgopal, S., Srinivasan, S., & Zheng, X. (2021). Measuring audit quality. *Review of Accounting Studies*, *26*(2), 559–619.

Suwarno, A. E., Anggraini, Y. B., & Puspawati, D. (2020). Audit fee, audit tenure, auditor's reputation, and audit rotation on audit quality. *Journal Riset Kuntansi Dan Keuangan Indonesia*, *5*(1, April), 61–70.

Tepalagul, N., & Lin, L. (2015). Auditor independence and audit quality: A literature review. *Journal of Accounting, Auditing and Finance*, *30*(1), 101–121.

Whelan, T., & Fink, C. (2016). The comprehensive business case for sustainability. *Harvard Business Review*, *21*.

Yebi, D. K., & Cudjoe, E. K. (2022). *Artificial intelligence as a Disruptive Business Model in auditing. A study of the impact of artificial intelligence on auditors' skills and competence, audit process, and audit quality* (pp. 1–79). Master Thesis. UEMA School of Business.

Zaman, R., Farooq, M. B., Khalid, F., & Mahmood, Z. (2021). Examining the extent of and determinants for sustainability assurance quality: The role of audit committees. *Business Strategy and the Environment*, *30*(7), 2845–3423.

Chapter 13

The Role of Social Media in Amplifying FinTech Brand Awareness

Tahreer M. Abu Hmeidan[a] *and Emad Masoud*[b]

[a]Applied Science Private University, Jordan
[b]Higher Colleges of Technology, United Arab Emirates

Abstract

The integration of social media with financial technology (FinTech) has revolutionised the financial services sector, introducing vast opportunities and significant challenges. Social media platforms, like Facebook, Twitter, LinkedIn and Instagram, have reshaped marketing strategies, consumer engagement and service delivery for FinTech companies. These platforms enable targeted advertising and personalised content, enhancing customer acquisition and retention through advanced analytics. Additionally, social media facilitates real-time customer support, fostering transparency and trust. Platforms such as Kickstarter and GoFundMe illustrate how social media promotes financial inclusion by enabling peer-to-peer lending and crowdfunding. Furthermore, data from social media interactions empower FinTech firms to predict market trends, assess credit risks and detect fraudulent activities. Social media sentiment analysis provides valuable insights for investment strategies. However, integrating social media with FinTech presents privacy concerns and the potential misuse of personal data, necessitating robust security measures and regulatory compliance. The spread of misinformation on social media can also destabilise markets. Despite these challenges, the synergy between social media and FinTech holds significant potential for innovation and growth. By strategically leveraging social media, FinTech companies can enhance operations and navigate ethical and regulatory landscapes to achieve sustainable growth. Understanding the FinTech audience, particularly Gen Z and millennials, is crucial for developing effective social media strategies. These demographics, characterised by their digital nativity and varying financial literacy, shape FinTech communication tactics. Market research and audience behaviour

From Digital Disruption to Dominance, 279–297

Published under exclusive licence by Emerald Publishing Limited
doi:10.1108/978-1-83549-608-420251014

analysis are essential for optimising social media use. Establishing a strong social media presence, aligning objectives with brand strategies and selecting appropriate platforms based on audience preferences are critical.

Keywords: Social media; FinTech; brand awareness; content strategy; user-generated content; community engagement

1. Introduction to Social Media in FinTech

The convergence of social media and financial technology (FinTech) has profoundly transformed the financial services sector, presenting numerous prospects and complexities (Ajouz et al., 2023, 2024; Alkhazaleh et al., 2023; Alkhwaldi et al., 2022; Rehman et al., 2023). This is a clear manifestation of digital transformation, where the integration of technology in financial services not only optimises operational efficiency but also reshapes customer engagement models (Shehadeh, 2024; Shehadeh, Alshurafat, & Arabiat, 2024; Shehadeh, Hussainey, et al., 2024). FinTech companies have greatly benefited from social media platforms like Facebook, Twitter, LinkedIn and Instagram. These platforms have significantly changed marketing strategies, consumer interaction and how services are provided. These platforms provide precise advertising and customised content, improving the process of attracting and keeping customers by utilising thorough analytics (Kumar et al., 2016). Additionally, social media enables immediate customer help, promoting openness and confidence (Malthouse et al., 2013). Platforms such as Kickstarter and GoFundMe demonstrate how social media promotes financial inclusion by facilitating peer-to-peer lending and crowdfunding, making money more accessible to a wider range of people (Agrawal et al., 2014).

Moreover, the data derived from social media interactions enable FinTech companies to utilise sophisticated analytics for forecasting market trends, evaluating credit risks and detecting fraudulent activities. Social media sentiment analysis offers valuable insights into public perceptions, which can be used to inform investing strategies. Nevertheless, the process of combining social media with FinTech is not devoid of obstacles. The important issues of privacy concerns and potential misuse of extensive personal data require strong data security measures and adherence to regulatory compliance (Acquisti et al., 2016). In addition, disseminating false information on social media platforms can result in fluctuations in the market and pose a risk to financial stability (Allcott & Gentzkow, 2017). Although there are obstacles to overcome, the combination of social media and FinTech has the potential to bring about substantial innovation and expansion. Through the strategic use of social media, FinTech companies can optimise their operations while successfully navigating the ethical and regulatory challenges to ensure long-term and sustainable growth.

1.1 Definition and Significance of Social Media in the FinTech Landscape

The fundamental significance of different FinTech concepts is in the user interactions inside the business environment and how companies actively involve users, workers and partners. This engagement facilitates conversations and exchanges that encourage and maintain the brand identity of FinTech. These tactics include blogging, utilising external social networks and microblogging on social networking websites. Social media transcends various cultural, social and economic boundaries and profoundly influences the lives of countless individuals. Technologies and platforms offer users a wide range of chances to utilise different services and interact with others. Social media frequently showcases the latest news and pertinent topics, broadening users' understanding and influence. Social media is made even more interesting by including healthcare services, customers' product opinions, financial services, retail services, finding employment and other ideas.

Furthermore, users often engage in economic transactions, exchange information and experience happiness while participating in the electronic marketplace and other social media platforms. Social media encompasses several company features, such as blogging and text messaging on social networking platforms. These features provide the benefit of easily accessible and unfiltered content, allowing participants to share unverified information (Kaplan & Haenlein, 2010; Kietzmann et al., 2011).

1.2 Utilising Social Media Platforms for Brand Awareness and Audience Engagement

Engaging in commercial activities within the FinTech sector involves distinct difficulties in establishing and promoting brand recognition not often experienced in other industries. The challenges encompass integrating three distinct sectors: finance, technology and regulatory frameworks. These challenges are characterised by a heightened perceived threat level, a significant barrier to adopting innovation, specific regulatory and security concerns, a niche target audience and the necessity to attract a younger demographic to replace an ageing customer base. Although the substantial use of social media by traditional businesses for purposes such as brand awareness, consumer engagement and reputation management has been well-documented, there is a noticeable lack of literature that expressly focuses on social media tactics in the FinTech industry.

2. Understanding the FinTech Audience on Social Media

As technology advances rapidly, it continuously reshapes businesses, creates new jobs and transforms existing ones. Social media has become the technological communication conduit that FinTech entrepreneurs have long anticipated. Before receiving strategic and financial support from venture capital firms, many young entrepreneurs – often millennials – emerged from the internet, using social media to learn about trends, receive news, obtain financial support and communicate. As social media's role in communication grows, traditional and modern financial companies seek to attract attention and announce innovations. They differentiate their products using instant messaging applications, blockchain, peer-to-peer lending and cryptocurrencies like Bitcoin. Maintaining these functional differences and utilising these applications daily to gain a competitive edge has become essential.

Institutions that effectively communicate with and provide exceptional services to Gen Y and Z in the financial world make these generations their brand advocates. The power of peer recommendations among these digitally active groups makes them crucial market players. Understanding the modern technology jargon used by Gen Y and Z and developing products that meet their expectations allow for innovative business models and promising financial strategies in the FinTech sector. The FinTech audience comprises two main categories: Gen Z, digital natives and financially savvy millennials. These groups are connected through technological devices such as SMS, social media and applications. While they share similar motivations and behaviours, their levels of financial literacy vary. The foundational factors of these generations, encompassing their technological orientation and the profound transformations they introduce, shape the development of FinTech tactics and communication via social media platforms (Wilkins et al., 2020; Berger, 2016).

2.1 Demographics and Characteristics of the Target Audience in FinTech

FinTech investors and stakeholders have high expectations for any startup joining their industry, which limits the type of material that should be created. Many individuals prefer to avoid generic content or general advice, opting instead for material specifically tailored to their business needs. This includes information on new projects, real-life examples from users in specific regions, investment data, emerging technologies like blockchain and stories of success from startups and entrepreneurs. This audience primarily focuses on mobile devices and places great weight on social media. Customising material based on the specific attributes and actions of the audience promotes exceptional quality. By 2020, the projected number of social media users is 5.5 billion. Key goals are platforms with a high-value business audience interested in FinTech, commonly known as FinTech+. The FinTech audience, particularly in insurance technology (insurtech), consists of knowledgeable early adopters who are very receptive and frequently engage in enthusiastic discussions on social media platforms (Chaffey & Ellis-Chadwick, 2019; Kotler et al., 2017).

2.2 Market Research to Understand Audience Preferences and Behaviours on Social Media

To maximise the potential of social media in reaching new target audiences, it is essential to research influencers who have a substantial influence over the desired followers. Influencers offer spontaneous input and foster open conversation, creating a more relatable experience. References from influential individuals with high levels of engagement hold significant value, frequently leading to a higher quantity of online references that endure longer than those from the wider community. This is especially accurate on platforms that employ intricate spam-detection algorithms like Instagram. When creating their media marketing strategy, firms must have a deep grasp of customers' and businesses' social habits and behaviours in their target market. Market research tools comprehensively analyse social media usage based on different demographic groups.

In contrast, net sentiment analysis offers valuable insights into audiences' attitudes towards certain trends and businesses. Social monitoring suites provide marketers with useful insights by identifying keywords and phrases, enabling them to optimise their strategy. When a company is unfamiliar with a platform, it is crucial to research to assess its compatibility. This involves monitoring conversations and sentiment levels related to specific keywords (Evans, 2020; Tuten & Solomon, 2017).

3. Building a Strong Social Media Presence

An organisation should establish a digital communications team including communications specialists, product managers, a development team, media relations experts, legal advisors and other relevant departments. This team's primary responsibility is to strategise, validate, monitor and communicate the company's desired presence on various social media platforms. Despite the widespread use of social media for communication, it is challenging to accurately determine a company's ideal target demographic, preferred online platforms and the most effective way to create a message that captures and maintains their interest. Organisations should perform a SWOT analysis on social media to determine whether and where they should establish a social media presence. In the current highly competitive digital landscape, establishing a robust and unambiguous social media presence has become imperative for engaging with existing and prospective clients and nurturing ongoing connections with them. Establishing a robust presence on existing or possibly new platforms is crucial for a firm to sustain a competitive edge.

Nevertheless, there is a need to achieve equilibrium. Having a presence on all available platforms might result in an organisation getting overwhelmed and unable to stay informed about the newest advancements and promptly reply to potential clients across various channels. While it is important to focus on communicating on the existing platforms used by organisations and clients, organisations should also consider the future direction of social media communications to sustain future growth.

3.1 Establishing Objectives and Goals Aligned With Brand Strategies

Social media management typically involves reshaping and strengthening current operations rather than introducing new responsibilities. This can provide significant advantages from the perspective of communication synergy. Potential benefits may encompass the efficacy of communication initiatives and the establishment of personal connections and integration into social circles, thereby boosting the exchange of ideas. The toolbox of social media assets provides diverse tools to assist various organisations in their go-to-market strategies, specifically tailored to each general purpose. Companies can carefully integrate several degrees of digital marketing communication tools using social media. Strategy in social media refers to the overall approach or plan while an objective is the purpose or reason. The 'how' of social media includes a detailed plan or a set of recommendations on various methods to execute the strategy effectively. It is crucial to build effective performance measures to prevent wasting time and money. When confronted with this circumstance, executives are eager to initiate their presence on social media. However, it is intriguing to observe the reaction of a company or marketer when we inquire about their objectives, strategies and measures for achieving success in social media. Another factor to consider is clearly expressing both 'soft' and 'hard' objectives. While it may seem vague, a 'soft' objective like 'empowering customers' can lead to the 'hard' objective of higher sales as customers are supported in making better-informed choices. Before engaging in a social media initiative, firms must formulate social media goals and objectives that align with their business brand initiatives. The selection of particular social media objectives for a FinTech is influenced by the brand's target audience persona (acquiring clients), the stage in the client's journey, their relationship and interaction with the brand (engaging clients) and the satisfaction of the clients, which can enhance the value of the brand–target audience relationship and foster client loyalty (satisfying clients). The objective is to synchronise the company's business and brand strategies with the extent and capabilities of communication social media platforms provide to various communication brands.

3.2 Selecting Appropriate Social Media Platforms Based on Audience and Features

Martínez et al. (2022) contend that each social media platform may be viewed as a micro-community of common interests. These platforms can serve as effective advertising and marketing tools for organisations targeting these consumers, given their extensive and easily accessible user bases. The choice of suitable social media platforms depends on the target audience a firm aims to engage in and their behaviours. Social media platforms are chosen based on the functionality and features the intended user demographic prefers. Gao et al. contend that the 17 most prevalent social media platforms in the United States boast a substantial user base, with each site having approximately 100 million subscribers. Businesses may have several goals when utilising social media platforms, including enhancing brand awareness, sharing video content, promoting events, providing product links and fostering user involvement. Businesses can enhance the visibility of their brand on social media by utilising a range of measurable criteria. Enterprises can entice consumers to their brand and merchandise. Enterprises can enhance their brands' visibility on Facebook, the most extensive social media network in the United States, with a user base of more than 2.2 billion individuals. Businesses can achieve optimal user engagement by increasing the number of followers as the size of the business's follower base can impact sales. Business posts are classified into 'follower' and 'non-follower'. This classification considers the overall duration of involvement and the number of comments, which includes likes, shares, engagements and interactions. Businesses can enhance user engagement by integrating platform-specific analytics with their products or brands. Businesses could advertise their products on Pinterest, a platform primarily used by female users to post visual information such as photos, pictures and videos. Enterprises can produce uncomplicated and motivating visuals on Instagram, a platform predominantly influenced by the millennial generation. Businesses can use visual narratives to highlight and prioritise their ethical values and principles. LinkedIn is a digital platform for businesses, allowing them to enhance their network by leveraging their employees' profiles, geographical information and company offerings. Regarding metric utilisation, many industries' key performance indicators (KPIs) are exhibited to demonstrate diverse platform classifications and industry categories. Entrepreneurs may leverage social media platforms to establish and enhance the identity and reputation of FinTech in the industry. Startups could utilise pertinent social media functionalities to get feedback at various stages of development and enhance the final product. Established financial institutions can utilise social media marketing as a complementary strategy to support the efforts of their current marketing department. Companies with constrained resources can commit the required personnel and financial resources to a social media marketing strategy easily evaluated by user engagement metrics such as likes, shares and clicks.

3.3 Developing Consistent Brand Voice and Visual Identity

The development of financial applications is always progressing. The unique and dynamic design promotes increased user confidence by creating smooth connections and easing user interactions. Three impactful ways to ensure consistent and unique brand messaging online include leveraging shapes and colour palettes and enhancing user and brand engagement through chatbots. FinTech possesses a clear advantage and gains from providing chatbot-generated leads that are swiftly followed up with in-person support discussions. A brand's visual identity is essential for developing and promoting brand recognition. Social media users are presented with significant content that appears in their news feeds regularly. Moreover, a significant number of users have restricted attention spans. The visual component functions as how the message is communicated, evoking inspiration as users navigate the newsfeed. Developing a unified voice necessitates accurately and uniquely representing the intended audience. It is recommended to carefully evaluate the suitable tone – positive or negative, formal or informal, factual or dynamic – that best connects with the brand. The chosen tone will influence all interactions with the target audience and create a unique brand that can be easily recognised through consistent messaging, recruitment efforts and customer engagement. To increase brand awareness on various social media platforms, a thorough strategy is essential, including building a consistent brand identity, using captivating visuals and promoting a consistent message across all communication channels. By doing so, the brand will be able to create a unique and recognisable image, effectively interact with the target audience, build trust and increase customer loyalty.

4. Content Strategy for Social Media

The objective of content strategy is to guide the progression of a business from its initial stages to the last steps of acquisition. This entails employing inventory management, comprehending the customer's path to purchase and formulating a social media plan (Kotler et al., 2017). Additional content creation and strategy recommendations for businesses involve developing and distributing content that corresponds to popular consumer search queries, directing traffic to all content through social networks, utilising publicly available data from external sources to enhance the value of content, employing data-driven blog posts to generate excitement on social media platforms, establishing enduring passive links through blog posts and employing contests, sweepstakes and promotions to stimulate customer engagement and encourage the sharing of links. Content strategy is crucial for shaping a brand's social media responses. It can take three main forms: Big block content (long-form pieces or detailed visual content like infographics, videos and slideshows), small block content (simple pieces or images and texts meant for easy sharing) and single pieces or visual content (standalone pieces or rich nodes) (Kotler et al., 2017). Big block content facilitates rapid sharing, as social network users typically spend less than 10 s reading updates. On social media, peripheral material intended for short reading and easy sharing is the most common. Compact content, intended for rapid assimilation, can manifest as cover images, showcased posts and shareable material.

4.1 Creating Engaging and Relevant Content

When creating content for FinTech products, it is crucial to have a deep awareness of consumer requirements (Wilkins et al., 2020). An approach that prioritises the needs and preferences of users guarantees that the information on social media platforms is appealing, easily shared and connects with a wider audience. This, in turn, leads to increased demand for the product. The material is designed to teach users about the advantages of adopting specialised FinTech. It relates to strategic goals and uses various forms to keep the audience interested and promote their response.

4.2 Incorporating Multimedia Content

Both business-to-business (B2B) and business-to-consumer (B2C) organisations should consider the nature and appropriateness of the content they send through social media platforms (Tuten & Solomon, 2017). Disseminating instructional information showcasing field competence helps cultivate commercial partnerships and establishes the company as an asset. The product uses and prospective benefits are properly showcased through clear and easily understandable pictures and examples, engaging and enlightening the audience. Storytelling may be effortlessly included in videos and images, establishing a strong bond between users and the brand (Kotler et al., 2017). Encouraging additional discussions and engagement can increase audience interaction and broaden the reach of shared content. Utilising visual content such as infographics, videos and images may greatly improve the visibility and engagement of posts, resulting in increased views and conversation. Visual content of superior quality, such as films, infographics and images, enhances user interaction and enjoys more visibility in followers' feeds, generating more views and attracting client interest.

5. Community Engagement and Relationship Building

Essentially, social media creates a sense of community and facilitates interaction between those who share similar interests. The traditional marketing approach of pushing products or services onto users is not well-received and is generally ineffective. Cultivating relationships is a gradual process that demands ongoing dedication although the enduring and robust relationships that ensue are highly valuable (Kaplan & Haenlein, 2010). This social networking method deviates from the conventional model as its primary objective is to establish relationships, comprehend needs and promote goods and services. Utilising social media solely as a platform for marketing broadcasts is not held in high esteem. It is crucial to provide multiple expectations to receive reciprocation. Through sharing information and actively participating in discussions, ties are strengthened and the social network transforms into a highly beneficial platform. Social media marketing extends beyond the acquisition of followers and the expansion of visibility. Establishing a community on social networks is essential to successful social media marketing (Kaplan & Haenlein, 2010). Disseminating information and making connections alone is insufficient; active participation and integration into a community are necessary to seize opportunities fully. FinTech companies should prioritise the establishment of rapport and cultivation of relationships with both customers and businesses. Engaging in social interactions and sharing knowledge without anticipating immediate gains from quick sales can frequently lead to increased future sales prospects. Enduring persistent aggressive sales solicitations in a commercial and recreational setting is undeniably challenging. Social networking requires a careful equilibrium, where one must demonstrate interest and provide advantages to their relationships without being excessively assertive.

5.1 Fostering Meaningful Interactions With Followers

Visual content should be developed to tell a story with which followers can empathise and react, with polls, quizzes, contests and other 'light' interactive content designed to foster early engagement and conversation perimeters (Kaplan & Haenlein, 2010). Brands equipped with lifestyle or corporate values are often better served on platforms such as Instagram and Facebook that can effectively highlight these corporate values through creative photography and video. Story features offer the best interface for promoting back-and-forth conversations. Each story should end with a direct call to action encouraging participation, such as 'Tag a friend who shares the same taste' or 'Swipe up if this meal makes you feel hungry'. Videos could explain the features of your innovative products and services and give a 'behind the scenes' look at your offices and the activities of your employees. Social media platforms prioritise posts that result in meaningful engagement (Kaplan & Haenlein, 2010). Therefore, organisations wishing to maintain a strong presence on social media may need to consider fostering conversations and connections with their audience to remain relevant in their followers' feeds. Yet, user participation is essential to produce engagement as a brand that only talks about its products and services by delivering its message like a one-way street is not ideally suited to effectively leveraging the communicative capabilities of social media. This means that having a product, service or brand primarily cultivated with user-generated content can be extremely beneficial in starting conversations.

5.2 Encouraging User-Generated Content

The 'social media marketing funnel' proposed by Kaplan and Haenlein (2010) emphasises the behaviours – the measures of success that include five fan-engagement strategies – 'communication', 'cooperation', 'community', 'co-creation' and 'entertainment' (5 Cs). The communication strategy refers to the social media page's capability to connect with customers by sharing stories while seeking to boost engagement rates and maintain direct communication with them. 'Cooperation' encourages participants to share content while working together with others; 'community' is the strategy that aims to manage social relationships that encourage the joining of the brand's page. 'Co-creation' is the strategy that engages customers in product and service development; finally, the 'entertainment' strategy is focused on the fun, humour or distraction capacity of electing, sharing and creating content by interacting with a brand's digital media. As consumers increasingly prioritise word-of-mouth opinions over brand advertisements, business–consumer interactions are becoming more liberal and relational. User-generated content, created by unpaid participants, humanises a brand. It also implicitly captures higher degrees of trust because it is relatively more authentic than brand-generated content. Thus, fan engagement strategies can significantly improve a brand's social media marketing effectiveness. Success in engaging fans bolsters followers' willingness to share content, express opinions, supplement customer feedback, participate in discussion forums, co-create solutions, mediate relationship-building, experiment with product/service innovations and more.

5.3 Collaborating With Influencers and Experts

To effectively collaborate with influencers and experts, involving them in your content is not enough. Instead, you should focus on building a genuine relationship with the influencer, which requires an investment from your brand and start by getting on their radar through positive feedback and engagement rather than immediately making requests (Kaplan & Haenlein, 2010). The approach to requesting the influencer to promote your product or service is closely related. Depending on the influencer, they may also be working with other brands. Therefore, when reaching out to an influencer to discuss a collaboration with them, be clear about your goals, allow for some flexibility within the influencer and incorporate their work style and tone of voice into the collaboration. Influencers can be cheaper and more effective than celebrities or other individuals with high followings because their communities are already interested in the field of the brand. Therefore, their followers are just the right people the company is targeting to sell their products to. Influencers and experts can be great assets for any brand, but both can be especially effective when engaging your community in the FinTech industry. Influencers often have many followers on their social media accounts, and their words carry weight with their community, which could be beneficial if they promote or engage the community with your products or services. Identifying and reaching out to influencers who are respected in the industry can require some effort, but in the long run, it can be well worth the time you spend on it.

6. Paid Advertising and Promotion on Social Media

Advertisers who use paid media are given comprehensive advertising statistics to track and analyse their campaigns continuously. The user is asking about the performance of their campaign. The analytics encompass many metrics such as demographic post reach, inorganic post impressions, engagement rates ad attribution to the Facebook pixel on Ad-Clicked or watched Landing Page Views, Ad-DVD Click, ad clicks, Video 25% Watched, Video 50% Watched and Video 75% Watched. Academic researchers have utilised advertising analytics data from Facebook's ads and company page interface to examine the impact of paid social media advertising on post-engagement measures (Smith et al., 2020a, 2020b). On social media, brands have increasingly adopted the practice of sharing content on their channels and investing in advertising and promotion to reach a wider audience. Paid media enables companies to precisely target specific audiences based on the extensive user information, user-generated content and events they engage with on the social network. Facebook, Twitter, Instagram, LinkedIn and YouTube are examples of social media platforms allowing paid media advertising (Jones & Brown, 2019). Advertisers are granted access to a web-based interface where they may generate campaigns, allocate an advertising budget, choose a specific audience to target (based on user profiles, interests or activities) and specify the type of their advertisement and the sponsorship level it will receive. As an illustration, a company may choose to produce a video advertisement for 'Sponsor Name' that will be displayed to a target audience of male users in the New York City region interested in sports. Users can choose their advertisement to be displayed either as a standard post in the news feed or as a suggested or sponsored post in the sidebar. Inorganic posts in social media can arise because of paid advertising or can follow paid advertising.

6.1 Utilise Targeted Advertising Options Offered by Social Media Platforms to Reach Specific Audience Segments

Utilising advertising on platforms like Facebook and LinkedIn enables organisations to target users on social networks who have indicated specific interests through their profiles (Johnson, 2018a, 2018b). Additionally, it enables precise and detailed targeting using the social media interface, allowing simultaneous advertising on Facebook and LinkedIn to a certain audience. This strategy is beneficial for targeting recruitment goals in the business through Facebook and in programming through LinkedIn. Utilising advertising on mainstream social media platforms or developing a proprietary social media platform enables organisations to publish tailored content. For instance, employing digital advertising on social media platforms and implementing recruitment strategies to attract interns to prestigious industrial brands can demonstrate brand members' internal organisation and communication. This revelation can allure prospective participants to a corporate workshop by persons acting as brand ambassadors.

Furthermore, it is advisable to use the targeted advertising possibilities provided by social media platforms to effectively reach certain sectors of the audience in addition to the various sorts of posting options accessible. LinkedIn provides businesses and other organisations utilising the platform with the option of paid advertising as a basic feature (Smith et al., 2020a, 2020b). This functionality enables the acquisition and precise targeting of advertisements to reach specific people on the LinkedIn platform. Facebook advertising enables advertisers to choose target individuals or persons on Facebook who are also part of their external network using custom targeting. The advertising features of LinkedIn and Facebook are valuable due to the behavioural insights and business-oriented data provided by LinkedIn as well as the personal-focused and relationship-rich information offered by Facebook. This allows researchers to combine various data points and create audience segments for targeted advertising.

6.2 To Maximise Visibility and Engagement, Experiment With Different Ad Formats, Such as Sponsored Posts, Carousel Ads and Video Ads

It is important to consider that the duration of your video should align with the recommended guidelines for the channel. Typically, video ads on LinkedIn, Twitter and Snapchat should not be longer than 30 s. However, there are no limitations on YouTube so that you can create longer films for advertising. Also, please consider the sound-off feature, accessible on all channels except for Messenger. The video ad format continues to be highly effective for engaging potential buyers, particularly on platforms like Pinterest. This ad format allows potential buyers to be inspired by your ideas and receive insights about your product or service by clicking on the ad before purchasing. If the journey to the goal conversion provides a terrific experience, it can result in a 70% boost to a brand's awareness.

Regarding sponsored content, the opportunity is consistently available if you desire to advertise your most recent post, release or news, specifically targeting individuals who already follow the brand. This is a more cost-effective alternative; however, to get the intended outcome, the information you intend to promote should be captivating for a broader audience. Therefore, it is recommended to have a clearly defined content strategy in advance. To enhance visibility and user engagement, it is recommended to perform experiments with different advertising formats, including sponsored posts, carousel adverts and video commercials. Carousel advertising is a highly effective means of showcasing multiple products. If you are an eCommerce company, you may want to showcase your most recent products in stock. Alternatively, you may seek to secure donations if you are a non-profit organisation. If that is the situation, the carousel advertisement is the most efficient choice for drawing attention to the benefits of the items or services you provide and attain a substantial level of user interaction with a minimal expense of approximately 20 cents by executing a suitable marketing campaign (Brown, 2021a, 2021b).

6.3 Set Clear Objectives and Budgets for Paid Social Media Campaigns and Monitor Performance Metrics Closely

To reap the advantages of the strategies employed by advertisers, which involve optimising budget allocation, swiftly targeting specific audiences and achieving KPIs related to recognition and consideration, it is important for a wide range of businesses, not just established ones, to heed this advice. Therefore, given these circumstances, social media advertising is expected to continue to expand and demonstrate the need for decision-support tools, both on the buyer and agency sides, to be consistently maintained due to ongoing performance pressure. At Facebook, four measures assess the success of candidates: reputation, customer preference, customer consideration and a composite measure. Collectively, these metrics aim to measure the calibre of a brand's audience – individuals who hold a favourable perception of the brand, who exhibit a preference for its products, who are inclined to consider purchasing the brand and who ultimately have a higher likelihood of generating additional sales for the brand. 'The ad effectiveness metrics are created by initially identifying the quintile of a brand's audience responses'. The utilisation of social media advertising is increasing to establish closer connections between businesses and brands with their customers. As social networks continue to enhance their advertising reach and effectiveness capabilities, numerous untapped possibilities may be explored using data-driven and strategic approaches. Business motivation, financial planning and precise target group definition are only a few hurdles (Smith et al., 2020a, 2020b).

7. Social Media Analytics and Measurement

Although social media in the business sphere has primarily been associated with advertising and marketing, organisations have overlooked its potential advantages in terms of customer relationship management (CRM) (Jones & Brown, 2019). When utilised in the context of big data, social media enables organisations to acquire valuable customer insights, assess the brand performance of their rivals and stimulate innovation through expanded customer co-creation possibilities. By utilising social media analytics, firms can better understand how to align their management processes to effectively cater to their client base (Smith et al., 2020a, 2020b). Users must possess enhanced capabilities to fully analyse many interactions to incorporate them into the organisation's core. This ability is crucial as it enables the identification of patterns and occurrences, which can greatly influence the opinions they form (Johnson, 2018a, 2018b). Social media analytics will gain the capability to provide the missing value that the company has been seeking by utilising established language models and machine learning algorithms from external vendors, third-party suppliers or internal data scientists to identify recurring patterns. In the modern era of social media, customers have unprecedented connectivity to websites such as Facebook, Twitter and Yelp, enabling them to access data easily. However, companies struggle to identify how to utilise the information they receive effectively. By comprehending the characteristics of various data types and their potential interactions and subsequently proficiently deploying social media tools, firms may stimulate stakeholders, gain insights from their feedback and regulate the discourse they generate (Brown, 2021a, 2021b).

7.1 Track Key Performance Indicators (KPIs) Such as Reach, Engagement, Click-Through Rates and Conversions

Social media analytics allows you to evaluate the efficacy of your paid advertisements and organic marketing efforts while also helping you find areas that may be improved (Jones & Brown, 2019). Engaging in sponsored advertising initiatives involves incurring financial costs. This investment must produce concrete results. The benefit of using paid advertising on different social media platforms is the capability to execute accurate targeting tactics. This allows you to efficiently target the right audience with customised content, reducing advertising costs and a lower cost per click (CPC). An effective method to connect with individuals who closely resemble your most loyal customers is by generating lookalike audiences based on their interests and online behaviours.

Moreover, focusing on smaller, more specific demographics is feasible by utilising the interests, habits and other information that Facebook users have shared on the platform. The ad management feature on social networking platforms, such as Facebook, Twitter, Instagram and LinkedIn, allows you to create and personalise the targeting of your advertisements. This enables you to capitalise on these opportunities and optimise your investment. You possess exclusive rights to the data from your website and social media platforms. It is an essential element of your 'owned media' that must deliver information to the rest of your marketing strategy. Social media analytics platforms, such as Buffer Analyze, Hootsuite Insights and Sensible Insights, allow you to monitor important data such as reach, engagement, click-through rates and conversions. To improve and maximise the effectiveness of your social media marketing strategies, it is important to understand the elements that trigger a significant reaction from your intended audience.

7.2 Use Social Media Analytics Tools to Gain Insights Into Audience Behaviour and Preferences

To optimise visibility and engagement, leverage the tailored targeting features offered by platforms like Facebook and Twitter. Align content with audience behavior to enhance effectiveness. An effective campaign should utilise a strategic blend of innovative components and advertising text to allure and engage the target audiences. Translate the effectiveness and wide audience of television advertising to Facebook and Twitter by producing visually appealing picture and video commercials that enhance brand visibility, capture attention and stimulate imagination. Attract notice and distinguish yourself with videos that adhere to the platform's standards as tailored video content can achieve the same level of effectiveness in prompting action while costing significantly less. Ensure your campaigns are current as users are consistently active and predominantly use mobile devices.

Furthermore, ensure that the social funnel is properly constructed and that advertisements target the appropriate audience. Advertisements should be tailored to elicit specific actions from your existing or target audience, and the targeting should align with the desired outcomes, emphasising preferences, social interactions, user engagement and conversions on your website. Due to the constantly changing nature of the Internet world, businesses are compelled to adopt and utilise all the available channels and opportunities within those channels to engage and establish connections with their audience effectively. Social media platforms, including Facebook and Twitter, offer various advertising options to efficiently target and attract specific audiences, increase engagement and manage expenses. In addition, social media analytics solutions offer up-to-the-minute statistics on the level of engagement your audience has with your content and advertisements. These technologies offer valuable information on the target audience, the effectiveness of the content, the success of conversion efforts and the performance of advertisements.

7.3 Analyse Data to Refine Social Media Strategies and Optimise Content Performance Over Time

Successful social media marketing contributes to the generation of leads, new sources of income and attendees, as well as the cultivation of valuable long-term relationships and the establishment of a brand persona through qualified involvement (Brown, 2021a, 2021b). These data are also crucial in developing a responsive and focused paid advertising campaign on these networks. Every platform provides valuable information. However, page managers should routinely monitor Facebook Insights. In addition, Facebook Business Manager offers the convenience of scheduling reports to be sent via email, which aids in time management. The marketing team's ability to define an audience directly impacts their success precisely and consistently in aligning a platform's algorithm with the intended viewers. Once the target audiences are narrowed down, data on the most efficient sorts of content also become helpful. By analysing periods of heightened posting, these data are used to make informed decisions about paid advertising investments and to promote effective content to Facebook users. Social media is crucial for digital marketing managers, serving many purposes, such as daily content delivery, paid advertising and metrics monitoring. Social media analytics may showcase the efficacy of ideas, guide successful paid marketing initiatives and substantiate the worth of marketing endeavours to investors. Marketing managers may encounter a surplus of data and a scarcity of established methods for effectively analysing that data. It is crucial to comprehend the nature and purpose of analysis. The quality of the brand account can be inferred from several factors, such as platform data and referral traffic, as well as the way people interact with different types of content. Determining which data to utilise for measuring return on investment can be challenging to ascertain without experience.

8. Compliance and Regulatory Considerations

Commercial speech, which includes advertising, can be regulated within reasonable limits under the First Amendment (Johnson, 2018a, 2018b). Traditionally, the commercial speech doctrine provides limited protection to commercial speech, which is not constitutionally protected. It also applies a less strict standard of scrutiny to regulations that aim to control commercial practices related to specific types of advertising or promotion. To qualify as commercial speech, the expression being analysed must be a type of advertising and marketing that promotes a company's self-interest while presenting an increased threat to society's well-being (Brown, 2021a, 2021b). However, regarding the coverage of paid influencer social media marketing under the commercial speech doctrine, factors such as credibility and believability indicate that the most impactful speech comes directly from the influencer. Therefore, influencers and advertisers must avoid presenting themselves as mere mouthpieces for the brand as this can harm consumers' attitudes and their intention to purchase when they perceive the brand to be endorsed by well-known spokespersons. The Supreme Court's protection of commercial speech in 1976 established that advertising impacts are considered honest and non-misleading speech, which is still protected under the First Amendment (Smith et al., 2020a, 2020b). Amidst the rapid expansion of social media, the industry must carefully evaluate the compliance and regulatory aspects that affect both social media firms and online consumers. This section examines the legal framework that traditional advertising and social media organisations must consider while engaging in paid advertising services and creating popular influencer-targeted marketing campaigns (Jones & Brown, 2019).

8.1 Ensure Compliance With Regulations and Guidelines Related to Advertising, Data Privacy and Financial Promotions on Social Media

Online or electronic operations, such as social media, inherently involve numerous external systems that governance must oversee. Against this background and in the context of data-driven marketing, social business model management requires governance to conduct a rigorous assessment for default by examining the exposure of their systems, content silos, data and other associated points of compliance containing knowledge, expertise, business social marketing workstream resources and assets capable of initiating, driving and delivering the command and control framework of relevance for the governance of social data engagements in measuring, evaluating and forecasting the fit from scope and direction of the value proposition through to business systems and data protection compliance, underpinning the full gamut of customer social data ecosystems on social media platforms, resulting in the outbound context of customer data silos by consensus decision-making run on privacy controls and safety measures at national, European or global level with in-place processes for governance of reporting to executive leadership levels (Smith et al., 2020a, 2020b). Every organisation or institution that participates in sponsored advertising must ensure adherence to mandatory regulations and guidelines, both internally and externally. The main responsibility of marketing is to combine control requirements with transparency duties to achieve that goal. Within the larger marketing system, paid social media is the initial platform where consumers encounter your brand's products and messaging. It generates targeted traffic to a desired destination and improves customer profiling. Management frequently utilises marketing social data to analyse social media metrics, perform analytics and manage performance on various social media platforms. These efforts are driven by the opportunities presented, the latest social engagement tools, interest and demand levels measures and consumer behaviour. Additionally, management considers the regulatory context, including advertising regulations, financial promotions, data privacy, business exposures and social media risk management, as outlined in Johnson (2018a, 2018b) study.

8.2 Work Closely With Legal and Compliance Teams to Mitigate Risks Associated With Social Media Marketing Activities

When formulating retail business plans, organisations must carefully consider the growing adoption of social recommendation systems by Chinese clients and their diminishing commitment to a single shopping platform. Since increasing clients typically leads to increased information, organisations must adopt a more sophisticated method for analysing social media data. They should persist in prioritising the collection of data that is pertinent to their business and its storage. However, they must adopt an innovative strategy to distinguish their companies. Additionally, the researchers discovered that public relations experts might efficiently leverage social media data to formulate innovative crisis communications tactics in the foreseeable future. By utilising the social media monitoring tool's daily data collection for 'Thursday', they could pinpoint significant events and achievements on social media. According to their research, social media milestones can indicate financial instability and could assist management in enhancing investor relations and public values.

Given that the lag duration spans from five to seven days, corporate executives should include these electronic indicators in their corporate strategy to enhance it (Brown, 2021a, 2021b). By 2020, most marketing operations will occur within social media. With regulators increasing their scrutiny of media operations, corporations should take proactive measures by collaborating with their legal and compliance teams to identify potential risks and implement safeguards to prevent significant liabilities. Additionally, they can establish internal or external task forces dedicated to managing social media risks. These task forces would collaborate closely with regional units to promptly address any risk-related concerns arising from actions on different social media platforms.

This would not only rectify the errors attributed to the regional units but also aid in devising a marketing strategy to mitigate the risks linked to the promotional channels utilised (Jones & Brown, 2019).

References

Acquisti, A., Taylor, C., & Wagman, L. (2016). The economics of privacy. *Journal of Economic Literature*, *54*(2), 442–492.

Agrawal, A., Catalini, C., & Goldfarb, A. (2014). Some simple economics of crowdfunding. *Innovation Policy and the Economy*, *14*(1), 63–97.

Ajouz, M., Abuamria, F., Al Zeer, I., Salahat, M., Shehadeh, M., Binsaddig, R., Al-Sartawi, A., & Al-Ramahi, N. M. (2023). Navigating the uncharted: The shaping of FinTech ecosystems in emerging markets. *Cuadernos de Economia*, *46*(132), 189–201.

Ajouz, M., Shehadeh, M., Jabarin, R., Sharar, S. A., Jawabra, S., & Salman, W. (2024, February). Is FinTech catalyst or constraint for banking performance? In *2024 2nd International conference on cyber resilience (ICCR)* (pp. 1–5). IEEE.

Alkhazaleh, A., Assaf, A., Shehada, M., Almustafa, E., & Allahham, M. (2023). Analysis of the impact of FinTech firms' lending on the expansion of service base companies in Jordan. *Information Sciences Letters*, *12*(8), 2891–2902.

Alkhwaldi, A. F., Alharasis, E. E., Shehadeh, M., Abu-AlSondos, I. A., Oudat, M. S., & Bani Atta, A. A. (2022). Towards an understanding of FinTech users' adoption: Intention and e-loyalty post-COVID-19 from a developing country perspective. *Sustainability*, *14*(19), 12616.

Allcott, H., & Gentzkow, M. (2017). Social media and fake news in the 2016 election. *The Journal of Economic Perspectives*, *31*(2), 211–236.

Berger, J. (2016). *Contagious: How to build word of mouth in the digital age*. Simon & Schuster.

Brown, C. (2021a). Maximising visibility and engagement through different ad formats: A comparative study. *Journal of Marketing Communications*, *12*(1), 45–58.

Brown, C. (2021b). The role of social media tools in managing customer feedback and engagement. *Journal of Interactive Marketing*, *29*(2), 87–103.

Chaffey, D., & Ellis-Chadwick, F. (2019). *Digital marketing: Strategy, implementation and practice*. Pearson.

Evans, D. (2020). *Social media marketing: An hour a day*. Wiley.

Johnson, R. (2018a). Integrating social media analytics into organizational processes: A framework for effective implementation. *International Journal of Information Management*, *38*(4), 187–201.

Johnson, R. (2018b). Targeted advertising options on social media platforms: A strategic approach. *Social Media Today*, *15*(3), 56–73.

Jones, A., & Brown, C. (2019). The role of social media platforms in paid advertising: A comparative analysis. *Journal of Social Media Marketing*, *7*(2), 89–104.

Kaplan, A. M., & Haenlein, M. (2010). Users of the world, unite! The challenges and opportunities of Social Media. *Business Horizons*, *53*(1), 59–68.

Kietzmann, J. H., Hermkens, K., McCarthy, I. P., & Silvestre, B. S. (2011). Social media? Get serious! Understanding the functional building blocks of social media. *Business Horizons*, *54*(3), 241–251.

Kotler, P., Kartajaya, H., & Setiawan, I. (2017). *Marketing 4.0: Moving from traditional to digital*. Wiley.

Kumar, A., Bezawada, R., Rishika, R., Janakiraman, R., & Kannan, P. K. (2016). From social to sale: The effects of firm-generated content in social media on customer behavior. *Journal of Marketing*, *80*(1), 7–25. https://doi.org/10.1509/jm.14.0249

Malthouse, E. C., Haenlein, M., Skiera, B., Wege, E., & Zhang, M. (2013). Managing customer relationships in the social media era: Introducing the social CRM house. *Journal of Interactive Marketing*, *27*(4), 270–280.

Martínez, J., Carracedob, P., & Comasc, D. (2022). An analysis of the blockchain and COVID-19 research landscape using a bibliometric study. *Sustainable Technology and Entrepreneurship*, *1*(1), 1–7.

Rehman, S. U., Al-Shaikh, M., Washington, P. B., Lee, E., Song, Z., Abu-AlSondos, I. A., Shehadeh, M., & Allahham, M. (2023). FinTech adoption in SMEs and bank credit supplies: A study on manufacturing SMEs. *Economies*, *11*(8), 213.

Shehadeh, M. (2024). Digital transformation: A catalyst for sustainable business practices. In A. Hamdan (Ed.), *Technological innovations for business, education and sustainability* (pp. 29–45). Emerald Publishing Limited.

Shehadeh, M., Alshurafat, H., & Arabiat, O. (2024). Inverting the paradigm: Digital transformation's impact on firm performance and the counterintuitive role of gender. *Competitiveness Review*. https://doi.org/10.1108/CR-11-2023-0299

Shehadeh, M., Hussainey, K., Alhadab, M., & Kilani, Q. (2024). Corporate narrative reporting on Industry 4.0 technologies: Do the COVID-19 pandemic and governance structure matter? *Review of Accounting and Finance*, *23*(5), 687–714.

Smith, J., Lee, C., & Brown, A. (2020a). Harnessing big data in social media analytics: Implications for customer insights and innovation. *Journal of Business Research*, *78*, 321–336.

Smith, J., Lee, C., & Brown, A. (2020b). Understanding the impact of paid social media advertising: Insights from advertising analytics data. *Journal of Digital Advertising*, *8*(4), 201–218.

Tuten, T. L., & Solomon, M. R. (2017). *Social media marketing*. Sage.

Wilkins, E. J., Smith, J. W., & Keane, R. (2020). Social media communication preferences of national park visitors. *Applied Environmental Education & Communication*, *19*(1), 4–18.

Chapter 14

The Influence of COVID-19 on the Adoption of Disruptive Technologies in SMEs Practices: UAE Context

Anas Al Mulla[a], *Fadi Alkaraan*[b] *and Tamer Darwish*[a]

[a]University of Gloucestershire, UK
[b]University of Lincoln, UK

Abstract

Disruptive technologies (DTs) becoming pivotal issues towards successful business innovation strategies. DTs are the emerging technologies that result due to change in the cost of how we access products and services. DTs offer small and medium enterprises (SMEs) a wide range of advantages including improved productivity, value addition to the business and improve the performance delivery to the end users. Organisations' digital readiness and future research topics should also address the effect of technology on ethics like data privacy and identifying algorithmic bias, as well as sustainable digital business transformation initiatives outside the crisis phase.

This chapter sheds lights on the socio-economic effects of the COVID-19 pandemic on the adoption of DTs in SMEs' accounting practices in UAE. Adoption of Artificial Intelligence (AI), cloud solutions, mobile accounting and robotic process automation of accounting are valuable and crucial instruments in relation to the absence of business continuity; their application contributes to remote work as well as increases efficiency. These technologies made it possible for SMEs to counter quick shocks in the market and supply changes, besides helping to cope with fluctuating cash flows. It was established that those companies that managed to adopt digitalisation strategies in the organisation were in a better place to deal with the effects caused by the pandemic. The results also pointed to a strong influence of an external environment concerning the implementation of DTs by policy-makers and market forces.

From Digital Disruption to Dominance, 299–311

Published under exclusive licence by Emerald Publishing Limited
doi:10.1108/978-1-83549-608-420251015

Keywords: Disruptive technologies; SMEs innovation; business innovation; accounting; technological innovation; UAE

1. Introduction

Digital technologies (DTs) are more critical for many accounting technology systems users as enabler for improving firms' capability. Accountants and auditors considered digital accounting as the most accepted new norm of the new accounting and financial services. DTs-oriented accounting techniques are affordable and suitable for small and medium enterprises (SMEs). Technology advancement answers the question of whether companies and markets will fail or succeed when the time comes for new adoptions (Chandra et al., 2019). Radicic and Alkaraan (2022) explored the relative effectiveness of open innovation strategies in a single and complex SME. The study of Alkaraan et al. (2024) investigates the influence of technologies adoption on green business strategies towards sustainability. Hussainey et al. (2022) examined the influence of governance on corporate reporting and technologies adoption.

DTs are more convenient to use in the long term as their innovation is less frequent. The technology has been on every transaction since COVID-19 striped. Almost every product and service in the UAE has adopted this as the world health organisations ruled that social distancing is one method of preventing the spread of COVID-19. The government of UAE saw a possibility of adhering to the rules of the World Health Organization (WHO) and still let their business stay open. Business scholars worldwide have highlighted the place of DT in enhancing productivity as far as small and medium business enterprises are concerned.

DTs been defined as the new way of doing business that overturns the traditional methods. For instance, nowadays, you don't need to visit a shop to buy things. The e-commerce platforms have pathways of bringing the items you need to your doorstep at a click of a button. Businesses worldwide have been rushing to adopt DT in a bit to maintain their competitive advantage over their competitors in the ever-competitive global market. Everyone wants to outdo the other (Shafi et al., 2020). The use of DT is not only for office work.

During this seismic global shift, Abu Dhabi talent technology has been helping thousands of employees and employers to transition from working at their office desks to their kitchen tables or to remote working. The technology sector of Abu Dhabi has cultivated a particularly innovative group of talent technology companies who develop smart, disruptive products and services that are enabling companies worldwide to attract, engage, manage and retain their workforce in these uncertain times. Specifically, there are nine technologies that are disrupting the operations of SMEs amid the COVID-19 changes. COVID-19 brought about many changes in the working environments of people. To prevent and reduce the spread of coronavirus, the government of UAE instructed companies to consider their employees working from home. As a result, remote working was adopted by many SMEs in Abu Dhabi, UAE, and thus, DTs in accounting had to be adopted by these SMEs.

Remote working brought about by COVID-19 has led to the bringing up of many DTs. Specifically, QuickBooks online, Xero, Microsoft Teams, teleworking, telecommuting and video conferencing are some of the DTs that were brought about by remote working. While the way of work has been evolving rapidly, the COVID-19 pandemic has accelerated the need of people to work remotely. During this seismic global shift, Abu Dhabi talent technology has been helping thousands of employees and employers to transition from working at their office desks to their kitchen tables or to remote working. The technology sector of Abu Dhabi has cultivated a particularly innovative group of talent technology companies who develop smart, disruptive products and services that are enabling companies worldwide to attract, engage, manage and retain their workforce in these uncertain times.

The government of UAE has prioritised COVID-19 victims seizing the opportunity to strengthen the capacity of the region's health care systems (Hong & Lee, 2020). UAE has embraced and expanded into other markets like e-tolling and fuel, i.e. companies that facilitate delivery of goods in urban areas. SMEs have been piloted by the government, which has introduced a technological platform in the delivery of services (Miceli et al., 2021). In the education sector, institutions have started offering online tutoring and online courses. The government of UAE commenced offering drone services in delivering of foodstuff and essential medication goods. The Software as a Service (SaaS) providers on the cloud computing services have made their services available to the government to aid in recovery support (Hong & Lee, 2020).

2. DTs and Accounting Implications

Atanasovski and Tocev (2022) found that every innovation in technology has forced accountants to innovate and adapt but ultimately improve the effectiveness of accounting systems. With new developments in technology, the role of accountants is rapidly changing, and therefore, accounting education must be revolutionised (Cited in Atanasovski & Tocev, 2022). The most rapid change in accounting relates to the implementation of robotic process automation (RPA) and Artificial Intelligence (AI). These changes affect the hiring, education and the day-to-day operations of an accountant. The development of accounting software has made accountants to hone their skills. With all the new technologies, accountants have found a way of remaining relevant.

Post-COVID-19 witnessed a rapid pace of technological change that has changed traditional procedures in accounting and all other businesses. DTs such as RPA, AI and blockchain have regulated existing business models and assisted UAE at the beginning of new models. Accountants must take the client on the journey as they employ new models advising clients on how the new models will affect the system as it delicate process. DTs ensure that all the calculations are correct and accurate, unlike the traditional methods. It also provides automatic invoices, which are taken care of immediately. By doing so, the innovations make it easy to acquire access to data files when you need them. Scholars have also identified that the software is more accurate and reliable than the accountant themselves. Accounting has changed from the invention of a calculator to the invention of computers and accounting software. Just like any language has gone through several changes throughout the years, so has accounting. In Abu Dhabi, accounting has taken a significant leap in using technology, and these are the examples the accountants use (Chandra et al., 2019). The United Arab Emirates has undergone various technological changes, and the main factors contributing are the supportive government policies and a tech-savvy population. The UAE has appointed a minister in AI and advanced services to help with technology's tremendous growth. Other institutions have also been established in Dubai like Smart Dubai, Dubai Future Foundation and initiatives like Area 2071 that support firms in technology-related fields (Sharma, 2014).

The Abu Dhabi Global Market and Dubai International Financial Centre are globally known to make the financial industry grow through the fintech company. Mamo Pay was founded in 2019 by Google employees, and it is a Dubai-based payment app that allows its customers to make payments and transfer money using phone numbers and emails, which simplified the use of traditional methods like the use of IBANs. Another programme in the UAE is the use of Tabby, a Dubai-based app that enables the population across Saudi Arabia and UAE to buy and pay for products through online and offline purchases. One can pay for the product in instalments. Bitex is a digital currency exchange used by the Indians and the United Arabs Emirates, which had the incorporation of block-chain technology (Musa et al., 2015). For a better adaptation of new technologies, the Central Bank of the UAE and other Financial Regulators have launched several days for consultation on the guidelines for adopting the new technologies (Tarhini et al., 2015).

The primary goal of AI in accounting is to mimic the actions of human beings. The only difference is that AI is fast and more accurate, thus giving no room for errors. In accounting, AI is commonly used in repetitive tasks such as sorting transactions, inputting and matching data from scanned receipts and invoices to transactions, recording data, reconciling accounts and tracking price changes and subscriptions. While AI tools have become widely accepted in customer service and marketing, their application within finance and accounting is still new, but growing quickly. By some estimates, it is estimated that the AI finance software market will grow to $10 million in the next few years. This expectation and customer demand is driving innovation and development to improve the technology and apply it to more and more complex tasks. AI completes rote tasks and lets the humans get back to what they're good at: strategic thinking, creativity and planning. Businesses will always need the critical decision-making capabilities of accountants and bookkeepers, whether they're using AI technology or not. With strategic implementation, AI can benefit a company in any number of ways. When you choose to implement AI technology within your finance department, you must do so with intention. AI-powered platforms are there to automate repetitive tasks, not solve big-picture problems. And it goes without saying that leveraging AI to manage elements of a business' finances can pose risks if it is implemented incorrectly; it's important to consider how your human finance professionals will work alongside AI to properly manage and maximise efficiency of both ends of the finance management spectrum.

New technology can be intimidating, but when it comes to AI in finance, the benefits far outweigh the costs. When correctly adopted, AI can benefit your finance team and entire company by saving you money, increasing efficiency and providing access to real-time financial data. Traditionally, financial reports are usually delivered a few weeks after a month closes due to the time it takes to enter and reconcile bank statements. Using AI reduces the amount accountants need to perform the month-end close activities, in turn, allowing them to deliver financial reports in a timely manner. When used in conjunction with machine learning, AI can provide insights into the financial performance of the company automatically. Besides, it can interpret the data with ease. Instant access into real-time financial data of a company could impact the sales negotiations of a business, the expansion plans, vendor partnerships, hiring decisions, fundraising efforts, infrastructure investment strategy. Using AI helps to unlock access to more accurate and up-to-date information. Besides, it encourages business growth. With real-time access to accurate financial data, a business can move from reactive to responsive. Instead of making changes at the end of the month, businesses can adjust their financial data in real time. Using AI changes the way a business is run. The technology still needs human oversight and financially savvy team members to make high-level strategic decisions about finances. However, decisions are made faster. If a business is performing poorly, AI will help the management make real-time decisions to strengthen its performance, and thus, this would encourage business growth (Al-Maroof et al., 2020). When humans perform repetitive jobs for long, they get bored. AI provided automation for these jobs. Accounting in banks has incorporated the use of AI systems. They can now be used to verify documents for loan approval, which is a repetitive and tiresome work for human beings (Javaid et al., 2020). In almost every sector of its application in business, the AI system betters each day. It has room for expansion and for growth into more accurate software to aid all problems encountered in business accounting (Shafi et al., 2020).

In SaaS, it involves licensing of software applications to clients mostly used by Microsoft office. Infrastructure as a Service (IaaS) involves a method of delivering everything to a client through Internet Protocol (IP)-based connectivity as part of demand services. Platform as a Service (PaaS) is the complex of the three and shares similarities with SaaS. Most businesses in Abu Dhabi have welcomed the use of the cloud. It is secure because in case there is loss of equipment or property destruction, the information will be available for review, unlike the old archaic methods used before the COVID-19 hit us (Shafi et al., 2020). Business-wise cloud computing has loads of benefits which include cost saving in that once you are on the cloud, easy access to your company's data will save time and money in those project start-ups. The cloud technology has been programmed to keep the utmost security as its job is to carefully monitor security careful 24/7. For business flexibility, cloud computing is the best ordeal. With the flexibility, one is able to work on their goal of client satisfaction (Papadopoulos et al., 2020).

SMEs can use cloud computing service provider resources to reduce extra costs in purchasing expensive systems and equipment. The cloud service provider will reduce your consumption cost, reduce the wages you had to pay to your staff and lower your cost of system upgrades and thus allow the business to make more of profit than loss (Tarhini et al., 2015).

Innovation of Tax Software is a software that has been automated to prepare personal and business accounting reports. This helps the taxpayer to complete their returns without using the actual paper forms. The accounting institution with the incorporation of this has helped reduce error and businesses that avoid paying tax penalties (Chandra et al., 2019). The use of accounting technology has helped companies develop a security system that tracks and records the transaction and keep them for future reference. They also make activities easier as they have individual reports and help management make loan decisions faster using current transaction information. It has also created jobs; for instance, after the creation of cloud technology by the accounting industries, the mobile accountant's vacancy has been created.

3. Benefits of Mobile Accounting to SMEs

The benefits include greater functionality in the sense that on your device, you can do this that would be done in an office, thus saving time. It also helps clients keep their records better as they don't receive mass papers (Papadopoulos et al., 2020). Benefits of mobile accounting to SMEs include the following:

- Helps in the monitoring of budget and expenses mobile devices have been fitted with accounting software's; hence, you can track and approve transactions while in the office, at home or on a vocation (Cao, 2021).
- Helps in easy creating, sending and managing of invoices and quotations: Xero, an accounting software fitted in some phones, helps the owners of SMEs to manage and create invoices using their phones to customers. This means that the owner of the enterprise needs not to be literate but to have just a small knowledge of the use of a smartphone (Islam et al., 2021).
- Saves your money and the general costs incurred by the enterprise: To begin with, mobile banking will save you unnecessary paperwork. The use of less paper is part of the corporate social responsibility of a business as it will amount to environmental conservation (Musa et al., 2015).

The use of AI has raised questions about the use of human labour in the years to come; likewise, the use of cloud technology, which big and small firms have incorporated, affects the position of competition in this institution. Nevertheless, cloud technology has eliminated the use of extra-human labour needed (Kumar & Ayedee, 2021). The business owners and the clients are not affected by these positive changes as they cut down the payroll, so the human force behind the desks is affected. The use of big data, which impacts accounting institutions helping with the analysis of information and dealing with the data set, has done away with the manual workforce from being part of the process (Qin et al., 2020).

To ensure better and stronger supply chain networks, managers must engage technology according to the analysis. This includes forecasting demand to create an order, maintaining the optimum stock and trying to identify an appropriate disruption. Blockchain can bring efficiency in supply chain, offer transparency and security, building trust for various transactions. Alkaraan et al. (2023) shed lights on a new era of strategic investment decision-making towards sustainable supply chains and circular economy (see also, Akaraan 2023a, 2023b, 2023c). Current issues in business innovation, investment efficiency, financial flexibility governance and business performance are widely addressed by prior studies studies. Reviewing these studies is beyond the focus of this chapter. For more recent debates, see Alkaraan (2017), Alkaraan (2021a, 2021b), Alkhwaldi et al. (2022), Alkaraan and Floyd (2020), Al-Araj et al. (2022), Abu-AlSondos et al. (2023), Shehadeh, Almohtaseb et al. (2023), Hatamlah et al., 2023, Shehadeh, Almajali et al. (2023), Wu et al. (2024, 2023) and Alkaraan (2022a, 2022b). Decision-makers should ensure that they rely on the data and information available when making decisions. DTs produce immense volumes of data, which, when analysed, can reveal handy information concerning the performance of organisations, business trends and consumer behaviour. Through technologies adoption including big data and Business intelligence (BI), managers are able to make efficient decisions that will enhance growth and the bottom line for their respective firms. It is essential that resources and tools are provided to support data analytics and make employees aware of how they should read these reports.

4. Conclusion and Managerial Implications

DTs can enhance the management of performance from a financial view by offering timely data. These tools should be used by managers to enhance strategic decision-making since they increase financial awareness concerning performance and trends. This is done by employing the use of computers and software to monitor the account spending, determine the expenditures and costs and predict the company's future financial health. The ability to analyse financial information in near real time enables managers to swiftly adapt when there are shifts in market conditions, including making the necessary strategic adjustments. SMEs benefit from new technologies since they reduce the overall cost of operation required by firms to achieve their pre-specified goals. Operations managers must understand which processes can be affected by the application of the technology for purposes of cutting costs by either avoiding repetition of certain tasks or expending limited resources. Managing cost by implementing effective cost control is a crucial factor that can enable SMEs to sustain themselves and stay afloat during the current challenging economic times.

It is critical imperative to improve on the existing technological supports. Managers should therefore focus on specialising in suitable and effective cloud accounting software applications, since cloud accounting solutions are now more than ever needed due to the need for remote information access, teams' cooperation and preparing for future disruptions. These are fairly secure and reliable systems that can accommodate as many users as is necessary for business continuity during remote working. Furthermore, specialised and complex work environments in the financial business domain can benefit from an increase in efficiency and accuracy by employing applications of AI, for instance, in document scanning for invoices, expenses and financial reports. They should consider using AI technologies to change the process by minimising outside intervention and increasing productivity levels so that personnel can focus on other valuable tasks.

It is necessary to enable the use of virtual collaboration software and other detailed remote work orientation. Business managers should ensure they incorporate the use of technology solutions in the virtual environment in a way that will enable consistent real-time reporting and effective decision-making through sharing of documents and other communication and project management tools. Proper training education should be incorporated to embrace technical advancement through the use of online learning programmes to create corps of well-equipped human resource. Through the optimisation of remote accounting processes, it becomes possible for managers to maintain efficiency and accuracy even when the work is being done away from the business premises. The adoption of such payment systems is essential if one is to improve the process of payment as a whole, guarantees a decrease in physical contacts and facilitates payments processes through the use of digital payments. They should adopt a digital payment system to enhance the likelihood of successful transactions for managers. This transition also fulfils the expectations from a newer and tech-savvy generation of customers but that also caters to shift towards contactless payments that have been brought down due to the current pandemic situation.

The strategic use of these tools in financial management recognises that cash flow and patterning involving finances can be predicted at the risk of market fluctuations. Managers should use data analytics to understand more about the business and customers who spend their money. This knowing enables efficient risk management and the identification of promising business prospects and strategic options. It is crucial to consider measures to overcome key barriers in the adoption of technology because small firms are the major affected segment due to financial constraints on constrained capital. Managers wishing to adopt continuous improvement should look for cheaper ways to implement this change, search for grants from the government or subsidies and possibly gain the introduction and implementation of the change in phases. Supervising employees in terms of adequate technological support like fibre connectivity and comprehensive accounting platforms in order to support remote working is another important factor. Managers must make changes in IT facilities towards the consideration of the necessity of having efficient technology for remote working because it is crucial for productivity and companies' competitiveness.

Decision-makers need to pursue skills update and courses in an effort to acquire skills to tackle technological developments within the short emerging trends. This covers such areas like update with the latest technologies, attending an exhibition or a conference of the profession or sub-profession or being an active member in the professional forum. It is critical to implement digital transformation plan. This requires embracing advanced technologies that seek to challenge the established industries such as the AI, cloud and mobile accounting. Specific goals of strategic planning should be aimed at the effective implementation of these technologies within the business processes as a way of enhancing efficiency and accuracy and strengthening the decision-making capacities of the businesses. For SMEs to remain viable and achieve successful performance objectives, they must place significant focus on the concept of innovation. Employers should support people in power to encourage ideas from bottom to top and encourage employees to try out different technology and approach. This can be done through seminars, focus group discussions, workshops, joint programmes and special partnership projects. Through such a diversification strategy, IT SMEs are able to distinguish themselves from others in the market and look for more opportune ways to tap the value-added services.

Decision-makers should determine what tasks can be best handed over to technology to help them cut on their time and costs such as data inputting, preparing invoices and displaying and analysing data. By introducing advanced technologies, such as AI and RP, productivity can be improved due to a decrease in the number of mistakes done manually, while at the same time, they can be relieved to allow them to carry out more complex tasks. This can lead to optimisation of functions and reduction of cost. The use of such technologies such as AI chatbots and customer relationship management (CRM) systems can a have a positive impact on customer service since customers will be provided with quick and personalised replies to their queries. It is high time that managers ensured that the aforesaid tools are utilised in the right manner with the aim of enhancing customer satisfaction and the loyalty that is accorded to them in the process. Furthermore, communication channels such as social media can also be utilised to interact with the customers, as well as capture their feedback and address them appropriately at that very same moment.

DTs in the workplace require upskilling and reskilling of human resources, to help the organisations adapt and grow. Decision-makers need to focus on reinforcing creation of training and development courses that will enable employee competencies to run new technologies required in workplaces. This entails the kind of training that one gets from an institution of learning in terms of operational skills in computers as well as other related technologies. Fostering continued learning culture saves its employees in terms of technology advancement because technological space is dynamic.

Decision-makers are central to the cultural transformation of organisations and the pursuit of innovation, particularly as it relates to strategy. This includes creativity, exploration and the ability to make enhancements continually. Managers must set conditions in which individuals, teams or an organisation encourage the innovative search for solutions, the taking of reasonable risks as well as learning from mistakes.

5. Suggestions for Future Research

Future research on DTs can enhance the knowledge level of future research on the determinants of technology adoption, the time-related effects of digitalisation and its various implications for SMEs and the economy. Comparing the application of different technologies with countries will further explain the possible variations that may exist in different regions due to the different economic model, cultures and policies. Depending on this broader perspective, some of the best practices and main challenges faced can be identified in order to present a more overall view of the digital transformation processes around the world.

Future research may focus on how different sectors in the economy: manufacturing, retailing, healthcare, education, among others. More studies should be made to determine the relationship that exists between the use of technology and trends that affect Key Performance Indicators (KPIs) and organisational success. Another issue is the usage of an overall perspective of both short-term advantages and long-term consequences for further analysis of the opportunities and threats connected with digitalisation. Further studies should pinpoint how using DTs to address crises may help an organisation thrive despite the nature of a crisis, be it an economic, natural or geopolitical one. Through the presentation of qualitative case studies of SMEs managing crises by implementing digital strategies, the authors can define factors that contribute to better coping and resourcefulness of such businesses.

Technology adoption on the other hand is a process through which technology is integrated fully within the main systems in use. Subsequent research must aim to understand the issues and solutions related to incorporating emerging technologies into SMEs. This entails putting into consideration such aspects as the degree of integration between new and existing systems and how data integration impacts on organisations in terms of cost, time and quality of the outcome, among others, and the extent to which standards and protocols are supportive of interoperability. Understanding these technical issues would ensure that organisations do not encounter problems during the implementation processes while, at the same time, take advantage of the technological advancement for improvement.

Future research may investigate the customer-oriented view of digital transformation further. It is thus important for SMEs to comprehend how technology adoption influences customers' experiences, satisfaction and subsequent behaviours. Future studies should examine how DTs can be used in SMEs to engage customers in a way that enables direct feedback and real-time data collection to be fed back to the business and how the business can adapt in real time to the ever-changing demands from the customer. Thereby, incorporating a customer perspective to the operation of SMEs can also improve their ranking within their industry and customer loyalty.

More studies should be conducted to provide future research understanding of the various environmental profiles of different technologies; this will make it possible for the SMEs to realise a win-win situation between the economic and ecological dimension factors. This includes examining the steps that green technologies and sustainable supply chain management initiatives can take to support sustainable ventures and goals.

References

Abu-AlSondos, I., Alkhwaldi, A., Salhab, H., Shehadeh, M., & Ali, B. (2023). Customer attitudes towards online shopping: A systematic review of the influencing factors. *International Journal of Data and Network Science*, *7*(1), 513–524. https://doi.org/10.5267/j.ijdns.2022.12.013

Al-Araj, R. E. E. M., Haddad, H. O. S. S. A. M., Shehadeh, M. A. H. A., Hasan, E., & Nawaiseh, M. Y. (2022). The effect of artificial intelligence on service quality and customer satisfaction in Jordanian banking sector. *WSEAS Transactions on Business and Economics*, *19*(12), 1929–1947. https://doi.org/10.37394/23207.2022.19.173

Al-Maroof, R. S., Salloum, S. A., Hassanien, A. E., & Shaalan, K. (2020). Fear from COVID-19 and technology adoption: The impact of Google Meet during Coronavirus pandemic. *Interactive Learning Environments*, 1–16. https://doi.org/10.1080/10494820.2020.1830121

Alkaraan, F. (2017). Corporate governance in Ireland: New challenges and opportunities. In V. Capizzi, U. Braendle, & A. N. Kostyuk (Eds.), *Corporate governance: New challenges and opportunities*. Virtus Interpress. ISBN: 978-617-7309-00-9.

Alkaraan, F. (2021a). Editorial: Recent debates on corporate governance and sustainability. *Corporate Governance and Sustainability Review*, *5*(3), 4–6. https://doi.org/10.22495/cgsrv5i3editorial

Alkaraan, F. (2021b). Strategic investment decision-making: Mergers and acquisitions toward Industry 4.0. In C. L. Cooper & S. Finkelstein (Eds.), Advances in mergers and acquisitions *(*Advances in mergers and acquisitions, Vol. 20, pp. 39–52). Emerald Publishing Limited. https://doi.org/10.1108/S1479-361X20210000020004

Alkaraan, F. (2022a). Editorial: Current issues in corporate governance and sustainability. *Corporate Governance and Sustainability Review*, *6*(2), 4–6. https://doi.org/10.22495/cgsrv6i2editorial

Alkaraan, F. (2022b). A new era of mergers and acquisitions: Towards synergy between Industry 4.0 and circular economy. In S. Finkelstein & C. L. Cooper (Eds.), Advances in mergers and acquisitions *(*Advances in mergers and acquisitions, Vol. 21, pp. 51–61). Emerald Publishing Limited. https://doi.org/10.1108/S1479-361X20220000021004

Alkaraan, F. (2023a). Editorial: Current issues in business innovation, governance structure and business performance. *Business Performance Review*, *1*(2), 4–6. https://doi.org/10.22495/bprv1i2editorial

Alkaraan, F. (2023b). Review of the book Organizational behavior and transformational leadership by S. S. Abu Mahfouz. *Corporate Governance and Sustainability Review*, *7*(4), 37–40. https://doi.org/10.22495/cgsrv7i4p4

Alkaraan, F. (2023c). Editorial: Corporate governance and sustainability issues. *Corporate Governance and Sustainability Review*, *7*(1), 4–6. https://doi.org/10.22495/cgsrv7i1editorial

Alkaraan, F., Elmarzouky, M., Hussainey, K., Venkatesh, V. G., Shi, Y., & Gulko, N. (2024). Reinforcing green business strategies with Industry 4.0 and governance towards sustainability: Natural-resource-based view and dynamic capability. *Business Strategy and the Environment*, 1–19. https://doi.org/10.1002/bse.3665

Alkaraan, F., & Floyd, D. (2020). Rethinking of the UK strategic public decision: Outsourcing accountability and governance perspectives. *Strategic Change*, *29*(6), 625–632. https://doi.org/10.1002/jsc.2370

Alkaraan, F., Floyd, D., Rahman, M., & Nuery, N. (2023). A new era of strategic investment decision-making practices in UK companies: Towards sustainable supply chains and circular economy. *Theoretical Economics Letters*, *13*, 666–682. https://doi.org/10.4236/tel.2023.133040

Alkhwaldi, A. F., Alharasis, E. E., Shehadeh, M., Abu-AlSondos, I. A., Oudat, M. S., & Bani Atta, A. A. (2022). Towards an understanding of fintech users' adoption: Intention and e-loyalty post-COVID-19 from a developing country perspective. *Sustainability*, *14*(19), 1261. https://doi.org/10.3390/su141912616

Atanasovski, A., & Tocev, T. (2022). Research trends in disruptive technologies for accounting of the future–A bibliometric analysis. *Journal of Accounting and Management Information Systems*, *21*(2), 270–288. http://dx.doi.org/10.24818/jamis.2022.02006

Cao, T. (2021). The study of factors on the small and medium enterprises' adoption of mobile payment: Implications for the COVID-19 era. *Frontiers in Public Health*, *9*. https://doi.org/10.3389/fpubh.2021.646592

Chandra, G. R., Sharma, B. K., & Liaqat, I. A. (2019). UAE's strategy towards most cyber resilient nation. *International Journal of Innovative Technology and Exploring Engineering*, *8*(12), 2803–2809. https://doi.org/10.35940/ijitee.L3022.1081219

Hatamlah, H., Allan, M., Abu-AlSondos, I., Shehadeh, M., & Allahham, M. (2023). The role of artificial intelligence in supply chain analytics during the pandemic. *Uncertain Supply Chain Management*, *11*(3), 1175–1186. https://doi.org/10.5267/j.uscm.2023.4.005

Hong, S., & Lee, S. (2020). Sharing economy and government. *Journal of Open Innovation: Technology, Market, and Complexity*, *6*(4), 177. https://doi.org/10.3390/joitmc6040177

Hussainey, K., Albitar, K., & Alkaraan, F. (2022). Corporate narrative reporting on Industry 4.0 technologies: Does governance matter? *International Journal of Accounting and Information Management*, 1834–7649. https://doi.org/10.1108/IJAIM-02-2022-0024

Islam, A., Jerin, I., Hafiz, N., Nimfa, D. T., & Wahab, S. A. (2021). Configuring a blueprint for Malaysian SMEs to survive through the COVID-19 crisis: The reinforcement of Quadruple Helix Innovation Model. *Journal of Entrepreneurship, Business and Economics*, *9*(1), 32–81.

Javaid, M., Haleem, A., Vaishya, R., Bahl, S., Suman, R., & Vaish, A. (2020). Industry 4.0 technologies and their applications in fighting COVID-19 pandemic. *Diabetes & Metabolic Syndrome: Clinical Research Reviews*, *14*(4), 419–422. https://doi.org/10.1016/j.dsx.2020.04.032

Kumar, M. A., & Ayedee, D. N. (2021). Technology adoption: A solution for SMEs to overcome problems during COVID-19. *Academy of Marketing Studies Journal*, *25*(1). (forthcoming).

Miceli, A., Hagen, B., Riccardi, M. P., Sotti, F., & Settembre-Blundo, D. (2021). Thriving, not just surviving in changing times: How sustainability, agility and digitalization intertwine with organizational resilience. *Sustainability*, *13*(4), 2052. https://doi.org/10.3390/su13042052

Musa, A., Khan, H. U., & AlShare, K. A. (2015). Factors influence consumers' adoption of mobile payment devices in Qatar. *International Journal of Mobile Communications*, *13*(6), 670–689. https://doi.org/10.1504/IJMC.2015.072100

Papadopoulos, T., Baltas, K. N., & Balta, M. E. (2020). The use of digital technologies by small and medium enterprises during COVID-19: Implications for theory and practice. *International Journal of Information Management*, *55*, 102192.

Qin, X., Huang, G., Shen, H., & Fu, M. (2020). COVID-19 pandemic and firm-level cash holding—Moderating effect of goodwill and goodwill impairment. *Emerging Markets Finance and Trade*, *56*(10), 2243–2258.

Radicic, D., & Alkaraan, F. (2022). Relative effectiveness of open innovation strategies in single and complex SME innovators. *Technology Analysis & Strategic Management*. ISSN 0953-7325. https://doi.org/10.1080/09537325.2022.2130042

Shafi, M., Liu, J., & Ren, W. (2020). Impact of COVID-19 pandemic on micro, small, and medium-sized enterprises operating in Pakistan. *Research in Globalization*, *2*, 100018.

Shehadeh, M., Almajali, D., Abu-AlSondos, I. A., Alkhwaldi, A. F., & Al-Gasaymeh, A. S. (2023). Digital transformation and its impact on operational efficiency and competitive advantage in Islamic banks. In *2023 International conference on business analytics for technology and security (ICBATS)* (pp. 1–6). IEEE. https://doi.org/10.1109/ICBATS57792.2023.10111266

Shehadeh, M., Almohtaseb, A., Aldehayyat, J., & Abu-AlSondos, I. A. (2023). Digital transformation and competitive advantage in the service sector: A moderated-mediation model. *Sustainability*, *15*(3), 2077. https://doi.org/10.3390/su15032077

Tarhini, A., Arachchilage, N. A. G., & Abbasi, M. S. (2015). A critical review of theories and models of technology adoption and acceptance in information system research. *International Journal of Technology Diffusion*, *6*(4), 58–77. https://doi.org/10.4018/IJTD.2015100104

Wu, W., Alkaraan, F., & Le, C. (2023). The moderating effects of corporate governance and investment efficiency on the nexus between financial flexibility and firm performance. *Journal of Financial Reporting & Accounting*. https://doi.org/10.1108/JFRA-05-2023-0234

Wu, W., Le, C., Shi, Y., & Alkaraan, F. (2024). The influence of financial flexibility on firm performance: The moderating effects of investment efficiency and investment scale. *Journal of Applied Accounting Research*. ahead-of-print. https://doi.org/10.1108/JAAR-07-2023-0192

